Faces of Moderation

FACES OF MODERATION

The Art of Balance in an Age of Extremes

Aurelian Craiutu

PENN

UNIVERSITY OF PENNSYLVANIA PRESS

PHILADELPHIA

A volume in the Haney Foundation Series, established in 1961
with the generous support of Dr. John Louis Haney.

Published by
University of Pennsylvania Press
Philadelphia, Pennsylvania 19104-4112
www.upenn.edu/pennpress

Printed in the United States of America
on acid-free paper
3 5 7 9 10 8 6 4 2

Cataloging-in-Publication Data is available
from the Library of Congress.
ISBN 978-0-8122-4876-0

Our world does not need tepid souls. It needs burning hearts, men who know the proper place of moderation.

—Albert Camus

CONTENTS

Prologue

In Search of an Elusive Virtue

> People offer advice, but they do not give at the same time the wisdom to benefit from it.
>
> —La Rochefoucauld

Many may still remember Barry Goldwater's famous words on the occasion of his nomination acceptance speech at the Republican National Convention in San Francisco in 1964: "I would remind you that extremism in the pursuit of liberty is no vice. And let me remind you also that moderation in the pursuit of justice is no virtue." After pronouncing these memorable words, Goldwater gracefully accepted the nomination of his party and went on to score a massive defeat at the polls. His extreme defense of liberty was seen by many in tension with his opposition to the Civil Rights Act, and this contradiction (in addition to other things, of course) was enough to send Goldwater to the ranks of political losers.

Nonetheless, it would be difficult not to have some sympathy for his immoderate position in defense of liberty at a critical moment during the Cold War when the fate of freedom in the world was uncertain, to say the least. We would be mistaken to characterize it, to use Senator William Fulbright's own words, as "the closest thing in American politics to an equivalent of Russian Stalinism." Goldwater was none of that, to be sure; he was an American patriot who believed in his country's mission to spread liberty in an embattled world during the Cold War. I have no intention of reassessing Goldwater's legacy here. I begin with his critique of moderation because in my view, it misrepresented in an unforgettable way a cardinal virtue without which our political system would not be able to function properly. This understudied and underappreciated virtue deserves a closer look to reveal its nature, complexity, and potential benefits.

This is precisely what I hope to achieve in the present book, which is part of a larger multivolume research agenda whose main goal is to bring to light the richness of political moderation in the history of modern political thought. The concept of moderation was already present, as it were, between the lines in my first book, *Liberalism Under Siege: The Political Thought of the French Doctrinaires* (2003). It came to the fore in a subsequent volume, *Elogiul moderației* (In Praise of Moderation), written for a general public and published in Romanian in 2006. Six years later, in *A Virtue for Courageous Minds: Moderation in French Political Thought, 1748–1830,* I began exploring in detail the tradition of political moderation in France (a second volume covering the period 1830–1900 in France will follow in due course). I argued that political moderation constitutes a coherent, complex, and diverse tradition of thought, an entire submerged archipelago that has yet to be (re)discovered and properly explored. This "archipelago" consists of various "islands" represented by a wide array of ideas and modes of argument and action; at the same time, it also includes elements and political strategies that were not shared by all moderates, or were shared only to varying degrees. The book ended (rhetorically) with a "Decalogue of Moderation" that emphasized the complexity, difficulty, and richness of this virtue. I argued that, far from being of mere historical interest, moderation may be particularly relevant in a post–Cold War age such as ours because it enables us to deal with the antinomies and tensions at the heart of our contemporary societies and allows us to defend the pluralism of ideas, principles, and interests against its enemies. I also insisted that moderation should be regarded as an eclectic virtue transcending the conventional categories of our political vocabulary. While moderation may sometimes imply a conservative stance embraced by those who seek to preserve the status quo, it would be inaccurate to claim that all calls for moderation are little else than conservative or "reactionary" attempts to maintain unjust social and political privileges or components of an ideological system by which modern elites seek to legitimize their power and domination.

The present volume has a different emphasis and examines select faces of political moderation in the twentieth century. It pays special attention to its shifting polemical and rhetorical uses in different political and national contexts and addresses the following questions: What did it mean to be a moderate voice in the political and public life of the past century? How did moderate minds operate compared to more radical spirits in the age of extremes? What were they seeking in politics, and how did they view political life? We will also take up a few more general questions: What are the characteristics of the "moderate mind"[1] in action? To what extent is moderation contingent upon the existence and flourishing of various forms of political radicalism? What do moderates have that others lack? Is moderation primarily a style of argument that varies according to context, circumstances, and personal character? Or does it also have a strong ethical-normative core? And, finally, are there any common elements of what might be called the "moderate" style?[2]

This volume does not aim to be—nor should be seen as—a work of political contestation; it is first and foremost a work in modern intellectual history, history of ideas, and political theory that contributes to contemporary debates on political virtues, radicalism, and extremism. Without treating moderation as a unitary block, I show its heterogeneity and diversity by focusing on the writings of representative authors (mostly European, with a few American exceptions) who defended their beliefs in liberty, civility, and moderation in an age when many intellectuals shunned moderation and embraced various forms of radicalism and extremism. Although their political and intellectual trajectories were significantly different, these thinkers may be seen as belonging to a loosely defined "school" of moderation that transcends strict geographical and temporal borders. I insist at the outset that there is no "ideology" (or party) of moderation in the proper sense of the word and that moderation cannot be studied in the abstract, but only as instantiated in specific historical and political contexts and discourses. What is moderate in one context and period may significantly differ from what is moderate at another point in time, which is another way of saying that moderation is not a virtue for all seasons and for everyone.

In treating such a complex subject as moderation, it is necessary to be as ecumenical as possible and examine a wide cast of characters including thinkers from all aisles of the political spectrum and from both sides of Europe (West and East). The last detail is particularly relevant today when the memory of the Cold War seems to be revived by recent political developments in Russia and the Middle East. Since the main focus of the book is on European political thought, the least represented here is the American political tradition. Nevertheless, the brief discussion of Judith Shklar's "liberalism of fear"[3] and Arthur Schlesinger Jr.'s "vital center"[4] and the occasional references to Edward Shils's writings on civility and Albert O. Hirschman's views on self-subversion should make it plain that American scholars, many of whom were of European extraction, brought important contributions to the debates on moderation and extremism in the twentieth century.

We will explore both well-known authors (such as Isaiah Berlin, Raymond Aron, and Michael Oakeshott) and lesser-known ones (such as Norberto Bobbio, Leszek Kołakowski, and Adam Michnik) whose selected writings had something important to say about political moderation in an age of extremes. Taken together, these thinkers do not offer a comprehensive account of this virtue, and the reader might wonder, for example, whether other major figures such as Hannah Arendt, Albert Camus, or John Maynard Keynes should not have been examined as well.[5] Needless to say, there is no shortage of worthy candidates. One thing is certain though: we need an open and ecumenical form of intellectual history, one that takes into account the creativity of both well-known and allegedly marginal authors whose works can illuminate the complexity and richness of the tradition of political moderation in the twentieth century.

The thinkers discussed or mentioned in these pages came from several national cultures (mainly France, Italy, England, Poland, and the United States) and belonged to different disciplines (political theory, philosophy, sociology, literature, and history of ideas). Not all of them identified themselves primarily as moderates; some preferred to be seen as liberals or conservatives, while others rejected all labels. What makes them fascinating and noteworthy is precisely their syncretism as illustrated by their different trajectories and ideas as well as by the fact that many of these thinkers, brave soldiers in the battle for freedom, refused narrow political affiliation and displayed political courage in tough times. Some of them started off their careers on the Left and then gradually embraced political moderation, moving toward the center or the center-right. A few of them exercised significant political influence as journalists—Aron, for example, wrote for *Le Figaro* and *L'Express* for over three decades, while Michnik has been the editor of the influential *Gazeta Wiborcza* for over two decades and a half now—or engaged intellectuals or politicians such as Bobbio who was a member of the Italian Senate. Still others such as Berlin and Shklar remained in the ivory tower of academia, even if they never lost interest in political issues.

Be that as it may, these thinkers paid a certain price for their political moderation because they refused to play the populist card or did not embrace trendy themes for short-term gains. As such, they lived at a slightly awkward tangent to their contemporaries with whom they had a complex relationship, punctuated by occasional crises and a few tense moments. Some of them were subjects of suspicion or even contempt, as demonstrated by the Parisian students in 1968 who thought it was "better to be wrong with Sartre than right with Aron." Finally, the thinkers studied here kept open the dialogue with their opponents even in the most difficult times. This was the case with Aron and Sartre, Bobbio and the Italian Communists, and Michnik and the former Polish Communist leaders.

Although the chapters of this book can be read individually as a series of intellectual vignettes, they are not intended as comprehensive studies of any of the aforementioned authors. Instead, the main focus is on the concept of political moderation, and each chapter illuminates a certain face of this elusive virtue as reflected in their writings. I examine how these thinkers conceived of moderation and, where applicable, how they practiced it. To this effect, I focus on their most relevant writings and comment on their intellectual and political trajectories only when they seem relevant to the larger topic of moderation. The mentality of our authors will remain obscure if we do not take into account how they related their ideas to the events that defined their lives, such as communism, fascism, the Soviet Union, the postwar European reconstruction, and the student revolts of 1968. The moderates discussed in these pages differed among themselves in several respects and belonged to different intellectual and spiritual constellations. Yet, at the same time, they also shared many important things in common such as their belief in dialogue, their rejection of Manichaeism and ideological thinking, their embrace of trimming and political eclecticism, and their opposition to extremism and fanaticism in all their forms.

The first chapter discusses the ethos of moderation broadly defined. I begin by examining a few misrepresentations of moderation and then comment on the challenges associated with studying and writing about this elusive and difficult concept. Next, I emphasize the potential radicalism of moderation as a fighting virtue before turning to trimming as a key face of moderation and exploring its role in combating ideological intransigence and dogmatism. I challenge the common view of moderation as a conservative defense of the status quo and claim that this virtue can also have its own radical side depending on circumstances. Finally, I focus on two essential aspects of moderation: as a synonym of civility and openness and as an antonym of fanaticism and dogmatism. As such, moderation appears as an essential ingredient in the functioning of all open societies because it acts as a buffer against extremism and promotes a civil form of politics indispensable to the smooth running of democratic institutions.

The second chapter examines the metaphor of the "committed observer"—*le spectateur engagé*—as a face of political moderation in the writings of Raymond Aron (1905–83). The choice of a French author for a book on moderation may seem surprising at first sight. Yet, a closer look at the French political tradition reveals that the latter has combined a well-known tendency to radicalism with a lesser-known but surprisingly diverse tradition of political moderation. Aron's writings such as *The Opium of the Intellectuals, An Essay on Freedom, Thinking Politically*, and his *Memoirs* are discussed here as examples of lucid political judgment in an age of extremes when many intellectuals shunned moderation and embraced radical or even extremist positions. As an engaged spectator raised in the tradition of Cartesian rationalism, Aron reflected on a wide variety of topics such as the philosophy of history, war and peace, and the virtues and limitations of liberal democracy while commenting extensively on the major political events of his time. His works shed fresh light on the relationship between moderation, engagement, responsibility, and political judgment. Among other topics discussed in this chapter are the role of intellectuals in politics, Aron's reading of Marxism, his analysis of the revolution of 1968 in France, and his intellectual dialogue with Hayek. I also illustrate Aron's political moderation by analyzing his critical attitude toward General de Gaulle and his uncompromising attitude during the Algerian crisis when Aron defended the independence of the former colony.

Chapter 3 focuses on the relationship between political moderation, freedom, monism, and pluralism in the writings of Isaiah Berlin (1909–97) examined in the larger context of the Cold War liberalism. Berlin is an obvious choice for a book on moderation given his endorsement of pluralism and vigorous critique of political idealism, utopianism, and monism. I explore these topics along with Berlin's anticommunism and opposition to determinism by focusing on some of his best known essays (such as "Two Concepts of Liberty," "The Pursuit of the Ideal," and "The Originality of Machiavelli"), his interpretations of Russian thinkers, as well as his extensive correspondence. In this chapter, I also link Berlin's works to those of other Cold War liberals such as Arthur Schlesinger Jr. (1917–2007) and Judith Shklar (1928–92) whose respective theories of the "vital center" and "liberalism of fear" he partly shared. Another common trait linking these authors was their views on the role of passions, vices, and reason in politics. They dreaded the presence of irrationality, cruelty, wickedness, and evil in history and attempted to understand their roots and mitigate their influence in reality. Finally, I explore

Berlin's moderate temperament by comparing it with that of two of his favorite authors, Alexander Herzen and Ivan Turgenev.

In Chapter 4, I turn to the writings of the Norberto Bobbio (1909–2004), the most prominent twentieth-century Italian political philosopher, in order to examine how constitutional liberalism and socialist democracy came to be reconciled in Italy and gave rise to an original yet still little-known form of "liberalsocialism," an important chapter in the history of political moderation in the twentieth century in which Bobbio and some of his friends (such as Guido Calogero) played an important role. The experience of fascism, the ideological divisions of the Cold War, and the slow and protracted democratization of Italian society during the 1960s and 1970s exercised decisive influence on Bobbio, who emerged as a strong advocate of constitutionalism, equality, and the rule of law. I examine his complex dialogue with the Italian communists and Marxists as well as the philosophy undergirding his politics of culture elaborated in *Politica e cultura* (1955) and other texts written during the Cold War; next, I consider Bobbio's views on political engagement and the role of intellectuals in society. Later in life, he argued that the most important virtue of intellectuals is *mitezza* (meekness), an important and intriguing face of political moderation. I argue that Bobbio's meekness derived from a particular *forma mentis* that could also be found at the heart of his philosophy of dialogue and politics of culture.

Chapter 5 focuses on the relationship between moderation, trimming, the politics of faith, and the politics of skepticism in the writings of the British political philosopher Michael Oakeshott (1901–90), best known for his critique of rationalism in politics and his theory of civil association sketched in *On Human Conduct* (1975). An attentive rereading of Oakeshott's writings shows that his target was not only rationalist socialism, but also those forms of conservatism that tend to evolve into rigid ideologies, thus losing sight of the complex nature of society and politics. After examining Oakeshott's distinction between "civil" and "enterprise" associations and his critique of political rationalism and ideological thinking, I focus on the affinities between moderation and conservatism in *Rationalism in Politics* (1961). Next, I turn to Oakeshott's posthumously published *The Politics of Faith and the Politics of Skepticism* (1996) in which he distinguished between two fundamental types of politics that, he argued, should be seen as the two poles between which modern politics have moved for the past few centuries. I draw on Oakeshott's reworking of the ideas of a classical seventeenth-century text, Halifax's "The Character of a Trimmer," and comment on his claim that we need a mixture between the politics of skepticism and of faith to navigate the troubled waters of modern politics.

The last (sixth) chapter turns to Eastern Europe and focuses on two concepts related to political moderation that were central to the anticommunist resistance in Poland: "new evolutionism" and "self-limiting revolution." The first became a key principle in the agenda of the Workers' Defense Committee (also known as KOR, founded in 1976), while the second defined the platform of the Solidarity movement beginning with the summer of 1980. The concept of "new evolutionism" was theorized by Adam Michnik, who developed it in the 1970s in a series of important essays collected later in his *Letters from Prison* (1987). In the footsteps of Leszek Kołakowski (1927–2009), Michnik presented a persuasive case for a reformist agenda while supporting the general goal of a limited gradual revolution. In so doing, he also argued for a creative form of "radical moderation" at a key time when all of Europe was struggling to end the Cold War. I pay special attention to Michnik's ethics of dialogue and political trimming as illustrated, among others, by his position on the dialogue between the Catholic Church and the Left in Poland as well as his conversations with Václav Havel and General Wojciech Jaruzelski collected in *Letters from Freedom* (1998). I also examine Michnik's controversial views on lustration and decommunization before concluding with a few reflections on the relationship between moderation and "inconsistency" in politics.

In the epilogue, I elaborate on the broad themes (metanarratives) of the book and highlight their contemporary implications for us today. I revisit the main arguments for moderation made in the previous chapters and reflect on how the hybridity of this virtue mirrors our world's ideological and institutional complexity. I argue that moderation should not be expected to always bring forth moral clarity and explain why there can be no ideology of moderation. As such, the latter must not be equated with tepidness or (always) seeking the midpoint between two opposing poles and opportunistically planting oneself there. In some cases, moderation is, in fact, the outcome of a long, arduous, and open-ended process of political learning, as the chapters of the present book demonstrate.

"A history book—assuming its facts are correct—stands or falls by the conviction with which it tells its story," Tony Judt once said (Judt and Snyder, 2012: 260). "If it rings true, to an intelligent, informed reader, then it is a good history book." I venture to say the same about a book in political theory or intellectual history, and especially about a volume on political moderation. The proper attitude for anyone writing on this difficult virtue is patience, and that is why I am inspired by the following words of Ortega y Gasset: "I am in no hurry to be proved right. The right is not a train that leaves at a certain hour. Only the sick man and the ambitious man are in a hurry."[6] These days, it is quite common to be pessimistic or cynical about the chances of moderation in the short term. It is equally normal to lament its political powerlessness in a world dominated by ideological intransigence in which in order to be successful and make headlines, it seems that one must often espouse mostly extremist and immoderate positions. Anyone writing about moderation seems therefore to face daunting challenges.

To tell a convincing story about the types of moderation espoused by the authors studied in this book requires that we clearly highlight the common themes shared by their political and intellectual agendas as well as the differences among them. My ambition is to rethink an old concept and through it, to identify a certain school of thought where few had perceived its existence before. This raises a few significant methodological questions and challenges. First, there is the danger of converting some scattered or incidental remarks into a coherent doctrine of moderation which has never existed in reality. A related risk might be the tendency to underplay the differences between the ideas, agendas, and temperaments of the moderates studied here and overplay, in turn, the affinities or similarities among them. Yet another problem might arise from the attempt to offer a series of individual portraits and intellectual vignettes that might have only tenuous links among them.

My hope is that the approach used in this book successfully avoids all of these problems. I admit from the outset that moderation is a particularly difficult concept placed at the heart of a complex moral and political field. When reflecting upon the nature of this virtue, rather than relying upon the instruments of analytical philosophy, we need to adopt a concrete way of thinking about politics that takes into account the complex interaction among ideas, passions, institutions, and events. What makes moderation a notoriously difficult subject is not only the virtual impossibility of offering a coherent theory of this virtue, but also the fact that moderates have worn many "masks" over time that are different and may sometimes be difficult to relate to each other: prudence, trimming, skepticism, pluralism, eclecticism, antonym of zealotry, fanaticism, enthusiasm, and the "committed observer." Equally important is that claims for moderation have been part of historical controversies and debates and thus carry with them a certain rhetoric and a plethora of connotations, some more obvious than others.[7] Among the concrete examples of agendas that claimed to be moderate one could mention the following: the *juste milieu* between revolution and reaction in postrevolutionary France, Ordoliberalism in postwar Germany, and social democracy in Sweden as a middle ground between pure free market capitalism and full state socialism. There were also several political movements that claimed to follow the principles of moderation: the Solidarity movement and the "self-limiting" revolution in Poland, Charter 77 in the former Czechoslovakia, and the doctrine of the "Third Way" in the United Kingdom in the 1990s.

Hence, the selection of the authors has been carefully thought out and the themes in each chapter have been chosen with the general goal of presenting a few faces of moderation that remain relevant to twenty-first-century readers. There are important differences among our authors that should not be glossed over. If they were all political moderates in one way or another, they had different temperaments and followed distinctive agendas dictated by the peculiar contexts in which they lived. While there may not be perfect ideological balance among them, I have included thinkers from different aisles of the political spectrum (Bobbio on the Left, Oakeshott on the Right, Berlin and Aron in the middle) as well as a few such as Adam Michnik or Leszek Kołakowski who are quite difficult to classify according to our conventional political categories.[8]

Since projects similar to this one may appear to contain an air of intellectual superiority, chimerical fancy, and even conceit, I acknowledge from the outset with Shaftesbury that "the Temper of the Pedagogue suites not with the Age. And the World, however it may be taught, will not be tutor'd" (2001: 1:44). Hence, my main goal is to continue a conversation about an important but still surprisingly neglected virtue that is worth having today in our heated political environment. Overall, in the following pages I offer a spirited tour of perplexities, not a doctrinal book or a political agenda. I therefore play the role of a tour guide who introduces the topic and reflects on the virtues and limits of political moderation through the voices of a few thinkers who wrote about it or practiced it.

I do not hope to convince everyone about the benefits of moderation, nor do I want to give the impression that I might be an unconditional defender of this difficult virtue. It would be ironical (and absurd) to write a book about the latter that attempts to definitively settle the debate. One of the main ideas of this volume is that moderation has not one but many faces tied to various shifting contexts. It is important to remember that what was moderate in the

1920s or 1960s may no longer be so today, at least not in the same manner. This does not mean, however, that we should embrace nihilism or relativism for lack of a better solution. As the moderates discussed here show, some choices are (were) more reasonable than others and ought to be pursued (with the proper discernment) in spite of their imperfection.

One of the tasks of political philosophers is to challenge and help enlarge the sense and range of possibilities. I prefer to let those who open this book find and follow their own path, allowing them to see their own sights and draw their own conclusions as they think fit. If I have a sense of the final destination, I am much less certain about the best ways of finding the elusive archipelago of moderation. The readers are therefore invited—and encouraged—to be active participants on this journey, which might, after all, turn out to be much more important and fascinating than Ithaca itself—in this case, the concept of political moderation. Without the appeal of the latter, however, we might have never started the voyage and set sail for the unknown.

CHAPTER 1

The Ethos of Moderation

> What then is the spirit of liberty? I cannot define it. . . . The spirit of liberty is the spirit which is not too sure that it is right; the spirit of liberty is the spirit which seeks to understand the minds of those men and women; the spirit of liberty is the spirit which weighs their interest alongside its own without bias.
>
> —Judge Learned Hand

When Things Fall Apart . . .

Yeats's hauntingly beautiful verses from *The Second Coming* offer one of the best introductions to a book on political moderation in the twentieth century.[1] Here is the Irish poet lamenting the unraveling of the center and the coming of anarchy:

> Turning and turning in the widening gyre
> The falcon cannot hear the falconer;
> Things fall apart; the centre cannot hold;
> Mere anarchy is loosed upon the world,
> The blood-dimmed tide is loosed, and everywhere
> The ceremony of innocence is drowned;
> The best lack all conviction, while the worst
> Are full of passionate intensity. (1962: 99–100)

"Surely, some revelation is at hand," the poet added. And what a revelation it was!

The "rough beast" whose hour came "round at last" and which slouched "toward Bethlehem to be born" was the herald of a bloody century whose balance sheet speaks for itself. Things did fall apart (and not only once) and the center failed to hold precisely when it was most needed. The "worst" proved to be extremely active and full of "passionate intensity." They started, among other things, two devastating world wars, embraced ruthless ideologies that justified the murder of almost a hundred million innocent people in the name of deceiving or criminal ideals, used extensive propaganda techniques and brainwashing methods, and were instrumental in creating mass-scale terror, forced labor, and extermination camps. As the distinguished Spanish essayist and diplomat Salvador de Madariaga once put it (1954: 5), "reason and liberty are precisely the two martyrs of our age." Many words such as equality and liberty had to change their ordinary meanings and were given new ones that sought to distort the reality on the ground. Reckless overconfidence came to be regarded as manly courage, while prudent hesitation and careful consideration of facts were deemed to be forms of treason or cowardice. Moderation was held to be a cloak for pusillanimity, and the ability to see and take into account all sides of a problem was denounced as incapacity to act on any. Fervent advocates of extreme measures were often deemed to be trustworthy partners, while their opponents were regarded with suspicion and dismay.[2] Albert Camus was right then to begin his account of revolutionary ideologies in *The Rebel* with a dark conclusion. In his view, "slave camps under the flag of freedom, massacres justified by philanthropy or the taste for the superhuman" (1956: 4) represented the dark side of the past century that nobody could excuse or ignore any longer.

The seeds of destruction, however, had been planted long before under our own eyes. In the wake of the Paris Commune whose bloodiest episodes brought back the memory of the revolutionary Terror, Rimbaud had proclaimed, "*Voici le temps des assassins*!" How prescient the poet was! If the nineteenth century was a century of hope, the one that followed, the most political century in history, turned out to be extremely violent and cruel. With the assassination of the Archduke Ferdinand in Sarajevo in 1914, Europe entered a long "age of anxiety" after a century of relative calm and prosperity. The drumbeat of barbarism sounded in the very heart of the civilized world before setting the entire world aflame. The Bolsheviks drew direct inspiration from the Terror of 1793–94 and invented a new style of politics that showed in plain daylight how fragile and unstable the hold of civilization is. For all the great and undeniable achievements of the past century—the rise of the average human life expectancy, the eradication of many illnesses, the conquest of the space, the outlawing of various forms of discrimination—the two totalitarianisms that originated in Europe (fascism and communism) constituted new forms of barbarism with a modern face that cast a long shadow over the entire world. Whether we like it or not, we are heirs to an epoch that produced Hitler, Stalin, Mao, and Pol Pot, larger-than-life tyrants whose hubris far surpassed the lust for power of their predecessors. Confronted with these distressing facts and numbers, even Voltaire's Candide would have paused for a moment to question the idea of progress and might have been inclined to abandon his proverbial sunny optimism.

Today, the decades from the 1920s to the 1960s may seem a part of another world reinforcing the belief that the past is a foreign country. But as we look at the world around us, we realize that this is a costly illusion. Simone Weil was probably right to argue that "modern life is given over to immoderation. Immoderation invades everything: actions and thought, public and private. . . . There is no more balance anywhere" (1997: 211). Our undeniable technological advances have not been matched by corresponding progress in the realm of morality. As Norberto Bobbio remarked (2002: 191), "we may be technologically literate but many of us are still morally illiterate. . . . Our moral sense develops, always supposing it does develop, much more slowly than economic power, political power, and technological power." That is why, as we enter our own (postmodern) age of anxiety fraught with new dangers and challenges, it might be timely and necessary to examine how twentieth-century European intellectuals responded to their challenges and sought to preserve the values of civilization threatened by the rise of totalitarian ideologies and secular religions such as Nazism and communism.

I am a child of that century, having been born during a postwar period known in the West as *les trentes glorieuses*; alas, the Eastern part of the old continent where I grew up was not that lucky. After the Iron Curtain fell over Europe, the entire world became divided into two separate worlds that waged a long and costly Cold War. Life under communism had many shortcomings, to use a euphemism, but it taught me at least two important lessons. The first one was that, after all, there is no fundamental distinction between the "brilliant" future envisaged by the founders of Marxism and the real communism that was offered to us as a gateway to a perfect tomorrow. What I saw with my own eyes was not a perversion of the ideals of Marx or Lenin; it was actually, for the most part, the realization or consequences of their own principles. The real communism that existed in Eastern Europe and the former Soviet Union implied not only the triumph of the proletariat, but also the monopoly of a vanguard elite showered with obscene privileges denied to the majority of citizens, the persistence of severe economic shortages for the masses, the strict punishment of dissenters, the conscious promotion of incompetence over competence, unrelenting official propaganda, and the omnipresence of the secret police that relied on constant spying and denunciation. The second lesson that life under a totalitarian regime taught me was about the fragility of freedom and the importance of political moderation as an antidote to zealotry and fanaticism.

Moderation, the subject of this book, is therefore, at least for some of us, a legitimate reaction to the violent age of extremes in which we have lived. It is one of those key virtues without which, as John Adams once said (1954: 92), "every man in power becomes a ravenous beast of prey." But I have also come to regard it as something much more than a circumstantial (contextual) virtue or a mere character trait. The argument offered in this book is that moderation, in its many faces, is a fighting and bold creed grounded in a complex and eclectic conception of the world. A great advantage of the latter is that can be shared by diverse actors on all sides of the political spectrum (not only in the center!) in their efforts to promote necessary social and political reforms, defend liberty, and keep the ship of the state on an even keel. Because it rejects ideological thinking, moderation implies a good dose of courage, non-conformism, flexibility, and discernment, as suggested by the image chosen as the cover of this book. Finally, as a tolerant and civil virtue related to temperance and opposed to violence, moderation respects the spontaneity of life and the pluralism of the world and can protect us against pride, one-sidedness, intolerance, and fanaticism in our moral and political commitments.

A Challenging Virtue

To be sure, this is not how moderation is usually perceived today when it seems particularly difficult to articulate a convincing and effective philosophy of this elusive virtue. At first sight, few ideas might seem more quixotic than moderation in modern politics. Why did so many intellectuals eschew it and fall under the sway of grand schemes of social and political improvement that led to mass poverty and terror? Following Plato's example, they searched for their own "Syracuse"—be that Moscow, Berlin, Havana, Beijing, or Tehran—or visited "Syracuse" in their own restless imaginations. Many of them willingly offered their services to tyrants, defended the indefensible—that is, cruel regimes that displayed no regard for human dignity and liberty—and defiantly ignored the lessons of history, often choosing authenticity and adventure over humility, decency, and moderation.[3] Others felt increasingly alienated in modern society and spoke as prophets of extremity, in search for radical cures to the ills of modernity. Some of them (Heidegger) took to task the legacy of the Enlightenment, while others (Foucault, Sartre, Derrida) spoke in the name of the ideas of the Enlightenment and used them in order to diagnose and criticize the malaise in our political and social institutions. Finally, a select few gave up politics altogether and retreated into their own mythical "Castalias" or withdrew into their hermitages of pure thought, often on the top of a "magic mountain," far away from the sound and fury of the world, preparing themselves for the appearance of the last gods.

Whatever the reasons for their political and existential choices might have been, one thing is obvious: these thinkers did not have much interest in moderation, which they regarded as a weak and insignificant virtue, incapable of quenching their thirst for absolute, authenticity, and adventure. This should come as no surprise as many are usually enthralled by allegedly strong virtues—courage, prowess, fearlessness, and so forth—which are seen as incompatible with moderation. These are the virtues of the powerful, those who lead and govern, the state builders, the "lions" of this world. For them, there is no limit to what they may do with the lives of others; everything seems permissible to them, even violence. Allegedly weak virtues are those practiced by ordinary, inconspicuous individuals, the "lambs" of the world, the poor and the humiliated ones. They do not make history; instead, the latter is made without them or, better said, above them.[4]

How are we to explain the general skepticism toward moderation? It may be useful to start with a commonplace. Moderation seems to be the touchstone of many contemporary democratic political regimes, since no regime can properly function without compromise, bargaining, and moderation, and the proper functioning of our representative system and institutions depends to a great extent on political moderation. And yet, among major concepts in political theory and history (justice, liberty, equality, natural right, or general will), moderation is unique in being understudied. As a virtue, political moderation finds itself in an awkward situation. On the one hand, it has rarely been examined as a self-standing concept, even if we have been familiar with the works of famous thinkers considered to be moderates such as Aristotle, Montesquieu, Burke, or Tocqueville; their ideas have rarely been seen as belonging to a larger tradition of political moderation broadly construed. On the other hand, moderation is one of those concepts that may suffer from semantic bleaching. Sometimes, it is used in a very loose or narrow sense that fails to adequately capture its political, moral, and institutional complexity. This happens, for example, when moderation is conceived only as a relative concept defining itself according to whatever forms of extremism it opposes or whatever the poles might be between which it seeks to carve a middle path. A similar situation arises when moderation is equated with a defensive posture or a philosophy for weak souls, *une philosophie pour les âmes tendres*, as Sartre once put it. Finally, moderation has sometimes been represented as an allegedly aggressive and coercive means of social control in the history of early modern Europe.[5]

The conventional image of this concept accounts to a certain extent for this curious and confusing situation. Moderation often appears as an ambiguous virtue whose genealogy and history are too vague to be properly defined or analyzed.[6] Not surprisingly, we tend to misrepresent or distort the true meaning(s) of moderation, often regarded as the virtue of tepid, middling, shy, timorous, indecisive, and lukewarm individuals, incapable of generating heroic acts or great stories. Sometimes, moderation is desired not as a good in itself but mostly for its consequences, including the control of one's desires, self-mastery, and harmony of the soul. In the first book of *The Republic*, for example, Plato showed the limitations of this narrow view of moderation embodied by an old and respectable character, Cephalus.[7] His moderation in old age, a time of freedom from the domination of appetites, was a weak virtue that relied only upon the "release from a bunch of insane masters" (329d), suppression of desires, and faithful obedience to custom and tradition. This type of moderation appears as an obstacle to the pursuit of a free and happy life rather than a means to it. To make things more complicated, sometimes we may even need to abandon moderation for a while. There are, in fact, goods and values that are more valuable, at least for a certain time, than moderation, and we may have to act sometimes with immoderation in order to achieve necessary reforms, even if such courses of action might be criticized as radical or uncivil. As such, moderation challenges our imagination and appears as a fuzzy concept that defies universal claims and moral absolutes and is very difficult to theorize in the abstract (unlike, for example, justice or rights).

Lately, there has been a slight revival of interest in moderation that should not go unnoticed. Harry Clor (2008) analyzed moderation as a political, personal, and philosophic virtue, while Peter Berkowitz (2013) and Paul Carrese (2016) made a strong case for linking conservatism and political moderation viewed as a constitutional imperative. Ethan Shagan (2011) argued that the ideal of moderation (used to describe a wide variety of positions from that of the Church of England to the Conformists and Puritans) functioned as an ideology of control and as a tool of social, religious, and political power in sixteenth- and seventeenth-century England. William Egginton (2011) discussed various aspects of religious moderation, while Julien Boudon (2011) traced briefly the history of the idea of moderation and ended with a few comments on the relevance of this virtue for contemporary French politics. Finally, in the pages of the *New York Times*, David Brooks has courageously defended political moderation as an indispensable virtue that might help us effectively tackle some of the most pressing issues we are facing today in an age of increasing ideological intransigence. To all this, one can add the passionate defense of Centrism put forward by John Avlon (2004 and 2014), whose work complements the detailed analysis offered by Geoffrey Kabaservice (2012) who documented the trend toward immoderation within the GOP in the last five decades. Finally, a special issue of the *Sociological Review* (2013) was devoted to the "sociologies of moderation" and brought together scholars from different fields who explored difference aspects of moderation. This issue was ably edited by Alexander Smith who has been studying the activism of grassroots moderates in Kansas, a state often seen as incompatible with political moderation.[8]

A Fighting and Civil Virtue

What is then the mentality of those who put moderation first? Moderates share a steady preoccupation with political evil and seek to avoid the extremes of cruelty, suffering, anarchy, and civil war. They tend to keep the lines of dialogue open and reach out to their political opponents in order to preserve the fundamental values of their communities. They do not see the world in Manichaean terms that divide it into forces of good (or light) and agents of evil (or darkness). They refuse the posture of prophets, champion sobriety in political thinking and action, and endorse an ethics of responsibility as opposed to an ethics of absolute ends. Sometimes, this involves significant personal risks and costs, including serving time in prison. If we are to look for a single word to characterize many (though not all) political moderates, then they might be described as trimmers who seek to adjust the cargo and trim the sails of the ship of the state in order to keep it on an even keel. Although their adjustments may be small and unheroic at times, they are often enough to save the state from ruin. In many respects, moderates are similar to the courageous tightrope walkers who must always be extremely careful to maintain their balance and sense of direction.

As a fighting creed, moderation is a combination of prudence, commitment, and courage far from the image of a lukewarm and indecisive mean between extremes with which it is often equated.[9] The intellectual trajectories of the thinkers discussed in this book confirm this point. Theirs was a bold form of moderation that proves that Nietzsche was wrong when dismissing this virtue as proper only to a conformist herd.[10] In reality, as Montaigne had noted (1991: 1261), it is much easier and less commendable to make one's journey "along the margins," that is, the extremes, "where the edges serve as a limit and a guide, rather than take the wide and unhedged Middle Way." Being a moderate (in the sense indicated in these pages) demands bold vision, audacity, and firmness as well as a certain degree of nonconformity. Our moderates did not propose a Parnassian retreat to a nonpolitical sphere—art, literature, religion—free from the impurity of politics. If they found themselves caught up between political parties, their political moderation was not incompatible with firm and passionate commitment, nor did it condemn them to powerlessness in the political arena. Their moderation sometimes required them to take sides—though not always the same side—and made some of them appear unpredictable, giving their choices "a provisional and skeptical cast."[11] Yet, their actions and initiatives were not devoid of a certain logic which can be described with the following words of Simone Weil. "If we know in what way society is unbalanced," she once wrote in *Gravity and Grace* (1997: 224), "we must do what we can to add weight to the lighter scale. . . . But we must have formed a conception of equilibrium and be ever ready to change sides like justice, 'that fugitive from the camp of the conquerors.'"[12] This is an excellent description of what moderates usually do for the sake of restoring balance and social harmony in times of crisis and a good illustration of the paradoxical nature of political moderation.

To restore equilibrium in society, moderates tend to adopt some of the soundest attitudes and principles of all parties and facilitate agreements between them in order to calm passions and heal wounds. They seek to protect and foster the balance between diverse social and political forces and interests on which political pluralism, order, and freedom depend in modern society. Sometimes this requires them to deftly adapt their strategies to shifting circumstances. To this effect, they reject an all-or-nothing approach and always keep an open mind, engaging in dialogue, and accepting new evidence and arguments on all sides, including from their opponents. In so doing, they remain faithful to one of their fundamental principles according to which their main duty is "to suppress the excesses and to condemn them publicly."[13] Far from being a synonym of soft-mindedness, timidity, and hesitation, this type of moderation is a fighting, courageous, and nonconformist virtue that refuses the litmus test of ideological purity and opposes zealotry in all of its forms. It is a strong and energetic form of moderation that must be clearly distinguished from the "counterfeits of pusillanimity and indecision" denounced by Burke (1992: 16). It thrives on partisanship and does not always search for a cozy (and ultimately illusory) political consensus on dividing issues. It radiates openness and generosity toward others and refuses to practice political vendettas; instead, it takes contrary opinions seriously and argues against them without going to extremes and without displaying excessive zeal.

At the same time, we must also be prepared to admit that without a certain degree of immoderation, even moderation might sometimes become ineffective or even counterproductive. Some form of immoderation may sometimes be necessary to reach the golden mean itself. "A grain of boldness is everything," the seventeenth-century Jesuit writer Baltasar Gracián once wrote. "This is an important piece of prudence" (1993: 74). Sometimes, a certain form of "fanaticism" sui generis may be justified as the political mobilization of the refusal to compromise on issues on which there can be no reasonable compromises.[14] Yet, although I am prepared to accept that there are causes that may sometimes be pursued for a while without moderation, depending on the context, I believe that fanaticism and extremism cannot be justified as enduring features of any civilized society, regardless of the causes they pretend to serve. Any defense of fanaticism works only in exceptional circumstances, and it is difficult to see how it could be applied to normal politics.

Might flexibility then be the virtue appropriate to the politics of open societies? As the opposite of rigidity and dogmatism, flexibility has something in common with political moderation, even if it is not the same thing. What I have in mind here is a particular type of flexibility—a certain form of "inconsistency"—adapted to an imperfect world in constant flux in which "one contradiction disappears only to give way to another" (Kołakowski, 1968: 217) making any universal synthesis of values impossible. In our ever changing world, contradictions between values and principles cannot be reconciled, and sometimes a certain form of flexibility and inconsistency sui generis might be the best way of dealing with them by allowing us to preserve a fragile equilibrium. That is why under certain circumstances, in order to preserve this balance, we might have to espouse a certain form of creative immoderation, while at other times we might need a peculiar brand of "fanatical moderates."[15] One could then claim that moderates are called to combine "a tough mind with a tender heart,"[16] and are often required to blend opposites in what might appear to others as an inconsistent manner.

A few interesting examples come to mind. The first one is a defense of a bold and robust form of moderation put forward by someone who lived through the darkest times of the twentieth century in Eastern Europe. A prominent literary critic and religious writer educated in interwar Romania, and author of one of the most interesting books (*The Diary of Happiness*) published since the fall of the Iron Curtain, Nicolae Steinhardt (1912–89) lived under two totalitarian regimes that had no place for political moderation.[17] In a very interesting essay published in Romanian, "Broad Liberalism: The Problem of Moderation and Violence," in 1937, at a point in time when the whole of Europe was rapidly descending into the abyss, Steinhardt argued that in order to prevent a tragic outcome, moderate ideas had to be affirmed and pursued with energy, force, and, if need be, even with a certain form of violence. In his view, "violent moderation" and "extreme center" were not oxymora as we might assume. "One can be a partisan of middling normality," Steinhardt wrote (2009: 535), "one may defend liberty and order, but with determination, strong convictions, and sometimes in a violent manner. We know that one can be a liberal and an extremist at the same time. But one can also be an extremist of the center," he added. For Steinhardt, moderation was such a mixed—and exciting—ideal requiring strong commitments and a firm determination to fight for the preservation of the fundamental values of our civilization. "Moderation," he believed (2009: 536), "cannot be defended or restored by verbal means, fear, or subtle conversations. . . . In order to promote liberty, the center must be as passionate as the extremes." There is notable difference between this energetic moderation defending an "extreme center" and moderation seen as a virtue suitable only to a "dead center" for lukewarm and weak souls.

The second example is better known and comes from the pen of a Nobel Laureate whose inspiring words were chosen as the epigraph to this book. At the end of *The Rebel*, after having exposed the shortcomings of many revolutionary projects that ended in tyranny and disappointment, Albert Camus made a moving plea for another type of radical moderation. Referring to "the extenuating intransigence of moderation" (1956: 303), he viewed the latter as a rebellious political attitude that does not avoid tensions but freely embraces them. Animated by the spirit of rebellion, the persons who embrace this bold form of moderation take the part of "true realism." They see farther than both the utopian revolutionary spirits who admit of no limits to their plans and the prudent bourgeois minds who are satisfied with the comfort of the known world. Moderation properly understood, Camus argued, "is not the opposite of rebellion." It is sometimes an unconventional form of dissent that "can only live by rebellion [and] is a perpetual conflict continually created and mastered by the intelligence" (1956: 301). Yet, this form of rebellious moderation is not a blank check to irresponsibility, for "it does not triumph either in the impossible or in the abyss. It finds its equilibrium through them." It starts from the recognition that while "excess is always a comfort, and sometimes a career," moderation is always going to be the more difficult choice because it is "nothing but pure tension" (1956: 301). "Whatever we do," Camus concluded, "excess will always keep its place in the heart of man" and our task is not to unleash "our crimes and our ravages" on the world, but "to fight them in ourselves and in others."[18] To achieve all this, we can turn to a virtue for burning hearts: moderation.

Even when the latter manifests itself as a fighting creed, it remains committed to civility, an essential virtue in our democratic and pluralist societies that cannot properly function without it. In the absence of civility and, implicitly, moderation, our open societies risk succumbing to extremism, violence, sectarianism, and fanaticism. As a face of moderation, civility polishes the edges and calms down passions, allowing us to affirm and negotiate our personal and political differences without invectives, open conflicts, or civil wars. It starts from the assumption that social, political, economic, moral, and cultural pluralism is an ineradicable aspect of our modern society and seeks to do justice to its diversity. It acts as a necessary restraint on the passions with which we pursue our interests and ideas by placing "a limit on the irreconcilability with which parochial ends are pursued" (Shils, 1997: 341). Last but not least, also like moderation, civility protects citizens from abuses of power committed by their rulers, while allowing (and encouraging) the latter to exercise their authority within the proper limits of the laws.

The strong correlation between moderation, civility (as a mode of social and political action), and manners warrants closer scrutiny. A distinction can be made between manners in general and civility as a particularly political virtue and face of moderation.[19] To be sure, there is much more to civility than polite manners. Civility presupposes that while we all are free to pursue our private ends, we are also called to abide by the requirements of the common good loosely defined. Civility, Shils argued (1997: 340), implies "a norm which gives precedence to the interest of the collectivity over the individual or parochial interest." This means only that the rules of civility are meant to allow us to pursue certain things in common that are essential for the preservation of our communities, in spite of our personal disagreements and differences and without ever being able to eradicate them.

In particular, good manners, civility, courtesy, and moderation are essential to the functioning of our parliamentary regimes in which, to use the words of a wise politician (Sir William Harcourt), the survival of the system requires to be able to constantly dine with the opposition.[20] Being courteous and civil does not mean, however, obliterating the differences that distinguish us from our opponents, nor does it imply what we ought to give up our ideas and ideals in an illusory pursuit of a fictitious common ground. It is a certain style of thinking and action that makes us regard our antagonists as reasonable opponents with whom, our differences notwithstanding, we can argue about the best ways of pursuing both individual and common projects and interests, rather than implacable enemies who must be eliminated from the public sphere. As such, civility requires that confident and often self-righteous claims to "moral clarity"[21] be tempered by the constant awareness of our own shortcomings and limitations, as well as of the virtues and merits of our opponents. It presupposes a persistent attempt and effort to try to understand the points of view of the latter and see the world for a moment through their own eyes. As a face of moderation, civility rejects the extreme partisanship and sectarianism that can be found in ideological politics operating according to the sharp distinctions between good and evil, Left and Right, "children of light" and "children of darkness," "friend and foe," "us and them," among which no combination or agreement is seen as admissible or possible.[22] Civility limits not only the losses inflicted by open political and social conflicts, but also the intensity of the latter and prevents pluralistic and open societies from descending into a ruthless war of all against all.

It is essential to remember that principled disagreement is different from hostility and partisanship, and that civility does not necessarily presuppose the reduction or disappearance of disagreement in open societies. If moderation and civility can lessen the ardor of ideological disputes by emphasizing what we share over what divides us, it might not be always possible to do that. For sometimes people are unwilling and psychologically unable to compromise their principles or interests, and any view that is more moderate may seem to them as a betrayal of their beliefs.[23] The question remains whether a refusal to moderate one's views constitutes a denial of civility or something else. Once again, the truth is in the details and there is no algorithm that can decide this issue in an abstract manner.

Yet, it is possible to regard civility as a necessary political virtue even (or precisely) in the midst of uncompromising (and sometimes unrelenting) antagonism between political positions and platforms bitterly opposed to one another and among which there seems to exist little chance for agreement. We should not then expect civility to be able to evacuate passion, anger, and disagreement from politics. But it is the task of civility (as a face of moderation) to calm and restrain passions when the game of politics becomes dangerously overheated and political actors tend to give priority to campaigning and winning over legislating and governing.

The Lost Art of Trimming

It is here that the close connection between moderation and trimming comes to the fore and requires further explanation.[24] Some moderates have been trimmers while others have not (the opposite also applies). Trimming as a face of political moderation is one of those concepts that challenge our imagination more than others and is bound to remain an essentially contested term. This is demonstrated first and foremost by the many meanings of the verb "to trim": to prepare, to put something in proper order (e.g., to trim one's mustache), to clip (for example, the dead branches of a tree), to cut something down to the required size, to balance a ship by shifting its cargo or an aircraft by adjusting stabilizers, to modify according to expediency, to adjust one's opinions, actions, expenditures (to trim one's sails), to adapt (opportunistically or not) to ever changing conditions and situations.

It was George Saville, Marquis of Halifax (1633–95), who penned the classical definition of the trimmer in his essay, "The Character of a Trimmer," written in 1684–85 and published in 1688 (under the name of Halifax's uncle, Sir William Coventry).[25] At the heart of Halifax's definition of the trimmer was the classical image of the captain seeking to keep his ship on an even keel by using different techniques to maintain its equipoise. "This innocent word *Trimmer*," wrote Halifax, "signifieth no more than this, That if Men are together in a boat, and one part of the company would weigh it down on one side, another would make it lean as much to the contrary; it happeneth there is a third Opinion of those, who conceive it would do as well, if the Boat went even, without endangering the passengers."[26] It is worth pointing out that during Halifax's time, the word "trimmer" had a pejorative connotation derived from the intense religious and political controversies of that period. It meant at the same time not only a "man of moderation" and a "man of Latitude," but also a "neutral" and uncertain person, and a "traitor."

Halifax's merit is to have given the term a more positive and civil connotation that is quite relevant for the study of political moderation. Instead of quarrelling with his reputation of a trimmer, he assumed it "as a title of honor, and vindicated, with great vivacity, the dignity of the appellation" (Macaulay, 1913: 1:234). Although he was for some time at the center of English politics, either at the court or in opposition to the latter, Halifax remained politically uncommitted and refrained from joining any political association, party, or group. As a trimmer, through his interventions and initiatives, he attempted to reduce the differences between factions instead of adopting and inflaming their political passions. His distrust of parties ran deep and stemmed from his belief that the intensity of political contest gives men "a habit of being unuseful to the public by turning in a circle of wrangling and railing, which they cannot get out of" (Halifax, 1969: 209). Furthermore, Halifax believed that the trimmers' independence of mind and unpredictability are incompatible with strict party discipline, which requires conformism and dogmatism: "Ignorance maketh most men go into a Party, and shame keepeth them from getting out of it" (1969: 209). On this view, trimmers can never be loyal members of any party and are often condemned to marginality.

It is this peculiar combination of flexible tactics, forward-looking attitude, and conservative interests that makes the position of a trimmer like Halifax unclassifiable and likely to be mischaracterized or misunderstood as opportunism. Trimmers like him go backward and forward and change sides quite often in such a way that in the end no side fully trusts them. They always leave open the possibility of dialogue with their opponents, and their changes of mind or course are such that their transitions are never absolute. They have nothing in common with those who fly from one extreme to another, and who regard the party that they have deserted with an animosity far exceeding that of implacable enemies. They tend to be severe with their friends and always in friendly relations with their moderate opponents. When they stay with a party for some time, they refuse to go all in, and they do not turn against that party after leaving. As trimmers both by intellect and constitution of heart and mind, instead of adopting and inflaming the passions of those whom they join, they try to diffuse among them something of the spirit of those whom they have just left.

Trimming and trimmers come in different shapes and nuances. As Cass Sunstein pointed out in a perceptive essay on this topic (2009: 1059–62), we must distinguish between trimmers about particular and simple issues and trimmers about large and complex political questions. It might be argued that almost any issue affords some degree of trimming and, in Sunstein's words (2009: 1063), "nearly any position could be described as trimming, because any position is likely to be between at least some imaginable poles." Trimmers also have many reasons to act that must be properly distinguished from each other. According to Goodheart, some trimmers try "to find common ground between extremes not for the sake of compromise but *because reason does not have a single location on the political spectrum*" (2013: 21, emphases added). Some trimmers are simply compromisers, while others are "preservers"; some trim on principle believing that trimming is justified along epistemological grounds (in light of our imperfect knowledge and limited information), while others trim as circumstances require for purely strategic reasons.[27] On some issues, for example, such as the rule of law or civil peace, they refuse to trim or to make any compromise. They pay due attention to the survival and security of their communities and when the danger of civil war or anarchy looms large, they do everything in their power to avoid the worst and attempt to restore the balance between competing groups, interests, and forces in society.

That is why trimmers as moderates are notoriously difficult to place on the scale of modern political ideologies. Although they share a number of affinities with both the conservative and liberal traditions, neither of these doctrines can fully claim them as their own (reliable) representatives. Trimmers are neither saints nor ideologues; they refuse the litmus test of ideological purity, oppose radicalism and zealotry, have a solid understanding of history and the irreducibly complex nature of politics, and are aware of the tragic nature of political events and of the inevitable plurality of social, moral, and political values and goods. By acknowledging the antinomies and uncertainty of political life as well as the complexity of moral life, trimmers (and moderates in general) successfully avoid the fixation on one single dimension of integrity, moral clarity, or the political good. They start from the assumption that the life of a statesman is merely a choice between evils and that, like most questions of civil prudence, political matters are neither black nor white, but gray. Political affairs admit exceptions and demand constant modifications that must be made not by an exact algorithm, but by the rules of prudence often (though not always) seeking the mean between deficiency and excess in each case.

Although trimmers sometimes change their political allegiances in response to shifting circumstances, and endorse certain means or courses of action that might counteract their initial agenda, trimming should not be equated with opportunism. As moderates concerned with the preservation of political equilibrium and liberty, they believe that the absolute domination of any single idea, principle, party, or group would spell the end of freedom and the rule of law in society. It is this final goal—the preservation of political balance between rival principles—and their opposition to Manichaeism rather than abstract theories of liberty, equality, or justice that tell them when compromise and accommodation are necessary, desirable, and possible, and when bolder action or extreme measures may be needed to save the community from ruin. Moreover, trimmers attempt to facilitate the dialogue and cooperation between various social and political forces, groups, ideas, and interests.

As such, trimming is an art of balancing different ideas, groups, and interests on which political pluralism, social order, and freedom depend in modern society. It poses a significant challenge to the practitioners of ideological politics who claim to stand on principle and whose black-and-white universe consists of sharp contrasts. Trimming also challenges inflexible politicians who seek ideological or moral clarity or purity at all costs and proudly march toward their goals, refusing to compromise their values under any circumstances. Because they are willing and prepared to adjust their beliefs and choices to changing situations, trimmers refuse most of the time to think of politics as an arena in which the forces of the good and evil fight against each other in an epic battle of historical significance. In most circumstances, trimmers prefer to engineer compromises between acceptable values and principles rather than try to achieve perfect moral clarity or definitive solutions to complex and contested political issues.

As moderates, trimmers have often been criticized for being impure, hesitant, opportunistic, timid, vacillating, or neutral; at other times, they have been seen as inconsistent, weak, or too ingenious in devising objections and pretexts. Either way, they appear to many as exotic voices in the wilderness, too weak to form a consistent political tradition, and thus share the disdain heaped upon moderates of all colors. As Henry Adams wrote in *The Education of Henry Adams*, as a cast, trimmers (whom he identified as the followers of Tocqueville and J. S. Mill) are timid and hesitant—and with good reason—and their timidity, "which is high wisdom in philosophy, sicklies the whole cast of thought in action" (1960: 192). They are often accused of dealing in contradictory and equivocating doctrines and practicing a continual seesaw of admissions and retractions. Their moderation and prudence, it is sometimes claimed, are nothing else than synonyms of weariness, and their works are time-bound and incapable of transcending historical circumstances. Moreover, trimming is difficult to define and explain whereas political doctrines such as conservatism, socialism, and communism are more easily understood because they are based on clear and unambiguous principles. In this regard, trimming shares a lot with Whiggism, whose ambivalent nature once triggered the following famous reaction from Disraeli: "A Tory and a Radical, I understand; a Whig—a democratic aristocrat, I cannot understand."[28] Hence, trimmers appear as exotic voices in the wilderness, perhaps too weak to form a consistent political tradition. We tend to distrust them because we are inclined to see them as moral chameleons who seek only personal advancement and seem therefore unworthy of our respect. Most often we are puzzled by such characters and do not know how to characterize their attitudes properly. Sometimes, we use the word "bipartisanship" to do so, but this might not be the best term to describe their moderate positions.

It would be unwise to ignore or dismiss all these critiques of trimming, which might contain a kernel of truth after all. At the same time, it would be difficult to deny that trimming, as Joseph Hamburger argued a few decades ago, constitutes an important and distinct political tradition "that can accommodate men with radically different outlooks in normal times. This tradition of moderation attracts those who are sensitive to crisis and who give priority to the problem of maintaining the legacy of rules and procedures and civilized habits that provide the framework within which party and even ideological politics is permissible" (Hamburger, 1976: 188). The meaning of trimming that I have in mind here is an essential face of moderation as an art of balance. It refers to adjusting one's opinions or viewpoints so as to moderate the zeal of opposing factions and keep the ship of the state on an even keel by offering necessary and timely concessions in order to prevent anarchy, violence, or civil war.

As both a disposition and an act of judgment, trimming has a close relation with political moderation. It is not a mere coincidence that many of the moderates discussed in this book were trimmers who pursued their aims by looking to both the Left and Right and were able to adjust their attitudes depending on what circumstances required in order to maintain the balance of their political communities. They believed that political reason is a computing principle by which we balance inconveniences and engage in give-and-take compromises that seek to preserve and reform at the same time. As trimmers, they were inclined to say, with Dr. Rieux, the hero of Camus's *The Plague*: "Salvation is just too big a word for me. I don't aim so high. I'm concerned with man's health; and for me, his health comes first" (Camus, 1991: 219). Their position was characterized by a fundamental modesty that prevented them from catching the malady that "consists in believing nothing and claiming to know everything" (Camus, 1974: 229). They had a good sense of priorities and paid due attention to the survival and security of their communities; when the dangers of anarchy loomed large, they did everything in their power to avoid the worst.

As such, their political moderation was an upshot of their belief that what matters above all in politics is, in Aristotle's words, "to have the right feelings at the right time, about the right things, toward the right people, for the right end, and in the similar way."[29] Sometimes, the essence of a moderate outlook lies not so much in *what* opinions one holds, but in the *manner* in which they are defended: "Instead of being held dogmatically, they are held tentatively, and with a consciousness that new evidence may at any moment lead to their abandonment" (Russell, 1950: 15). To give just one example, a moderate spirit on the Left such as Camus was not afraid to claim in 1957, in the aftermath of the Hungarian failed revolt, that "today, conformity is on the Left" and took this colleagues to task for using a defective vocabulary, "capable merely of stereotyped replies, constantly at a loss when faced with the truth" (1974: 170–71). Camus's example shows that far from being an expression of opportunism, trimming (as a face of moderation) can be grounded in a robust sense of moral requirements and possibilities that go beyond what deontological rules and categorical imperatives may prescribe. As moderates, trimmers accept that not every action admits of a mean; this is the case not only with theft, murder, slavery, on which no compromise is ever justified or acceptable, but also with more ambiguous examples such as lying or using dubious means to achieve commendable ends in politics. Furthermore, there can be no moderation and trimming about the principles of what is scientifically known to be true or what is universally acknowledged to be beyond dispute; moderation and trimming are about things that are neither demonstrable nor scientifically known. They concern particular things that are uncertain and open to deliberation and are by nature controversial and unsettled, requiring experience and prudence.

Hence, trimmers understand that the science of government is by definition practical and extremely complex and the real effects of ideas and policies are not always immediate; they are also prepared to take into account the unintended consequences of human actions. Furthermore, they accept that liberties and rights vary with times and circumstances, and cannot be settled upon any abstract or universal rule. Sometimes, it is extremely difficult to hit the intermediate accurately and we need to content ourselves with the lesser of two evils in order to be moderate; in other cases, we need to incline toward the excess or toward the deficiency, depending on circumstances. That is why trimmers tend to be skeptical toward grand schemes and abstract theories and favor a flexible and pragmatic agenda that is open to dialogue and compromise and does not view politics along the lines of the "friend-foe" or "us versus them" distinctions. They fear opposite excesses and reject single-mindedness and calls for absolute moral clarity in politics. "The moderate doesn't try to solve those arguments," David Brooks wrote (2012). "There are no ultimate solutions. The moderate tries to preserve the tradition of conflict, keeping the opposing sides balanced. She understands that most public issues involve trade-offs. In most great arguments, there are two partially true points of view, which sit in tension. The moderate tries to maintain a rough proportion between them, to keep her country along its historic trajectory."

This explains why trimmers (and moderates in general) tend to espouse, in Michael Oakeshott's terms, a "politics of skepticism" different from "politics of faith" of their radical or extremist opponents.[30] They refuse the posture of seers or prophets and are aware that the world contains both good and evil in varying proportions at different times. They are skeptical toward visions of politics based on passionate calls for moral or religious purity. Their instinct is to explore and understand what each side has to say and to figure out what, if anything, might be derived from each position that might have some value.

Sometimes, trimmers accept that certain issues must be left undecided while at other times a certain form of clarity may be achieved. They are aware that good and evil coexist in such a way that nothing is so evil that it does not contain some grain of good, just as nothing is so good that it does not contain some dose of evil. Distrusting any vision of politics that has a messianic or soteriological ring, trimmers believe that the most important aim of politics is to reduce suffering, the intensity of conflict, and the level of violence. To achieve all this, one needs only an imperfect understanding of reality and must remain as close as possible to the facts themselves, and avoid letting oneself be carried away by abstractions and utopian ideals.

But trimmers (and moderates in general) are not supposed to be indifferent spectators located in a hypothetical center; it bears repeating that their natural home is not necessarily the middle party. If they are located most of the time between political parties, they may still choose one side or another, though not always the same side. Hence, their unpredictability and alleged inconsistency, which are often wrongly interpreted as lack of principle, make them difficult to understand in the eyes of their critics.[31] In reality, trimmers fight with determination for preserving the constitution of a country and defending liberty against its opponents. As such, trimming as a face of moderation is perfectly compatible with firmness and resolute action, and trimmers think no precaution would be too great to avoid social chaos or civil war. They do not shy away from recommending tough measures that might sometimes be necessary to avoid the latter. At the same time, they seek to promote possible compromises and agreements that could heal the open wounds of the body politic. In general, trimmers tend to support the party that they dislike least, even when they do not entirely approve of its principles. Although their actions always have a provisional and skeptical cast, they are guided by a few values and principles, and they search for solutions that may be healing and can promote agreements and compromise. Trimmers believe in the supremacy of laws and constitutions,[32] which they consider as powerful antidotes to arbitrary and unlimited power and adore "the goddess Truth,"[33] without becoming fanatics of law and truth. Standing for balance and moderation—they often (though not always) seek "a wise mean between barbarous extremes"[34]—they abhor any form of idolatry and, feeling the complexity and uncertainty of everything human, distrust those who view politics as the pursuit of certainty, or the search for absolute moral clarity or purity.

To sum up, one might then claim that the ethos of moderation (and trimming) is similar in many respects to the elusive spirit of liberty described by

Judge Learned Hand in the epigraph to this chapter. Just like the spirit of liberty, the ethos of moderation (and trimming) cannot be properly defined, but can be described only with approximation. It is the spirit that is never entirely sure that it is in the right, yet knows quite well what it ought to avoid and what it should oppose in most circumstances. It is the spirit that when hesitating between two parties or agendas chooses to adhere to that which it dislikes least, though in the whole it may not entirely approve of it. And it is the spirit that reaches out to others seeking to understand their values and perspectives and strives to find a balance between the irony of the "jester" and the seriousness of the "priest."[35] It is finally the spirit that admits, in the words of another moderate (Ortega y Gasset), that "life is perplexity" and quite mixed and that our duty is not to try to simplify it. On this view, we must refuse to devote ourselves to the feverish affirmation of any single idea, value, corner, or aspect of life at the expense of all others.[36] This complex art of balance will be the subject of the following chapters, which focus on the intellectual and political trajectories of several exemplary political moderates who managed to remain non-captive and independent minds in dark times.[37]

CHAPTER 2

The Lucidity of Moderation

Raymond Aron as a "Committed Observer"

> Freedom flourishes in temperate zones; it does not survive the burning faith of prophets and crowds.
>
> —Raymond Aron

"Notre dernier professeur d'hygiène intellectuelle," our last teacher of intellectual hygiene: this is how the famous anthropologist Claude Lévi-Strauss referred to Raymond Aron (1905–83) a year after the latter's death at the age of seventy-eight.[1] Lévi-Strauss was not the first one to praise Aron's political acumen. In the spring of 1968, the venerable Jean Monnet, one of the founding fathers of what is today known as the European Union, had written to Aron to congratulate him on his courageous public critique of Charles de Gaulle's unfortunate remarks during a press conference in which the General arrogantly referred to the Jews as "an elite people, sure of itself and overbearing." Monnet praised Aron's unique combination of passion, responsibility, and courage in the following unforgettable words: "It is a privilege to live in a civilization which makes possible the existence and expression of opinions like yours."[2] Henry Kissinger said much the same in his foreword to the English translation of Aron's memoirs.[3] If Aron elicited praise from so many different quarters, one of the main reasons must have been his political moderation, a rare and difficult virtue that he practiced like no one else in postwar France. Aron was a peculiar type of intellectual simultaneously at home among academics, journalists, writers, and, to some extent, politicians. He wrote for influential newspapers, taught in prestigious academic settings, such as the Sorbonne and Collège de France, and was read and respected by those in positions of power and influence, without ever becoming an establishment person in the proper sense of the term. Nonetheless, Aron was the preferred target of relentless criticism from the Left until the mid-1970s, when his name was on the blacklist of the Parisian intelligentsia, attracted to the ideas of Mao, Stalin, Che Guevara, and the Ayatollah Khomeini, among others.[4]

In this chapter, I turn to some of Aron's most important writings in order to explore his political moderation. After providing a brief overview of the main themes of Aron's works, I focus on the twin issues of political judgment and engagement, with special emphasis on the metaphor of *le spectateur engagé* ("committed observer").[5] To further illustrate Aron's moderation, I discuss his intellectual dialogue with Marx and Hayek and end with a summary of the main tenets of Aron's political vision. In this chapter, I pay special attention to one of Aron's favorite books published in 1981, *Le Spectateur engagé*. Reedited in the United States two decades ago as *Thinking Politically*, it features a series of dialogues between Aron and two younger interlocutors, Dominique Yolton and Jean-Louis Missika. Aron played the role of an engaged spectator for almost five decades, and to understand his political engagement and trajectory, one must read this book along with Aron's memoirs (now finally available in French in a complete edition)[6] and a few other texts discussed in this chapter.

The Battle for Civilization Against Barbarism

For Aron, the three years he lived in Germany between 1930 and 1933 were an eye-opening experience that constituted his real political education.[7] Germany taught Aron an important lesson about the power of irrational forces in history and reminded him of the fragility of the institutions and values of Western civilization.[8] What struck Aron in the early 1930s was the rapidity with which his contemporaries were slowly losing faith in the capacity of liberal democratic institutions to meet their real needs. He was dismayed by their increasing disregard for the rule of law and legality and their preference for emergency measures instead of laws.[9] Such trends, Aron believed, posed significant threats to the future of liberal democracy and the Western civilization in general.

It was during Aron's sojourn in Germany, while witnessing one of the most tragic events of the twentieth century (Hitler's rise to power), that he conceived for the first time the idea of being a critical spectator engaged in the fight to save civilization from barbarism.[10] That attitude, he understood later, did not presuppose detachment from reality; it demanded instead that one try to grasp the ideas that make events possible and motivate peoples and their leaders to act in a certain way. In the context of interwar Europe, such a position required that one respond firmly to the fascist demagoguery not only by a contrary form of propaganda, but also by reflecting on the sources of totalitarianism, highlighting its revolutionary nature and its originality, and contrasting it with the "human ideal of revolution" (Aron, 2005: 140). Fascism and communism, Aron wrote in 1943, were two forms of secular religions that sought to occupy in the souls of people the place that once belonged to religious faith, now gone.[11] As Manichaean religions of collective salvation with an immense potential for mobilization and violence, they admitted nothing that would be superior in authority to the objectives of their movements. They relied on a "permanent mobilization" (Aron, 1985a: 374) on the part of their believers and required their total commitment, providing an *ersatz* of true religion and offering a final distant but alluring goal along with an unambiguous principle of authority meant to put an end to the prevailing social and political chaos. Aron understood early on the danger that these secular religions posed and was particularly worried by the fact that self-proclaimed providential figures, demagogues, populists, and adventurers could arise at any moment and destroy centuries-old institutions and norms, because the soil had already been prepared for their arrival. They exercised huge influence over disintegrated and desperate masses ready to abandon themselves into the hands of charismatic and populist leaders promising salvation. The logic was a perverse one: "Collective beliefs give birth to prophets and the Caesars invent their own religion" (1985a: 378).

An excellent case in point was the lecture Aron delivered in June 1939 at the Société française de philosophie in Paris, titled "États démocratiques et états totalitaires."[12] In this important text, he outlined the differences between the two types of states (democratic and totalitarian), showed the limits of pacifism, and highlighted the conditions of survival of modern democracies. Since the totalitarian states were revolutionary in both their ideology and means, Aron believed that the democratic regimes should (and could) play an essentially "conservative" (2005: 62) role that they had to assume in full awareness of their duties and risks. This task required heroic virtues that had to be reawakened and kept alive through deliberate efforts and concerted action.[13] When people no longer believe in the worth of the regime under which they live and consider it not worth fighting for, it is all the more important (and urgent) to stand up for the values and principles of the endangered liberal democracy.

L'Homme contre les tyrans, originally published in 1944 in New York in the collection "Civilization" directed by Jacques Maritain, came out in Paris two years later. It is, in my view, one of the best expressions of Aron's political moderation as a fighting creed, and one can only regret that this book is not better known and discussed today. Containing pieces that had originally appeared as articles in *La France libre*, this book is a genuine intellectual and political tour de force that also includes substantial essays on key figures of the French political tradition such as Montesquieu, Rousseau, and Constant. Written with verve, the book deals with important matters such as political liberty, despotism and tyranny, the weaknesses of democracy, bureaucracy and fanaticism, enthusiasm, violence, and war. In a chapter titled "The Birth of Tyrannies," Aron examined the originality of totalitarian regimes, which he ascribed to their combination of technical rationality, effective propaganda, charismatic leaders, and a detailed administration of things.[14] These types of popular despotisms offered a mixture of personal and arbitrary power, absolute authority, popular consent, and popular enthusiasm. Their leaders cultivated military virtues—virtues of action, self-denial, and devotion—rather than liberal ones, such as respect for persons, rule of law, and individual autonomy. The Leviathan state that emerged from this chaos was never going to be a state of parties freely competing for power, but a totalitarian state dominated by a single party unwilling to allow for any legal opposition or political contestation.

The proper response from the defenders of liberal democracy to this threat, Aron argued, was not resigned pacifism, but a conscious effort to rekindle the faith in the values of Western civilization, the rule of law, constitutionalism, and parliamentarism. It is interesting to note that in *L'Homme contre les tyrans*, Aron resorted to the same definition of civilization (as the opposite of barbarism) that Ortega y Gasset, whom he greatly admired, had previously used in his influential book *La rebelión de las masas* (1929). Civilization, Aron wrote, quoting the Spaniard, amounts to a sustained effort to reduce violence and contain its effects as much as possible.[15] In Aron's view, in order to save liberal democracies from the threats posed by the new forms of barbarism, many things were required, from the cultivation of discipline, self-restraint, and civility to defending those values that make possible the peaceful life in common: devotion to the common good, trust in one's fellow citizens, and respect for legality and the rule of law. Trying to save liberal democracy also required a "morality of heroism" (Aron, 2005: 219); people must want to win and should be prepared to fight for the very principles and values that sustain their life together as free and equal citizens under the empire of just laws. Furthermore, Aron insisted on the key role that a certain form of "conservatism" (2005: 79) broadly defined could play in the defense of the values of the Western civilization. He added that this was, appearances notwithstanding, a liberal and forward-looking form of conservatism, one that sought to save individual freedom, dignity, and autonomy from its enemies and was not fixated dogmatically on conserving an obsolete form of tradition or a particular set of rigid institutions and practices.

Can the Intellectuals Think Politically?

The question that preoccupied Aron was whether intellectuals in general are able to think politically and how can they develop informed and balanced judgments on complex political matters. These questions had preoccupied many French intellectuals for some time. In *La Trahison des clercs* (1927), a book that Aron reviewed a year after its publication, Julien Benda had famously claimed that most intellectuals—*les clercs*, in his own words—tend to defend political and moral ideas that flatter their pride and suit their sentiments rather than reason. He also noted with skepticism the desire of the "clerks" to belong to powerful groups that participate in the "intellectual organization of political hatreds."[16] One implication of Benda's book was that intellectuals tend to succumb to attractive political myths while being extremely good at finding intelligent justifications for them. This, he insisted, was proof of mere rhetorical dexterity rather than sound political judgment.

Benda's book also raised for Aron an interesting question: what constitutes good (political) judgment? If one were to ask the experts, they would say that having sound judgment amounts to being able to predict and quantify facts and study them rigorously with the aid of exact statistical methods. A second possible answer would be that there is no recipe for good political judgment, given the particularly fluid nature of politics and the inevitable constraints of the political sphere. On this view, applying principles of rational analysis and logical inference from natural sciences to politics, a field dominated by passions and interests rather than reason, would be a misunderstanding of the nature of politics. In this sphere, in which one of the highest virtues is prudence, it is important to know when to act and when to refrain from acting; exceptional circumstances do matter, and human actions often have unintended consequences that cannot be explained with the aid of equations and models. A third related response might be that good political judgment is inherently impressionistic and resembles the judgment of an artist trying to grasp the essence of reality. In order to understand facts, the artist sometimes takes the liberty of "imagining" and "reshaping" them to fit his (or her) affective and intellectual proclivities. Yet another possible answer would be that good political judgment presupposes (most of the time) a rebellious rejection of the status quo and an uncompromising search for radical political solutions to our present problems.

Aron was quite familiar with the latter type of political judgment from reading and commenting on his fellow intellectuals with whom he tried to engage in a responsible dialogue on some of the most pressing issues of his age such as totalitarianism, the Soviet Union, the Algerian crisis, the Cold War, and the reform of the French universities. As he soon discovered, this turned out to be more of a monologue, especially when it came to his colleagues on the Left, many of whom embraced systems of thought that aspired to be total and claimed to be in possession of universal truths, confidently predicting the course of the future. They also tended to justify their faith in absolute terms, which made dialogue highly difficult.

The reality on the ground confirmed Aron's intuitions. Beginning with the late 1940s and throughout the 1950s, prominent thinkers on the Left such as Maurice Merleau-Ponty and Jean-Paul Sartre, along with their disciples, mixed Marxism, phenomenology, and existentialism into a new ethics of authenticity and choice meant to overcome individual and class alienation in modern (capitalist) societies with a view to achieving what Marx had called "the true recovery of human nature through and for mankind."[17] In their works, Aron detected the pernicious effects of the excess of speculative intelligence, sometimes accompanied by a good dose of "irresponsible metaphysics," which, in his opinion, was often the cause of poor political judgment. These thinkers acted like moralists in politics and freely borrowed concepts from authors as different as Hegel, Marx, and Kierkegaard without paying sufficient attention to the incompatibility between them. Thus, they endorsed a deterministic view of history that ended up justifying the ruthless practices of the existing Marxist-Leninist regimes around the world. "The question for the moment," Merleau-Ponty wrote in response to his critics questioning his views on violence, "is not to decide whether one accepts or refuses violence, but whether the violence with which one is involved is 'progressive' and tends toward its own abolition, or whether it tends to perpetuate itself."[18] Such an analytical and ultimately rhetorical distinction, which condoned forms of violence that paved the way for an allegedly more humane future, made little sense in Aron's eyes. It was based on a confused understanding of the relationship between means and ends and worked with a questionable view of history that judged reality from the perspective of that which does not exist yet and considered the latter as more real and important than the former.

As Aron explained in "Fanaticism, Prudence, and Faith," many thinkers on the Left, although genuinely concerned with abstract issues such as justice, inequality, and exploitation, tended to ignore real politics and were reluctant to study in detail the actual functioning of political systems. The most radical among them were even ready to purchase a distant and alluring redemption at a high price that implied the sacrifice of the present for the sake of an abstract, radiant, and uncertain future. This, Aron argued (2001: 342), was a "betrayal of the 'eternal' Left," a movement that was the heir to the Enlightenment and had traditionally placed intellectual freedom above everything else in its attempt to understand and improve the actual functioning of concrete political institutions.

When reflecting upon the political and social events of his time, Aron refrained from using vague concepts such as alienation or domination, which, in his opinion, had little explanatory power. All social and economic regimes, he claimed, involve a certain degree of domination, but that is not what makes them different; nor would putting an end to alienation ever be able solve the enigma of history. Aron believed that Sartre's musings on man's solitary condition in the universe in *L'Être et le Néant* were valuable from a philosophical point of view and expressed the views of a genuine moralist, but they were unlikely to have any tangible impact on improving the condition of the working classes. The solution for reducing the *Angst* felt by the solitary individual facing an allegedly meaningless and hostile universe was not the proletarian revolution envisioned by Marx, with its dreams of universal liberation from the "shackles" of the bourgeois world through a temporary dictatorship of the proletariat.

In this regard, the peculiarities of French history and culture played an important role in the creation and spread of alluring narratives of social and political deliverance. Aron noted that it was characteristic of the majority of French intellectuals to be "in love with ideas and indifferent to institutions"

(2001: 43). Many of them showed little respect for—or interest in—facts and did not seek to understand the social and political universe to which they belonged, its institutions and practices. They were impatient with (or bored by) complexity and imperfection and often resorted to political myths and secular religions to make sense of the world in which they lived. Aron criticized the tendency of many French intellectuals to denounce too quickly the capitalist civilization as excessively rationalistic and antiheroic without attempting to grasp the functioning of its institutions and improve them. His target was those who preferred to categorically condemn the existing order rather than seeking to understand it first and who believed that "reform was boring and revolution exciting" (2001: 43). The French have also displayed a particular fascination with revolution and violence ever since their great revolution of 1789. "The myth of the Revolution," Aron wrote (2001: 65), "serves as a refuge for utopian intellectuals; it becomes the mysterious, unpredictable intercessor between the real and the ideal." At the same time, he also acknowledged that the fascination with the idea of a total revolution expresses a certain form of nostalgia that will continue to exist as long as modern societies and their institutions are (seen as) imperfect or unfair.

As Aron noted in *The Opium of the Intellectuals* (2001: 213–35), the limitations of the industrial civilization, the power of money, the need for tough (and sometimes unpleasant) compromises, and the constraints of economic rationality and success challenge the susceptibilities of intellectuals. The latter tend to become overemotional and espouse a form of intellectual and political evangelism, while also claiming to be more competent than ordinary citizens in judging the flaws of their societies. In reality, some of them are more or less indifferent to—and ignorant about—economic matters, while others view with skepticism the progress of technology and are ultimately uninterested in understanding the actual logic and functioning of the market and representative institutions. As late as 1960, for example, Merleau-Ponty confidently affirmed that the advance of modern society made the old ways and institutions of parliamentary and political life "decrepit."[19] He also claimed that capitalism prevents any form of progress toward the disappearance of classes and stifles the development of a genuine intersubjective world. Another illustration of this form of political impressionism was the attitude of those who, without being familiar with the basics of economics and sociology, felt confident nonetheless to indulge in endless diatribes against the rationalization of the soul and the allegedly ruthless bourgeois commitment to efficiency and productivity. "A century after the publication of *The Capital*,"

Aron remarked surprised, "Sartre has nothing to say about the socioeconomic structure of our epoch" (1975: 208), unlike Marx who devoted thirty-five years to studying economics. Instead, Sartre's philosophical and literary works abounded in suggestions for dealing with increasing human autonomy and reducing individual alienation in modern society. A consensus emerged among Sartre's followers and admirers that the great enemy of "being" was "having," and consequently, to paraphrase a famous line from Marx's *Economic and Philosophic Manuscripts*, "the less you *are*, the less express your life, the more you *have*, the greater is your alienated life."[20]

These radical critiques shared two other important features. First, they had a bohemian and apolitical ring manifested by their uncompromising critique of modern society for preventing individuals from being "true" to themselves. Second, they tended to conflate the "real" and "ideal" emancipation of the proletariat, while being poorly familiarized with the actual condition of the latter. Aron believed that many of the workers' grievances and alienation were bound to subsist even if the means of production were to be collectivized and placed in the hands of the state, as Marx and others recommended. In his view, the allegedly scientific Marxist explanation of the poverty of the working class and the theory of alienation were wrong to attribute the entire responsibility for oppression to the pattern of ownership and the free market forces. This explanation, Aron argued, was an example of the monist error according to which everything in society can be explained by referring to the economically dominant class that is always and "by definition in possession of the power" (2001: 343). In reality, this analysis had an inadequate sociological grounding and was little else than a form of pseudoscience imbued with a good dose of ideological faith immune to criticism, open debate, and refutation.

To his credit, Aron was never blind to the imperfection of the Western parliamentary democracies, but made a clear distinction between those shortcomings endemic to them (and hence impossible to eliminate entirely) and those that could be reformed by means of gradual steps. Striving to create a genuine social intersubjectivity, as some existentialists aspired, might have been an exciting philosophical ideal in the footsteps of Descartes and Husserl, but it made little sense as a concrete political agenda in postwar France, confronted with more pressing challenges such as constitutional reform, the war in Algeria, the possibility of nuclear war, and economic recovery. Consequently, Aron criticized those "captive minds" who refused to think politically and embraced instead a literary image of a "desirable society" (1997b:

154) that rejected the formal liberties of the bourgeois democracy as obsolete and argued that only a radically different type of society could guarantee "real" liberties worthy of human beings. This attitude, Aron insisted, is a common trait of intellectuals who tend to form opinions based on emotions and self-imposed moral imperatives rather than a careful analysis of each particular situation. Sometimes, they conceive of their political engagement only (or primarily) as a pretext for self-aggrandizement or as a decisive moment in a heroic battle between the forces of light and those of darkness.

In this regard, Aron's argument bore some affinities with Hayek and Schumpeter's explanations for the intellectuals' general hostility to capitalism.[21] In *The Opium of the Intellectuals*, Aron made a seminal distinction between three types of social criticism pursuing various agendas and based on different assumptions. The first type he dubbed "technical criticism" seeking to offer practical and limited solutions to concrete social and political problems. This form of criticism, when exercised responsibly, can be an example of thinking politically as long as it starts from what "is" and relies on facts rather than imagined data. "By technical criticism," Aron argued (2001: 210), "one puts oneself in the place of those who govern or administer, . . . suggests measures which might attenuate the evils one deplores [and] accepts the inevitable constraints of political action." Different from this form are two other types, moral and ideological criticism, which tend to gloss over political facts and reject the existing order in the name of an imaginary society whose contours remain fuzzy and imprecise.[22] Aron acknowledged that each of these types of criticism has its own role and justification as well as its own pathologies. In particular, he was skeptical about the last two forms of criticism because in his opinion, they largely offer only vague and impressionistic accounts of reality that provide no substantive guidance for social and political reform.

In his memoirs, Aron candidly acknowledged that he, too, had occasionally fallen into these traps in his diatribes against his opponents on the Left. Yet, even when he did so, he stopped short of endorsing Manichaeism or grounding his arguments in an ideal order against which existing institutions are always likely to be found defective. In his view, this type of impressionistic criticism cannot articulate an effective agenda for change and is bound to remain at the level of abstract theory and speculations divorced from social reality and real politics.

The Principles Undergirding Aron's Political Moderation

Aron never believed that a political science *more geometrico* à la Hobbes would ever be possible or desirable and understood that not all types of claims in politics can be demonstrated and defended rationally. Anyone writing on politics, he argued, must always ask and start from the following fundamental question: "What would I do if I were in the place of the statesman at the helm of the state?"

Several fundamental principles defined Aron's political outlook and method.[23] The *first* principle has to do, as we have already seen, with thinking "politically" as opposed to thinking "ideologically." In order to understand the nature of the political sphere, Aron argued (2005: 1233–37), one must first study the nature of the political regime, that is, the organization of powers in the state and the dominant ideas about authority and legitimacy, before examining the social classes and the relations between them. Aron's emphasis on the primacy of the political went hand in hand with his (Aristotelian) claim that it is vitally important that one always start from what "is" rather than what "ought" to be. This means several things: taking popular beliefs, opinions, and conventions seriously; trying to understand the historical and political contexts in which people make concrete choices and the motivations of these choices; studying carefully the diversity of existing political regimes, mores, customs, traditions, and the habits of the heart.[24] Our opinions, Aron insisted, must always be based on a careful consideration of facts and should take into account the complex ways in which changing circumstances affect people's decisions, strategies, and goals. This explains why political thought should never be detached from reality. According to Aron, we should study with the aid of proper methods the functioning of real political and economic institutions such as parliaments, markets, interest groups, and political parties. The analysis of facts and institutions is inseparable from the assessment of risks, priorities, and possibilities and must consider the interplay among structural constraints, luck, political crafting, leadership, and unique circumstances.

At the same time, Aron admitted that "raw observation is hardly instructive and utopia of little use in practice" (1984: 237). One cannot determine what *should* be solely on the basis of what *is* any more than one can limit one's perspective to the examination of allegedly pure facts. For the latter are always influenced by our value judgments, which, in turn, are defined by our environment, upbringing, and culture. Thinking politically, on this view, is not a neutral stance or a form of relativism; it implies making concrete choices for specific political regimes and particular institutional arrangements. In the end, it amounts to making a fundamental decision. "To think politically in a society," Aron argued (1997b: 44), "one must make a simple but fundamental choice. This fundamental choice is either the acceptance of the kind of society in which we live, or its rejection. . . . From this fundamental choice flow decisions."

One example would suffice to illustrate this point. It is sometimes argued that, since Realpolitik involves a certain degree of deception and violence, it is impossible, in fact, to make a clear-cut difference between good and bad political actors in international politics. From this, it is then inferred that there may be little or no moral difference between, say, the policies of Stalin and Mao and those of Churchill and Roosevelt. Such a difference, Aron believed, always exists in reality, and thinking politically requires that one acknowledge this distinction without resorting to clever but ultimately superfluous arguments or sophisms. Thinking politically involves taking sides (after carefully considering the facts) rather than avoiding them or pretending to be neutral between two evils. When asked to judge the Stalinist regime, Aron insisted, it was absurd to claim that one could be simultaneous/sly for and against it, as Francis Jeanson did in his (in)famous diatribe against Camus in *Les Temps modernes*. In Aron's view, such an ambiguous position was not only logically incoherent, but also politically irresponsible insofar as it eschewed making a clear commitment while seeking to justify (through a sophism) what was unjustifiable.[25]

There is an interesting upshot of this principle worth highlighting here. When reflecting on political events, Aron argued, we must free our political analysis, as much as possible, of all forms of ideological thinking and sentimentality, stay clear of moralizing, and refrain from applying inadequate criteria to judging political matters. Aron admitted that political activity is by nature impure and cannot be judged with concepts such as moral clarity or the precepts of any particular morality or religion. In other words, politics are "not coterminous with the activities of good Samaritans" (1997b: 244) and should never be reduced to a simple conflict between good and evil. In politics and public life in general, we are often required to choose between what is acceptable and reasonable and what is detestable and unreasonable (1997b: 242) rather than between good and evil. Hence, it is not an accident that Aron rejected perfectionism in unambiguous terms. "In political affairs," he once said (1997b: 264), "it is impossible to demonstrate truth, but one can try, on the basis of what one knows, to make sensible decisions." In times of great crises, even truth may be "prosaic and insufferable" (1997b: 82).

Aron always searched for the right tone when addressing different matters that could not be judged from one single perspective or analyzed with one particular method. For example, writing about economic issues requires a different approach and tone than commenting on international relations or politics in general. When dealing with economic questions, Aron tried to be clear and remain as close as possible to the facts while on political topics, he reflected as a person who observed and attempted to find the most reasonable solutions for the entire community, based on the available information. He always wrote in his usually balanced, nonpartisan, and moderate style even when treating events that he disliked or disapproved of (the Vichy regime),[26] or when his country faced tragic events (the Algerian crisis). "Political analysis gains by divesting itself of all sentimentality," Aron insisted (2001: 345). "Lucidity demands effort: passion automatically goes at a gallop." Lucidity is particularly needed when one attempts to figure out the least bad solution in each context and sort out the better from the worst possible outcomes. Historical existence, Aron added in an important essay on Max Weber and modern social sciences, is made up of "uncertain struggles in which no cause is pure, no decision without risk, no action without unforeseeable consequences" (1985b: 370).

An excellent example of thinking politically in a non-sentimental, objective, and non-moralizing way can be found in Aron's reflections on the Algerian independence, an issue that polarized the entirety of French public opinion for almost a decade and generated many emotional reactions from all sides of the political spectrum. Aron recognized early on that denying Algeria's independence would have been both morally illegitimate and economically disastrous for France. Although he was not at all blind to moral considerations, he defended Algeria's independence primarily (though not exclusively) on economic and political grounds rather than moral ones. Aron pointed out that denying the independence of the colony would have required a military and economic commitment that France was unable to sustain at that point in time (the whole decade of the 1950s marked the decline of its military power). On this topic as on many others, Aron preferred to think politically and refused to embrace an ethics of absolute ends obsessed with moral clarity. "I based my policy on reality," he once confessed. "The policy that I recommended could just as easily have been based on moral principles, because they were compatible. . . . My purpose was to analyze a political problem in order to demonstrate that a given solution was the least bad. . . . The avoidance of a national tragedy, that is, a civil war, depended upon the courage of the politicians."[27]

The *second* principle of Aron's political moderation is his defense of social, political, and methodological pluralism. "Plurality," Aron wrote in his *Memoirs* (1990: 85), "is immanent in the historical world. . . . We do not grasp in a single perception a large whole, a global culture, or even a macro-event like the French Revolution. This plurality is bound up with the plurality of human nature itself, simultaneously life, consciousness, and idea, and with the fragmentary nature of determinism." One must therefore study and take into account a plurality of factors, motivations, and viewpoints when analyzing complex social and political phenomena. This, Aron acknowledged, is never an easy task. To understand the forces at work in political life one must pay attention not only to structural factors that define the realm of the possible, but also to contingency, political leadership, the winds of fortune, and human nature. Here is a revealing passage from an important text of Aron that sheds light on these factors: "One must consider (1) the plurality of goals, from short-term to distant, from tactics to strategy; (2) the actor's knowledge of the situation, as well as the relative effectiveness of means; . . . (3) the nature, lawful or unlawful, praiseworthy or not, of the end or means in relation to religious, mythological, or traditional beliefs; and (4) the duly psychological motivations of the act, which is sometimes appropriate but sometimes apparently irrational with respect to the actor's objective" (1984: 48–49). In other words, when analyzing politics, one must take into account the plurality of the goals, the possible tensions between them, as well as the different perspectives and strategies of individual actors.

Far from being incoherent, this plurality is a permanent feature of the political and social sphere. Since individuals and groups in society pursue a wide range of interests, we must always pay due attention to the inevitable conflict between their ideas as well as between economic growth, division of labor, economic productivity, equality, freedom, and justice. Seeking a fictitious harmonization of all these values and principles would be futile and harmful, Aron argued (2001: 346). What responsible politicians do instead is to try to achieve a reconciliation or compromise between them, while being aware that any solution can be only an imperfect and temporary one. Aron viewed with skepticism the confidants of Providence who embraced the ethics of absolute ends, claimed to have a clear and infallible knowledge of the future, and operated with a Manichaean view of politics ignoring the ineradicable pluralism of values and ideas that define our modern society. At the same time, what distinguished his position from that of other romantic intellectuals searching for authenticity in politics was his exquisite ability to grasp and interpret the antimonies at the heart of modern society, the inescapable trade-offs that people face in our daily lives, and the constraints that "weigh as much on those who govern as on those governed" (1997b: 251).

The *third* principle undergirding Aron's political moderation is the rejection of all forms of historical determinism, including Marxist dialectical materialism and Spenglerian pessimism. All philosophies of history, Aron remarked, are "secularized theologies" (1985b: 109) and must be interpreted as such. History is "neither progress nor decadence, neither movement toward a final end nor the endless repetition of the same facts or the same cycles" (1984: 55). Aron criticized those who were certain of knowing in advance the evolution of history or being able to predict it; his moderate and prudent approach admitted the existence of a margin of indeterminacy in all political and social events. Every political situation, he argued (1984: 237), "always allows for a margin of choice, but the margin is never unlimited;" human beings are never fully determined, nor are they ever entirely free to choose. Social scientists and philosophers should therefore try to elucidate, from the study of past and contemporary societies, the goals, ideals, and preferences of the people and the means they choose to achieve them. Such a study is always bound to be influenced by prior preferences and desires, but it also retains a scientific side. "The outcome is never a moral or political imperative," he argued (1984: 238), "but an indication of diverse possibilities (as to goals) and degrees of probabilities (as to means)."

In "Three Forms of Historical Intelligibility," Aron demonstrated the shortcomings of all attempts to find patterns of historical and political intelligibility in history with a view to predicting and influencing the direction of the future. He took issue with the use of vague terms such as the "goal of History" and reminded us that no one can comprehend the historical totality from a privileged Archimedean point.[28] In any attempt to reach this point, he confessed (1984: 65), "even one inspired by idealism, I suspect a new incarnation of the monster." For Aron, positing the idea of an overt or hidden meaning of history amounted, in fact, to adopting "a theological position"[29] at odds with scientific analyses of historical events and patterns. He preferred instead to embrace what he called "probabilistic determinism" (1984: 61) based on the belief that, far from advancing inexorably toward a certain goal, the actual development of history always remains open-ended and impossible to predict or control. This is all the more true given the plurality of values and principles underlying human action and the unique and complex nature of ever changing political contexts.

In the inaugural lecture at the Collège de France delivered in December 1970 and titled "On the Historical Condition of the Sociologist," Aron recommended endorsing an "active" form of pessimism as an effective antidote to a misplaced form of idealism that can often be quite misleading and even dangerous. History, he reminded his readers, does not obey the dictates of reason or the desires of men of good will. Even the twin ideas of reason and progress as the end goal of history, Aron wrote (in "Three Forms of Historical Intelligibility"), cannot—and should not—be identified with a coming period or with a particular set of institutions "without creating fanaticism and unreason" (1984: 61). No philosophy of history can predict with any certainty that the future will favor a certain political doctrine or group that enjoys special status or claims to have a special mission in history.[30] Nonetheless, if we may never be certain of acting "rationally," that is, in keeping with the alleged laws of history, we can always try at least to make reasonable decisions and choices in specific contexts based on trial and error and using the available information at any point in time. In the end, however, we will not be able to escape the conflict of values and must acknowledge the existence of important differences between political regimes.

The *fourth* principle undergirding Aron's political moderation derives from the awareness of his own fallibility and limited knowledge that fueled his skepticism and led him to criticize the "millenarian politics" of self-confident political actors who embraced uncritically a specific regime or political agenda and proclaimed their inevitable success in light of an alleged ineluctable historical trajectory. Aron believed that we must admit the limits of our knowledge in order to escape this form of Promethean pride and determinism; consequently, he insisted that unfolding events should be interpreted neither with "the certainty of victory nor with a cry of despair" (1990: 206). Identifying the goal of history with a coming period, a specific class or set of institutions is particularly problematic because it requires an act of faith often accompanied by a form of radicalism (bordering on fanaticism) that seeks to justify the worst forms of cruelty in the name of allegedly bright ideals. By attributing absolute value to a particular regime, class, or nation, the true believers in a final goal in history often end up justifying absolute power and ruthless cynicism with regard to the means chosen for attaining their goals. They claim that ethical rules have only a historical and transitory basis and see themselves as engaged permanently in an epic struggle with the forces of darkness whose outcome is bound to determine the whole course of history. All forms of millenarian politics, Aron claimed, are subject to the law of overcommitment, and many of them, having unlimited confidence in the power of human reason, end up justifying the use of violence in the name of achieving a perfect future society, free from the ills afflicting the present one.

To millenarian politics, which are a form of "politics of faith" gone astray, stands opposed a "conservative" form of politics defined by Aron as the type of politics that denies "the possibility of a final regime that would overcome the contradictions of previous regimes and be immune to the constituent laws of human societies as such" (1984: 242). Yet, in his view, the dichotomy between millenarian and conservative politics did not exhaust the realm of possibilities. Aron acknowledged the existence of a third type—"progressive politics"—that refuses "to proclaim exclusively a final goal to history or its complete regularity" and allows for "irregular and undefined transformations toward a goal situated on the horizon, . . . justified by abstract principles" (1984: 246). Although this type of politics may sometimes display excessive faith in the power of reason, it is, more often than not, a moderate form of politics based on the assumption that history consists of a plurality of regimes succeeding each other, or is a history of variations on a simple theme, whatever the diversity of their concrete forms.[31] The proponents of this type of politics tend to view the activity of governing as detached from the pursuit of perfection and claim that the most important aim of politics is to improve the material conditions in which people live by reducing the level of poverty and suffering that they experience. Yet, Aron suggested, even this form of politics has its own limitations and in times of crisis may become ineffective. It is worth noting that in his essay on this theme originally published in 1949, Aron placed more faith in non-millenarian progressive politics than he did elsewhere in his later writings, especially in *The Opium of the Intellectuals*.

The *fifth* and last principle of Aron's moderation has to do with his refusal to admit that normal politics are Manichaean, cast in black-and-white contrasts. He was aware that nothing is so evil that it does not contain some good, just as nothing is so good that it does not contain some evil. No choice is clear, perfect, or cost-free, and every decision requires careful thinking and adequate evaluation of alternative paths. That is why he did not seek cheap rhetorical victories and refused to consider himself a moral authority entitled to give lessons from the pulpit to his fellow citizens. Aron's rejection of moral posturing should also be linked to his tendency to self-doubt, skepticism, and self-questioning. While acknowledging the need for difficult and costly trade-offs in politics, he was perfectly aware that there are rarely heroes on one side and villains on the other. Because Aron believed that politics always involve a mixture of heroism and cruelty, saints and monsters, progress and reaction, reason and passions, he accepted the fact that liberal democracy is by nature, to use the words of another moderate studied in this book (Adam Michnik), "an eternal imperfection, a mixture of sinfulness, saintliness, and monkey business,"[32] a regime that, in spite of its patent shortcomings, is capable of improvement and needs constant nurturing. Aron insisted that in nearly all things one must always make prudent distinctions and exceptions, because circumstances endlessly change and require novel methods and approaches. To judge by the book would amount to a serious misunderstanding of political life, because every tiny difference in each case can have significant effects. Or, to discern these small differences requires a perspicacious eye and sound discernment. Political affairs cannot be properly judged from an Archimedean point above the sound and fury of the world, but ought to be resolved and considered day by day, step by step, in *media res*.

Aron and the "Elusive Revolution" of 1968

To understand how Aron applied these principles, we turn next to the events of May and June 1968 in Paris when France came close to a real revolution as students and workers demanded "real" liberties as opposed to the "formal" ones guaranteed by the Constitution of the Fifth Republic.[33] Aron's attitude toward the events of 1968 is worth examining here not only because it was misunderstood and misrepresented by his critics, but also because it illustrates well his bold form of moderation that was dismissed by Sartre in a famous piece following the May uprisings as a cowardly form of conservatism.[34]

If Aron's analysis of those events was, in general, lucid and on the mark, it lacked the self-righteousness and certainty of those who worked with a Manichaean interpretation of the world. Still, his words left no room for ambiguity: "I do not know of any other episode from the history of France that gives me the same degree of irrationality."[35] In his opinion, the actors of 1968 and their supporters encouraged the "sacralization of delirium" (2005: 611) and fell prey to utopianism and psychodrama,[36] while forgetting the cautionary lessons of a century and a half of violence and revolutionary fervor. The participants in the events, Aron claimed, relied on an incoherent mixture of ideas combining pre-Marxist utopian socialism with strong libertarian proclivities. One of the issues that triggered strong controversies was whether political liberties in modern society are mere formal freedoms, as Marx and his disciples claimed, or whether they have a firmer foundation and a substantive content. Most of these themes had previously been touched upon by Herbert Marcuse, who had denounced the values of commercial society, its forced consumption patterns along with the waste and alienation that it tends to produce. "In this domain," Aron wrote (1990: 324), "the revolutionaries made friends by popularizing an ideology that did not coincide with the ideology of any of the parties: quality against quantity, a comfortable life against the pursuit of a high standard of living."

Not surprisingly, the French students did not have a coherent agenda for political reform, and their flamboyant slogans gave the impression of a "collective delirium" that threatened to bring about the decomposition of the entire French society. Aron believed that the demonstrators made a confusion between anarcho-syndicalism and *l'autogestion*, and ignored the inevitable and ineradicable tensions between the requirements of economic rationality, the rhetoric of authenticity, and the possible humanization of industrial society. In his view, the idea of a libertarian revolution opposed to any form of domination was an untenable blend of pre-Marxist socialism and anarcho-syndicalism that lacked an adequate understanding of the inevitable constraints facing the political and economic spheres in modern society. Without being a dogmatic partisan of the status quo, Aron pointed out that the relentless contestation of hierarchies and the rejection of technological rationality were unlikely to usher in the discovery of an effective and original "third way" between—or beyond—communism and capitalism. In his view (2005: 610), promoting the self-management of enterprises and universities could not offer a viable middle ground between Soviet communism and socialized capitalism.

It was a mark of his political moderation that Aron refused to apply a black-and-white approach when interpreting the events of May and June 1968. He understood that the radical language used by political actors and groups transcended party programs and signaled a larger discontent with larger forces at work in modern society that could not be ignored or dismissed by any responsible politician. While he criticized the radicalization of students and workers, Aron also acknowledged in unambiguous terms the urgent need for reforming the sclerotic French university system and implementing much-needed political reforms. He did not limit himself to the common narrative about the events as "revolution or psychodrama," "carnival or tragedy," and interpreted them instead from a larger sociological point of view. He sought to understand why the revolts occurred in France and what the popular discontent with the de Gaulle regime revealed about the deeper causes of *le mal français*.

The diagnosis that Aron proposed was accompanied by a call to sobriety and responsibility to all the actors involved in the events. The country, he claimed, lacked intermediary bodies, and its presidential republic had not given the opposition and the other social groups sufficient institutional leeway for voicing their demands. Reviving and strengthening these *corps intermédiaires* should therefore have been a priority for all the major political actors involved in the resolution of the crisis. Aron also noticed with dismay that many decent intellectuals on the Left, who had previously been anti-Stalinists, applauded and endorsed the violent means used by the demonstrators in the streets. This reminded him of the Jacobin clubs, the Paris Commune of 1871, and the revolutionary climate in Russia in the months leading up to the Revolution of November 1917. Aron was equally surprised to discover that many French teachers and civil servants, unlike anywhere else in the world in 1968, willingly broke the law and showed profound contempt for legality, being ready to condone the curtailment of seminal civil and political liberties.

Among Aron's opponents and critics, the prevalent attitude was that he had not understood them.[37] They regarded his attitude toward the revolutionary *journées* as conservative or reactionary and challenged his claim that the events did not represent a true revolution. Some took Aron to task for the harsh words—irrationality, psychodrama, carnival—he chose to describe the events. Others dismissed him as a rigid defender of the Gaullist establishment, while a few went so far as to suggest without any proof that he was a paid agent of the CIA or other secret services. Referring to the manifestation of support for de Gaulle on May 30, 1968, an American historian did not have any hesitation to claim that "intellectuals like Raymond Aron marched beside the lumpen dregs created by the colonial wars—the secret societies, parallel police, hit men, strike breakers, *anciens combattants*, and hired thugs that had rallied to de Gaulle's summons" (Ross, 2004: 59). Such a tendentious account had, of course, nothing to do with the reality on the ground. Moreover, what

Ross conveniently forgot to mention was not only that respectable people on the Left such as Kostas Papaioanou marched with Aron on that May day on the Champs-Élysées, but also that he had been a lucid and persistent defender of the Algerian independence and a critic of some of de Gaulle's actions.

It would be difficult to deny that the two camps in the events had little love for each other, and it is important to remember that students had famously avowed that they preferred to be wrong with Sartre than right with Aron. Nonetheless, a close examination of Aron's position in 1968 shows that the situation was much more nuanced than his critics would have us believe, and that he clearly understood that the events marked a genuine political crisis in France that caught its political and academic elites by surprise. He chose to play the unpopular role of a trimmer concerned with keeping the ship on an even keel in times of social and political unrest. Aron's political moderation came to the fore when he was invited to comment on the governance of the universities. His attitude with regard to the French academic system was a perfect example of his lucid political moderation that did not seek a lukewarm and comfortable middle between extremes. A critic of the students' political demands in the streets, Aron sided firmly and unambiguously with the reformers when it came to proposing changes for improving the academic curriculum. In this regard, he was, in fact, firmly on the side of those who had complained about the sclerosis of the French academic system and called for urgent reforms. Aron paid special attention to what happened within the French universities because he considered them as a representative microcosm of the entire French society. It should not be forgotten that he had left his prestigious and comfortable tenured position at the Sorbonne a few months before the events of May 1968 as a protest against the refusal of the administrators to upgrade the curriculum and improve the selection of students.

"Whenever I discussed the future or questions of reform at university meetings," Aron remembered (1997b: 215), "I was always on the side of the reformers. But as soon as I saw that honorable and decent teachers were being treated in a shabby manner, I defended them. I didn't agree with them, but I defended them." Aron leaned to the Right on the question of the selection of students by arguing for a more rigorous selection in admission to university. He criticized the French *baccalauréat* as too difficult an examination for the completion of secondary studies and for being an inefficient means of selection for admission to the university. He also took to task the famous *aggrégation* because in his opinion, it did not guarantee the quality of education and failed to provide adequate training in research. But Aron also leaned to the Left when pushing for greater autonomy for universities and a more open and competitive selection of both students and professors. He denounced the absolute autonomy of professors who behaved like uncontested masters in their chairs, while often remaining ignorant of what their colleagues and students were doing. To his credit, Aron refused to give the same course over and over again, as many of his colleagues were accustomed to, and pushed for the adoption of a more rigorous selection system for professors. Last but not least, he criticized the French university system for being overly bureaucratic and centralized and lacking effective channels for consultation. Its highly centralized structure favored instead the politicization and radicalization of faculty and students at the expense of dialogue and compromise.

Hence, it was not a mere coincidence that in 1968, in a volatile and conflict-ridden environment, Aron pushed for substantive academic reforms and advocated the depoliticization of French universities. Although he called for the prompt return to legality and enjoined his fellow citizens to respect the rule of law and the legitimate outcome of democratic elections, his attitude was far from being conservative, as some argued.[38] Aron believed that these measures (along with others) offered the only possible way of distinguishing between those who genuinely wanted to reform the French academic and political system and those who were satisfied with the status quo, in spite of their misleading rhetoric.[39] In the end, what Aron rejected in the events of 1968 was not the demands for justice or reform (which he supported, as we have already seen), but the romantic and puerile rhetoric of self-realization and overcoming alienation with which the students and their supporters among intellectuals tried to respond to the serious crisis of the French universities. Such a mixture, Aron believed, was not an effective way of changing the system of higher education in France. He also thought that in their attempt to "go to the people," the intellectual leaders of 1968 failed to articulate a coherent political reformist agenda. The famous *comités d'action* that sought to combine discipline and self-realization, centralism and self-government lacked a coherent political agenda and ended up having no enduring institutional legacy. Last but not least, Aron was taken aback by the allegedly irresponsible attitude of many of his colleagues who showed little regard for legality and were attracted to various forms of socialism and communism based on a romantic cult of authenticity, autonomy, and violence that had little appreciation for the actual working of representative institutions.

A Man Without a Party

Aron's position as a moderate isolated in the middle along with the civil and combative manner in which he defended his views puzzled his contemporaries. "My passion for analysis," he once said (1997b: 301), "has led me to criticize almost everyone in politics, even including those who, in general terms, think as I do. . . . Oddly enough, although I write in moderate terms, it frequently happens that I do so in a wounding way or at least in a way considered irritating." Some saw in him primarily the skeptic who on the last page of *The Opium of the Intellectuals* called for "the arrival of the skeptics so that they may extinguish fanaticism" (2001: 324). Others regarded him as a political moderate incapable of devoting himself to a great cause. In reality, Aron was neither devoid of passion nor a skeptic who endorsed apathy or indifference to public life. His entire career shows, in fact, the bold, fighting, and courageous face of moderation and the challenges of being a "committed observer" in an age of increasing ideological intransigence.

What makes Aron as a *spectateur engagé* an excellent case study for a book on political moderation is that he managed to carve out an original path between the Left and Right while both aisles of the political spectrum (with very few exceptions) ignored or dismissed his lessons.[40] He spent his entire life going to the Left while speaking the language of the Right, and going to the Right while speaking the language of the Left.[41] "To me," Aron wrote (2001: 342), "loyalty to one party has never been a decision of fundamental importance. . . . According to the circumstances I am in agreement or disagreement with the action of a given movement or a given party. . . . Perhaps such an attitude is contrary to the morality (or immorality) of political action; it is not contrary to the obligations of the writer." Sometimes, for example on the Algerian war, Aron's positions were closer to the Left than to the Right. This point was recognized by one of his critics, Michel Contat, in an article published in *Le Monde* in 1980. According to the latter, Aron belonged to the family of the Left because his arguments were always "directed to the Left, as though he wanted to remove their blinders."[42] On the issue of communism, however, Aron was seen as a conservative because he denounced the logic, principles, and practices of communist regimes in unambiguous terms and with remarkable firmness and clarity. At the same time, he always paid a lot of attention to the ideas of those who disagreed with him, Sartre being the most famous example in this regard, although not the only one.

Aron's position on Marxism is a good case in point and an excellent example of his moderation, lack of dogmatism, and openness to dialogue. He regarded Marxism as a global interpretation of history predicated upon two (contestable) main assumptions: the preeminence of class struggle and the priority of the relations of production vis-à-vis the forces of production. From his materialistic interpretation of history, Aron claimed, Marx drew a radical conclusion unsupported by logic or facts, namely that every progressive spirit must be on the side of the proletariat (identified with light and goodness) in the fight against the bourgeoisie (equated with the forces of darkness and evil). Because Marx thought that the endpoint of history was communism, he believed that any rational person must embrace the latter in order to be on the side of progress against the forces of reaction. Aron was uncomfortable with this conclusion because he saw in it a giant leap of faith. It was a form of idolatry of history which "arrogates to itself the right to ignore the brute facts or to give each of them the meaning which will fit in with an allegedly definitive system of interpretation" (2001: 193). As such, Marx's theory of communism belonged to the realm of prophecy rather than science and stood in sharp contrast with the more scientific side of his works and his reputation as a perceptive sociologist of nineteenth-century capitalism. It is no coincidence, Aron noted, that none of the main forms of Marxism had been able to reconcile the prophetic side of Marxism and its accompanying moral condemnation of capitalism with historical reality and the real facts about capitalist production that contradicted Marx's theory of labor value and his predictions of diminishing returns and the growth of the proletariat.[43] In the end, Aron confessed (1997b: 41), "after having studied Marxism for almost an entire year, I concluded with regret that, in this form, it was not acceptable. The analysis of history does not permit one to determine the policy to follow and to foresee, as an end result, a society from which contradictions among men would be eliminated." On the contrary, it teaches us humility and modesty and reminds us of the limits to our knowledge, the gaps in our information, and the fallibility of our methods of interpretation. This lesson stood in sharp contrast to the overconfident tone of those like Sartre and his colleagues on the Left who believed in the existence of a dialectical reason acting in history in the inevitable direction predicted by Marx and Engels.

If Aron was a critic of many of the ideas of the Left, he was far from being a conservative spirit in the conventional meaning of this term. He sought to maintain his intellectual and political independence and transcend the conventional political categories of Left and Right. He once described himself as "a man without party, who is all the more unbearable because he takes his moderation to excess and hides his passions under his arguments."[44] Early on in his career, in an article from January 1933, Aron offered the following revealing self-portrait: "I am neither of the Right nor the Left, neither communist nor nationalist, no more radical than I am socialist. I do not know whether I will find companions" (1990: 71). In this regard, he followed in the footsteps of Ortega y Gasset, one of the authors for whom he had a profound appreciation. "Aligning oneself with the Left, as with the Right," the Spaniard once wrote, "is only one of the numberless ways open to man of being an imbecile: both are forms of moral hemiplegia."[45] Ortega's claim was a passionate *cri de cœur* against political extremism and intellectual servitude as well as a plea for preserving one's intellectual independence and autonomy in an age of increasing ideological conformism. In an essay on Ortega written in 1983, Aron explicitly referred to the latter's rejection of both the Left and Right, considering it consistent with his own political vision. "Had I remembered this formulation," Aron confessed (1988: 363), "I would have found a better answer to those who asked me whether I was on the Right or the Left."

Much like Ortega, Aron often felt uncomfortable with aligning himself to a particular group, even if both thinkers were staunch defenders of liberal democracy and could be regarded as conservative liberals (in the European sense of the term). Some of Aron's contemporaries took him for being a man of the Right or a devoted Gaullist, even if in reality he was not an unconditional supporter of the General, nor was his mind always in sync with some colleagues on the Right in their common fight against communism. Although Aron's ideas evolved over time as he became one of the most vocal critics of communism in France, it is fair to say that he maintained his independence of mind throughout his career.[46]

One of the most remarkable things about Aron is that he was not always in agreement with those for whom he voted or whose ideas he partly shared. The best examples of his independence of mind were his complicated relations with Charles de Gaulle and his intellectual dialogue with another prominent liberal thinker, Friedrich von Hayek. While sharing the same strong commitment to the fundamental principles and values of the French Republic as de Gaulle, Aron never became a card-carrying Gaullist or a confidante of the General, and did not unconditionally endorse all of his initiatives. He did not shy away from taking distance from de Gaulle's misguided policy toward Germany after 1946, which sprang out of fear and risked blocking the initiatives of the Americans and the English, aiming at creating a unique administration of the four occupation zones in postwar Germany. The General who famously proclaimed *Plus jamais de Reich* was clinging to the idea that Germany remained the greatest danger in Europe at the very moment when the real threat started coming, in fact, from a former ally in the East, the Soviet Union. Aron went so far as to criticize on more than one occasion what he called a certain form of "Gaullist fanaticism" that went against the main principles of his own political moderation. "To be truly Gaullist," he once claimed, "it was necessary to have faith in de Gaulle and to be ready to change one's opinions to agree with his. I could not do it, but that didn't prevent me from being André Malraux's *directeur de cabinet*."[47]

The careful choice of words on Aron's part is proof of both his moderation and non-dogmatic attitude toward the man with whom he had closely collaborated in London during the war. Aron's ambivalence can be traced back to a famous article he published in London in 1943, titled "L'Ombre de Bonaparte." As he came to know de Gaulle better, Aron realized the dangers of replacing democratic legitimacy with the legitimacy of "a man chosen by History." Such a step, he averred, would have jeopardized the constitutional edifice of the country and might have derailed democracy in France. On the position of France toward NATO, their disagreements were even stronger. Unlike de Gaulle, Aron was convinced that France had no choice but to side with the United States on this issue, given the escalation of the Cold War and the growing threat posed by an increasingly belligerent Soviet Union. On the subject of the Algerian independence, the two did not see eye to eye either. In a famous article, "Farewell to Gaullism," from 1959, Aron criticized the General's strategy of small concessions, while also admitting that he represented "our last hopes for an honorable peace" (1990: 260). Finally, he strongly criticized de Gaulle after the General described the Jews as "an elite people, sure of itself and overbearing" in a famous press conference in 1967.

Under the Fifth Republic, Aron's attitude toward de Gaulle was defined by the principle "solidarity in times of crisis and independence in normal times." While he thought that the General's foreign policy—"la politique du joyeux célibataire international"[48]—was sometimes unnecessarily provocative, Aron recognized that its main initiatives were in line with the general interests of the French Republic and the free world. At the time of the Liberation, Aron noted, de Gaulle's government was "much the best and . . . it was necessary to support it." A decade later, de Gaulle's return to power, "even though the circumstances were unpleasant, was rather desirable" (Aron, 1997b: 101), because thanks to his prestige, he had a better chance than anyone else to find a solution to the Algerian crisis. As the latter degenerated, the General "had dirtied his hands as little as possible" (Aron, 1990: 255). Moreover, de Gaulle sought to strengthen the democratic republic, even if his constitutional plan gave the president of the Republic the opportunity "to exercise an absolute and limited power."[49] As such, he was a perfect example of the charismatic leader who had "historic ambitions comparable to those of Washington" (1990: 258) and was committed to a democratic form of republicanism. In an article published on the first anniversary of de Gaulle's return to power, Aron offered the following balanced assessment: "The Fifth Republic exists, and in present-day France, General de Gaulle is the best possible monarch in the least bad of possible governments. He possesses personal power, but he restored the Republic in 1945. He manipulated the 1958 revolution in order to produce an authoritarian republic, not fascism nor a military despotism. He wants to save the remnants of the French empire, but he has granted the territories of black Africa the right to independence" (1990: 258).

If we turn now to Aron's defense of liberal democracy and open society, we notice that it overlapped with that of other prominent Cold War thinkers such as Isaiah Berlin, Karl Popper, and Friedrich von Hayek, who, for all their ideological and methodological differences, shared a common commitment to freedom, pluralism, and the rule of law. Yet, Aron has arguably remained to this day the most misunderstood thinker from this group. He was taken to task by his critics for being the official apologist of capitalism, although in reality he was never a dogmatic defender of the status quo and emphasized time and again the importance of both civil *and* social rights, liberty *and* equality. In his memoirs, Aron described himself as "an egalitarian in the moral sense of the term," and recognized that he loathed the type of social relations in which status hierarchy stifles the development of a certain minimal sense of social solidarity. He went on to add that for all his appreciation of equality, beyond these feelings, he did not know "what is implied by social justice, nor what distribution of income, wealth, prestige, or power would meet the requirements of equity" (1990: 480).

In the 1950s, Aron mounted a powerful challenge to the ideas of the Left in *The Opium of the Intellectuals* (1955), one of his best-known (and most polemical) books in which he criticized the three great "myths" of the Left:

the myths of the revolution, of the proletariat, and of progress. He resorted to a complex and nuanced sociological analysis of modern societies that sought to identify and evaluate the economic and social conditions that allow freedom and pluralism to survive. In so doing, Aron spent a great deal of time and energy—arguably greater than any other twentieth-century social scientist, perhaps with the exception of Max Weber—studying the interplay among economics, social relationships, class relationships, political systems, and international relations. The main targets of Aron's critique were those who considered their values and principles as the only acceptable ones for interpreting the world. In "Fanaticism, Prudence, and Faith," the essay published as a response to the critiques of *The Opium of the Intellectuals*, Aron labeled this attitude "doctrinairism," which he defined as the tendency to attribute universal value to a particular doctrine and specific set of institutions.[50] In all of its forms, he argued, doctrinairism fails to acknowledge and honor the pluralism and complexity of the social and political world. After highlighting the tensions existing between the three principles at the core of the Left—liberty, organization, and equality—Aron pointed out that, while the Left in the Western world strove to free individuals from immediate servitude and economic poverty, it simultaneously submitted them to an ever more dangerous form of servitude to an all-powerful communist state in the Eastern camp. At the same time, another myth of the Left perpetuated the illusion that the irresistible movement of history is "a continual process of accumulating gains" (2001: 21) toward full social justice, full employment, and economic equality.

A few years later, Aron the trimmer turned his attention to the ideas of the Right, even if his critique of the latter was not comparable in tone and sharpness to his account of the myths of the Left. He was convinced that liberty must be protected not only against its enemies, but also against its own overzealous defenders. Conservatism, Aron claimed, comes in two forms. The first starts from the premise that all regimes contain within themselves insurmountable tensions that cannot be fully solved, only mitigated through prudent reforms. The second form of conservatism starts from the assumption that there is an eternally valid and attainable order—a final synthesis of all values—that could solve these antinomies. It is against this second type of conservatism that Aron reacted, noting that conservatives in this mold may sometimes be as intolerant and dogmatic as their counterparts on the Left. They tend to adopt a revolutionary cast of mind when "having confused a particular order with eternally valid order," they become "revolutionary in relation to the established one" that they dismiss as "established disorder,"[51] holding no promise of redemption.

Aron's essay, "On the Right: Conservatism in Modern Societies," included in *Espoir et peur du siècle* (1957),[52] challenged an obsolete form of conservatism out of sync with the legitimate demands for equality in modern democratic societies. In *Essais sur les libertés*,[53] Aron took to task the conception of freedom held by those intellectuals (in both the liberal and conservative camps) who focused exclusively on one aspect of liberty as freedom from state's interference. Although Aron was aware of the importance of this definition of freedom, he put forward an equally strong defense of liberty that differed in several regards from that of Friedrich von Hayek and the other members of the Mont Pelerin Society (founded in 1947 to defend the principles of the free market economy and open society), while also sharing a common commitment to freedom, pluralism, and the rule of law in the fight against communism. Aron refused to refer to "freedom" and "liberty" in the abstract; instead he preferred to write about "liberties" in the plural,[54] and chose to analyze them in the larger context of the modern society characterized by economic growth and technological progress. While Aron believed that the goal of a free society ought to be the limiting of the government by men and increasing the power of the laws,[55] he took distance from the one-dimensional interpretation of these principles offered by Hayek, starting with his concept of negative liberty opposed to any form of welfare state. Aron disagreed with Hayek and his disciples and believed that a moderate welfare state respecting the principles of constitutionalism was not a priori incompatible with political freedom and the rule of law.

If this was a civil disagreement among independent spirits situated on the same side of the barricade during the Cold War, it was nonetheless a real intellectual exchange in which Aron did not shy away from taking his colleagues on the Right to task for occasionally putting ideology ahead of facts. In *Essais sur les libertés* and his important review of Hayek's *The Constitution of Liberty* written in the 1960s, Aron examined in detail the limitations of all approaches which focus on a single aspect of liberty, either as freedom from constraint or freedom to participate in political life.[56] In particular, he took distance from Hayek's tendency to equate liberty with obedience to general and impersonal laws. Liberty, affirmed Aron, depends on the universality of the law, but it is also much more than absence of constraint: "All power involves some element of the government of men by men; liberty is not adequately defined by sole reference to the rule of law: the manner in which those who hold this power are chosen, as well as the way in which they exercise it, are felt, in our day, as integral parts of liberty."[57] Liberty and power have a variable character that delineates the ever shifting limits of the individual sphere that must be protected against the encroachment by the state or other groups. As such, there can be no objective, eternally valid definition of constraint and liberty, since general rules, too, may sometimes be oppressive. Aron believed that for all the brilliance of his analysis, Hayek neglected this important point when drawing a stark distinction between obedience to persons, which he equated with domination, and submission to abstract and universal rules, which he equated with liberty. Such a distinction, Aron insisted, was an expression of the very type of ideological thinking that Hayek himself opposed in his writings. In spite of his courageous and honorable defense of the principles of open society, Hayek went too far in equating political freedom with absence of interference and encroachment upon individuals' private affairs.

"Even today," Aron argued in 1961, "as much as it is legitimate to consider both respect for and the enlargement of this [private] sphere as one of the goals, eventually as the primordial goal, of the social order, it is also unacceptable to refer to this *sole* criterion in order to judge *all* actual societies" (1994: 89, emphases added). While negative liberty (as absence of constraint and freedom from interference) is central to the functioning of open society, along with the existence of impersonal rules and the rule of law, it would be an error to posit either of them as the unique criterion of freedom. In reality, Aron argued, neither negative liberty nor the rule of law can ever serve as the single standard by which we can judge how free a society is in reality. Individuals must also have the opportunity to participate in the making of the laws and ought to be able to achieve a decent standard of living if they play by the rules of the game accepted by everyone. After insisting that there is no perfect or sole definition of constraint and liberty, Aron went on to argue for a combination of negative and positive liberty.[58] A free society, he believed, may be called more or less free in keeping not with one, but several related criteria. For example, the power of rulers should be limited and used strictly to achieve clearly defined goals. In turn, citizens must be free to pursue their own interests and plans, unimpeded by the state, and ought to have a say in the making of the laws through their freely elected representatives.[59]

Thus, it was a mark of Aron's political moderation that at a time when the development of the welfare state was seen with skepticism by many classical liberals engaged in the fight against collectivism and communism, he was not reluctant to acknowledge the importance of *both* social and political rights in modern society. Such a mix of rights, in his view, was demanded and justified by the complex nature of modern Western industrial societies, which have a threefold ideal: "bourgeois citizenship, technological efficiency, and the right of the individual to choose the path of his salvation."[60] None of these three ideals, Aron believed, may be sacrificed, but at the same time "we must not be so naïve as to believe that is easy to achieve them all" (1970: 48).

This thesis of Aron was clearly articulated in the last lecture he gave at the Collège de France on April 4, 1978, titled "Liberty and Equality." He spoke at length about "social liberties" and admitted that, as long as there will be people who obey and individuals who rule, the first ones must retain the right to organize in order to protect themselves against those in positions of command. Western welfare states, Aron claimed, must grant and guarantee a modicum of social rights in order to make real and tangible the civil and political rights and freedoms enshrined in their constitutions. The same can be said about citizenship, a concept that during the Cold War had been related to "positive" liberty and was therefore viewed with skepticism by classical liberals. Aron chose a different path. "Individuals in a democracy," he admitted (1997b: 248), "are at once private persons and citizens. What bothers me most is that it seems to me almost impossible in France to have courses in citizenship in the schools. . . . Our societies, our democracies, are citizens' countries." The functioning of free societies depends to a great extent on the education of their members as citizens as well as on the viability and strength of the institutions that make possible their life together.

Consequently, it was his deep awareness of the fragility of liberal institutions that led Aron to emphasize not only the centrality of mores to the preservation of liberal democracy—a lesson he had learned from Montesquieu, Tocqueville, and Aristotle—but also the need for a distinctive type of liberal civic education meant to cultivate certain traits of character suitable to (and required from) citizens living in modern liberal democracies. Among these traits, he included concern for the common good, civic mindedness, respect for diversity, and pluralism. In his last lecture, Aron referred on several occasions to the "moral crisis" affecting our liberal democracies today, but his was not the lament of a conservative mind displaying a nostalgia for a bygone past. We may be freer than before in our choices, Aron claimed, but we no longer know for sure where to locate virtue and how to think of it in our societies. If we are to remain free, our efforts at protecting individual rights against encroachment by the state must be accompanied by a reconsideration of our civic duties.[61]

This approach distinguished Aron from the perspective of Hayek and Friedman, who remained closer to a type of classical liberalism exclusively focused on rights and a negative conception of freedom. Aron's position was, however, unambiguous. He rejected the once fashionable theory of the convergence of capitalism and communism and believed that capitalist liberal societies could be peacefully reformed, in spite of their inherent shortcomings. As Robert Colquhoun remarked, the convergence thesis was a "theory which had been attributed to him by superficial readers but which he always rejected" (1986: 384). Aron never ceased to see in the Soviet Union first and foremost an "ideocracy" (rather than another form of industrial society) whose ideological underpinnings dictated its social, economic, and political priorities. This became obvious in the third volume of Aron's trilogy on modern industrial societies, *Democracy and Totalitarianism*, which contains both an implicit and explicit critique of the once famous convergence theory.[62] In the middle of 1970s, in an exchange with a "true believer"[63] who embraced a militant form of Marxism and naïvely believed in the possibility of liberal reforms in the former Soviet Union, Aron unambiguously declared his skepticism toward that optimistic scenario. In his opinion, it was possible for the Soviet Union to borrow the techniques and vocabulary of the Occident and still maintain intact for some time its authoritarian administrative foundations and ideological orthodoxy that ultimately made genuine reforms impossible. Furthermore, in a response to Alexander Solzhenitsyn who had declared (in May 1975) that the Western world had lost the "third world war" without even waging it, Aron politely begged to differ, taking distance from the excessive pessimism of the famous Russian dissident. Aron remarked that this hypothetical war had not taken place precisely because the Western democratic world had managed to affirm the superiority of its political principles over those of the communist camp. "In this historical rivalry," Aron wrote (1997a: 1543), "the Occident has not lost yet. It still possesses the greatest stock of scientific and technical talents indispensable to the survival of billions of human beings on our planet."

Aron the Political Educator

Arguably the most enduring legacy of Aron has to do with his image and role as a genuine political educator and skilled practitioner of dialogue and the art of balance. As Pierre Manent remarked, Aron was a true "political educator"[64] who showed his contemporaries how to think about politics *sine ira et studio* by combining accuracy, respect for facts, impartiality, responsibility, and passion. If Aron engaged critically with those with whom he disagreed such as Jean-Paul Sartre, he never wrote against them personally, distinguishing clearly between ideas and persons, thinking and action.[65] The liberal party to which he belonged in spirit did not exist, and much like Tocqueville, Aron, too, was condemned to being a marginal figure in his own country.[66] But if he was a moderate of a peculiar breed with a keen sense of intellectual and political independence, he was also a *bold* moderate who never sought refuge in a lukewarm center. Aron took firm and clear stances on all the great and difficult questions of his time: fascism, communism, decolonization, Algeria, May 1968, the role of the United States and the former Soviet Union in the world.

On all of these issues, Aron's judgments, controversial as they may have been, were lucid and balanced rather than emotional, and all things considered, he proved to be a far more reliable judge of modern politics and society than Sartre, Merleau-Ponty, Althusser, or Foucault. His reasoning was always surprisingly simple, unencumbered by the philosophical anxieties that plagued many existentialists and ultimately led some of them to espouse dogmatic views on political issues. Without ever turning into an inflexible defender of the status quo, Aron unambiguously affirmed the superiority of the free society over all forms of closed society, beginning with communism:

> I have chosen the society that accepts dialogue. As far as possible, this dialogue must be reasonable; but it accepts unleashed emotions, it accepts irrationality. . . . The other society is founded on the refusal to have confidence in those governed, founded also on the pretension of a minority of oligarchs that they possess the definitive truth for themselves and for the future. I detest that; I have fought it for thirty-five years and I will continue to do so. The pretension of those few oligarchs to possess the truth of history and of the future is intolerable. (1997b: 252)

Aron analyzed each political situation with a mixture of attachment and detachment, reason and passion, being attentive to the particular constellation of factors defining each context. He had no patience for sophisms such as Merleau-Ponty's puzzling statement that there was as much "existentialism" in the stenographic record of the Moscow debates as in all of the works of Koestler. The claim that one might be simultaneously anti– and pro–Soviet Union prompted Aron to remind his readers that while philosophers were playing with words in Paris, millions of people were sent to labor camps or left to starve simply because they dissented from the communist orthodoxy. In his eyes, one had to make a simple choice: either break with communism or embrace its ideology. *Tertium non datur.*

Another explanation for Aron's political lucidity might be his peculiar brand of rationalism. In one sense, as Edward Shils pointed out (1985: 14), Aron was not a rationalist in the conventional sense of the word. "I was a disciple of Kant," the Frenchman confessed (2002a: 263), "and there is in Kant a concept to which I still subscribe: it is the idea of Reason, an image of a society that would be truly humanized. We can continue to think, or dream or hope—in the light of the idea of Reason—for a humanized society." Aron was committed to exploring through critical and rational analysis the effectiveness of various agendas, ideas, and policies, while regarding all claims about truth to be provisional and open to criticism. Yet, he remained skeptical of what he called *la politique de la raison* (2006–7: 905) that is, a type of politics that pretends to know in advance the development of history, and claims to be capable of steering the latter toward the alleged final goal. As an avid reader of Kant, Aron was conscious of "the crooked timber of humanity" and retained a skeptical attitude toward the idolatry of scientific progress professed by some of his contemporaries convinced that the progress of science and technology could significantly improve the condition of humanity in the short run. Yet, for all of his awareness of the fragility of human condition, Aron believed that even in difficult times, one can (and ought to) remain committed to reason by upholding the ideal of a decent society. He recognized that, notwithstanding the limits of our knowledge and reason,[67] we always have concrete possibilities for responsible action in our imperfect world. Furthermore, Aron retained confidence in rational inquiry and individuals' ability to see the differences among illusions, emotions, hopes, and demonstrable truths. He refused to despair of his contemporaries, even though his century gave him many reasons to question the power of reason.[68]

As such, Aron's chastened rationalism was inseparable from—and reflected his—political moderation. He refused the posture of a seer or a prophet who interprets secular history as sacred history with a predetermined end goal. As an editorialist for *Le Figaro* for thirty years, he believed that a well-informed journalist must not seek to indoctrinate his readers, but ought to give them the basic facts that both politicians and administrators should use in making their decisions. When Aron shared his own preferences, he did it with his characteristic "icy clarity"[69] and detached attachment, aware of the fact that he lacked a certain capacity for performance that is an important prerequisite of success in politics. As he put it in his memoirs, "Intelligence, knowledge, and judgment are not enough. Performance is also required, of which I would have been most probably incapable" (1990: 476).

Finally, no account of Aron's moderation would be complete without mentioning his unique capacity for—and openness to—dialogue. The many insults whose target he was did not alter his belief in the value of dialogue, nor did they diminish his intellectual generosity toward his critics. The rage and incivility of some of those who disagreed with Aron—critics and enemies alike—bothered him little, and he learned to accept them as they were, even in their immoderation.[70] As an American colleague once remarked (Shils, 1985: 13), the most remarkable thing about Aron is that he "was never abusive even when he was abused; he wrote polemics, but they were factual and logical, and he never insulted his adversaries as they insulted him." Aron's lifelong public dialogue with Sartre—in fact, more of a monologue, since the latter chose to ignore Aron's critique—is an eloquent proof of his intellectual openness, honesty, and generosity.

Another sign of Aron's moderation is that he was not afraid of questioning his own stances and expressed reservations even toward some positions that he sometimes endorsed and whose limitations he openly recognized. One such attitude was skepticism. In the foreword to *The Opium of the Intellectuals*, Aron wondered whether the greatest danger facing modern societies might turn out to be not so much the ideological fanaticism of professional revolutionaries as the extreme form of skepticism of those who had previously dreamed of a sweeping transformation of society and saw their hopes dashed afterward. These disillusioned revolutionaries, Aron noted, tended to minimize and underestimate the stakes of political debates under the guise of a false equanimity that verged into cynicism. "Those who have dreamed of a radical revolution," he argued (2001: xxiii), "find it hard to accustom themselves to the loss of their hope. They refuse to distinguish among regimes from the moment none of them is transfigured by the hope of a radiant future." In Aron's view, this form of disillusioned skepticism and cynicism was an ineffective cure for the problems faced by Western societies. He went to great length to teach his fellow countrymen how to admire liberal democracy without being blind to its faults, how to love liberty without being dogmatic in its defense. *La société de consummation* and liberal democracy, Aron argued, must be appreciated for what they are worth; they must be neither rejected due to imaginary or real faults nor idolized for their imaginary virtues. After all, neither production nor consumption can give ultimate meaning to our individual lives; the vital things in life remain beyond the realm of supply and demand, that is, beyond the economic order ruled by private property and free markets.[71]

As the last great representative of a distinguished tradition of European liberalism,[72] Aron attempted to disintoxicate minds and calm fanaticism in dark times. In many of his writings, he sought to explain how ideologies came to be so attractive and influential and were able to produce an explosive combination of despair and hope with large-scale implications. While he criticized the grand soteriological narratives that characterized many social and political movements, Aron took their ideas seriously and chose to leave it to his readers to draw their own conclusions about the direction of the future. "The liberalism in which I seek and find my spiritual home," he once remarked (1984: 81), "has nothing in common with a philosophy for tender souls." In fact, it required a good dose of courage to swim against the current, stand alone in the eyes of public opinion, and take adequate decisions in rapidly evolving circumstances.[73] Aron strove to act reasonably, "according to the lessons, however uncertain, of historical experience, in conformity with the partial truths he assembles rather than by reference to a falsely total vision" (1984: 81–82). He understood that politics always involve the inevitable exercise of power for maintaining order and security, with all its ensuing risks and costly choices in an environment fraught with uncertainty and in constant flux.

It is Aron's political moderation along with his sobriety and intellectual responsibility that make him relevant today, in an age when doctrines and ideas are again mixed, after having lost their previous sharp contours and identities. The age of ideological extremism is hopefully over, and with it also disappears the conception of politics as secular religion and the pursuit of certainty against which Aron wrote memorable pages during the Cold War. With the benefit of hindsight, we may no longer claim that the freedoms brought forth by liberal democracies around the globe are merely formal ones devoid of substance. Liberal regimes are not perfect, to say the least, but their institutions have proved to be working decently well compared to others; as such, they must be analyzed without unjustified enthusiasm or theatrical indignation for their imperfection. As Leo Strauss once put it, the grandiose failures of the past make it easier for us "to understand that wisdom cannot be separated from moderation and . . . requires unhesitating loyalty to a decent constitution and even to the cause of constitutionalism. Moderation will protect us against twin dangers of visionary expectations and unmanly contempt for politics" (1968: 24).

Strauss's quote can be interpreted as a nice gloss on Aron's writings. Some of Aron's themes, such as his critique of the theory of convergence between communism and capitalism or his rejection of all forms of *marxismes imaginaires*, were linked to the context of the Cold War and may or may no longer present great interest to younger readers today. Other topics, including Aron's defense of freedom, his critique of ideological intransigence, and his analyses of the relation between freedom and equality in modern society, continue to speak to us today. He believed that at all times we must strive to preserve and nurture the pluralism of ideas, principles, and interests essential to freedom in modern society. Equally relevant remains Aron's interpretation of the limits of political engagement.[74] He had little patience for the once fashionable idea of engagement as an end in itself or as a response to "existential" imperatives, and in the footsteps of Benda, he criticized his fellow intellectuals for uncritically enlisting their ideas and persons in the service of larger entities such as state, race, party, or nation. For all of these reasons (and many others), Aron remains our contemporary and, to quote again Lévi-Strauss, our indispensable professor of intellectual hygiene at the beginning of the twenty-first century.

CHAPTER 3

Moderation as an Antidote to Monism

Isaiah Berlin's Cold War Liberalism

> The middle ground is a notoriously exposed, dangerous, and ungrateful position.
>
> —Isaiah Berlin

"The Bird in the Golden Cage"

Isaiah Berlin (1909–97), a moderate mind, was born and lived, some might say, in the wrong century, an era of tyrannies and political immoderation. Making sense of this age of anxiety and extremes has been a daunting task for historians, political scientists, sociologists, and philosophers. Looking back at his own life, Berlin was surprised by the mere fact that he should have lived "so peacefully and so happily through so many horrors."[1] The disruptions of the last century "were not natural disasters, but preventable human crimes" (Berlin, 2014) caused by ideas and political doctrines. Yet, understanding those ideas that altered the course of history always requires a considerable effort of empathy of which not many are capable.

Berlin was a fortunate exception in this regard. He had all the required qualities that made him one of the most persuasive champions of the power of ideas in history. Neither a professional historian nor a philosopher, he was an original combination between the two, excelling at writing essays rather than long treatises. He looked for insights in literary works, often ignored or underappreciated by political theorists, and was a notoriously unsystematic thinker. An intellectual fox, he followed a dazzling diversity of interests and paths that earned him the unflattering image as the "Paganini of ideas."[2] Berlin mixed biography, ideas, history, and arguments in his writings to the point that the latter often appeared to be more like carefully crafted jewels and personal impressions than tightly argued pieces. He started his career as an analytical philosopher, but after becoming disenchanted with the apolitical and abstract method of philosophizing practiced in Oxford during the 1930s, he moved on to studying the history of ideas. A couple of decades later, Berlin became the holder of the most prestigious chair in political theory—the Chichele Chair in Moral and Political Theory at Oxford—and subsequently accepted the presidency of the newly founded Wolfson College, which he successfully led for a decade. He did not like to see himself as part of the academic mainstream and deftly cultivated an elegant air of marginality that suited him well. For all the accolades received from many universities across the world, he remained an idiosyncratic academic, skeptical and ironical enough to elicit both the praise and envy of his colleagues and rivals. If he distrusted some aspects of academic life, he also enjoyed a few others, benefitting from the opportunities it provides for leisurely study and dialogue.

Berlin had not one but several identities, layered on top of each other, and an amazing ability to adjust himself "rapidly and easily"[3] to almost any group of persons he happened to interact with. Inducted into the greatest halls of fame—he served as president of the British Academy and received such prestigious prizes as the Lippincott, Erasmus, and Agnelli awards—Berlin was a public intellectual "in the Russian mold and in English idiom" (Ignatieff, 1998: 205); his Jewish roots played an important role in his life, without ever turning him into a committed Zionist. "His deepest loyalties," Berlin's biographer wrote, "were not conveniently layered one on top of the other. They were in conflict. . . . What made him magnetic company for his friends . . . was in fact sharply divided: a fox who longed to be a hedgehog; a solitary thinker who longed for society; a liberal, often torn by the displeasure his middle course earned him from his friends on the left and right" (Ignatieff, 1998: 203). The masterful manner in which Berlin combined all these identities made him one of the most admired citizens of what Tony Judt once called "the Twentieth-Century Republic of Letters." He relished being an intellectual, that is, "someone who wants ideas to be as interesting as possible," combining in a highly personal way academic erudition and analytic arguments with digressions and personal impressions. The Cambridge historian and cultural critic Stefan Collini may have been right then when claiming that "probably no one in our time has come nearer to being regarded as the academic equivalent of a saint than Isaiah Berlin."[4]

Berlin was no stranger to the world of comfort and refinement or the temptations of social and intellectual snobbery so typical of the Oxbridge circles. This consummate Oxford insider, who had once been ironically described by Anna Akhmatova as a "bird in the golden cage,"[5] was fascinated not only by ideas, but also by power and prestige. He loved the orderliness and peace of bourgeois life and was at home among aristocrats, politicians, and eccentric dons alike. For example, Berlin was a close friend of Chaim Weizmann, who encouraged him to immigrate to Israel in 1948; he also corresponded and met several times with Winston Churchill and John F. Kennedy. Berlin was also on familiar terms with prominent American journalists, academics, and dignitaries, from George Kennan and Arthur Schlesinger to Hamilton Fish Armstrong and Joseph Alsop. A short diplomatic stint during World War II took him to Washington, where he witnessed how important political decisions were made, and to Moscow as the Iron Curtain was about to fall over Eastern Europe. In Moscow, Berlin had the privilege of meeting two of Russia's most important writers, Anna Akhmatova and Boris Pasternak.

Individualistic and aristocratic at heart, Berlin was often skeptical and quite reserved in political matters, even though he enjoyed making political points under the guise of historical scholarship. In a letter to Jennifer Hart, he acknowledged that he liked "the history of ideas and in particular the personalities associated with ideas" (2009: 411–12), but admitted that he was far from practicing a conventional type of political theory. Ignoring the conventional distinctions and borders between philosophy, political theory, and intellectual history, Berlin's own version of the history of ideas was, in the words of an Oxbridge colleague (Collini, 1997: 4), a form of "high-altitude aerial photography" seeking broad patterns and the company of the leading minds of mankind, "a kind of All Souls of the mind." He was skeptical toward the conventional way of doing political theory that limits itself to a narrow subject matter and assumes that the task of the theorist is to analyze concepts only in an abstract manner. Berlin combined abstraction and synthesis like few others and deftly applied this method to the study of the Enlightenment and romantic thinkers and ideas. He was as much a historian of ideas as he was a moralist and always acted as a mediator between the texts he studied and his readers. Berlin wanted to challenge those thinkers who claimed that individuals may be seen only as parts of a larger whole and may be sacrificed for the sake of larger and nobler ends. His intention was to discourage extremist projects and fanatical ideas that often originate in "blind adherence to outworn notions, pathological suspicion of any form of critical self-examination, and frantic efforts to prevent any degree of rational analysis of what we live by and for" (Berlin, 2000: 34–35). In particular, doctrines of historical inevitability became special targets of his essays in which he defended a robust conception of individual liberty.

Yet, if Berlin's analyses were never neutral, he managed to eschew, for the most part, the more extreme forms of partisanship that can be found in the writings of many of his contemporaries from Isaac Deutscher and Eric Hobsbawm to Jacob Talmon and even, up to a certain point, Friedrich von Hayek. Berlin wrote about key figures of the Counter-Enlightenment not because he had a secret admiration for their ideas, but because he wanted to understand the flaws in the arguments put forward by the defenders of the Enlightenment whose values he endorsed for the most part. If he was interested in politics, he never assumed that the latter represented the whole of life, and he did not forget that there were other equally important dimensions of life that require the historian's attention. He was much more interested in exploring personal character and individual actions and motives to action along with the beliefs that determine people to (sometimes) die for them.

One can find several recurrent themes in Berlin's writings from liberty and pluralism to political moderation. The latter, I believe, is key to understanding his political outlook even if he never wrote explicitly on this elusive concept. Berlin preferred instead to argue against various forms of immoderation among which the most dangerous one, in his view, was the craving for unity and symmetry at the expense of experience. His moderation combined a principled rejection of monism, a strong commitment to liberty, and an unambiguous aversion to violence and disorder with a sincere admiration for deep convictions and occasional longing for faith. Yet, the very word "moderation" rarely appeared in his writings, although its spirit was present in many of them. It behooves us then to try to reconstitute from a wide array of texts and letters what kind of political moderate Berlin was, what his reasons for embracing moderation were, and what role this virtue plays in his writings. Needless to say, I focus here only on those aspects of Berlin's thought that might help us understand better his political moderation.[6] I begin by examining first his belief in the power of ideas before considering his views on pluralism and his anticommunism. I then place Berlin's work in the larger context of Cold War liberalism and compare it with the "liberalism of fear" espoused by a kindred and younger spirit, Judith Shklar (also born in Riga, like Berlin). I conclude by outlining the main tenets of Berlin's moderate political vision.

Berlin's Main Idea

Berlin's embrace of a moderate and skeptical form of liberalism came from a long study and engagement with some of the ideas that had shaped the course of modern Europe. His intellectual project was an attempt to redefine political liberalism in light of the tragic lessons of the twentieth-century's failed political soteriologies. In this respect, along with Karl Popper, Jacob Talmon, Hannah Arendt, Arthur Schlesinger, and Raymond Aron, he became a prominent representative of what is today known as Cold War liberalism, even if he was never entirely satisfied with this label and sometimes protested against it.[7] These thinkers were anxious to understand how freedom could be preserved in an age dominated by radical ideologies and increasing bureaucratization.

What distinguished Berlin and singled him out among his peers was his peculiar way of practicing intellectual history and political theory. He was fascinated by ideas as much as the personalities associated with them, and had a particular knack for studying the complex ways in which different individuals promote their intellectual and political agendas. He admitted being interested in reflecting mostly on those who did not hold the same views as him. "I am bored by reading people who are allies," Berlin once confessed, "people of roughly the same views, because by now these things seem largely to be a collection of platitudes because we all accept them, we all believe them. What is interesting is to read the enemy, because the enemy penetrates the defenses, the weak points, because what interests me is what is wrong with the ideas in which I believe—why it may be right to modify or even abandon them" (1998a: 90). In another interesting dialogue with the Iranian-born philosopher Ramin Jahanbegloo published in the early 1990s, he admitted (echoing a point made by John S. Mill) that he was interested in exploring the views of thinkers who held contrary views because understanding how our opponents think can always sharpen and improve our own arguments and ideas. "Clever and gifted enemies," Berlin believed, "often pinpoint fallacies or shallow analyses in the thought of the Enlightenment. . . . If you believe in liberal principles and rational analysis, as I do, then you must take into account what the objections are, and where the cracks in your structures are, where your side went wrong: hostile criticism, even bigoted opposition, can reveal truth" (Jahanbegloo and Berlin, 1992: 70–71).

One idea in particular caught Berlin's eye early on, he confessed in "My Intellectual Path" and "The Pursuit of the Ideal," two essays that are essential for understanding the nature of his political moderation and his defense of liberty and pluralism. Studying both ancient and modern philosophers especially from the Enlightenment period, Berlin was surprised to discover that they all shared a monist belief—the "Platonic ideal," as he called it—characterized by three main assumptions: first, that "all genuine questions must have one true answer and one only, all the rest being necessarily errors; . . . that there must be a dependable path towards the discovery of these truths; [and] . . . that the true answers, when found must necessarily be compatible with one another and form a single whole, for one truth cannot be incompatible with another" (1998b: 14). As an inveterate reader of philosophy from Plato, Aristotle, and the Stoics to the *philosophes*, Berlin was struck by the claim that to all true moral and political questions there can be only one true and correct answer discoverable by reason and that can be reached through inferences from apodictic axioms about human nature and the world. The implication that the rest must necessarily be errors that ought to be discarded or eliminated if progress is ever to be achieved in the realm of knowledge also troubled his skeptical and moderate sensibility.[8] According to this monist point of view, the truth is always one (surrounded by many false answers and widespread ignorance) and the ideal world is one of harmony and devoid of contradictions between values and principles; as such, diversity and conflict are almost always unambiguous signs of imperfection and error. Once discovered with the proper method, the truth is definitive and universal and is supposed to make all rational individuals happy and free.

Berlin described this as "the belief that somewhere, in the past or in the future, in divine revelation, . . . in the pronouncements of history or science, or in the simple heart of the uncorrupted man, there is a final solution" (1998b: 237–38) which could (and should) be endorsed by all rational individuals. The miraculous thing about this solution is that it promises to reconcile all the values in which human beings have believed over time in such a way that they become compatible with each other and form a harmonious whole. In their passionate quest for the truth, the philosophers belonging to this tradition of thought have displayed a great deal of metaphysical optimism by believing that ultimate questions about virtue, truth, justice, or goodness could be answered by resorting to an overarching, universal, and timeless standard. Berlin noted that there was very little or no skepticism at all about the possibility of achieving such harmony and absolute knowledge. Confident in their ability to understand complex issues about human behavior and society, many of these Enlightenment thinkers (and not only them) were led to believe in the possibility of a rational organization of society based on the premise that human needs and interests might be objectively identified and fulfilled by using proper rational methods and right criteria. Accordingly, it was assumed that entire societies could be transformed and changed in a relatively short span of time if only enough people were prepared to accept and follow the principles and priorities set by a vanguard in possession of those timeless standards.

The only thing that remained to be done, Berlin wryly noted, was to eliminate all obstacles (human and material) to progress before the process of building the radiant future could begin in the earnest. This could be done in one step through violence or gradually through persuasion, threats, reeducation, disenfranchisement, dispossession of property, relocation, coercion, blackmail, denunciation, and, if necessary, terror. Among the obstacles often invoked by the proponents of a perfect society were human vice, stupidity, ignorance, material interests (broadly defined), and class interests. The emphasis on the latter has been particularly evident in Marxism, which proclaimed that in order for progress to be achieved, it was necessary to remove first the traditional enemies of progress (usually the bourgeoisie), establish a temporary "dictatorship of the proletariat," and then entrust the management of society to "disinterested scientific experts whose knowledge is founded on reason and experience" (Berlin, 1948: 43). Marxism was only one of the movements imbued with this monist perspective, along with scientism and utopianism. All these doctrines and movements assumed that once all the correct answers to complex issues could be figured out, the results would represent the final solutions to all the problems in life; correspondingly, there should (and could) be no incompatibility or contradictions between these values and principles.

To be sure, Berlin was not the first one to remark that such a *Weltanschauung* made possible by the advance of science and the rise of political ideologies in the modern age had considerable potential for fostering various forms of extremism and fanaticism. As a political moderate, he came to be skeptical toward the Platonic ideal that had flourished in Enlightenment circles and then dominated the social and political vision of many nineteenth- and twentieth-century political thinkers and politicians. What made Berlin's position original was the connection he drew between monism and the assumption that all forms of monism are detrimental to liberty in one way or another. In so doing, he might have underappreciated the semantic ambiguity of monism and the fact that there might exist some forms of monism not necessarily related to authoritarian or totalitarian practices. Although it can be argued that Berlin's understanding of monism left little room for discriminating nuances and that he drew too close a link between monism and totalitarianism, in reality he was fully aware that monism, which he took primarily as a useful heuristic device, can come in many different shapes and colors, not all of them connected to totalitarianism. Moreover, monism not only is linked to the philosophical belief in the possibility of a final synthesis of values, but also can be derived from scientist or rationalistic outlooks, equally inimical to individual liberty. To these stronger forms of monism one could add a few softer ones, such as any doctrine strongly committed to an overarching good that overrides all other goods or values. What they all have in common is their faith in a single supreme criterion for evaluating the good society and the belief that values can be brought in harmony with each other through specific methods or techniques.

Berlin rejected the belief in the possibility of a final harmony of values as a "fallacy"[9] and found the notion of a "perfect life" or "perfect society" questionable, to say the least. He doubted that moral, social, and political questions could ever have definitive, unambiguous, and universal answers discoverable with the aid of allegedly correct and precise methods, as is the case with geometry and exact sciences. He was equally skeptical that, once found, putting these solutions into practice would be only a matter of technical skill to be left to the discretion of technocrats. All this, Berlin insisted, is not merely impossible in practice, but also flawed in theory. The belief that there must somewhere be a set of discoverable "true" answers to our problems and questions on how we ought to live and that they all form a coherent and harmonious synthesis is conceptually problematic, if not altogether false as a guide for political reform and our daily lives.

Yet, the worship of oneness, the longing for absolute certainty, and the belief in the possibility of a final synthesis of values, in Berlin's view, represent a form of *philosophia perennis* (1999: 38) not confined to the thinkers of the Enlightenment. It can also be found in many other quarters, religious or secular, which all share the belief that there must exist a clear and discoverable path that may help perceptive and disinterested thinkers, endowed with correct methods and instruments, find the correct answers to complex topics. The latter include not only controversial political and social questions concerning justice, rights, or the redistribution of resources, but also moral and philosophical issues regarding morality and religion that had been the object of intense philosophical debates for centuries and are bound to remain open-ended questions regardless of our best efforts and intentions to solve them. According to Berlin, the belief that one can answer these questions in a definitive manner is unjustified and unrealistic. "I do not know why I have always felt skeptical about this almost universal belief, but I did," he acknowledged in an important text written in the last decade of his life. "It may be a matter of temperament, but so it was" (1999: 39). To think otherwise would be a costly illusion that could lead to gross distortions of facts and might have nefarious consequences, especially concerning individual liberty, rights, and autonomy. Moreover, there is no guarantee that, even if such solutions to our social problems were available, we could come up with the proper and effective means and techniques to find them in a timely manner. Most of the time, it is impossible to estimate the real costs of such solutions, not to mention other unforeseeable side effects. Last but not least, the belief in the possibility of a final synthesis of values tends to foster strong forms of faith that undermine or weaken one's capacity for self-examination, doubt, and skepticism.

A second risk follows from here. Once the select members of the vanguard believing in their special mission are officially entrusted with the task of bringing about a perfect world free of the sins of the past, there is likely to be no limit to what they would feel entitled to undertake in the pursuit of that goal. "If you are truly convinced that there is some solution to all human problems," Berlin claimed in a short text conceived as his message to the twenty-first century, "that one can conceive an ideal society which men can reach if only they do what is necessary to attain it, then you and your followers must believe that no price can be too high to pay in order to open the gates of such a paradise" (Berlin, 2014). No expense will be seen as too costly and no human life will be regarded as sacred or too precious to sacrifice in the pursuit of such a "bright" ideal. Gas chambers, labor camps, induced famine, show trials, civil wars, and genocides could all be justified in the name of final goals and ends demanded by the logic of history, or in light of emergency circumstances that require exceptions to the rule. Once the first eggs are broken and the habit of breaking them becomes entrenched in society, it will be very difficult, if not altogether impossible, to stop or reverse this process, even if it turns out that the promised and much vaunted omelet remains as elusive as ever.[10]

Third and most importantly, it would become possible to force people to follow a certain path in accordance with an alleged universal moral vision or final goal of history determined by a particular elite. This would, however, be politically dangerous and morally objectionable since the select few that form this vanguard might have a wrong set of values or narrow class interests that could clash with the general long-term interests of society and the common good. As Berlin wrote to George Kennan in 1951, "What we violently reject is . . . the very idea that there are circumstances in which one has a right to get at, and shape the characters and souls of other men for purposes which these men, if they realized what we were doing, might reject."[11] The respect for individual liberty goes hand in hand with the recognition of human dignity as a fundamental principle and is incompatible with treating human beings as sheer material to be conditioned and shaped at will. It is also often at odds with granting the conscious direction of human affairs to qualified experts, visionary leaders, prophets of a radiant future, or self-proclaimed elites, regardless of how knowledgeable or virtuous they may be (or pretend to be), and regardless of how good or pure their intentions are in theory.

Pluralism, Liberty, and Moderation

In "The Idea of Freedom," a long and dense essay published in *Political Ideas in the Romantic Age*, Berlin denounced those theories that give "unlimited power to any person or body which feels itself in possession of the right rule for the government of men" (2006: 140). His main justification for rejecting these doctrines, which he considered (rightly or wrongly) to be derived from Rousseau's ideas, had to do with their paternalism and unlimited potential for manipulation, humiliation, and curtailment of individual autonomy and liberty. Failing to treat people as ends in themselves (or paying lip service to this principle) and denying them the right to freely choose their own path and plan of life represent a serious affront to their dignity as human beings and infringe upon their basic liberties and rights.[12] Berlin insisted that respecting individuals' fundamental right to be treated as ends in themselves and unique persons is a categorical principle of our Western liberal civilization that may never be tampered with or compromised under any circumstances. This was the basis of his notorious anti-Procrusteanism,[13] at the core of which lies a very simple idea, namely, that human beings may never be coerced into following patterns of behavior and thought imposed from outside without their consent. "Man must be free," Berlin wrote (2006: 144), "uninterfered with, acting by his own volition, pursuing ends which are his, and solely his, for motives which are his own, in ways which he perceives to be best."

In his regard, the greatest dangers come from several groups. First, there are those who seek to impose political and ideological conformity upon others, the high priests of this world who admit no dissent and dream of a perfect order which was revealed to them. Next come those who see themselves entitled to break an unlimited number of eggs in order to build a radiant future and a perfect omelet. They are often indistinguishable from those who, believing themselves to be engaged in a heroic effort to build an earthly paradise, constantly invent new myths and reasons to legitimize their use of violence and oppression. And finally, these are those who believe not only that the course of history is determined by iron laws, but also that they are the only ones to know them and, as such, feel entitled to punish and wipe out any opponents. What all these groups have in common beyond their differences is that they regard individuals as mere abstractions or numbers, to be accounted for by "standard formulas and neat solutions," and adjustable at will. The outcome of treating people like ideological abstractions, as mere caryatids for the upper rooms of history, to use Berlin's words, is always the same: "a terrible maiming of human beings, . . . political vivisection on an ever increasing scale, . . . the liberation of some only at the price of enslavement of others, and the replacing of an old tyranny with a new and sometimes far more hideous one" (2008: 193).

Berlin's rejection of Procrusteanism deserves special attention here because it is directly connected to his endorsement of pluralism, liberty, and political moderation as well as to his enduring interest in the political doctrines of romanticism. The basic assumption of the latter is that every human being has a unique spirit and personality as well as a particular set of passions, desires, and creative impulses that seek to express themselves spontaneously, but rarely manage to do so. This doctrine of self-development was articulated, among others, by Johann G. Herder and Wilhelm von Humboldt, who emphasized in their writings the importance of free choice, free expression, and spontaneity for the self-development of all individuals. According to this view, it would be wrong and inadequate to try to indiscriminately apply general principles of behavior and a single model of development without taking into consideration the specific conditions of each individual, group, and context.

The main lesson that Berlin took from these thinkers was that each of us can (and must) find a model for ourselves, but only after a long search and arduous process of self-discovery by dint of which we come to choose our own goals that suit our nature. These goals are not to be derived from universal standards or timeless laws, but must reflect an inner imperative that allows each of us to try to fulfill our own vocation and nature as we think best.[14] In a long letter to Myron Gilmore from December 26, 1949, Berlin singled out the vanity and futility of any "search for general principles of permanent reliability" (2009: 152) in setting the allegedly right priorities in our lives. Such a search for universal criteria to decide what the good life is for each of us represents a costly illusion because it is practically impossible to evaluate with accuracy the diversity of human goals, paths of life, and ideals with the aid of any single universal measuring rod or criterion. It does not matter whether this standard is linked to a transcendent value or principle; what is certain is that any attempt to impose a single pattern of perfection and a unique set of values on all individuals, irrespective of their uniqueness and particular condition, is bound to have nefarious consequences in the long term. This has to do with respecting individuals' rights to self-direction and self-development, on which, in Berlin's view, there may be no compromise. These rights are sacred and must be unconditionally respected.

Berlin's political moderation connected to his theory of pluralism and liberty can therefore be best understood in light of his anti-Procrusteanism and deep-seated skepticism about the possibility of a final synthesis of values, which, as already mentioned, he considered theoretically incoherent and practically impossible.[15] "If there were a final solution," Berlin wrote, "a final pattern in which society could be arranged, liberty would become a sin"[16] because it would threaten to destroy the harmony of the world. But once the belief in the existence of such a harmonious whole is challenged or rejected, then we must admit that some values will inevitably clash or conflict with others. There will be enduring disagreements about philosophical, moral, social, and political issues since there is "no single universal overarching standard that would enable [us] to choose rationally between them" (1998b: 315). The only reasonable solution to all this is pluralism, a doctrine that starts from the assumption that "human goals are many, not all of them commensurable, and in perpetual rivalry with one another" (1998b: 241).

The pluralism of values mirrors and corresponds to the nature of the human condition, which presupposes liberty, creativity, diversity, spontaneity, conflict, tragedy, and sometimes luck. It reminds us that the search for moral certainty and clarity is often illusory in an ever changing, imperfect, and uncertain world in which we are part of a larger scheme of things than we cannot fully understand and in which we can at best attain only intermittent glimpses of the truth. We must constantly engage in trade-offs being aware that rules, values, principles should not be pursued intransigently, but "must yield to each other in varying degrees in specific situations" (Berlin, 1998b: 15). No matter what, there will always be profound disagreements between what people take to be the true or best answers to their deepest social, political, and moral questions. We cannot have equality, justice, and absolute freedom at the same time; trade-offs between these values are necessary and unavoidable in setting our social priorities if we are to prevent tragic situations and avoid inflicting suffering upon other human beings.

It might then seem surprising and even counterintuitive that Berlin took this to be the most important lesson to be drawn from Machiavelli's *The Prince*, the classical textbook of Realpolitik, which not many would be inclined to place in the pluralist tradition.[17] Among the many faces of the Florentine author proposed over the centuries, Berlin's account of Machiavelli stands out because it presents him as a defender of pluralism of values and principles and a key participant in a long-standing debate about their incomparability. By examining how princes behave in normal and exceptional political circumstances, Berlin's Machiavelli concluded that there are two equally valid ideals, outlooks, and moralities—the pagan and the Christian ones—among which we have to decide in politics, but lack absolute criteria for our option. We are therefore compelled to make choices between these two outlooks without having at our disposal "an infallible measuring-rod which certifies one form of life as being superior to all others" (1998b: 314).

By teaching that not all the supreme values pursued by mankind are necessarily compatible with one another and juxtaposing (at least) two different outlooks and incompatible moral and political philosophies, Berlin's Machiavelli undermined forever the belief that "somewhere in the past or future, in this world or the next, in the church or the laboratory, in the speculations of the metaphysicians or the findings of the social scientist, or in the uncorrupted heart of the simple good man, there is to be found the final solution of the question of how men should live" (1998b: 321–22). If such a single final solution does not exist, then multiple answers to the question of what the good life is are possible and it is inevitable that people will have different and often conflicting views on this issue. In other words, there are several systems and clusters of values among which we may choose, but we lack a single criterion in order to make a rational choice between them. Machiavelli, Berlin claimed (1998b: 316), had perhaps unintentionally uncovered a disquieting truth at the heart of modern liberalism, namely "that not all ultimate values are necessarily compatible with one another." After Machiavelli, according to Berlin (1998b: 323), serious doubt was cast upon all forms of monism and people lost their certainty that there may be a final solution to the old question regarding the good life and the existence of a clear path to it.

Berlin's study of Vico and Herder, the German romantics, and the Russian writers reinforced his belief that not all of the supreme values pursued by mankind are necessarily compatible with one another. The encounter with Vico's work was particularly important because it taught Berlin an essential lesson about cultural pluralism. Every society has its own vision of reality, a specific understanding of the good life, and a special relation to its past expressed in its art, religion, literature, and forms of social life. That is why the values of different cultures are not always comparable and may sometimes be, in fact, incompatible with each other. Each brings a unique contribution to the plurality of the world through its own values, customs, traditions, institutions, and lifestyles. Every society, culture, and nation has its own center of gravity within itself, its own unique ideals, standards, and ways of life. From here, Berlin assumed that it would be extremely difficult, if not altogether impossible, to find universal values beyond a minimal set of core principles such as respect for human dignity and avoidance of suffering. There are no immutable rules and criteria for judging the excellence of various cultures and nations based upon any one single criterion on which we might all agree. There are as many different types of perfection as there are types of culture, and there are many equally valuable ends pursued by people belonging to different cultures.

Three major implications of Berlin's embrace of pluralism are worth highlighting in connection with his political moderation. First, the existence of a plurality of values shows the impossibility of formulating a coherent and universal political morality and a theory of the good life or society based on a single overarching principle or value, be that liberty, equality, or justice.[18] It is indicative of Berlin's political moderation that, while he believed that freedom and justice are fundamental values without which no liberal society can subsist, he refused to elevate liberty and fairness to the rank of absolute principles against which all others ought to be evaluated. Second, outlining the image of a perfect society is likely to be as futile an endeavor as searching for the quadrature of the circle as long as human values are plural, incomparable, and sometimes incompatible. No form of moral or political reasoning, however rigorous it claims to be, can ever achieve perfect moral clarity and eliminate the possibility of conflict between the different values and principles embraced by different individuals and cultures. Hence, we are bound to live with a significant degree of moral unclarity, as it were, and should use prudence and moderation when addressing complex moral dilemmas. Reason itself may sometimes be powerless to guide our actions when facing tough choices between incommensurable values. Incommensurability of values does not imply relativism though; it means only that it is impossible to use a common (Procrustean) yardstick to properly asses and compare them.

Finally, by embracing the idea that values are plural, incommensurable, and sometimes incompatible, Berlin was led to reject all forms of historical determinism as well as softer forms of social and political meliorism that work with a definite goal of history in sight. History, he liked to repeat, borrowing a sentence from one of his favorite authors (Alexander Herzen), has no predetermined libretto or endpoint; it is and will always remain unpredictable and open-ended. The idea that history has a predetermined goal is a dogma not supported by experience. It can be dangerous insofar as, as Berlin put it (1998b: 43), "[a] fanatical doubt in almost any dogma can be of help to determined men, by justifying ruthless acts and suppressing doubts and scruples." This, he believed, also applies to the blind faith in concepts such as capitalism, socialism, or communism, whose legitimacy cannot be ascertained solely based on abstract models, theories of value, or concepts such as the invisible hand, historical materialism, and class struggle.

Berlin's "Moderate" Anticommunism

Because the deterministic theory of history was central to Marxism and communism, Berlin felt compelled to take issue with it early on, beginning with his biography of Marx written in the 1930s. He continued to discuss this topic in the heated context of the Cold War, when many still believed in the existence of inexorable laws of history and a predetermined future. Berlin did not suffer from any Hamlet-like ambivalence in this regard, and his position on communism was devoid of any ambiguity. As Alan Ryan once put it, Berlin "was anti-communist as only a Russian could be" (2013: 65). He denounced in unequivocal terms the cynicism, high costs, and moral corruption brought about by the Soviet regime based on a minute organization of all available natural and human resources in keeping with the needs of a highly centralized command economy. Yet, if Berlin was a defender of negative liberty (freedom from interference) and a convinced pluralist without being a relativist, he was also a political moderate who resented being caged into a doctrinal corner and refused the posture of a propagandist in the ideological battle against Soviet Union and its satellites.[19] His anticommunism was informed by his political moderation and his distrust of zealotry, ideological simplicity, and political Manichaeism.

The story is, however, not as simple as it might seem at first sight. Berlin's famous essay "Two Concepts of Liberty," originally prepared for his inauguration as the Chichele Professor of Moral and Political Theory at Oxford in 1958, had been regarded by many as an anticommunist manifesto, and not without some good reasons. As Berlin recalled decades later in a letter to a critic, he "merely wished to stress the perversion of the concept of liberty in an Orwellian manner, as a synonym for total control, indeed, oppression" (2015: 14). But Berlin firmly rejected the accusation of engaging in "Cold War rhetoric," which he saw as "both a slur and completely unjust." He claimed that he was merely describing what everyone who was sane and honest could easily see and reiterated an obvious point, namely, that for all their limits and imperfection, the constitutions of liberal states had managed to preserve civil liberties much more successfully than communist states. Several years before, in a letter to the editor of the *New York Times* (June 30, 1949), Berlin stressed the incompatibility between any form of democratic belief and the Marxist doctrine and argued for "a sharply critical approach to doctrines which even today tend to be swallowed whole by the fanatical Marxist sectaries, both orthodox Communists and the heretics whom they have excommunicated" (2009: 100).

Berlin's visit to the Soviet Union in 1945 was a major moment in his career. There he met both Boris Pasternak and Anna Akhmatova, and these meetings strengthened his awareness of evil and convinced him of the high stakes of politics and the heroism involved in the act of preserving one's moral dignity in the face of persecution and in a climate of constant terror and denunciation. The visit also reinforced in him a sense of responsibility to those living behind the Iron Curtain and dispelled any illusions about the allegedly democratic nature of Stalin's regime. As Berlin confessed to Hamilton Fish Armstrong in a letter from August 16, 1951, he decided, however, to follow the policy of publishing nothing about the Soviet Union directly under his name, fearing that such an act would have harmful consequences for his friends who lived there.[20]

It is then all the more interesting that he refused to pay heed to all calls for a stronger faith coming from the quarters of the zealous friends of freedom in the fight against communism. Fearing hard-liners and fundamentalists, Berlin repudiated the role of a conventional Cold War warrior, which seemed to him to lack the humility and sophistication proper to a political moderate. Although he advocated a policy of containment, much like George Kennan, with whom he exchanged a few important letters during this period, he did not view the battle in which he was involved as simply one between the forces of goodness and the forces of evil, as many others did. Berlin's anticommunism lacked the fervent zeal of those who saw themselves engaged in an all-or-nothing crusade against communism and thirsted for absolute moral clarity and purity. It displayed his fear of simplicity and one-dimensional thinking as well as his *penchant* for nuances and moderation.

All this came to the fore in a memorable letter Berlin sent to his friend Herbert Elliston on December 30, 1952:

> I do not think that the answer to Communism is a counter faith, equally fervent, militant, etc. because one must fight the devil with the devil's weapons. . . . If you have a truth you must certainly teach it or testify to it, but not say: "There must be a truth somewhere; what we need is irrefutable principles; what we need is something stronger than what the other side has." If we have it we shall use it; and either we or they will win. If we haven't it we haven't and it is then no use looking around at the available models—Catholic, Protestant, Democratic, Socialist, Liberal, and Existentialist etc. to see which is the most effective antidote to corrosive doubt or destructive totalitarianism. If you really don't believe in anything very much then I daresay we probably shall lose the battle—certainly doubt is no solution and nothing to live by. (2009: 349)

The main point made by Berlin in this passage is that we are likely to lose the flexibility necessary to effectively fight against extremists of all sorts if we are "hypnotized by the blood-curdling threats of the enemy into a frame of mind similar to his own" (2009: 351). Such a transformation, he feared, would spell the defeat of the true friends of liberty across the globe. "I see no point in defeating the other side," Berlin concluded his plea for political moderation (2009: 351), "if our beliefs at the end of the war are simply the inverse of theirs, just as irrational, despotic, etc."

At the very end of his long essay "Political Ideas in the 20th Century," Berlin made a similar point that is worth quoting here in full because it complements the ideas of the previous quote and illustrates well his political moderation:

> What the age calls for is not (as we are so often told) more faith, or stronger leadership, or more scientific organization. Rather it is the opposite—*less Messianic ardour, more enlightened skepticism, more toleration of idiosyncrasies, more frequent ad hoc measures* to achieve aims in a foreseeable future, more room for the attainment of their personal ends by individuals and by minorities whose tastes and beliefs find (whether rightly or wrongly must not matter) little response among the majority. What is required is a less mechanical, *less fanatical application of general principles*, however rational and righteous, a *more cautious* and less arrogantly self-confident application of accepted, scientifically tested, general solutions to unexamined individual cases. (2002: 92, emphases added)

"Less Messianic ardour, more enlightened skepticism, more toleration of idiosyncrasies" along with a "less fanatical application of general principles" however rational they may be: this was what Berlin recommended for the fight against communism at a point in time when Cold War rhetoric reached a dangerous peak and many of his contemporaries called for the opposite, namely more intransigent partisanship, less skepticism, absolute moral clarity, no compromise, and no toleration of idiosyncratic spirits. Worth noting in the above fragment is the use of comparative terms (less, more), which are relative, contextual, and tentative, at the antipodes of absolute universal standards or principles (ought or ought not, shall or shall not, etc.), which are rigid, categorical, and unconditional.

At the same time, Berlin was realistic about the impossibility of reforming Stalinism, a cynical and cruel regime that used the state apparatus and official propaganda for the ruthless management of human beings. Writing under the pseudonym "O. Utis" about Stalin's "art of government" in *Foreign Affairs* in the early 1950s, Berlin offered a sobering diagnosis of a brutal regime whose capacity for survival depended on having complete control over public opinion and putting into practice a large apparatus of universal surveillance and repression. He explained the sudden switches of Moscow's official line as ad hoc and ideologically driven responses to "the need to steer between the Scylla of self-destructive Jacobin fanaticism, and the Charybdis of post-revolutionary weariness and cynicism" (1952: 203). As such, the two poles of fanaticism and apathy between which the regime oscillated corresponded to the alternation between terror and limited liberalization. "An open attempt to modify—let alone cancel—any Marxist principles in such central and critical fields as political theory, or even philosophy," Berlin wrote, "is therefore out of the question" (1952: 207). No ambiguities or uncertainties about the official doctrine were permitted. As long as this intolerant policy was in effect and the system followed a zigzag path, allowing only for short breathing spells but without the possibility of a serious and lasting change of course, the regime was likely to survive in spite of the recurrence of terror. "Those who believe that such a system is simply too heartless and oppressive to last cruelly deceive themselves," Berlin warned. "The Soviet system, even though it is not constructed to be self-perpetuating, certainly bears no marks of self-destructiveness. . . . A human life can be lived—with moments of gaiety and enthusiasm, and of actual happiness—under the most appalling and degrading conditions" (1952: 213).

It is indicative of Berlin's moderation and complex understanding of moral clarity that while he entertained no illusions about the possibility of liberalizing the Soviet communist regime, he also called for less Messianic ardor in the ideological fight against it on a world scale. He thought that we should begin by carefully studying the real nature and functioning of Marxism and Stalinism in an effort to understand better their inner logic and nature. While Berlin believed that the phrase "democratic Marxism" was an oxymoron and that it was both "possible and desirable" to refute Marxism, which abounds in "errors and distortions," he also thought that "if Marxism were to be refuted, . . . it must first be understood."[21] In particular, Berlin claimed, Marx deserves to be studied as "the father of economic history and the originator of a new approach to social history" (2009: 99).

These details show that Berlin's political moderation implied a keen sense of proportions and careful attention to context and nuances combined with a lack of illusions and a good dose of realism. Radical calls for ideological or political purity from both camps left him unmoved and unconvinced for at least two reasons. First, he resented their self-righteous and, at times, hypocritical tone, which was too often a cover for dubious ambitions and dangerous political crusades; second, he doubted that such calls could ever be effective even if they were legitimate. It is often the case, Berlin noted, that what such calls normally achieve in practice is to delegitimize even the best and most generous intentions. To demand ideological purity and moral clarity on issues that are bound to remain messy or blurred would amount to misleading others and deluding ourselves at the same time. This could promote an undesirable form of doctrinairism or moral absolutism that would threaten the very pluralism and liberty that such calls for moral clarity were originally meant to advance and defend. It is not a mere coincidence that Berlin found Arthur Koestler's *Darkness at Noon* "morally askew" and sought to keep distance from its author.[22]

This was one of the reasons why Berlin was unwilling to go as far as Hayek, who described the development of the welfare state as a dangerous and fatal step toward totalitarianism in the West. In the aforementioned letter to Herbert Elliston from December 30, 1852, Berlin teasingly referred to "the wicked Hayek" with whose ideas he declared himself, however, in general sympathy, although Berlin thought the famous Austrian economist had been "quite wrong in assuming that political liberty is indissolubly tied to economic private enterprise."[23] Such a strong link, in Berlin's view, was an example of ideological thinking and a misguided search for political clarity, reflecting precisely the shortcomings of the counter-faith which he found ineffective and in tension with the spirit of true liberalism. If Berlin regarded negative liberty (freedom *from* interference) as essential to the preservation of open society in the West, he also acknowledged the importance of a modicum of positive liberty (self-determination, self-rule, and freedom *to*) for securing a dignified life for all individuals. Liberal democracy, he believed, is nothing more than a continuous and fragile articulation of diverse interests and is made possible by a constant search for compromise among diverse groups in society. As such, it is a mixture of sinful and pure motives, a combination of elevated sentiments and material interests.[24] The age, Berlin concluded, did not call for grandiose plans, tougher leadership, or more scientific organization of society; in reality, the opposite seemed to be the case. For where there is ardent faith and the state or a particular group has a monopoly on virtue and truth, there is also often a great deal of ideological or religious intransigence.

Moderation, the "Vital Center," and Cold War Liberalism

Berlin's position that advocated less Messianic ardor in the fight against communism may have appeared to some as inconsistent with his commitment to individual liberty during the Cold War.[25] But a closer look reveals that it was, in fact, perfectly consistent with his political moderation, which reflects the fact that, as a famous Oxonian colleague of Berlin once put it, "we are doomed to inconsistency, to live in a state of tension, uncertainty, permanent risk" (Kołakowski, 1968: 155). Berlin was aware that when people feel lost in the complicated labyrinth of life, with its unsolvable tensions and paradoxes, they attempt to save themselves by trying to simplify and reduce reality to a few manageable patterns and clear ideas. Yet, they can never change the fact that life is a mixture of complexity and perplexity, and the more possibilities we are confronted with, the more perplexed and challenged we are likely to be.[26]

As a historian of political thought, Berlin knew well that moderation comes in various colors and shapes, some more attractive than others. His own political moderation overlapped to a certain extent with—and differed in other respects from—that of other twentieth-century thinkers who fought to stave off collectivist threats around the world. Most visible is the connection with the agenda of other Cold War liberals—liberalism is taken here primarily in the European sense of the word[27]—who belonged to the same "party of memory"[28] that denounced cruelty and oppression. They all defended a skeptical and dystopian "liberalism of fear" concerned less with achieving justice and more with avoiding the worst forms of political evil and the pathologies that had previously torn apart the fabric of the western world. In this regard, Berlin shared important affinities with Arthur Schlesinger Jr.'s defense of a "vital center," Daniel Bell's theory of the "disjunction of realms" in *The Cultural Contradictions of Capitalism*, and Lionel Trilling's critique of postwar American liberalism in *The Liberal Imagination*.

After the war, many thinkers coming from various ideological quarters and belonging to different social and cultural groups felt compelled to engage with the rise of collectivism in all of its forms. Because the memory of concentration camps and gulags was still fresh on their minds, they wanted to understand what had made possible Europe's descent into barbarism and what could be done to prevent its recurrence in the future. The growing power of the Soviet Union bent on spreading its ideology across the entire world and confidently proclaiming the imminent victory of communism in the Third World added to the mounting challenges faced by the advocates of open society in the Western world. These thinkers, some of them secular and liberals, other conservatives and religious, insisted that we could neither predict the course of history nor anticipate what we might know, need, or do in the future.[29] Troubled by the combination of faith and reason in these historical prophecies, they reminded Marx's followers that there is an unsolvable tension between the prophetic and scientific side and aspirations of Marx's doctrine. Its ambitious account of the meaning of history confidently proclaiming the need for new revolutions and announcing the imminent arrival of a radiant future renewed their skepticism toward all forms of historical prophecy. While reinforcing their sense of humility, these prophecies also gave them a renewed sense of the urgency and importance of their mission of protecting liberty during the Cold War.

In an influential book published in 1949, Schlesinger outlined a passionate defense of a "vital center," a term that he used to refer to the liberal democracy threatened by its international enemies, left and right. In his view, this was not the classical middle of the road solution—which the American historian equated with the "dead center"—but a dynamic, fluid, and open-ended coalition of various friends of freedom determined to fight for the preservation of liberal democratic regimes. The vital center that united the "hopes of freedom and of economic abundance" was supposed to include both members of the noncommunist Left and the non-fascist Right that shared a common faith in the values and principles of open society: civil liberties, rule of law, constitutionalism, pluralism, a belief in the integrity of the individual, and free elections.

The mission of the United States, in Schlesinger's view, was to make sure that this "vital center" would hold and benefit from the fact that political moderation had been a part of the American culture for a long time, although the latter has had its own implacable enemies and overzealous partisans of freedom as well. "By tradition," Schlesinger wrote,

> American liberalism is humane, experimental and pragmatic; it has no sense of messianic mission and no faith that all problems have final solutions. It assumes that freedom implies conflict. It agrees with Madison, in the Tenth Federalist, that the competition among economic interests is inherent in a free society. It also agrees with George Bancroft who wrote: "The feud between the capitalist and laborer, the house of Have and the house of Want, is as old as social union, and

can never be entirely quieted; but he who will act with moderation, prefer fact to theory, and remember that everything in the world is relative and not absolute, will see that the violence of the contest may be stilled." (1962: xv–xvi)

By extolling the virtues of a vital center based on a grand coalition of forces in defense of freedom, Schlesinger wanted to energize a base that seemed, at least in his eyes, to lack a sense of direction after the war. "The best must recover a sense of principle," he wrote in 1948, "and, on the basis of principle, they may develop a passionate intensity."[30] To this effect, the American thinker advocated "reasonable responsibility about politics and a moderate pessimism about man" (1962: 160) and reminded his readers that democratic politics demand a sense of humility and the conviction that every form of power requires solid opposition and relentless correction. He recommended pragmatism as opposed to ideological thinking and utopianism and was interested in shifting the focus away from sentimental and ideological politics to taking tough decisions under the burden of civic responsibility. He also emphasized the need to forsake any form of utopianism or millenarianism and advocated instead a policy of imperfection based on gradual reforms. "Let us not sentimentalize the millennium by believing we can attain it through scientific discovery or through the revision of our economic system," Schlesinger wrote. "We will not arise one morning to find all problems solved, all need for further strain and struggle ended. . . . Given human imperfection, society will continue imperfect. Problems will always torment us, because all important problems are insoluble: that is why they are important. The good comes from the continuing struggle to try and solve them, not from the vain hope of their solution" (1962: 254).

It is important to stress that this was not a conservative agenda, but one that sought to offer a realistic program committed to building and protecting a social and political order based on the assumption that as long as we are going to live in free societies, we would not be able to eliminate or solve forever their tensions, strife, and contradictions. Nonetheless, implementing such an agenda was far from being an easy task, as the wounds of war had not healed yet and the Iron Curtain that fell in Eastern Europe promised new tensions and military conflicts around the entire world. Although Schlesinger must have been aware by 1949 that the Americanization of the world was in full spate and was probably an unstoppable phenomenon, he did not ignore that free societies could survive only if enough people believed in their values and principles deeply enough to sacrifice themselves for them. As the old order and beliefs were beginning to fade, open societies were going through a crisis of confidence and had to counteract the rising cynicism and fears about the future of their values. "Our democracy," he wrote in the late 1940s, "has still to generate a living emotional content" and freedom had to become again a "fighting faith" (1962: 245). The vital center was precisely supposed to serve as the core of this new creed.

Undergirding Schlesinger's defense of a vital center was a nuanced vision of compromise and political moderation that shared important affinities with the ideas of Berlin and the other thinkers studied in this book.[31] Moderation in defense of the principles of open society, he argued, is the opposite of fanaticism: "The thrust of the democratic faith is away from fanaticism; it is toward compromise, persuasion and consent in politics, toward tolerance and diversity in society. . . . Its love of variety discourages dogmatism, and its love of skepticism discourages hero-worship. In place of theology and ritual, of hierarchy and demonology, it sets up a belief in intellectual freedom and unrestricted inquiry" (1962: 245). The proper response to the fanaticism of the communists, he argued, was not the overzealous attitude of the most fervent anticommunists who felt that they were called to participate in a moral and political crusade against communism. "Nothing is more superficially attractive," Schlesinger wrote, "than the notion that 'hard' men, affirming their anti-communism day in and day out, provide, in the cant phrase, the best 'bulwark against Communism'" (1962: 227). His invitation to moderation overlapped with Berlin's position on the dangers of calls for an intransigent and strong "counter-faith" in the fight against communism.

At the same time, other political thinkers subjected the concept of democracy to renewed scrutiny and explored its virtues and limitations from different ideological perspectives, but with a common focus on the concept of open society and the relationship between liberty and equality. They denounced totalitarian democracies across the globe, which displayed, in their view, an unreasonable yearning for unity and solidarity and a discernable propensity to violence and intolerance. The term was coined in the 1950s by Jacob Talmon, who drew a famous distinction between "liberal democracy" and "totalitarian democracy," both of which had roots in the philosophy of the eighteenth century. On his account, totalitarian democracy offered a messianic vision of a "pre-ordained, harmonious and perfect scheme of things, to which men are irresistibly driven, and at which they are bound to arrive" (1961: 2). This type of democracy rooted in the Rousseauian general will developed "a pattern of coercion and centralization" (1961: 249), which in spite of its professed ideas, eventually evolved into an illiberal direction, ending with terror and mass-scale violence. By seeking to remake all the existing traditions and institutions deemed to be flawed beyond reform, totalitarian democracy came in full collision with its liberal rival and became, in Talmon's words (1961: 3), "an exclusive doctrine represented by a vanguard of the enlightened who justified themselves in the use of coercion against those who refused to be free and virtuous." Liberal democracy, he argued, proceeds differently. It acknowledges uncertainty, imperfection, and limited knowledge and works with the assumption that individuals may not be coerced into following a predetermined path and that they are capable of reaching a state of order and prosperity through a gradual process of trial and error.[32] In this regard, Talmon followed in the footsteps of Karl Popper's influential *The Open Society and Its Enemies*, the locus classicus of this line of argument.

If Talmon's polemical book, an outcome of Cold War mentality, voiced strong skepticism toward direct democracy in the Rousseauian mold, it did not reject some of the latter's most important undergirding assumptions that affirmed the importance of equality, rule of law, and majority rule. There was, however, a noted ambivalence toward the latter, an uncertainty also shared by those who had previously professed social-democratic leanings like Karl Popper.[33] These thinkers refrained from defining democracy simply as the government by the majority of the people because they could not forget that Hitler had come to power in 1933 as a result of democratic elections that reflected, for better or worse, the will of the majority of the German people at that time. Similarly, another "democratically" elected leader such as Stalin presided over a regime in the East that called itself popular while practicing constant terror against its own citizens and allowed for no dissent from the official doctrine of the party. Instead, Popper linked democracy to liberal constitutionalism and defined it as a form of government whose institutions provide effective and peaceful means by which rulers may be elected and dismissed by citizens in a nonviolent manner, in keeping with established rules and traditions of behavior. Central to such a form of government are rational debates, political pluralism, and an open competition for power based on publicity, the rule of law, and parliamentarism.

In his political writings, Popper endorsed a policy of gradual social and economic reform based on what he called piecemeal social engineering. As he put it confidently in a later book, *The Poverty of Historicism*, "We can do much more now to relieve suffering and, most importantly, to increase freedom. We must not wait for a goddess of history or a goddess of revolution to introduce better conditions into human affairs" (1964: 80). Yet, while the main focus of these Cold War liberals (including Berlin) was on negative liberty broadly defined as absence of interference, some of them tried to combine this form of liberty with a more positive type of freedom,[34] and displayed measured sympathy for a moderate form of welfare state, a position flatly rejected by Hayek. What they all opposed, however, was utopianism, which they considered to be the essence of communism. A good number of these critics objected to the messianic message of communism, which they regarded as a form of secular religion, offering a false promise of salvation in this world.

The other Cold War moderate liberal with whom Berlin had close affinities was Judith Shklar (1927–92), a legendary professor of political theory at Harvard who shared with him the experience of exile. In their countries of adoption, they both cultivated and enjoyed a certain degree of "optimal marginality" that allowed them to maintain their independence while becoming over time respected voices in academia. Shklar also shared with Berlin the experience of totalitarianism that exercised decisive influence on her personal life and gave her professional career a sense of urgency and commitment that others lacked. Like Berlin, she sought to understand the nature and legacy of political ideologies that had made possible the horrors of World War II. Noting that the time of great narratives had come to an end in the postwar period, she surmised that with them were gone, too, "the last vestiges of utopian faith required for such an enterprise" (1957, vii). Too many false hopes had been entertained, too many wild dreams had been pursued starting from the idea that "man can do with himself and with his society whatever he wishes" (1957: 5). History, she argued, cast a long shadow on this unbound optimism, which required a big leap of faith that the new generations were unable and unwilling to make any longer.

Like Berlin (and Aron), Shklar displayed little sympathy or patience for unnecessarily sophisticated theories of "unhappy consciousness" or permanent revolution and viewed with skepticism radical critiques of society, prophetic claims, and grandiose concepts such as solidarity and fraternity. Although Shklar was a liberal, left of the center, she was quite suspicious of the jargon of authenticity and alienation and the ethos of romantic rebellion that influenced many left-wing movements and doctrines from Sartre to Marcuse. The ethics of authenticity pushed to extremes, Shklar claimed, recognize no duties to others and demand nothing but constant self-creation, which is a Herculean and superhuman task. The search for authenticity, she went on (1957: 142), "does not lead to cooperation; in fact, it militates against it." With its emphasis on the need to break through the banality of everyday life, it sees normal politics as "mere barriers to genuine political relationships" (1957: 151) and manifests no real interest in the world of social institutions and the concrete practices of governments, displaying instead a particular penchant for "the politics of 'extreme situations' and of dramatic violence" (1957: 149). If the politics of authenticity could at best act as an instrument of personal liberation, they do not provide an effective basis for political freedom and a politics of responsibility at the level of the entire political community. As such, Shklar believed that the ethics of authenticity were bound to remain futile if considered from a purely political and collective point of view. Much the same, she argued, could be affirmed about the ethos of romantic rebellion, which praises individual heroism and elevates "great men" above the common morality who consider themselves to be free from the shackles of tainted social conventions and self-righteously pretend to act as the eternal and disinterested allies of the oppressed.

The definition Shklar gave to radicalism in *After Utopia* was reminiscent of Oakeshott's famous critique of political rationalism discussed in Chapter 5. Radicalism, she asserted, is not to be equated with readiness to indulge in—or taking part in—revolutionary violence, as it is often assumed. It is rather the perfectionist belief that people can always "control and improve themselves and, collectively, their social environment" (1957: 219) through rational methods and rules capable of giving them complete mastery over their social and political environment. Such a belief, she argued a decade after the end of the war, had been falsified by previous developments that had delegitimized any romantic and demiurgic conception of politics; the new age called for a more modest (and moderate) agenda that properly takes into account human fallibility and the complexity of the social and political world. In another influential book, *Ordinary Vices*, published three decades later, Shklar argued that "most politics are not a question of stark choices at all; they involve bargains, incremental decisions, adaptations, rituals, display, argument, persuasion, and the like" (1984: 242). Most of the time, we have to choose between "ordinary vices" and virtues and are called to "defend the bad against the worse,"[35] a point with which Berlin and the other moderates discussed in this book wholeheartedly agreed.

Another important point of convergence between Shklar and Berlin had to do with their belief that literature and stories may help us understand the complex nature of political life better than normative and abstract theories.

Their skepticism toward grand theorizing and big narratives was an important facet of their political moderation along with their penchant for realism. As a recent commentator remarked, for Shklar (and, one could add, for Berlin as well), to be realistic about politics meant "not just paying attention to what is real but [also] to the political role of the imagination: what is possible, what is imagined, what is expected" (Forrester, 2012: 256). One of Shklar's (and Berlin's) main questions was whether we can really comprehend the values and judgments of others when we do not share them or feel compelled to reject them. A moderate mind, she suggested, might be better suited to enter into the ways of thinking of others and empathize with them, even when disagreeing with them.

A skeptical by nature, Shklar shared Berlin's curiosity about moral psychology and was interested in studying the motives that drive individuals and influence their actions. She thought there is an intimate connection between character formation and the ethos of pluralist societies and was committed to promoting those virtues that sustain the values and practices of open societies.[36] But she did it in a peculiar manner that owed a lot to her beloved predecessors Montaigne and Montesquieu. What attracted Shklar to the two French thinkers was the fact that they rejected perfectionism and reflected on human vices, mostly cruelty and betrayal, in order to draw relevant political conclusions for building a humane form of government. Her appreciation for these two writers also led her, in turn, to ask what a political theory that "puts cruelty first" might look like and what are the implications of focusing on avoiding cruelty,[37] two questions that also preoccupied Berlin, albeit in a different manner. On their view, "the first public obligation is to avoid extremes of suffering" (Berlin, 1998b: 15), especially the suffering of innocent ones. Therefore, "putting cruelty first" and securing the conditions of a decent society defined both Shklar and Berlin's agenda of political moderation and reflected their steady preoccupation with preventing people from inflicting suffering upon their fellow human beings. While it would be unrealistic to assume that the propensity to cruelty can ever be entirely uprooted from human nature, they insisted that we should always try to temper and moderate its effects as much as we can.

"A Little Dull as a Solution" or a Bold Attitude?

This was a point that Berlin shared not only with Shklar, but also with Oakeshott, an author with whom he had a tense relationship. If there was little admiration between the two Englishmen, they did have, however, something important in common: both attempted to take politics off the pedestal on which the ancients and their modern admirers had placed them. They believed that politics must start low and aim relatively low, by seeking first and foremost to reduce as much as possible the amount of suffering and violence in the world. The reality of which politics are made is a mix of ordinary vices and virtues, including irrationality, incoherence, and inconsistency, that allow for little or no moral clarity at all. In general, politics are not dramatic or grandiose and imply gray areas, significant risks, and messy compromises. In stressing all of these points, Berlin reminded us that most of the time (though not always) the best thing we can do is to endorse policies seeking to mitigate evil without being able to entirely eradicate it from the face of the earth. There is only so much that political action can do, and we should never think that politics could ever solve our inner conflicts or help us achieve authenticity or salvation.

To some, Berlin acknowledged, such a modest (and moderate) task may appear "a little dull as a solution" (1998b: 16), unable to quench the thirst for absolute, risk, and adventure experienced by those who romanticize politics and are prepared to fight and die for their sacred ideals. This may very well be the case. As a recent commentator claimed, for all of its obvious virtues, Berlin's insistence on pluralism "does not have the drama, the compellingness, the eros of some of actual philosophical claim[s] about the nature of the good" (Beiner, 2014: xviii). There seems to be something "deflating" about Berlin's idea of pluralism because as a philosophical position, the latter is derivative from—or parasitic upon—non-pluralistic, monist philosophies of the good life. It remains an open question how useful it is to argue that the ends pursued by human beings are diverse and often come into conflict with each other. This claim, Beiner suggested, may not take us too far and might even leave some among us longing for radical solutions that express an authoritative or radical view of life.

And yet, the minimalist and moderate agenda advocated by Berlin (and Shklar) was far more than a mere defensive position. What did it entail beyond skepticism toward ambitious and elusive visions of political happiness?

We must remember that Berlin's political moderation was, in fact, a bold, sophisticated, and learned response to the lessons of history that reflected his enduring concern with limiting cruelty and violence and his profound awareness of the implications of human fallibility and epistemic uncertainty for building the institutions of a decent society. The distinctiveness of his moderation lies in its emphasis on sensibility, ethos, and style rather than institutions; in fact, his writings contain surprisingly little analysis of institutions or principles, such as rule of law and balance of powers. In Berlin's case, political moderation was accompanied by a constant effort to understand himself, his own complex identity, along with his own political and moral commitments. He believed that zeal even in the pursuit of noble causes must always be tempered by the awareness of our fallibility and limited knowledge, and he liked to quote a *boutade*—"Surtout, Messieurs, point de zèle"[38]—attributed to "the wicked Talleyrand," which resonated with him.

Berlin defended imperfection, variety, and diversity against homogeneity and violence; he took delight in contemplating and trying to grasp the "variety of life and the comedy of human character."[39] Life's fundamental diversity, he insisted, is the most powerful argument against utopianism or monism; to ignore human and cultural diversity amounts to trying to impose an artificial order on society by forcing individuals into predetermined patterns that do not fit their nature, desires, and interests. As a political moderate, Berlin believed that human diversity should not be regarded as disruptive of—or a danger to—social order, but could serve as a means of improvement if properly nurtured and managed. A society in which people would pursue the same goals would mean the end of human life; its creative tensions, conflicts, and differences reflect the irrevocable spontaneity of life and constitute a real engine of progress. Life's diversity, complexity, and murkiness must then be protected against those who have an excessive craving for unity, simplicity, clarity, and purity—"an infantile and dangerous illusion" according to Berlin—which often give license to inflicting suffering on other human beings.[40] And one of the best means we have to achieve this security is political moderation.

Let it be understood that moderation entails making risky choices and tough trade-offs between conflicting and sometimes incompatible values and principles, with every choice presenting significant opportunity costs and, at times, irreparable losses. As Berlin reminds us, multiple claims for social justice have to be constantly balanced with those for liberty and noninterference, and the best we can hope to achieve is a decent and fragile equilibrium that requires relentless efforts on our part in order to be maintained. It will never be more than a precarious and uneasy equipoise, to be sure, one "constantly threatened and in constant need of repair." Nevertheless, Berlin insisted, this fragile balance should suffice most of the time to avoid extremes of suffering and cruelty, and this explains why in his opinion, achieving this goal must be seen as the first requirement of any decent society. His moderate ideal does not celebrate extremism as a form of life,[41] along with imaginary virtues and larger-than-life heroes searching for great adventures and the earthly paradise here and now. It has a much more modest ambition—avoiding the greatest evil—and affirms that life is worth living even if we are not great individuals equal in prowess and virtue to the unforgettable heroes of antiquity whose deeds earned them literary immortality.

Once again, Berlin's opposition to any form of Procrusteanism plays a fundamental role here, accompanied by his rejection of historical determinism and utopianism, another important facet of his political moderation. To be sure, he was opposed to the view that history has (or might have) a predetermined libretto and doubted the possibility of grasping and describing the complexity of the world with the aid of abstract formulas or universal laws. As already mentioned, a leitmotif in all of Berlin's writings was the claim that there is no "final" answer to moral, social, and political questions since "no solution can be guaranteed against error" (2002: 93). He saw this point as an invitation to moderation that reflects the pluralism of values as an ineradicable fact of human existence and reminds us that conflicts and tragedies can never be entirely eliminated from the stage of history. At the same time, he was also aware that human beings will always remain responsive and attracted to utopian doctrines promising to deliver them from the suffering, pain, and poverty that are inseparable from living in society.

For all of its inherent limitations, Berlin believed that the baseline version of his "liberalism of fear" was an ideal worth fighting for and pursuing for several important reasons. It has a chastened quality (lacking any sense of self-righteousness), a moderate agenda, and a realistic goal: promoting and preserving the uneasy equilibrium of ideas, forces, interests, and groups in society that is often threatened and needs constant nurturing. Such a moderate ideal manifests a particular sensitivity to the lessons of history and is unlikely to be seduced by unreasonable hopes and utopian aspirations that often have unintended and perverse results. It starts from the assumption that not every conflict can or should be depicted or understood as a cosmic struggle between the forces of good and evil in which there can be no compromise or middle-of-the-road solutions. Equally important, it does not rely on the alleged virtues of heroic leaders and "great" men who see themselves as inspired artists called to create a new social order and who consider themselves entitled to mold human beings much like artists play with various colors and elements to create vast panoramas. Finally, Berlin's moderate vision does not dismiss the gray hues of ordinary life as baseless or lifeless contingencies to be replaced with the perfect geometry of abstract models or the stark colors of strong ideologies. It assumes that tensions, contradictions, and antinomies cannot be eliminated from reality any more than alienation, irrationality, and malice. To dream of a final triumph of reason, fraternity, or solidarity that would put an end to alienation, exploitation, ignorance, and error is to look for a universal and definitive remedy that exists only in the bold dreams of visionaries, but never in real life.

In spite of its subdued tone, there was a certain grain of boldness in Berlin's political moderation that was not a synonym for indecisiveness and weakness. In his view, moderation entails willingness to compromise and commitment to reason and requires that one recognize one's limits and learn how to cope with uncertainty, ambiguity, complexity, and imperfection. Yet in Berlin's case, acknowledging this point did not amount to embracing political neutrality or endorsing apathy. "I do not see," he wrote to a friend six decades ago (2009: 350), "why it is not possible to believe in the various ends in which we do believe with as much fervor and self-dedication as Communists believe theirs." His moderation was inseparable from his lifelong commitment to toleration and individuality, his defense of the widest possible degree of self-determination and autonomy, and his plea for increasing the area of individual choice and decision. Against the invasive attempts of all the "engineers of human soul" and technocratic followers of Saint-Simon who sought to manage the most minute details of social life and elevate efficiency above other principles, Berlin unambiguously and courageously affirmed the values of all "nooks and crannies of life" (2002: 90), in which individuals ought to be left to freely pursue their own ends as they think fit as long as they play by the legal rules. This was a principle for which Berlin fought to the very end of his life and on which he was never willing to compromise. This is all the more significant since as he once wrote to a friend (Philip Toynbee), "all principles are flexible and subject to interpretation, unless there is some point at which you are prepared to fight against whatever odds, and whatever the threat may be."[42]

As such, Berlin's political moderation was the opposite of the softness, cowardice, and opportunism often attributed to moderates. It will be recalled that he ended his inaugural lecture on two concepts of liberty by approvingly quoting these memorable words of Joseph Schumpeter: "To realise the relative validity of one's convictions and yet stand for them unflinchingly, is what distinguishes a civilized man from a barbarian."[43] This, in fact, can also be applied to the other moderates studied in this book. Berlin and Aron may have differed in many respects, but on several key topics their views did converge. One such issue on which they held more or less similar views was the revolution of 1968. Both Aron and Berlin disliked the jargon of authenticity and sincerity applied to politics and behind the rhetoric of authenticity they suspected a great deal of complacency and political irresponsibility. They were also remarkably firm in rejecting the utopian pretentions of communism and the conceptual core of Marxism, but the manner in which they did it—that is, without becoming zealots defending the opposite truth—bore the stamp of their political moderation. They belonged to the family of moderates who play a key role in times of crisis, but remain independent spirits who, when the battle threatens to become too intense, seek to calm down passions and engineer compromises, save lives, and avert chaos. Not surprisingly, these moderates end up being caught between all fires, being too skeptical to convince the committed ones and too independent to renounce their freedom of thought and become regimented members of an official party.[44]

Moderation, a Matter of Temperament or of Principle?

The question remains: can such a moderate agenda inspire and speak to those who crave for more heroic solutions and entertain bolder dreams of changing the world? In other words, how attractive can be the type of political moderation advocated by Berlin and others in his mold? After all, we should not forget that many individuals proved to be ready to live and die for a set of dogmas, but few or almost no one has been prepared to die for moderation. To be sure, a certain temperament does come into play here, for such a moderate agenda seems to be particularly appropriate and attractive to those who sense that their beliefs may sometimes not be right or true, but remain nonetheless motivated to defend their ideas in spite of being aware of their own fallibility. It is no accident that this moderate agenda is sustained by a sense of humility, the rejection of self-righteousness, and a profound mindfulness of one's limited knowledge and potential for error and violence.

Would it then be accurate to say that moderation might be more a matter of personal temperament than an expression of a coherent political outlook? Berlin would have paused a while before trying to answer this question and would have probably resorted to examples from Russian literature to make a point. The portrait of Ivan Turgenev that Berlin sketched in a seminal essay, "Fathers and Children," included in *Russian Thinkers*, could be construed as a vicarious self-portrait of the Oxford don and a comment on his own political moderation. Like the famous Russian novelist, Berlin was "amiable, skeptical, courteous, too self-distrustful to frighten anyone. . . . He advocated no particular doctrine [and] had no panacea for social problems" (Berlin, 2008: 270). His irony was wedded to his "tolerant skepticism" and "velvet touch" (2008: 292) that made him immune from all forms of fanaticism or extremism. Like Turgenev, Berlin believed that no issue was closed for ever, that every thesis must be carefully weighed against its antithesis, that the search for moral clarity is fraught with significant dangers, and that absolutes of every kind are little else than forms of "dangerous idolatry" (2008: 295) which we should oppose most of the time.

Yet, temperament alone would not be able to fully account for the complexity of Berlin's political moderation. There were several key principles that defined his political sensibility and outlook. As already mentioned, Berlin's writings display a steady preoccupation with finding a moderate and principled course between relativism, determinism, utopianism, and moral absolutism. He was a realist sui generis fond of repeating a famous aphorism of Kant—"Out of timber so crooked as that from which man is made nothing entirely straight can be built"—which he used for the title of one of his best books, *The Crooked Timber of Humanity*. But Berlin was not a realist in the usual sense of the term; in fact, he drew an important distinction between two types of realism, which is worth discussing here briefly. The first form of realism remains at the level of (narrowly defined) facts that it observes and describes faithfully without seeking to go beyond them. As such, it can undergird and inspire a managerial and bureaucratic conception of politics that Berlin flatly rejected for its narrow vision and philistinism. In some of its more radical incarnations, this first type of realism displays an excessive confidence in the efficiency of purely scientific procedures applied to the study of society, which, according to Berlin, is often in reality "one of the marks of lack of realism" (1997: 36). The second form of realism that Berlin thought to be superior to the first one not only seeks to study and understand the facts, but also requires and cultivates, among other things, "imaginative insight."[45] Such a type of realism refuses, for example, to endorse causes pursued by ruthless means and never forgets that politics always retain a potential for cruelty and tragedy that must be limited as much as possible. Yet, being realistic in this second sense may not guarantee sound political judgment either because this form of realism often tends to underestimate the ideas of those visionary and romantic dreamers whose longing for absolute and penchant for radicalism can still teach us important lessons about immoderation. No discussion of moderation would be complete without trying to understand the theories of those who adhere to various political ideologies with an absolute faith in the rectitude of their principles accompanied by total intolerance toward their opponents. By studying the worldviews of these ideological crusaders, we also stand to learn a great deal about the virtues and limits of moderation.

Much like another hero of his, Alexander Herzen, Berlin embraced a form of realism that made it impossible for him to ever become a party man, prone to ideological intransigence and moral or political crusading. If the experience of the New Deal reinforced his commitment to welfare-state liberalism and his appreciation for Roosevelt's statesmanship, his relationship to politics was that of an interested and curious observer rather than an active participant. Joshua Cherniss was right to claim that "Berlin admired political courage and respected political activists, but he was too moderate, tentative, and ironical to be capable of activism himself" (2013: 77). Berlin never joined, for example, Margaret Thatcher's bandwagon, although some of his ideas were cherished on the Right before or during her tenure in office. His short incursions into the world of journalism and diplomacy made him fearful of the notoriety he quickly achieved and determined him to make, according to his own confession, "a rapid retreat into . . . temporary trappism" (2009: 164). But such a choice had its own price. As Berlin wrote to Kay Graham on January 11, 1950, he was resigned to remain isolated in the middle, between those who have strong moral and political certainties and feel to possess moral clarity on both the Left and Right. "It obviously does not do to have a political position at all unless it is a good crude, simple thing, painted in bright colors," he confessed (2009: 167). "Nuances are merely a nuisance and cannot possibly be articulated and are treated as confusion or evasion or just specious preciosity of some sort, unworthy of the great critical moral questions, which ought to drive one into one lobby or another."

Reading Berlin's learned essays in the history of political thought, some may then be inclined to think that he remained, to use his own words, "ensconced in the grey misty gloom of the island monastery of Oxford, absorbed in academic studies of the most minute and unworldly kind" (Berlin, 2009: 165), and that he took little interest in the political issues of his day such as the creation of the European Community and NATO, the debates over nuclear disarmament, or the student revolts of 1968. But a cursory look at his correspondence shows a rather more complex picture. We now know that Berlin followed, albeit with detachment, the debates on Britain's integration with Europe, the American foreign policy, and the controversies on American imperialism. He acknowledged that he suffered from "a perhaps unreasoning sense of admiration for U.S. foreign policy" (2009: 167) which seemed to him to be holding a reasonable middle ground at that time (1950s) between the extremes of isolationism and straightforward imperialism.

When it comes to domestic politics, Berlin's moderation also played a role in defining his preferences. He once described his own position as occupying the "extreme Right Wing edge of the Left Wing movement, both philosophically and politically."[46] This was not an incoherent position after all, but an expression of his nuanced political moderation, for it was possible to defend liberal and social-democratic principles at the same time as opposing communism. If Berlin supported the moderate Left in British politics, the manner in which he did it was not devoid, however, of some interesting ambiguities. His writings contained, in fact, several ideas and themes that were construed as conservative in the context of the Cold War, beginning with his famous distinction between negative and positive liberty. Berlin was aware of the distance that separated him from those who always emphasized the need for moral and political purity on both aisles and were unwilling to accept the imperfection of the world. These purists, working with bright contrasts, were reluctant to acknowledge the inevitable constraints and burdens imposed by the exercise of power and the limitations of human nature. Berlin disliked all forms of conformism and indoctrination, being too liberal and civilized to wage ideological crusades against his opponents, but also too ironical and skeptical to fully commit himself to a particular group or party platform. In fact, nothing was more alien to him than the spirit of Napoleon's words approvingly quoted by no one else than Lenin toward the end of his life: "On s'engage et puis on voit." Such a form of blind commitment was based on the dogmatic belief that there are somewhere simple final answers to all human problems waiting to be discovered by the select few. Berlin believed the contrary: if a question was serious and agonizing, "the answer could never be clear-cut and neat"[47] and little or no clarity at all could be achieved with regard to that problem. He feared those who always thought that they had a recipe for action and possessed an inner certainty about what is the "right" course of action. Such people, he thought, teach us a memorable lesson about the dangerous power that ideological abstractions have over human lives.

Berlin's opposition to generalizations and abstractions, which was an important facet of his anti-Procrusteanism and political moderation, owed a great deal to his intellectual encounter with the writings of Herzen. The latter always maintained that the real center of society is never the collectivity but the individual, and insisted that individual lives may never be sacrificed on the altar of "big ideas," however attractive they might look in theory. Berlin, too, believed that human lives and relationships are far too complex and obscure to be accounted for—controlled or directed—with the aid of standard formulas, equations, or neat solutions. He warned that all attempts to transform individuals and fit them into a rational scheme of things and abstract ideals may have perverse effects, including the maiming of human beings. Particularly dangerous are those doctrines and theories that defend historical inevitability and refer to the laws of history as an alibi for justifying the pursuit of power for power's sake. In so doing, they transfer responsibility from the shoulder of individuals onto an abstract entity called history with the aid of "general principles of permanent reliability" (Berlin, 2009: 152).

As a political moderate, Berlin disagreed with these doctrines because they tend to "bear down too cruelly upon actual human beings in actual situations" (2009: 350). One must therefore judge each situation and individual only on its (or one's) own merits, giving up most of the time the search for general principles regulating what ends individuals may pursue and prescribing the means they should use to achieve those ends. "Ends are not demonstrable," Berlin maintained (2009: 350), "they just are held and in a healthy society there are a great many of them, occasionally colliding with each other, and this needs a machinery of conciliation." General moral principles can therefore be applied only in rare circumstances when the question at hand is liberation from specific or universally acknowledged wrongs. Such general principles are often used by individuals prepared to go all the way in their pursuit of their principles and values, no matter the costs involved.

Last but not least, Berlin took distance from those who predicted that we are witnessing the end of the bourgeois idea(s) and civilization or the end of the creative impulses of modernism.[48] He equally had little patience for the self-proclaimed engineers of the human soul who attempt to force the variety of life into distorting straitjackets. His anti-managerial liberalism sought to debunk the claims of scientific rationalism applied to human affairs and opposed the tendency to narrow the horizon of human activity to quantifiable proportions so that human beings could be more easily combined as interchangeable parts of large social patterns.[49] Like Aron, Berlin believed that people are always able to make free choices and he was convinced that there will always be a certain margin of liberty and room for individual choice. It is no mere coincidence then that he refused to interpret political conflicts exclusively in terms of competing interests—a common tendency among social scientists—preferring instead to refer to conflicts between plural and incommensurable values held by different human beings in particular circumstances. He reaffirmed the Kantian belief that human beings are ends in themselves and argued that we should always concentrate on attainable ends rather than distant and highly uncertain ones that have unquantifiable and unforeseeable costs. Berlin understood that the fanaticism that accompanies the pursuit of distant future goals always goes hand in hand with a lack of respect for real persons by refusing to treat them as ends in themselves.

Life, Berlin once claimed, may be seen through many windows, none of which is absolutely clear or opaque; although some of these lenses are more revealing or distorting than others, one should never put one's entire faith in any one of them. To do so and uncritically embrace a doctrine announcing the final triumph of one supreme value over all others amounted for him to a willful and regrettable betrayal of the intellect. To be sure, Berlin did look through many windows of life and tried to see as many sides as possible of each issue. Unlike many political theorists, he used literature and imagination as precious sources of valuable insight into human nature and society. It is no accident that two of his favorite authors were Herzen and Turgenev, from whom he arguably learned more than from the Enlightenment philosophers whose writings he also studied and admired.

As a perceptive reader of his works once put it, although Berlin might have sometimes been single-minded about some of his ideas (in particular, monism), he was "in the end a compromiser and not a fanatic" (Ringen, 2002: 26). Berlin defended his ideas vigorously, but did not stick to them at any cost, sensing that on most issues only an extremist mind could aspire to—and claim to be in possession of—absolute moral or political clarity. If he loved liberty, he was never an ideologue of freedom and capitalism, despite his greater sympathy for the party of liberty over the party of equality. On some issues, he could not cross unreservedly to either side in the conflict of ideas and classes, and in the thick of the fight he continued to speak to both sides. At the same time, he was never a relativist since he believed that there is a minimum of universal moral and political values—respect for individual rights and human dignity—without which societies could scarcely survive. Such values, he insisted, are worth defending everywhere and in any circumstances but without ideological zealotry.

What distinguishes Berlin's voice among the other moderates is a trait that he had in common with his beloved Turgenev, the Russian writer whom he much admired and whose novel *Fathers and Sons* (1862) he considered a masterpiece chock full of political insights. Turgenev had seen a revolution unfolding under his own eyes in Paris in 1848 and subsequently became a gradualist, old-style English liberal who rejected revolutionary upheaval and violence. His ambiguous attitude toward the younger generations in Tsarist Russia and, particularly, toward the main hero of his novel, Bazarov, notorious for his political radicalism, was more than a literary ploy. To some, Bazarov appeared as the first Bolshevik *avant la lettre,* coarse, restless, and brusque, while others underplayed his militant side. We do not know—and cannot tell for sure—whether the liberal-minded Turgenev, who cherished the achievements of the European civilization, meant in reality to praise or denigrate his main character who vituperated against them. Be that as it may, Turgenev spoke to radicals and criticized them at the same time, while trying to convince the older generations of the need for social and political reform.

Berlin, too, tried to see the many aspects of each issue in each case, but much like Turgenev,[50] despite his greater sympathy for the party of progress and enlightenment, he maintained to the end a degree of hesitation and uncertainty consistent with his political moderation. That is why Berlin may be described as a twentieth-century reincarnation of the Russian writer.[51] Most of the time—though not always (as was the case with communism)—he could not cross unreservedly to either side in the conflict of ideas and principles mainly because he refused what he considered to be simplistic views of moral clarity along with simplifications and vulgarizations of ideas *ad usum populi.* He liked to leave some doors open, seeking to avoid falling into what Flaubert once called *la rage de vouloir conclure,* the source of many misguided political judgments. In the end, Berlin failed to please everyone and could not entirely and always shed away the charge of softness that his opponents leveled at him. He deftly cultivated the image of a moderate in the middle, comfortable speaking to both sides without properly belonging to either of them. In so doing, he came to understand that the genuine spirit of moderation is the one which is sometimes ambivalent, not sure that it is right, but constantly seeks to understand the reasons of others' beliefs and tries to enter into the minds of those who pursue different, often radical ideals. It is no mere coincidence that Berlin wrote illuminating essays about authors whose political sensibility he did not share, but who had important things to teach him about politics and human nature.

Although some of us may disagree about the accuracy of some of Berlin's interpretations or arguments,[52] everyone would agree that his essays were never doctrinal or simplistic. For Berlin did not propose an ideology of moderation, nor did he aspire to grandiose syntheses or all-encompassing visions of the good life or the just society. He believed that such things are beyond the grasp of human beings and pursuing them would be a costly adventure. As such, his writings are a necessary reminder about the risks and challenges that accompany the blind search for moral clarity. Although Berlin's political moderation is nourished by his strong belief in the power of ideas,[53] there is nothing abstract about it. It was rather the lesson of experience that taught him, in the words of a contemporary, "the curse on salvationist creeds: to be born out of the noblest impulses of man, and to degenerate into weapons of tyranny" (Talmon, 1961: 253). Berlin understood that the yearning for salvation and the unchecked pathos for truth may coexist with the passion for freedom and equality, but he chose to maintain throughout his life a skeptical distance from them.

To conclude, while Berlin's moderation had a distinctive boldness, it deliberately refused to transform itself into a fighting creed serving a particular value, principle, or political doctrine. If he viewed himself as pleading for a form of "liberalism," this term must be taken in a broad sense as a set of ideas and principles advocating "a society in which the largest number of persons are allowed to pursue the largest number of ends as freely as possible" (Berlin, 2009: 350) and which provides an arena for open criticism and the possibility of peaceful change. He was much less political than Aron, Bobbio, or Michnik, and enjoyed cultivating at times, like Oakeshott, an air of aesthetic detachment from political affairs. Yet, Berlin never forgot the potential for violence and abuse inherent in politics and from his academic Parnassus, never tired of restating the importance of a few basic truths that he held to be essential to protecting freedom and maintaining pluralism in modern society. He acknowledged the spontaneity of life and chance and honored the complexity of the world rather than attempting to simplify it.

George Kateb once offered the following portrait of Judith Shklar, which may also be used (up to a point) to describe the essence of Berlin's political moderation with whom Shklar shared important affinities. Kateb referred to

Shklar as a "pessimist" and a "moderate," adding that she was a moderate "because she [was] a particular kind of pessimist: not sour, not cynical, but shrewd and, where possible, forbearing."[54] This seems to me, *toutes proportions gardées*, an apt description of the moderate temperament of Berlin as well. He was an anti-utopian thinker who advocated a robust conception of individual freedom and dignity. He emphasized that we must oppose all attempts to treat human beings as material to be molded and conditioned at will if we are truly committed to respecting individuals and protecting them against all forms of individual and institutional bullying. Finally, Berlin recognized that some of the greatest threats to the values and principles of open society may sometimes come from naïve idealists, unaware of the potential for corruption within their own minds and hearts, or among their fellow colleagues and citizens.[55] We should then be grateful to Berlin for encouraging us to remain vigilant and skeptical toward all forms of zealotry and insisting that we avoid becoming fanatical or dogmatic in our moral and political commitments.

CHAPTER 4

Meekness as a Face of Moderation

Norberto Bobbio's Politics of Dialogue

> We are like travelers in a labyrinth and act as if there were an exit. But we don't know yet where that might be.
>
> —Norberto Bobbio

Predisposed to Moderation

Holding joint degrees in jurisprudence and philosophy, Norberto Bobbio once described himself as "a man of reason" (1981: 161) and a moderate "unsuited to politics," suffering from the academic's "typical professional deficiency, that of being an eternal doubter" (2002: 141). He was not afraid to end some of his books with "expressions of doubt" (2002: 141) and confessed to have had a "natural inclination to expect the worst" (2001: 30), rarely giving in to optimism. Toward the end of his life, in a series of essays dedicated to old age, he acknowledged that he "had not found wisdom" yet and modestly admitted that he had "barely reached the foot of the tree of knowledge."[1] In other writings, Bobbio confessed to be "chronically disenchanted by . . . temperament or by calling" (2002: 160) and admitted having always had a sense of insecurity that generated anxiety and fostered his "inclination to extreme pessimism."[2] He attributed the "incompleteness" of many of his writings to this aspect of his personality as well as to the fact that he "attempted to plough different fields at the same time," often jumping from one to another "without waiting for the seed to give all its fruits" (2001: 69).

Yet, all these statements must be taken with a grain of salt. As Perry

Anderson remarked (1988: 6), Bobbio was "a figure of outstanding moral and political significance" with a truly prodigious scholarly output and a distinguished public career. Richard Bellamy (2014) went as far as to claim that Bobbio was "the model of the engaged intellectual" deeply dedicated to the cause of democracy in his country and who saw himself simultaneously as an objective analyst of the present condition and a fervent advocate of liberal values. To be sure, any reader of Bobbio's works is bound to be impressed by his clarity of vision and independence of mind, two traits that made the Italian thinker one of the most lucid defenders of the principles of open society in the second half of the twentieth century.

In several important ways, the intellectual trajectory of the Italian political philosopher born in Turin in 1909, five years before the onset of World War I, resembles that of two other thinkers studied in this book, Raymond Aron (who was four years his senior) and Isaiah Berlin (born the same year as Bobbio). Although, much like Aron, Bobbio founded no school of thought and did not cultivate disciples, he, too, managed to exercise a major influence over his contemporaries, at home and abroad. Bobbio shared Aron's political passion and talent for dialogue and, like him, engaged in substantive exchanges with his Italian Marxist and communist colleagues, challenging their unconditional allegiance to the Soviet Union and seeking to convince them of the need to embrace constitutionalism and liberal values and institutions. Another common trait that Bobbio and Aron shared was the political moderation, civility, and equanimity with which they engaged in public and scholarly debates.

Raised in a bourgeois family, Bobbio received a typical middle-class education—classical high school followed by university—that prepared him for what he referred to in his intellectual autobiography as "a peaceful life during one of the most dramatic periods of European history" (2001: 44). His formative years were marked by the rise of fascism and the gradual descent of Europe into barbarism. The crucial period was the twenty-month War of Liberation from September 1943 to April 1945, which Bobbio described as the decisive period for his generation. When Mussolini fell from power on July 25, 1943, Bobbio was thirty-four, "practically at the mid-point of [his] life's journey, as Dante defined it" (2001: 45). He had already began his academic career some nine years earlier at the University of Camerino, only to be arrested a year later (in 1935) for participating in the antifascist activities organized by the "Justice and Freedom" group.[3] In 1939, Bobbio was appointed to the University of Siena, where he was promoted to the rank of Professore

Ordinario in January 1942. Nine months later, he joined il Partito d'Azione (the Action Party), which had been active in the antifascist Resistance.[4] This was, in his own words, a "party of intellectuals with a liberal and democratic background."[5]

Unfortunately, the Action Party failed to gain many adherents among the Italian electorate in the immediate postwar context marked by political confusion and ideological uncertainty. For one thing, the political platform of the party was quite hybrid and arguably too heterogeneous. Some of its members, like Guido Calogero (1904–86) and Aldo Capitini (1899–1968), wanted to bring it closer to the principles of *liberalsocialismo* as a third pole between conservative liberalism and revolutionary Marxism and communism.[6] The second manifesto of liberalsocialism ended, for example, by reaffirming the key tenets of the latter—"securing the effective functioning of liberty and building socialism though this liberty" (Calogero, 1972: 224)—which, it was argued, were in keeping with the "eternal ideal of the Gospels." As such, Calogero claimed, liberalsocialism was nothing but "a form of practical Christianism, of service to God applied to reality" (1972: 226). Others wanted to keep the agenda of il Partito d'Azione closer to the platform of the movement Giustizia e Libertà created by Carlo Rosselli (1899–1937) in Paris in 1930.[7] The policy proposed by the Action Party advocated a synthesis between liberty and justice that distanced itself from all forms of totalitarianism while remaining close to the ideals of the Left. As Bobbio put it (2001: 51), "it considered itself a dialectical negation that was also an affirmation of all that communism represented in the defeat of fascism and as an antithesis of capitalism." A few decades later, in *Ideological Profile of Twentieth-Century Italy*, Bobbio acknowledged that, in spite of its original contributions, "the non-Marxist socialism of Carlo Rosselli and, thanks to Guido Calogero, of the liberalsocialist wing of the Action Party was and remained a minority current" in Italy during the second half of the twentieth century (1995: 174). The reasons for their lack of success had to do with both the eclectic nature of these doctrines affirming the complementarity between liberalism and socialism as well as the peculiarities of the Italian postwar social and political context.[8]

Bobbio ran in the elections of 1946 for the Constituent Assembly, campaigning against both the Communists and the Christian Democrats and lost, lacking "both the calling and the experience to be a speaker at political rallies" (Bobbio, 2002: 66). Two years later, the Action Party suffered a crushing defeat at the polls and dissolved in 1948. The dissolution of the Action

Party, which had inherited the liberal socialist values of Piero Gobetti and Carlo Roselli, made room for the more powerful Christian Democratic, Socialist, and Communist parties that would dominate the Italian scene for the next four decades or so.[9] The economic reconstruction was to be the work of the Christian Democrats, who reaped the political benefits of their economic successes. The failure of Bobbio's left-of-center party was attributed by historians either to the fact that the Action Party disposed of too many independent-minded intellectuals prone to creating factions, or to the fact that it was torn between two wings, a socialist and a democratic one, between which existed a climate of distrust.[10] With the benefit of hindsight, it is obvious today that the Action Party, which was "neither communist nor socialist," was in reality "split between different identities" (Bobbio, 2002: 68) that could hardly be reconciled and harmonized among themselves. The party was simply too eclectic to be centrist in the usual sense of the term. It could be better described as reformist and not revolutionary, yet its platform was not sufficiently convincing and clear for enough voters to rally behind it. Moreover, its understanding of economy and civil society was inadequate and the party had weak roots outside of northern Italy. As such, il Partito d'Azione was unlikely to succeed in the conflict-ridden context of postwar Italy.

Rather than lamenting the European catastrophe as the end of a turbulent period in the history of the Old World, Bobbio embraced the postwar period as the beginning of another period "worthy of being viewed with some hope," as he once wrote to Carl Schmitt, with whom he had an interesting correspondence from 1946 to 1953 (they developed, in Schmitt's own words, "a particular form of friendship").[11] In March 1948, Bobbio was offered the chair of philosophy of law at the University of Turin that had previously been occupied by Gioele Solari, a distinguished historian of philosophy of law and influential teacher who had supervised Bobbio's dissertation in 1931.[12] From Solari, who had the habit of "elevating political questions into philosophical ones" (Bobbio, 2002: 21), he learned how to inspire his students to question commonplaces and received ideas and put the study of the law in the service of the *civitas*. In Turin, Bobbio taught legal theory until 1972, and, from 1973 to 1979 he offered courses on modern and contemporary political thought, as successor to Alessandro Passerin d'Entrèves, himself a former student of Solari.

For Bobbio, those were the most productive years of his life that brought him wide national and international recognition. He authored over thirty books during his long and distinguished career, only a few of which were translated into English, among them *Which Socialism?* (1976/1998), *The Age of Rights* (1990/1996), and *The Future of Democracy* (1984/1987). As both an academic and respected public intellectual,[13] Bobbio saw himself as continuing a tradition of thought that had distinguished precursors in Italy (such as Carlo Cattaneo, Pietro Gobetti, or Carlo Roselli) and contemporaries (such as Luigi Einaudi). Two other thinkers exercised a lasting influence upon him: Thomas Hobbes and Hans Kelsen. Bobbio met the eminent Austrian jurist only once in Paris in 1957 and was deeply influenced by his procedural conception of democracy outlined in his *General Theory of Law*, a book that emphasized the importance of rules and procedures for providing a free and peaceful social cooperation.[14]

At least until the end of the 1950s, Bobbio embraced the principles of liberal socialism in the tradition of the antitotalitarian Left that took distance from both Manchesterian economic liberalism and authoritarian socialism and communism.[15] He defended the values of political liberalism (pluralism, the autonomy of civil society vis-à-vis the state, and individual rights) along with key aspects of economic liberalism such as private property, free economic initiative, and free exchange. Bobbio was in broad agreement with the liberal socialists' focus on the need for a modicum of social protection and social rights and a certain degree of wealth redistribution, but he also remained open to ideas coming from other intellectual quarters, especially republicanism. For example, he had a strong admiration for Carlo Cattaneo, whose "militant philosophy" he examined in a book published in 1971 and who suggested to him a new way of combining federalism (self-government), liberalism (limited state), and democracy (political participation). Bobbio also owed a great intellectual debt to Benedetto Croce, whom he praised as "the man who awakened Italians' will to combat dictatorship" and articulated "a genuine conception of history as the history of freedom" (1995: 1933). Thanks to the presence of individuals such as Croce and Einaudi, Bobbio argued (2001: 49), "liberal culture continued through the years of dictatorship almost with impunity."

During his long career, Bobbio also contributed to many Italian newspapers, beginning with the Action Party's daily newspaper, *Giustizia e Libertà* (spring 1945–fall 1946), then directed by historian Franco Venturi, continuing with *La Repubblica*, a small journal that Bobbio and his friends founded in mid-1946 to express support for the republican form of government, and ending with the Torinese daily *La Stampa* in the 1970s. Bobbio proved, in fact, to have remarkable journalistic skills that were complemented by his academic tone. He usually wrote once a month, tackling important topics of interest to general readers such as political ideologies, political pluralism, the organization of the state, and the international scene.[16] At the same time, Bobbio found it "very difficult to take on the guise of opinion-maker and leader-writer" (2002: 154). He tried to be moderate and evenhanded in his approach, but was unable to avoid controversies and clashes with prominent political figures such as the socialist leader Bettino Craxi (in whom he saw the first example of a plebiscitarian leader in postfascist Italy) and later the populist mogul Silvio Berlusconi. All this led Bobbio to doubt that he had "the necessary attributes for being a good journalist" (2002: 152), and he feared that journalism might be in the end a monumental waste of time for him.[17]

In 1984, President Sandro Pertini appointed Bobbio as Life Senator (a kind of Italian peer sui generis), and Bobbio, accepting this honor, joined as an independent the Socialist group in the Italian Senate. This prestigious appointment was a well-deserved (and somewhat paradoxical) recognition of the political acumen and wisdom of a moderate mind who ironically had claimed that he "never had any real political vocation" (2002: 21). Bobbio's proverbial moderation did not leave him after being elected to the Upper House, where he felt, in his own words, "a fish out of water in Parliament" (2002: 151). He sought to discharge as best he could his duties as a member of the Senate Legal Affairs Committee from 1984 to 1988, but again, when faced with the need to take crucial decisions, he acknowledged that he always found himself to be hesitant and lacking the doctrinal confidence of many of his colleagues. "I would ask myself who was really right?" Bobbio recalled (2002: 151–52). "I was always assailed by doubts. . . . I was always doubtful when there was a decision to be taken. I am an indecisive person, even in small things in life. I love to debate the pros and cons, rather than come to a conclusion." He had never been very sure of himself and psychologically had always considered himself "to be a little old" even in his youth (2001: 4).

A few days after the massacre in Beijing's Tiananmen Square in June 1989, Bobbio wrote a powerful indictment of the communist utopia titled "L'utopia capovolta" ("The Upturned Utopia") in which he unambiguously admitted that "the first utopia that tried to enter into history, to pass from the realm of words to that of things, not only came true but is being upturned" (Bobbio, 1989b). In 1994, just before the elections that brought Silvio Berlusconi's Forza Italia to power for the first time, Bobbio published a short and incisive book, *Left and Right*, which became almost overnight a best-seller, over two hundred thousand copies being sold across Europe. In his widely acclaimed book, he argued that the Left and the Right would continue to remain relevant as universal political categories on our political map. The attempt to reconcile the claims of liberty and equality, he argued, far from becoming irrelevant in future decades, is likely to remain the key issue of modern politics and the main dividing line between political parties. In the response to his critics, Bobbio embraced the label of eclecticism that had been applied to him, adding that, in his view, eclecticism meant "looking at a problem from all sides" and "is an approach which is reflected at a practical level in [his] political moderation" (1996: 93).

Bobbio's "Politics of Culture" and His Rejection of "Third Way" Theories

Bobbio was deeply preoccupied by the twin issues of cruelty and political evil and sought to understand the mental habits that make the latter possible.[18] The experience of fascism, the ideological divisions of the Cold War, the brutal repression of the Hungarian Revolution of 1956, and the gradual transformation of Italian society during the 1960s and 1970s described in his *Ideological Profile of Twentieth-Century Italy* led him to articulate a strong defense of the constitutional rules of the game against those who denied their relevance altogether or were ready to abandon them in search for allegedly higher forms of justice.

Soon after the end of World War II, Bobbio became aware that the Soviet Union, far from being the bright hope of mankind as its propagandists and zealous friends claimed, was, in fact, a despotic and cruel regime that committed grave abuses of power and used a bellicose rhetoric seeking to expand its political influence and domination around the world. As the ideological warfare between two opposite camps was gaining ground in Europe, the dialogue between communists and anticommunists became ever more difficult and fraught with dangers, fears, and misunderstandings. The political and ideological context was marked by uncertainty to such an extent that at the time, as Bobbio recalled decades later (2002: 92), "The choice between the old liberal civilization and the new communist civilization was not so easy as it is now." The communists emerged reinforced from the war, having played a key role in the antifascist movements all across Europe, and especially in Italy. This explains why six decades ago, "the choice between apologia and condemnation" (Bobbio, 2001: 53) was much more difficult and complex than it is for us today. The question that many asked then was whether, in spite of its obvious limitations, the communist experiment might not succeed in the end.

Bobbio had never visited a communist country until 1955 when he joined an Italian delegation invited to China for a month-long visit. On their long trek to Beijing, the Italians also stopped for a day in Moscow but did not manage to see much there. Still, it was an unforgettable journey that had a profound effect on Bobbio because it allowed him to see communism as it actually was, a previously unknown reality that required special hermeneutical skills to understand. At the end of an exotic and demanding journey that involved carefully organized trips into the country and official meetings with select individuals and groups that limited themselves to repeating the orthodox party line, he acknowledged that he felt deeply ambivalent about what he saw in China. On the one hand, it was impossible to deny the great changes brought about by the revolution that gave the impression of "a people who had woken up after a long sleep, leaping from the Middle Ages straight to modern times" (Bobbio, 2002: 88). On the other hand, Bobbio and his non-communist colleagues were worried about the severe limitations on freedom and democracy, the omnipresent self-censorship, the crushing of dissenters, and the delirious cult of Mao's personality. A genuine commitment to democracy, he believed, was simply incompatible with unanimity. Enforcing unity and stifling opposition and open debate, something that the Chinese regime had been consistently doing, went against the spirit of democracy that the Italian thinker cherished so much.

As a supporter of the principles of the open society, Bobbio was not—and could not afford being—an indifferent spectator in the polarized and conflict-ridden context of the Cold War. With regard to the "demonic face" (Bobbio, 1993: 215) of the Soviet regime and other communist regimes, he believed that there was no place for doubt: it was impossible to achieve political liberty in the absence of political contestation and through temporary dictatorship, however defined and justified. No compromise was possible on the primacy of freedom and the use of revolutionary violence; the question of liberty, Bobbio insisted, must always come *before* the conquest of power, not after.[19] The same "no compromise" logic, he added, applies to the relationship between noble ends and immoral means. The higher the ends, the greater the temptation will be to invoke dubious and ultimately violent means for achieving them.[20] In particular, Bobbio showed no willingness to compromise on what he considered to be a key trait of the open society: the rule of law. His strong defense of liberal democracy as "the rule of law *par excellence*" (1987: 156) was a principled response to his colleagues on the Left who had become increasingly skeptical toward liberal rights and the rule of law. In particular, Bobbio was concerned about the eroding consensus on the principles of the Italian Constitutional Charter, itself the outcome of a complicated and fragile compromise among various political groups in the early postwar context.

Bobbio insisted that a genuine commitment to the principles of liberal democracy required that all political actors and commentators take into account and address the shortcomings of democratic regimes as much as possible in a non-biased and non-ideological manner. "I am a convinced democrat," Bobbio acknowledged (2001: 68), "so convinced that I continue to defend democracy when it is inefficient, corrupt, and risks plunging into one of the extremes; either war of everyone against everyone else or rigid order imposed from above. Democracy is where extremists do not prevail (and if they prevail, then democracy is finished)." Democracy, Bobbio opined, cannot properly function without firmly allying itself with liberal principles, among which the rule of law, freedom of speech and association, and pluralism play a key role. While the ideal model of democracy is monist and presupposes "a centripetal society," in reality a democratic society has not just one center of power, "but a plethora of them" (1987: 28) interacting with each other. Democratic regimes work particularly well when a multitude of centers of power and intermediary associations coexist, none of which is so powerful that it can eliminate the others from the political scene.[21]

It is in this context that Bobbio's position on anticommunism must be understood as a part of a twofold agenda that included a strong defense of liberal democracy and a condemnation of all forms of Cold War anticommunist ostracism. Bobbio was under no illusion with regard to the limits of communism and Marxism, which, in his view, gave insufficient attention to limiting power, protecting political pluralism, and enforcing the rule of law. He remained committed to the principles and values of the moderate center-left and believed in the enduring relevance of the classical concepts of Left and Right.[22] This was all the more true since the great divisions in society revolve around the disagreements between egalitarians and inegalitarians. Bobbio took issue with those who dream of a future society in which such differences would be considered irrelevant with regard to the distribution of economic advantages. Such dreams, he claimed, are unrealistic because unlike the other three sources of discrimination—class, gender, and race—that have been attenuated over time, economic inequalities are much harder to deal with in the long term and can never be entirely eliminated.

In affirming the continuing relevance of the categories of Left and Right, Bobbio criticized those "third way" doctrines that sought to combine the principles and values of socialism, communism, and capitalism and positioned themselves as alternatives to the once dominant paradigms. His interest in the debates on these issues is confirmed by the fact that he devoted no fewer than seven widely read articles to this topic in 1978–79. Bobbio reminded his readers that the concept of a "third way" had traditionally had several meanings and was embraced by many political groups, among which there were significant political differences.[23] To give just two contrasting examples, Edward Bernstein's classic book *Evolutionary Socialism* (1899) defended a process of gradual reform and evolutionary change and was predicated upon the assumption that a "third way" between capitalism and revolutionary socialism was both possible and desirable. On the other end of the political spectrum, pseudo-fascist and corporatist parties and movements in various parts of Europe (such as Spain under the regime of Primo de Rivera) also claimed to offer a "third way" beyond the allegedly discredited Left and Right, arguing that historical developments had dissolved old alliances and required new coalitions and syntheses.

In the case of the Italian Left, the discourse about the need for a "third way" was, in Bobbio's opinion, an undeniable sign that the thinkers on the Left, exceedingly dissatisfied with the present, were also quite uncertain about their priorities, being more or less clueless when it came to devising new concrete institutions to deal with present and future challenges. Bobbio criticized the semantic imprecision of the term *terza via* that allowed many groups to (falsely) claim that they could offer a novel and superior path to existing alternatives. In so doing, they often turned their backs to existing parties and ideologies, often with a mixture of defiance, presumption, and arrogance. In particular, Bobbio believed that abandoning too easily the ideals of social democracy and ignoring its achievements to date was an error pregnant with significant implications for the future of the Left.[24] Another problem faced by those searching for a "third way" was that they had not been able to indicate clearly what their new (post-ideological) society would look like. Most of the time, the "third way" was defined negatively rather than positively and consequently remained an indeterminate and vague idea, which, in Bobbio's opinion (1981: 150), did not represent in practice a real advancement compared to the principles of social democracy. As such, he concluded, the doctrine of the "third way" was most often a figment of the imagination of its proponents who risked building "castles in the air" (1981: 126) while wrongly dismissing or underplaying existing institutions, norms, and practices.

It is important to stress that for all of his unambiguous language and opposition to the main tenets of communism and his rejection of "third way" doctrines, Bobbio did not like to define himself as a "militant intellectual" (2001: 84). He refused to act as a Cold War intellectual in the proper sense of the word and remained untouched by the spirit of political crusades marked by Manichaeism, ideological intransigence, and zealotry. The ambiguity and complexity of the position occupied by the Italian thinker deserve careful consideration. As Nadia Urbinati remarked (2003: 588), "Bobbio could not be an anti-Communist for the simple reason that he was not a Cold War intellectual. By the same token, however, he could not be a Communist sympathizer either." He had little sympathy for abstract normative judgments on communism and anticommunism and believed that such issues could not be judged outside of the historical contexts in which political passions emerge and beliefs are formed. Such contexts matter a great deal, and understanding them is an indispensable first step and precondition of sound political judgment. What Bobbio rejected was the idea that strict ideological criteria could decide who would be allowed to take part in dialogue and who should be excluded from it. According to the Cold War logic, the defenders of open society faced the following dilemma in dealing with their opponents: either suppress the liberty of those who adopted illiberal positions, or attempt to preserve their liberty but make it impossible for them to ever become a majority. Such a dilemma was particularly acute in postwar Italy, and Bobbio's merit is to have refused to accept the conventional terms in which political debates were carried on. In his view, the Cold War logic of argument was questionable because it was likely to foster even more ideological intransigence and fanaticism, with corrupting effects on both the public and political life.[25]

Nevertheless, if Bobbio (acting as a moderate) rejected the "either-or" ideology of the Cold War and did not succumb to the temptation of political sectarianism, he was never politically neutral or indifferent. Instead of what he called the "politics of politicians" (1955: 36) responsible for the division of the world into two hostile blocs engaged in a dangerous nuclear arms race, he endorsed (beginning with the early 1950s) a different type of politics—the so-called politics of culture—supposed to create and maintain civil harmony and cooperation across and beyond ideological differences and camps. Its agenda may have appeared utopian, but in reality it was in itself a powerful criticism of—and a symbolic challenge to—the then dominant Manichaean Cold War politics that sharply separated the forces of "light" from the forces of "darkness" between which no dialogue was deemed to be possible or effective. "Culture," Bobbio affirmed (2002: 123), "is intellectual balance, critical reflection, discernment, and horror of all simplifications, Manichaeism, and partiality." If the existence of the Berlin Wall and the Iron Curtain could not be ignored any longer, it was argued, one could still act *as if* they did not exist in reality. The main idea was that a consistent and strong emphasis on culture could go a long way in that direction.

By focusing on culture, Bobbio followed in the footsteps of Benedetto Croce who had previously argued that "the only way for an intellectual to be involved in politics was to become involved in culture."[26] Bobbio took active part in the European Society of Culture from its very beginning in 1950. The society's raison d'être and stated goal were to overcome the division of the world into two armed blocs by going beyond the simplistic logic of "aut aut, avec ou contre, oui ou non" and putting up "moral resistance" to the divisive patterns of the Cold War (Bobbio, 1955: 33). As a result, the proponents of the politics of culture refused to recognize the division of Europe into two parts separated by the Iron Curtain. "Our Europe," the Italian academic remarked (2001: 91), "was not Europe of the West or of the East. It was the Europe of culture that knew no national borders."[27] The politics of culture affirmed the existence of a unified European spirit across borders and ideological divisions and thus stood in stark contrast to ordinary politics predicated upon the division of the Old World into two incompatible hostile camps.

Those like Bobbio who endorsed the politics of culture believed that the conflict between the two rival camps was not inevitable. They acted based on the assumption that there were enough interests and groups whose agendas, far from being incompatible, overlapped to a certain extent, which made dialogue and cooperation possible. This strategy was a response to two extreme positions in a highly politicized and polarized environment. On the one hand, it challenged the politics of fear, jealousy, and rancor based on blind partisanship and superstition that could be found on both sides of the Iron Curtain in the first decades of the Cold War. On the other hand, it questioned the apolitical stance of those intellectuals who were (or claimed to be) above the fray, detached from the institutions of the society in which they lived.[28] For Bobbio and the other members of the European Society of Culture, it was "not a question of synthesizing opposites but of transcending them," as they were not interested in "reconciling on a higher plane what is good in one with what is good in the other" (Bobbio, 2001: 93). The latter was, in fact, the agenda of those seeking a third way between capitalism and communism that, as we have already seen, Bobbio rejected as an illusory and phony synthesis.

Appearances notwithstanding, the politics of culture was anything but apolitical, and the emphasis on affirming the autonomy and importance of culture in the framework of social life carried strong political connotations while seeking to distinguish the politics of culture, in both its style and content, from the reviled ideological politics of ordinary politicians. As Bobbio himself acknowledged, it was necessary to conceptualize culture as "a political fact"[29] and pursue "una vera e propria opera di impegno politico" (1955: 37) by actively participating in debates with opponents holding widely different views. "Culture means moderation, thoughtfulness and circumspection," he argued (2002: 79); it presupposes "assessing all the arguments before giving an opinion, checking all the accounts before taking a decision, and never giving an opinion or taking a decision in the style of some oracle on which a final and irrevocable decree is to be made."

The members of the European Society of Culture agreed that an effective politics of culture must involve, above all, a vigorous defense and promotion of liberty as philosophical principle as well as of the "strategic institutions of liberty" (1955: 38) meant to translate this value into practice. Free culture, they insisted, means unimpeded culture, freedom of speech, and exchanges of ideas, which explains why the preferred meaning given to freedom was absence of interference or impediments, be they physical, moral, or political. Related to liberty was also the concept of truth. As Bobbio noted (1955: 39), "the fight against moral impediments is [also] a struggle for the defense of the truth" and "the commitment of the men of culture is above all a commitment to the truth." Hence, Bobbio and his colleagues unambiguously condemned censorship, the falsification of facts, and the use of spurious arguments and demanded that all intellectuals and writers, regardless of the country in which they live, be allowed to enjoy unlimited freedom of movement and thought.[30]

At the same time, the European Society of Culture insisted that its politics of "defending the conditions of existence and development of culture" (1955: 37) implied a constant struggle against all forms of intolerance and "a position of maximum openness toward different philosophical, ideological, and mental positions" (1955: 36). Its main belief was that it ought to promote what all intellectuals shared rather than what divided them. Thus, the politics of dialogue gave voice to the intellectuals' determination to break the silence that had previously reinforced isolation and monologue. This open form of politics emphasized toleration, the duty to understand the needs and interests of others, and the moral obligation to render oneself open to the arguments put forward by others and resist the temptation to view them as wrong simply because they differ from our own beliefs.[31]

Equally important was the relationship the proponents of this form of politics drew between culture, moderation, and civility. Culture, Bobbio wrote (1955: 40), means "not only method and rigor in intellectual work, but also caution, circumspection, reserve in judgment: that is, to control all the testimonies and examine all the arguments before affirming something, and refuse to pronounce oneself rather than doing it in a hurry." This, he explained, amounted to promoting a civil form of politics that challenged the self-righteous pundits who searched for absolute moral clarity and were quick to divide the world into two irreconcilable camps (the good and the bad ones). The politics of culture also refused to transform human knowledge and science into absolute knowledge and prophecy and required that people be allowed to use their critical spirit against any form of dogmatism and orthodoxy. When the rights to free speech, freedom of movement, and free thought are unrecognized or trampled upon, Bobbio insisted (1955: 40), "the resistance against dogmatism and the defense of the critical spirit become a duty" for any intellectual committed to upholding the ideals of a free and decent society.

Bobbio's Philosophy of Dialogue

Bobbio felt particularly suited to this type of politics of culture whose ethos had little to do with the moral Manichaeism and political crusades of Cold War politics that operated with an intransigent black-and-white picture of reality.[32] As a political moderate, he considered his task to be that of a mediator called to "sow the seeds of doubt and not to gather certainties" (2002: 79). This required a set of special skills and a particular temperament that he was fortunate to possess. Reaching out to individuals of different ideological persuasions and starting a dialogue with them demanded then (and still requires today) a particular form of courage and fortitude that not everyone has. It also presupposes a particular style of discourse that avoids making reproaches and tirades against alleged "scoundrels" and traitors with whom no dialogue is conceivable.[33] "I learned to respect other people's ideas," Bobbio confessed, "to pause before the secret of every conscience, to understand before arguing, and to argue before condemning."[34] He had always been a person "more interested in dialogue than conflict" (2001: 41) and loathed extremist or intransigent positions on all sides.

Much like his politics of culture, Bobbio's openness to dialogue was in itself an act of defiance to the prevailing partisan politics of his age. "I believe that it is in my character not to exaggerate disputes or exasperate differences," he wrote in his intellectual autobiography, "but rather to seek out where people whose ideas differ from my own are right. I have always sought to have a civil debate with everyone: both Catholics and communists. . . . I have endeavored to use a method of reasoning that weighs up the pros and cons, without closing off all space for another's position, and that does not make it impossible for him to respond with his own arguments" (2002: 83). Bobbio's realist vision of politics started from the assumption that politics presuppose a constant management of conflict between competing interests and political agendas. Certain conditions must, however, apply, if this agenda were to be successful. "If we believe that political struggle is an antagonism that rests not on a discussion over social and economic issues, but on a theological, moralistic or philosophical disputation," he argued, "any agreement would be unthinkable."[35]

Bobbio's politics of dialogue bore the mark of his moderate personality that managed to combine two fundamental commitments which defined his political philosophy: the first one to liberal democracy and constitutionalism and the second one to dialogue and toleration. This dual commitment had first manifested itself in one of Bobbio's early and best books, *Politica e cultura* (1955), an excellent illustration of his political moderation. His invitation to dialogue, the subject of the opening essay in that volume, was a principled position demanding that others, in turn, remove their ideological lenses and temper their excessive attachments to their ideas in order to engage in a frank and uninhibited conversation with people of different political persuasions about issues of common concern. "Talking to each other is not enough to constitute a dialogue," Bobbio believed (2001: 41). "Those who talk to each other are not always actually talking to each other; each person may be talking for himself or for the audience that is listening to them. Two monologues do not make a dialogue." A genuine dialogue is supposed to be open-ended and unpredictable for no one can know in advance the conclusions that one might reach in the end; it has no trace of didacticism or self-indulgent moral posturing and involves challenging commonplaces and received ideas, myths, and dogmas. A true exchange of ideas is not supposed to reaffirm one's certainties but to examine critically one's thoughts and, when appropriate, to nuance or even refute them. That is why "the purpose of dialogue is not to demonstrate that you are cleverer, but to reach an agreement or at least mutually clarify your ideas" (2001: 49). On this view, the antithesis of an authentic dialogue is a monological exchange in which one seeks to always have the last word, or in which arguments are presented only in order to refute others' positions or stubbornly defend one's image or reputation. Bobbio had no patience for this type of univocal exchanges. He believed that our duty is to try to understand and properly present the contrasting positions in each case, explaining the main claims put forward by all participants without distorting them. This would be a principled position that entails neither a superficial reconciliation with one's political opponents nor indifference toward their agendas. A genuine commitment to dialogue always reaffirms the belief in reason and pluralism and presupposes respect for others' ideas, however different they might be from ours.

As a moderate, Bobbio had a notorious aversion to political sectarianism and zealotry and thought that objectivity was an obligation for any public intellectual who must eschew embracing hasty or intransigent partisan stances.[36] In his opinion, the greatest possible sin was "il rifiuto di comprendere," the refusal to understand, something that occurs when one begins to think ideologically by simplifying the world into two camps—friends and foes— among which one must choose and among which no dialogue or collaboration is possible. In so doing, one ceases to question one's ideas, using deliberately an ambiguous vocabulary, and lending the weight of one's authority and prestige to a dogmatic set of ideas and beliefs held to be universally valid.[37] According to Bobbio, *comprendere* implies a combination of moderation, discernment, circumspection, balance, and critical reflection that shuns Manichaeism and assesses all the arguments before giving an opinion. Hence, the model for any responsible intellectual is not the prophet who uses oracular language and is careless about facts or invents them, but rather the scientist who carefully examines the world around him (or her) and seeks to understand it as best he (or she) can. Unlike the prophet who speaks with confidence and is unwilling to revisit his (or her) intuitions, the responsible politician "examines, investigates, ponders, reflects, controls, and verifies" (Bobbio, 1955: 19), and is not shy of admitting his (or her) own perplexities and concerns. The lack of transparency about our main concepts,

Bobbio remarked, is often a considerable obstacle to mutual understanding and civility. Before entering the political arena, any intellectual has the right not to accept on blind faith the terms of the political debate proposed by others; these conditions must be subject to close and unbiased scrutiny and should be constantly reviewed and, if necessary, revised.[38] To comprehend requires, among other things, to achieve clarity on the terms of the debate in which contrasting positions are presented and justified in order to gather political support.

Two of Bobbio's essays stand out in this regard and deserve particular consideration. The first one, "Invito al colloquio" ("Invitation to Dialogue"), written in 1951, at the beginning of the Cold War, represents one of the best expressions of Bobbio's lifelong commitment to dialogue, civility, and political moderation and a good place to start examining the latter. The second one, written four decades later, "Né con loro né senza di loro" (literally, "Neither With Them Nor Without Them"),[39] illustrates quite well the philosophy of dialogue which Bobbio practiced for a long time. In both these texts, Bobbio explained why the conversation with the (Italian) communists, difficult and frustrating as it may have been, was both inevitable and necessary in spite of the heated Cold War rhetoric that discouraged genuine dialogue between rival camps. The fact that Bobbio regarded the Italian communists in the 1950s and 1960s as legitimate interlocutors rather than implacable enemies with whom no exchange was possible was neither an accident nor a form of political blindness or self-delusion on his part. Rather than a lack of moral clarity, it was a conscious (and courageous) political decision as well as an expression of his belief that a serious reckoning with the economic, social, and political agenda of the communists required the latter to be included in a wide social and political dialogue on the new constitutional framework of the country.[40]

It is important to remember how challenging and difficult this dialogue was at a point in time when ideological polarization made it extremely hard for rival camps to debate issues of common interest *sine ira et studio*. Tearing down the wall that divided non-communists from communists was virtually impossible, and Bobbio went a long way to prove that the dialogue between them on key issues was, after all, possible, even in the most critical moments of the Cold War. Because of his political moderation and lack of dogmatism that allowed him to challenge communism's principles without resorting to ideological clichés or engaging in a moral crusade, Bobbio managed to reach out to the other side better and more effectively than others who tried the same. "By neutralizing his interlocutors' weapon—ideological propaganda—which would provide them with ready-made answers," Urbinati remarked (2003: 589), "Bobbio forced them to discuss their own doctrine, and go to the foundation of the Marxist theory of democracy and its criticism of liberal democracy." To this effect, he focused on several related topics on which he opened a line of dialogue with the communists: the theory of the state, democracy, individual rights, and liberty. In the ensuing exchanges, Bobbio offered, in Perry Anderson's words (1988), a "serene but severe critique" of the traditional Marxist conceptions of these terms, and took his colleagues on the Left to task for underestimating the importance of constitutionalism and the rule of law. Bobbio predicted that the Italian communists would gradually come to accept and appreciate the importance of the separation and limitation of powers for the effective functioning of all democratic regimes. History proved him right in this regard.

Although Bobbio was not a communist and never thought of becoming one, he did not refer to communism as "the opium of the intellectuals," to use Raymond Aron's famous phrase. He admitted that communism could not be ignored or dismissed too easily as the "empire of evil" as long as it had been the principal agent behind enormous social, economic, political, and cultural changes. The legitimate appeal of communism and socialism, Bobbio pointed out, came from the idea of saving people from poverty, political dependency, and economic servitude. Furthermore, the communists had played a key role in the antifascist resistance, above all in wartime Italy, and had also contributed to the creation of the rules of the game in the postwar period. Beginning with the early 1950s, Bobbio began a dialogue with the Communists and the Christian Democrats on the best ways of consolidating the institutions of the nascent Italian democracy. In this respect, he followed a tradition initiated by Guido Calogero and his colleagues in the Action Party a decade before. While holding a negative view of the Soviet regime that had transformed itself, the official propaganda notwithstanding, into a totalitarian democracy incompatible with the ideals of socialism, the members of il Partito d'Azione viewed the Italian Communists as opponents with whom they needed to establish "a dialogue on the major themes of liberty, social justice, and above all democracy."[41] The Communists were thus considered to be partners with whom a dialogue on the future of the Left was both indispensable and desirable for its potential long-term benefits.[42]

Bobbio reminded his fellow Marxist colleagues and critics that the issues of justice, equality, and liberty could not be dealt with "by armed criticism but by critical weapons in the spirit of a debate and not a crusade, with the intension of definitively winning over its activists to democracy" (2001: 83). He lamented the fact that the majority of Marxists had traditionally been uninterested in studying the actually existing forms of socialism and communism and had spent much more time condemning various aspects of life under real capitalism or imagining what an ideal communist society might look like. In so doing, they had ignored studying how concrete cases might force them to reconsider key tenets of the Marxist theory. Bobbio believed that these cases were highly relevant and could not be glossed over because they teach us important lessons about the shortcomings of Marxism, above all the absence of concrete proposals as to what should replace capitalism.[43] Marxism, Bobbio argued, displayed an exaggerated and unwarranted hostility to liberal rights, in the footsteps of Marx's radical critique in *On the Jewish Question.* Marx and his followers also showed a misplaced strong skepticism toward the state, which they regarded as nothing more than an organ of the oppression of one class by another. This, too, Bobbio believed, was overstated and inaccurate. He also criticized Marxists for focusing mainly or exclusively on *who* has power and devoting insufficient attention to *how* power ought to be exercised after being conquered. Having espoused a rigid form of historical materialism, Marx was not interested in analyzing different forms of government and types of state government that he identified with dictatorship; nor was he particularly attentive to classical themes such as limited power, separation of powers, balance of powers, and pluralism.

Hence, in Bobbio's view, Marxism's main shortcomings stemmed from its weak political element and its theory of power that left no room for constitutionalism. But there was an additional problem: Marxism offered an unsatisfactory theory of individual freedom, focusing instead on achieving a loosely defined form of collective freedom.[44] In his exchanges with the Italian Communists, Bobbio proved relentless in his call to realism and his insistence that the means and ends pursued by both socialists and communists must be reformulated in such a way that they become fully compatible with civil liberties and individual rights. With regard to the latter, Bobbio remarked, the burden of proof was not on the defenders of liberal democracy, but rather on those who criticized and dismissed what they called "bourgeois" or merely formal liberties. "Without the recognition and protection of human rights,"

Bobbio maintained (2001: 82), "there is no democracy; without democracy there can be no minimum conditions for the peaceful resolution of social conflicts. . . . Subjects become citizens when they are attributed fundamental rights."

All of these topics were present in an interesting exchange that Bobbio had in the mid- 1950s with the influential Marxist philosopher Galvano Della Volpe (1895–1968), a proponent of a scientific alternative to the Gramscian Marxism within the Italian Communist Party, over whether socialist legality could be based on anything other than traditional liberal individual rights. Thinking within a Marxist tradition that had traditionally rejected the rhetoric of individual (liberal) rights, Della Volpe and his like-minded communist friends were deeply skeptical about the effectiveness and legitimacy of such rights and believed that the democratic principles, being superior to the liberal ones, could dispense with the latter in practice. Drawing on Rousseau's theory of positive freedom, Della Volpe rejected the definition of liberty as freedom from interference, commonly known as negative liberty, and challenged Benjamin Constant's assertion that the latter alone is suited to the commercial and pluralist ethos of modern societies.

Bobbio disagreed with Della Volpe and his colleagues and sought to persuade them of the importance of liberal principles which, he insisted, express a permanent necessity: to fight against abuses of power, no matter who commits them and how they may be justified. Regardless of who exercises power—the aristocracy, the bourgeoisie, or the proletariat—power and sovereignty must always be limited and ought to be exercised with corresponding moderation and prudence. On Bobbio's liberal account that followed in the footsteps of Constant, popular sovereignty does not replace the need for individual guarantees and liberal restraints on political power.[45] The Italian Communists were prone to forget this seminal point, and Bobbio thought that their dogmatic position on this topic was influenced by their unconditional admiration for the Soviet Union which had transformed itself by then into a classical case of a totalitarian regime and closed society. This unconditional allegiance to Stalinism, Bobbio claimed, also gave Italian Communists a biased perception of individual rights "merely as 'bourgeois rights' which the proletarian state could do without" (2001: 83). Not surprisingly, the Communists accepted as a dogma Marx's derivation of liberal rights—rights to equality, security, liberty, and property—from the material base of society. They did not take sufficient critical distance from Marx's rejection of the state as an organ of class rule and oppression, and shared his belief that a new allegedly scientific form of administration would eventually be able to replace party politics.

Bobbio thought that these positions reflected a disquieting inclination toward ideological thinking that misunderstood and simplified the complex nature of the political. In both his long response to Della Volpe and his answer to Palmiro Togliatti,[46] the general secretary of the Italian Communist Party who had intervened (under a pseudonym) in the debate in the journal *Rinascita*, Bobbio insisted that only a combination of negative and positive liberty was able to bring forth significant social and political progress in postwar Italy. He claimed that both meanings of liberty are "legitimate, each in its own sphere" and warned his colleagues of the futility of trying to figure out "which of the two liberties is the true freedom" (1955: 173). Such an attempt would start from a controversial premise, namely that there must be somewhere a single criterion of truth and a single legitimate mode of understanding liberty, all the others being flawed. This, Bobbio believed, was not a sound way of thinking about freedom; the latter involves simultaneously autonomy (participation) *and* non-interference in varying degrees, which can be properly evaluated only in different social and political contexts, not in the abstract. Thus, Bobbio concluded (1955: 177–78), "the democratic institutions (above all, universal suffrage and political representation) are a corrective, an integration, an improvement of liberal institutions; they are neither a substitution nor something that surpasses them."

The astute response Bobbio gave to Togliatti and Della Volpe nicely illustrates his political moderation. He began by acknowledging the importance of Marxism that allowed his generation to rethink the significance of key concepts such as political participation, justice, and the common good. Without the influence of Marxism, Bobbio admitted, "we would either have sought a haven in the refuge of interior life, or would have put ourselves at the service of the bosses." Then, he went on to argue that, important as it might have been in the antifascist movement, Marxism alone could not deliver on its ambitious promises of social transformation in the postwar political and economic context. Preserving the key achievements of the European liberal civilization was a priority in the new circumstances, and this task fell into the hands of a particular elite entrusted with a specific mission described by Bobbio as follows:

> There were only a few of us who preserved a small bag in which, before throwing ourselves into the sea, we deposited for safekeeping the

> most salutary fruits of the European intellectual tradition, *the value of enquiry, the ferment of doubt, a willingness to dialogue, a spirit of criticism, moderation of judgment, philological scruple, a sense of the complexity of things*. Many, too many, deprived themselves of this baggage: they either abandoned it, considering it a useless weight; or they never possessed it, throwing themselves into the waters before having the time to acquire it. I do not reproach them; but I prefer the company of the others. Indeed, I suspect that this company is destined to grow, as the years bring wisdom and events shed new light on things.[47]

Worth noting in this fragment is Bobbio's emphasis on cultivating openness to dialogue and exercising prudent judgment along with a proper sense of (the complexity of) reality and a genuine critical spirit, all of which are essential ingredients of political moderation. They are all the more important when judging the limits of existing regimes and assessing how to go about reforming them and maintaining political community. It is imperative to acknowledge, Bobbio insisted (1955: 28), that "the liberal-bourgeois civilization has posed in irrevocable terms the question of individual liberty" in its long and arduous confrontation with religious authorities and the absolute state. Its centuries-long struggle to protect individual liberties and rights against the claims of the state and the church had brought forth religious toleration, division of powers, political pluralism, parliamentarism, and the rule of law, all significant achievements in their own right that may not be dismissed as irrelevant by the Marxist critics of liberal regimes.

The Role of the Intellectuals

Bobbio's dialogue with the Italian Communists was important in yet another respect. It reminded and convinced him that political actors often tend to grant their ideas the aura of myth by presenting them as dogmas to be accepted without critical scrutiny. Bobbio believed that the role of intellectuals on both aisles of the political spectrum is to question these myths and accepted truths by submitting them to the light of reason and testing them against the evidence of facts. Their mission is "to spread doubt rather than gather certainties," he argued (1955: 15), and the best way of remaining true to their task is to refuse to think ideologically and withstand the temptation of self-righteousness and political intransigence. Intellectuals betray their mission when they accept on blind faith the arguments put forward by politicians, use in a dishonest way a purposively ambiguous language, and adopt a sectarian point of view that interprets the world in Manichaean terms based on the "friend-foe" distinction. In short, their duty is to make "il gioco di nessuno, che è poi il vantaggio di tutti" (1955: 11), the game of no one that is in the advantage of everyone in the long term.

In an important article, "Intelletualli e vita politica in Italia" written in 1954 and included a year later in *Politica e cultura*, Bobbio drew a seminal distinction between four types of intellectuals and political engagements. There is some overlap between these forms, and sometimes it may not be easy to distinguish them clearly in practice. The first group consists of the intellectuals who aspire to remain "al disopra della mischia" (1955: 132), untouched and above the fray. They witness the battle between factions with a mixture of sadness and dismay, "horror and shame" (1955: 132) and do their best to avoid being contaminated by what they perceive to be the fanaticism of all the combatants. They wait instead for the end of hostilities in order to safely descend from their pedestals into the public arena. The alleged advantage of this position is that it gives the impression—or perhaps the illusion—that one can view all historical events from the standpoint of universal history and thus one may become free, at least to some extent, from the politicians' alleged idiosyncrasies, passions, interests, and nearsightedness.

The second type is the intellectual who seeks to be "né di qua né di là" (1955: 133), neither here nor there, and whose prototype is Erasmus. This is someone who chooses neutrality, being unable or unwilling to fully commit oneself to any side. To anyone who claims that one may not remain neutral and must therefore make a choice, these neutral intellectuals respond that their choice is precisely *not* to make a choice and that their only commitment is to "the truth that the fanatics have abandoned" (1955: 133). These persons may retain a sense of dignity and composure, but they are rarely capable of making headlines or history; the latter is, in fact, made without them or, better said, above their heads. The intellectuals belonging to this group tend therefore to stay out of political controversies because the latter seem to them futile or excessively partisan. Yet in so doing, their excessive prudence risks condemning them to irrelevance, "an adventure with a sad end" according to Bobbio (1955: 143).

The third type is precisely the opposite of the passive intellectuals who withdraw from public or political life; the individuals belonging to this third type want instead to be "e di qua e di là," both here and there. This is the group of intellectuals who tend to get involved wherever and whenever "positive values are present" (1955: 134) and are ready to fight against the injustices of this world. They can be found on all sides of the political spectrum and are aware that no political party may ever claim monopoly on the truth which explains why political Manichaeism is alien to their mode of thinking. The originality and difficulty of their position stem from the fact that these engaged intellectuals are simultaneously committed to dialogue, liberty, and toleration and tend to be intransigent about their values and principles, which are held to be supreme and non-negotiable. To their credit, they seek to unveil facts as they are in reality, not as described by different political groups. This is a demanding attitude that presupposes firmness and determination to "combat lies, thwart absurd propaganda, reestablish the facts in their naked truth, [and] defend liberty where it is threatened, although in this battle one might find oneself side by side with faces that are hardly reassuring" (1955: 134). This was in part the position adopted by the proponents of the politics of culture and the European Society of Culture in the 1950s. The danger always lurking in the background, Bobbio warned, is that the intransigence regarding one's values might in the end surreptitiously turn into a form of "moral pedantry" (1955: 135) and an unhealthy obsession with achieving absolute moral clarity. The solution he recommended to combat this temptation was to adopt "maximum openness, which is a form of mental generosity, toward the opposing set of values" (1955: 135).

The last group, by far the most ambitious one, comprises those individuals whose vocation is to indicate the possibility of syntheses between different values and principles. If these intellectuals place themselves above all parties, they do so not with a detached or reproaching attitude, as was the case with the previous types, but with the desire to serve as responsible guides and mediators among conflicting groups. They see themselves capable of transcending the usual partisanship and sectarianism of political parties and aspire to occupy a higher platform that might allow them to see, most of the time, better and farther than others. The agendas defended by the intellectuals belonging to this group differ among themselves. Some may embrace "third way" theories and advocate a diverse mix of policies proposing different syntheses between liberalism and socialism, individualism and universalism, or personalism and solidarism. Others may reject such mixtures but still believe in the possibility of finding some form of common ground. What all these agendas have in common, however, is the fact that they usually tend to promote abstract ideals that have a considerable capacity for self-delusion. In claiming to be placed on an allegedly higher platform, these intellectuals risk placing themselves outside of history, or above it, thus losing touch with it.

Looking back at his own political involvement in the Action Party in the 1940s, Bobbio had plenty of reasons for being skeptical about the effectiveness (and desirability) of a party of intellectuals. Such a party, he remarked with a touch of humor and irony, is a "monstrous phenomenon" (1955: 137), difficult to imagine operating effectively in a normal political system. It usually lacks mass organization and a powerful leadership in order to make its voice heard and respected in the political realm. Bobbio insisted that the word "monstrous" be used here as a descriptive rather an axiological term, suggesting the unnaturalness of such a party of intellectuals who seek to be at the same time players, commentators, and referees. They work at the confluence between the politics of culture pursuing long-term goals and the ordinary politics of political parties seeking to gain power. The members of such a party of intellectuals, Bobbio believed, often make two major mistakes. First, they believe that they may be able to promote and pursue an effective and genuine politics of culture with the means of ordinary politics. Second, they make no distinction between a *cultural* third force (a "third way" doctrine, for example) and a *political* one and tend to identify the latter with the center that they distrust and dismiss as uninspiring.

None of the four types of intellectuals discussed above adequately reflect the kind of political and public engagement espoused and preferred by Bobbio. He was particularly critical of that attitude that tends to present each problem in dichotomic terms, *aut-aut*, as a radical option—communist or anticommunist, for or against the market, for or against the state—thus leaving no room for a middle solution, which may sometimes be possible and desirable. Yet, if Bobbio dismissed the arrogant or romantic pretentions of intellectuals to serve as enlightened guides of democracy, he was not prepared to recommend a withdrawal into the ivory tower either. On the contrary, he believed that intellectuals true to their vocation must remain involved in the affairs of their communities by always fighting against all forms of dogmatism and doctrinairism.[48] Intellectuals must not passively resist or withdraw from the political realm but should embrace, in Bobbio's view, "una filosofia militante" (1955: 16), a militant form of moderation. This may not be a philosophy or agenda in the service of a party or a church; it represents instead "a philosophy fighting against the attacks on reason, regardless of the quarters from which they come" (1955: 16). As such, it is a militant philosophy fighting against any form of blind faith, superstition, and censorship.

If intellectuals should not be directly involved in political conflict, they must always try, on Bobbio's account, to be present and stand for "positive values" regardless of where the latter may be found. He believed that such values never exist only on one side but can be found in varying degrees on all sides of the political spectrum.[49] This last qualification is important because it points to the dangers of overcommitment, blind faith, and ideological zealotry that are common among intellectuals. Bobbio insisted that if they are to remain true to their mission, intellectuals may never enter in complicity with the official propaganda and should refrain from embracing any form of political sectarianism. As already mentioned, their main duty is to try to "understand" (1955: 20) as best they can the complexity of the issues they deal with before voicing their opinions and making a commitment to one group or party. Bobbio believed that culture can make a significant difference in this regard by helping "defeat the myths, break the close circle of powerlessness and fear, in which the contagious inferiority of ignorance comes to light" (1955: 20).

It is essential therefore for intellectuals not to let themselves silenced by the "zelatori di ogni ortodossia o pervertiti di ogni propaganda" (1955: 20), that is, the dogmatic spirits on all sides who will always try to accuse independent intellectuals of either being unable to commit themselves to a "noble" cause, or having betrayed the "right" one, whatever that might be (progress, revolution, the proletariat, equality, or freedom).[50] Because intellectuals are often led by their hubris to espouse utopian or immoderate attitudes, Bobbio asserted, they must also exercise prudence, patience, and modesty in order to resist the temptation of becoming excessively self-righteous, partisan, and ideological in their commitments.[51] Not only should intellectuals resist the temptation to simplify reality by reducing it to easy and comfortable contrasts or slogans that match their political agendas, but they must also challenge those who pretend to know *the* truth and claim to be entitled to lead others to it. If and when they practice this Stoic form of skepticism by refusing to uncritically embrace the agendas, principles, and values of any single group, intellectuals are able to keep the dialogue open between rival parties and sometimes even convince them to reexamine their own positions with an open mind.[52]

Meekness as a Face of Moderation

It should be obvious by now that the habit of moderation coexisted in Bobbio with—and undergirded—his firm belief in the principles of liberal democracy. He remained to the very end a perceptive and steadfast defender of a moderate Left committed to the "four great freedoms" of modern individuals (Bobbio, 1989b): the right not to be arrested arbitrarily and to be judged in accordance with clearly defined penal and judicial rules, freedom of the press and of opinion, freedom of assembly and association. It is also important to note that similar to Raymond Aron in France, Bobbio was one of the most lucid analysts and critics of the ideas of the Left in European politics. As the intensity of the Cold War was waning in Europe in the mid- to late 1980s, he lamented the fact that his friends on the Left still lacked clear ideas about the real benefits and limitations of liberal democracy and were confused about whether to reform democratic institutions or replace them (1987: 64). Their unrelenting critique of "bourgeois democracy" often paid little or no attention to the machinery and real constraints of politics (at both the national and international levels) and thus risked becoming a mere cliché or an empty slogan as long as it did not sketch a credible political alternative.

Bobbio maintained a healthy skepticism toward—and distance from—these radical positions on the Left. Although he never turned a blind eye to the shortcomings of democratic regimes around the world, he steadily refused to offer catastrophic visions of the future of democracy. He believed that the broken promises and challenges faced by many countries in building viable democratic regimes did not erase in the end the fundamental distinctions between democratic and autocratic regimes. In spite of the obvious imperfection of many existing democracies, Bobbio argued, the minimal basic content of the democratic states has not been compromised. These states still contain "guarantees of the basic liberties, the existence of competing parties, periodic elections with universal suffrage, decisions which are collective or the result of compromise . . . or made on the basis of the majority principle, or in any event as the outcome of open debate" (1987: 40). For all their obvious flaws, these imperfect democracies "can in no way be confused with an autocratic state and even less with a totalitarian way" (1987: 40) as some radical voices argued. Having lived through tough times and experienced the dark sides of a populist dictatorship, Bobbio was convinced that a" bad democracy" was still preferable to a "good dictatorship" and "to have ten bickering parties is better than having one 'monolithically' united under the infallible leadership of its *duce*" (1987: 71). In this regard, he was in full agreement with the other moderates—Aron, Berlin, Oakeshott, and Michnik—studied in this book who all stood firmly behind the (imperfect) institutions of liberal democracy even when criticizing them.

Bobbio's political moderation originated from a particular *forma mentis* that predisposed him to this elusive virtue and gave him a refreshingly humane perspective on what politics can and cannot do. He was aware that the political sphere occupies an important and transformational role in our lives but admitted at the same time that politics are not everything and must play only a limited role in society.[53] The lives of ordinary people, Bobbio once remarked, "are lived out in most cases in areas which lie outside the one occupied by politics" and which politics never manage to invade entirely. If the political sphere were to take over and dominate the other spheres of society, "it is a sign that the individual has been reduced to a cog in a car engine and has no clear idea of who the driver is and where he is driving" (1987: 73). In other words, there is a realm beyond or outside politics that is even more important than the political sphere and must be duly protected against the undue interference of the latter.

Bobbio benefitted from being a university professor accustomed by professional habit to critically discuss every topic, including the most controversial ones, and ready to subject all issues to the test of logic and reason. He was famous for his capacity to make subtle distinctions and his unique eye for possibilities to reach compromise on a wide array of issues. As a moderate, he had serious reservations about Manichaean approaches to politics that divide the political universe into mutually exclusive interests and groups; to the logic of either-or, he often preferred that of neither-nor. "Today," Bobbio wrote in 1992 as many were celebrating the liberal end of history, "we need prudence and patience more than ever, and we must resist the temptation to say 'all or nothing.' Neither hope nor despair" (2001: 55). He also rejected all types of consolatory utopias and was convinced that there are no final miraculous solutions to our social and political dilemmas. The best thing we can do, he once admitted, is to take "one step at a time" (2002: 144) in our pursuit of justice and equality and exercise prudence and moderation in our choices and actions. As Bobbio wrote in "Reply to My Critics," included in *Old Age and Other Essays*,

> I am a moderate, because I am fully persuaded of the ancient maxim *in medio stat virtus* ("the middle way is best"). By this I do not mean

> that extremists are always wrong. I do not do so, because to assert that moderates are always right and extremists always wrong would be to think like an extremist. An empiricist must restrict himself to saying "for the most part." My experience of both public and private life has taught me that, "for the most part," the solutions provided by people who avoid clear-cut "either-or" approaches are, if not better, then at least less imperfect. (2001: 8)

A little over a decade before his death, Bobbio candidly acknowledged that, as he was reaching the end of his life, he got the impression that he was still at the starting block when it comes to understanding good and evil. "All the big questions remain unanswered," he confessed with modesty (2001: 58), before adding that he believed that, in spite of our best efforts, all the fundamental questions regarding the meaning of life and the good life are bound to remain open-ended and unanswered in the end.

The moral and political virtue that reflected Bobbio's metaphysical modesty was *mitezza*, best translated as meekness (it must be added that there is no perfect English translation of this word). It is not a mere accident that Bobbio gave the pride of place to an unconventional virtue such as meekness, which was a key facet of his political moderation. Compelling philosophical reasons and his own biography prompted him in this direction. "My choice of meekness," he acknowledged (2000: 34), "is not a biographic selection. Of itself it is a metaphysical choice, because it is grounded in a conception of the world that I could not otherwise justify." At the same time, the priority given to meekness also had a strong historical justification, "as a reaction to the violent society in which we are forced to live" (2000: 34). Too often, history has proved to be, in Hegel's own words (quoted by the Italian thinker), "a huge slaughterhouse"[54] with no regard for innocent lives and in which power-hungry individuals and groups often invoked the reason of state to justify their ruthless pursuit of selfish agendas and interests. That is why, Bobbio's ideal city is not the one imagined and described in painstaking detail by the utopian engineers of the human soul who proposed rigid forms of justice, solidarity, equality, and fraternity. Instead, he suggested, it is a city where meekness and "the kindness in the customs" could become "universal practice" (2000: 33).

Yet the question remains: how can a virtue such as meekness be effective in curbing the universal appetite for power and the inclination to violence inherent in human nature? To understand the peculiarity and complexity of meekness, it is best to start with the distinction Bobbio drew between "strong" and "weak" virtues. The first type includes courage, prowess, fearlessness, and liberality, which are typical of the powerful, those who found, lead, and govern states, the so-called lions of this world. For them, Bobbio remarks, there is no limit to what may be done; everything seems permissible, nothing appears to be forbidden, and they may use violence when it suits their goals. The category of "weak" virtues includes those practiced often by inconspicuous individuals, the "lambs" of the world, the poor and humiliated ones who will never become rulers and whose voice is rarely heard. These are those who do not make history; history is made above them, in their name, or without their participation or consent.[55] Meekness, Bobbio argued, is to be included among the so-called weak virtues and is "the least political virtue" or "the most apolitical of virtues" (2000: 28). Nevertheless, in his view, *mitezza* is not to be conceived as a virtue of the weak because a meek person can possess, appearances notwithstanding, real strength.[56] Unlike a submissive person who is often passive and abandons the struggle due to weakness, weariness, or fear, the meek never entirely yield and are neither inert nor docile. They seek instead to curb and "repudiate the destructive life out of a sense of annoyance for the futility of its intended aims" (2000: 29).

We can best understand the nature and complexity of Bobbio's *mitezza* by looking at its antonyms. The list is long and includes, among others, arrogance, self-righteous moral posturing, aggressiveness, greed, and abuses of power, along with the inclination to oppression, violence, and domination. Meekness is, above all, an antonym of submissiveness, apathy, or docility and represents "the opposite of aggressiveness."[57] Meekness is also the contrary of haughtiness, which is showy arrogance: "A meek person does not show off in any way, including his meekness" (2000: 28). He or she is detached "from those things that generate greed in most people" (2000: 30) and lacks the stubbornness and obstinacy that often perpetuate quarrels over trifling matters. Last but not least, a meek person is strongly opposed to violence and the cult of brute force. The paradox is that the opposition to violence is mounted in the name of a feminine virtue that has little to do with either the daunting prowess of the lion or the proverbial cunning of the fox. "Meekness," Bobbio acknowledged (2000: 34), "has always seemed desirable to me precisely because of its femininity. . . . The practice of kindness is bound to prevail when the city of women is realized." As such, meekness can serve as antidote to fanaticism and the *libido dominandi* of the powerful. It is not an accident that the Italian thinker chose a man of moderation, Erasmus, and his Christian humanism as a model for his own political moderation. Erasmus's primary virtue was meekness which he deftly used to oppose the religious fanaticism of his contemporaries and their unbridled lust for power.

It might be useful to take a closer look at the relationship between meekness and nonviolence, the subject of an interesting debate between Bobbio and Giuliano Pontara, who offered an arguably more political interpretation of *mitezza*. According to Pontara, nonviolence is "the channel through which meekness becomes strength,"[58] and the meek persons are nonviolent individuals who do not entirely repudiate the rules of normal politics, but seek only to humanize them. They do not engage in conflictual relations with others aiming to conquer, destroy, or defeat. As such, through their actions the meek disprove of the Machiavellian definition of politics as being the exclusive domain of the fox and the lion in which might makes right. They are not vindictive and do not bear grudges, nor do they resent or hate their opponents. Above all, the meek are not power-hungry and are rarely the ones to begin a quarrel, but they are not afraid to engage in political battles and controversies when necessary. Far from frightening them, the perspective of fighting for a worthy cause often energizes and motivates them.[59] "The meek are never first to start the fire," Bobbio agreed with Pontara (2000: 30), "and when the others do, they refuse to let themselves be burnt, even when they are unable to extinguish the fire. They traverse the fire unscathed, and endure internal storms without becoming angry, maintaining their moderation, composure, and openness." When they decide to engage in political fight, the meek consider conflicts "in such a way that the solution will never be zero-sum, but rather a solution in which all sides profit by it and hence is accepted by all."[60]

It is worth repeating that on Bobbio's account, meekness is not to be confounded with humility, modesty, or mildness, all of which are personal virtues that can be appreciated irrespective of—and independent from—the relations with others in social life. "We are humble and modest for ourselves," Bobbio wrote (2000: 231). "We are meek in respect of others." Meekness seeks to curb the zeal of passions and resentment and acts as a break upon our arrogance and the obsession with total moral clarity or purity in political affairs. By eschewing the pursuit of certainty in politics, the meek accept that their judgments can at best be prudent approximations of reality incapable of offering exact definitions and strong foundations. If the meek do not usually have a high opinion of themselves, this is not because they lack self-esteem, but because of their propensity to believe more in the lowly rather than lofty nature of humanity. As such, meekness complements—and is related to—imperfection, self-restraint, and civility.

If, as a social virtue, meekness contains real power, its force comes paradoxically from its apparent fragility, generosity, and openness that, to use Bobbio's own words, radiate "only in the presence of the other" (2000: 24). It is not a mere coincidence that he defined *mitezza* as "a positive inclination toward others, . . . an attitude toward others that does not need to be reciprocated for it to be fully actualized."[61] As such, meekness implies constant openness to dialogue, pluralism, and toleration, along with genuine respect for the ideas and values of others. The meek never venture to put the interests of others upon purely speculative grounds and tend to stay away from abstract schemes that would impose an artificial order and transform society into a vast political laboratory. They simply "let others be themselves [and] do not engage with others intending to compete, harass, and ultimately prevail" (2000: 29). For the meek, political life is never a winner-take-all game and the world is not to be divided simply between winners and losers. Simplicity and charity are two other complementary virtues that often act as preconditions of meekness and warn us against embracing the spirit of contest, competition, or rivalry in an immoderate way. Finally, the meek practice moderation and prudence because they are aware of the complexity of history and have a keen sense of—and appreciation for—the multiplicity of opinions, ideas, and interests in our free societies.

The Labyrinth of Moderation

In his political autobiography, Bobbio discussed three metaphors that might be used to describe the human condition: the fly in the bottle, the fish in a net, and the labyrinth. While he acknowledged the powerful connotations of the first two metaphors, he clearly preferred the third one. "Those who enter a labyrinth," he wrote,

> know that there is a way out, but they do not know which of the many paths that open up before them at different stages is the one that leads to it. They grope their way forward. When the way is blocked, they turn and take another path. Sometimes the path that seems the simplest is not the right one. . . . They need a great deal of patience, but

> they can never let themselves be deceived by appearances; they need to take one step at a time, and when confronted with a fork with no basis for a reasoned choice, they are obliged to take a risk while always being ready to retrace their footsteps. The nature of a labyrinthine situation is that no way out is absolutely assured. When the path is the right one in the sense that it leads to a way out, it is never the final way out. The only thing that a man in a labyrinth learns from experience . . . is that there are paths with no way out: the only lesson in the labyrinth is the lesson of the dead one. (2002: 167–68)

It is not a mere coincidence that Bobbio liked this metaphor so much. For the labyrinth describes quite well the paradoxes faced by all political moderates exposed to the cross fire of extremes. To successfully advance a moderate political agenda one needs to have similar qualities to the virtues of the hopeful wanderers in a labyrinth: a belief in the existence of a final destination, patience in finding and reaching the exit, good judgment, quickness of spirit, and openness to dialogue. Like the travelers seeking a way out of the labyrinth, the moderates must be attentive to detail and be ready to quickly amend their mistakes when necessary. They should display a good dose of realism and ought to be flexible by avoiding rigidity and dogmatism. Since overconfidence can lead the moderates astray at any moment, they must also be prudent and humble. To paraphrase Bobbio (2001: 167), even if they feel that a way out exists after all, they still do not know where that exit might be. Relying upon abstract theories or ready-made formulas does not lead them far in the labyrinth of political life, at the heart of which lies the struggle for raw power and supremacy.

In Bobbio's case, as we have already seen, moderation was a gateway to a larger and bold vision of a free, open, and decent society. Firmly situated within the political tradition of the Left, the Italian thinker practiced a form of political moderation that had a remarkable lucidity of purpose and mission and did not fall prey to the sirens' songs of political ideologies. In spite of his ultimately unfair image as a hesitant spirit, Bobbio demonstrated that moderates are capable of espousing firm positions and taking tough stances when necessary. He was neither neutral when neutrality was inappropriate, nor afraid of recommending bold measures when circumstances required them. His example proves that it is always easier to recognize moderates in action than to offer a theory of moderation and that sometimes it may be more appropriate to define moderation by looking at what it opposes in practice. The antonyms of moderation, Bobbio reminded us, are extremism, zealotry, and fanaticism rather than radicalism. Moreover, given the complexity of moderation, it is impossible to prove in an apodictic manner that moderation is always superior to other virtues or that it constitutes a moral absolute in all circumstances. The best we can do to orient ourselves in the labyrinth of moderation is to be prepared to make tentative and rational arguments defensible in light of our limited historical and personal experiences, knowing all the way, in Burke's words, that "no lines can be laid down for civil and political wisdom." Yet, moderates are also aware that if "no man can draw a stroke between the confines of day and night, yet light and darkness are upon the whole tolerably distinguishable" (1993: 149).

The most common objection against the political moderation of thinkers like Bobbio is that their agendas are little more than oxymora—"liberal socialism," enlightenment *and* pessimism, tolerance *and* intransigence—an eclectic "bouquet of hybrids" (Anderson, 1988) that cannot quench the purists' thirst for absolute and might not even work well in practice all the time. Yet, this can also turn out to be the moderates' greatest strength. As one of Bobbio's Spanish disciples remarked (Ruiz Miguel, 1994), his thinking was full of creative tensions and interesting paradoxes: an Enlightenment pessimist, a dissatisfied realist, a historicist analytical philosopher, a restless positivist, a formalist empiricist, a believing relativist, and a liberal socialist. Hence, the charge of eclecticism should not be an insurmountable problem as long as this concept is defined and justified as "looking at a problem from all sides" (Bobbio, 1996: 93) in order to grasp life's complexity and find adequate means for coping with it. Those who hope to find their way out of the labyrinth of political life must often embrace a certain form of syncretism, which means examining political problems without ideological blinkers or preconceptions from all sides. In Bobbio's case, such a form of eclecticism is reflected by his political moderation, a word that he was "not ashamed of using, as long as it is interpreted positively as the opposite of extremism and not negatively as the opposite of radicalism" (Bobbio, 1996: 93).

Thus, Bobbio's writings point to a paradoxical aspect of moderation that is often neglected or underappreciated; under certain circumstances, this elusive virtue can have its own *radical* side, especially on the Left. As such, contrary to its common image, moderation is neither a virtue of the powerful and the strong nor a mere endorsement of the status quo or an ideology of social and political control. Moderation is precisely the opposite: the weapon of the meek who seek to alter the balance of power in society through nonviolent means. The ethics of politicians, Bobbio claimed, "are still the ethics of power," and anyone who tries to resist the logic of dirty hands and the maxim "the ends justify the means" risks being considered "a visionary [and] a utopian" (2001: 168). And yet, moderation *can* humanize and mitigate the effects of the ruthless pursuit of power because it challenges the idea that might always makes right.

The radicalism of moderation is all the more surprising when accompanied by modesty, self-restraint, and humility. It is revealing that Bobbio, who put forward a bold series of proposals for changing the constitutional structure of his country, refused to consider himself a moral authority entitled to give lessons ex cathedra to his fellow citizens. "I have never wanted to hold up my personal preferences as general criteria for right and wrong," he once wrote (1996: 85), "although I do not believe I could ever renounce them." Bobbio's rejection of moral posturing was accentuated (and motivated) by his propensity to doubt and self-questioning that was an integral component of his political moderation. We should not forget either his mordant sense of irony that gave a humane touch to his political commitments through which he tried to reconcile the preoccupations of the scholar with the concerns of a responsible citizen.

Six decades ago, at the beginning of the Cold War, Bobbio allowed himself a rare moment of optimism when claiming that the future seemed to belong to those who refused to demand absolute moral clarity in politics and saw the world not in stark contrasts, but in shades of gray. He also predicted the fall of communism in the former Soviet Union.[62] Our times, Bobbio argued, seem to vindicate those who try to insinuate doubt into the beliefs and ideas of the zealots in all camps and trim the sails in order to keep the ship of the state on an even keel. They may be accused of being overly critical and skeptical and favoring no one, but, in reality, they make the game of no one, which is another way of saying that, in the long term, their trimming may benefit everyone. One of the greatest challenges faced by political moderates is that they must often put on the mantle of intellectual mediators and trimmers in conflict-ridden contexts in which the majority of political actors conduct themselves according to an "all or nothing" logic and view politics only through the lenses of the "friend-foe" dichotomy. Under such circumstances, keeping the dialogue open is a courageous and exacting attitude, not devoid of a certain form of heroism, and one that is likely to make the moderates suspect in the eyes of purists on all sides.[63]

Bobbio knew all this quite well and his long exchange with Della Volpe ended with a remarkable profession of faith. He suggested that moderation properly practiced is always a principled position that has nothing in common with the opportunism of those who seek only short-term gains and promote the interests of a particular faction or group. The agenda of moderation excludes "either-or" options and searches for mixed solutions and complex hybrids meant to promote and maintain the balance and stability of the community at large. This is true, above all, of the very concept to which Bobbio dedicated his entire life: political liberty. "Against the reactionaries," Bobbio wrote six decades ago (1955: 194), "we continue to defend the liberty of the moderns from that of the ancients. But let us not forget that it is equally important to protect it, against the overzealous progressives, from the liberty of subsequent generations." Such an argument for a middle ground between the two types of liberty may have seemed unconvincing back then, but with the benefit of hindsight, it is obvious today that Bobbio's words could not have been more on the mark. Finding a middle between the two types of liberty was as necessary then as it is now, and the best means to achieve it was—and still is—political moderation. It would be, indeed, quite difficult to find a more convincing argument for the enduring relevance of this virtue for courageous minds, which Norberto Bobbio practiced with elegance and perseverance in difficult times.

CHAPTER 5

Moderation and Trimming

Michael Oakeshott's Politics of Skepticism

> The business of a government [is] not to inflame passion and give it new objects to feed upon, but to inject into the activities of already too passionate men an ingredient of moderation.
>
> —Michael Oakeshott

Neither Too High nor Too Low

Born at the outset of a century that will be remembered in history for its unprecedented cruelty and destruction, Michael Oakeshott (1901–90) must have had few reasons to feel at home in a world dominated by anxious prophets of extremity, confident heralds of salvation and doom, and self-righteous philistines. A philosopher and bohemian spirit interested in exotic topics such as love, poetry, and horse betting (on which he coauthored a book), he might have easily sought refuge in philosophy, theology, literature, or art in order to escape the terror of history. Instead, Oakeshott chose what in hindsight appears as a much harder route. He proceeded to rethink the nature and ends of politics in the hope that by entering into a conversation with his contemporaries, he might be able moderate their propensity to radicalism and zeal for perfection. Central to Oakeshott's political thinking, culminating in his masterpiece *On Human Conduct* (1975), were his defense of moderation and lifelong opposition to all forms of ideological politics, whether they came from the Left or the Right. He was a political moderate keenly aware of what was afoot in his own age and ready to stand up for the values he cherished.[1]

For all of his romantic longings and bohemian sensibility that came to light so vividly in his recently published *Notebooks* (2014), Oakeshott had a distinctive political temperament, complemented by a strong penchant for introspection, irony, and, at times, hyperbole. His writings represented an effort to know and discover himself, which he considered as the highest and most difficult task.[2] Here is, for example, an interesting Socratic fragment from Oakeshott's notebooks: "To discover yourself. Sometimes this is achieved only formally—the discovery of a vocation, or a skill. But to discover yourself fully is to find freedom; and until this discovery is made all freedom is frivolity" (2014: 326). He often looked more patrician than he really was and preferred to maintain a certain distance from real politics. Although generally regarded as a conservative, Oakeshott did not identify himself with a political party and made a point of writing with the independence of someone who seeks to read into the nature of things and tries to understand them without taking on the role of a *maître à penser*. Nevertheless, he was often reluctant to use the word "intellectual," was skeptical toward academic fashions, and had few illusions about the effectiveness of intellectuals' political ideas. To be sure, Oakeshott's deflationary critique of the involvement of intellectuals in politics was quite ecumenical and spared no one. If he was harsh with his colleagues on the Left who imagined politics as a vast enterprise to improve mankind and reshape human nature, he also thought that many of his friends on the Right had succumbed, often unbeknownst to them, to the same rationalistic fallacy. What singles out Oakeshott's critique and makes it relevant for us today is that it was made in the name of a virtue that had been conspicuously absent from much of the twentieth-century politics—moderation and, in particular, a face of it, trimming. And it is in light of this last concept and his distinction between the politics of faith and the politics of skepticism that I interpret his work here, as a companion to the political moderation discussed in the other chapters of this book.

Oakeshott's defense of this old Aristotelian virtue was centered on several dichotomies that can be found, in different forms, in his works. The first one is that between the "politics of faith" and the "politics of skepticism," which appeared in his writings from the early 1950s. Oakeshott devoted to this topic an entire (undated) manuscript with this title; it was completed most likely by 1952, but it was left unpublished at the time of his death (the book came out posthumously only in 1996). He returned to this theme in other essays from the 1950s, most notably in "On Being Conservative," a text in which he opposed the "politics of skepticism" to the "politics of passion" and raised legitimate questions about our restless and self-indulgent age contaminated (in his view) by the virus of rationalist planning and a growing taste for melodramatic politics. In a series of lectures given at Harvard in 1958, he focused on the difference between the "morality of the individual" and the "morality of the anti-individual," which became three years later, in his essay "The Masses in Representative Democracy," the contrast between the morality of the "true" and "incomplete" individual (*manqué*). In *On Human Conduct* (1975), it was the distinction between civil and enterprise association, *universitas* and *societas*, that came to the fore and assumed center stage.

What all of these dichotomies share in common is a chastened view of politics, different from the romanticized image of politics advocated, for example, by Hannah Arendt and her disciples who were eager to bring something of the glamorous ethos of ancient politics into the commercial modern world.[3] True to his commitment to moderation, Oakeshott sought to put politics and political participation in their right place, neither too high nor too low, and he did it by pointing out both their worth and inherent limits. For all of his early interest in philosophical idealism manifest in his writings from 1920s and 1930s, Oakeshott's mature discussion of politics was, in fact, remarkably down-to-earth, showing a surprisingly keen appreciation for—and sustained interest in—current political events. He disliked the prevailing utilitarianism and bureaucratization of modern politics and criticized the understanding of politics as "who gets what, when, and how," because in his view, that was a narrow and vulgar way of thinking about political matters. Politics, he believed, are not so much about innovation and distribution of resources as about conservation and making constant and reasonable adjustments to a reality in permanent flux. Oakeshott rejected the all-consuming modern obsession with increasing productivity and welfare and regarded as shallow that conception of the good life that claims there is nothing worth pursuing beyond the enjoyment of material goods.[4] Greatness, he believed, cannot be derived from material wealth alone; the latter tends to foster bourgeois philistinism, intellectual mediocrity, conformity, and complacency, which characterize the "middle mind" and the rationalist spirit.

The main question is how we conceive of the ends of politics. The latter can be regarded as the pursuit of a single, comprehensive end or of multiple heterogeneous ends that form (and obey) no comprehensive pattern.

Oakeshott was particularly concerned about what might happen if and when politics were to engage in the exclusive pursuit of a single goal or issue, be that wealth, truth, equality, unemployment, war, or ethnic purity. The lessons of history, he remarked, suggest that the consequences would be less than desirable: "artificial unity, narrow overmastering purpose, the devotion to a single cause and the subordination of everything to it."[5] Oakeshott left no doubt about which type of politics he preferred. He had little appreciation for "the Puritan-Jacobin illusion that in practical affairs there is an attainable condition of things called 'truth' or 'perfection'" (1993b: 116) that must be the universal goal of all political actors. He also made a strong case for a moderate type of politics that blends skepticism and faith and avoids the self-righteous tone of those calling for higher forms of moral clarity and purity. According to the latter, the "truth" and those who claim to possess it are to be clearly distinguished from—and opposed to—"error" and those who dissent from the allegedly official truth. This maximalist type of politics, Oakeshott believed, is flawed because it neither reflects nor matches the moral complexity of the world with its gray hues. In the real world, he argued (1993b: 116), truth appears not so much as the opposite of error as the contrary of lies. One thing worth noting about Oakeshott's position is that it does not allow us to read a simple political program into his ideas. If he described himself as a conservative, as we shall see below, his conservatism was sui generis and unlikely to convince more conventional spirits on the Right.

Oakeshott's realistic view of politics offers a corrective to two influential conceptions of politics advocated in the twentieth century. The first one aimed at politicizing every aspect of human life and ascribed to politics an almost demiurgic role. The second one was an idealized and romantic form of politics, linked to the pursuit of the good life and a putative common good, often drawing upon the writings of ancient authors. Distancing himself from the fascination with the classical Greeks and Romans venerated by Leo Strauss and his disciples as well as by Rousseau's admirers on the Left, Oakeshott believed that most classical authors had an excessively elevated notion of politics that, for all of its virtues, is ill suited to our modern times. The ancients' use of nature as a normative yardstick for individual and collective behavior, he remarked, is as questionable as their idea of an authoritative and architectonic highest good at which politics must always aim. Equally problematic (in Oakeshott's view) was the alleged obligation of everyone to take part in political activity in order to be considered a good citizen.[6] Such an obligation, he wrote, echoing a point made by one of his favorite authors

(Hobbes), was a dangerous misrepresentation of the duties of modern citizens. Politics, Oakeshott believed, are a second-rate form of human activity compared to the salvation of one's soul or the creation of great works of art. "A general interest and preoccupation with politics," he noted, "is the surest sign of a general decay in society. A universal preoccupation with rights, interests, affairs of government, political questions in general is fatal to the public peace and individual happiness."[7]

Nevertheless, what politics can offer is "something of value relative to [man's] salvation" insofar as politics, which are neither an art nor a science, can create the necessary conditions for peace and security and can protect us against abuses and oppression. In Hobbes's footsteps, Oakeshott sought to offer a theory of limited politics tailored to the particular conditions of the modern world.[8] If politics must play a role, he believed, it must necessarily be a limited and well-circumscribed one. "The things political activity can achieve are often valuable," Oakeshott wrote (1993b: 93), "but I do not believe that they are ever the most valuable things in the communal life of a society." Political action involves a certain degree of "mental vulgarity" because of "the false simplification of human life implied in even the best of its purposes" (1993b: 93). Oakeshott never agreed with Hannah Arendt's idea that "true" politics occur only when we participate in the public realm for noninstrumental reasons and perform with virtuosity our role as citizens in order to create something "durable." Such a romantic view, he believed, was an illusion and a conceptual error pregnant with potentially dangerous consequences.

In another text, "Contemporary British Politics" (1948), Oakeshott affirmed a similar disenchanted (and moderate) view of politics when describing the latter as "a limited activity, a necessary but second-rate affair" (1948: 486). This does not amount to a denial of politics, as some might be tempted to infer from the author's skeptical tone; Oakeshott's main point was different. He maintained that "the most a politician can do is to ensure that some, and these by no means the most important, conditions in which the good life can exist are present and, more important still, to prevent fools and knaves from setting up conditions which make any approach to the good life impossible except for solitaries and anchorites" (1948: 486). On this view, unlike literature, philosophy, and art, the main task of politics is not to endow life with splendor and greatness but, more modestly, to provide the framework for "the gradual readjustment of human relationships . . . by fallible men" (1948: 489). In normal times, politics are not a superior form of activity; literature, art, and philosophy should be the outlets for the superior intellects called to create the values of their societies. These artists, poets, and philosophers—the "salt of the earth"—should not be compelled to leave their lofty retreats in order to bring their wisdom down into the political realm. Their main business is rather "to stay where they are, remain true to their genius, which is to mitigate a little their society's ignorance of itself" (1993b: 96). Politics, Oakeshott maintained, should never aim that high: their chief business must be "attending to society's arrangements" (1991: 45) and institutions and making the necessary adjustments in due course. In times of crisis, however, when societies are in danger of destruction, politics tend to assume new dimensions and renewed importance, which might lead some to believe in the superior significance of political activity. Yet, it is precisely in those moments that we may not forget that the work of protection, vital as it may be to the entire polity, is never of primary importance compared to creating and enforcing the rules of interaction among individuals.

Moderation, Pluralism, and the Rules of Civility

Writing in the first decades of the Cold War, Oakeshott noted that many tendencies that became prominent after 1945 had been injurious to civility. The rise of ideological politics characterized by Manichaean and monist conceptions of the world was a major factor in this regard, and the zealous promoters of this type of politics spent a lot of time insisting that government should promote a single comprehensive purpose to be strictly followed by all citizens, regardless of their own interests and preferences. Oakeshott was among those who disagreed with this view. The task of government, he believed, has little or nothing to do with human flourishing and achieving glory. It should be strictly confined to creating and upholding a neutral framework within which citizens can pursue many single goals that express their own real desires and respond to their actual needs.

To understand why Oakeshott felt compelled to invent a new vocabulary to convey this simple idea, we should examine briefly his distinction between civil and enterprise associations that undergirds his conception of limited politics and reflects his skepticism and commitment to political moderation.[9] In the third essay of *On Human Conduct*, which sums up his entire political philosophy, Oakeshott drew a seminal distinction between two forms of political association that he called *societas* and *universitas*. Its novelty derives from its focus on exploring the type of membership and the relationships that obtain between citizens that can be conceptualized in two different ways. Individuals may be assigned to play a purely instrumental role as active (or productive) members of an "enterprise association" conceived as a corporation in managerial and purely utilitarian terms. But membership can also be seen as involving duties, obligations, and rules that are not meant to prescribe to groups and individuals what ends to pursue, but leave them free to choose those that match best their own desires, interests, and needs. On this view, the task of government changes and the latter is expected to act only as an impartial referee, whose main duty is to ensure that the rules of the political game are legitimate and fair and are properly enforced and obeyed by all the members of a "civil association." The basis of the latter is consent, legal authority, and the rule of law (1975: 158), and the task of government is to be "the custodian of a *respublica* composing a system of civil law, to adjudicate disputes about the meanings of its component laws . . . and to redress injury" (1975: 313). In most cases, the government of a civil association does have a democratic constitution, but this does not tell us much about the quality and nature of the constitutional regime. For Oakeshott, the most important thing was that *civitas* and *societas* (as self-sustaining modes of association) had become joined in various ways in modern states that are a complex and sometimes unstable mixture of civil and enterprise association. At the same time, Oakeshott acknowledged that as the result of the rise of rationalism in politics, the irresistible trend has been in the direction of the state conceived of an enterprise association, with a managerial and monistic understanding of its purpose.[10] As a result, "the member of such a state enjoys the composure of the conscript assured of his dinner. His 'freedom' is warm, compensated servility" (1975: 317).

Two important implications of Oakeshott's theory of civil association are worth mentioning here because they are linked to his political moderation. The first concerns the concept of pluralism. For all of the differences (and personal dislike) between Oakeshott and Berlin, a certain affinity exists between their views on pluralism and their critique of the monist illusion of Western rationalism according to which there is only one single truth that must be searched and can be discovered if the proper methods are used to this effect.[11] Both thinkers denounced from different perspectives the illusion that there is somewhere a set of final solutions discoverable by reason to the question of how we ought to live. Oakeshott was particularly concerned with the implications of conceiving politics as a search for truth or as a pursuit of an illusory common good. As an admirer of Hobbes, he was skeptical that there can be "a *summum bonum civile* discernible to Civil Reason from which impeccable conditions of civil intercourse and the rules in which they should be formulated could be inferred or otherwise derived" (1975: 176). Oakeshott doubted that we could ever achieve objective knowledge of how we ought to live. Our views are partial, and the judgments we make are often little more than the expression of selfish and limited standpoints that do not express universal values.[12] The pluralism and imperfection of the external world mirror our inner plurality as well as the fallibility of our judgments. "I find myself full of contradictions," Oakeshott confessed in the footsteps of Montaigne, "a seething mass of unresolved contradictions, impulses which deny one another, desires which oppose one another" (2014: 196). We are multiple selves in the same way as the world contains many perspectives, among which it is often difficult to discern the true from the false ones. The recognition of this type of pluralism is implicitly an acknowledgment of imperfection and the need for prudence and moderation in our political and moral judgments.

The second important feature of Oakeshott's theory of civil association has to do with the concept of civility. The task that he set for himself was to investigate how civil associations can protect the fabric of our civilization and its complex ways of life. The topic of the fragility of civilization was a recurrent theme in his essays and books, as it was in the writings of Aron and Berlin. The diagnostic as to what makes civilization fragile may have varied from case to case, but the underlying concern seems to have been the same: on what terms can we live as free and equal citizens under the empire of fair and legitimate laws in modern, pluralistic, and diverse societies? In Oakeshott's case, the answer to this question was connected with his views on the task of government and, more importantly, with his theory of civil association, at the heart of which lies the concept of civility.

One of the distinctive things about Oakeshott's ideal type of civil association is that it is designed in such a way as not to impose a uniform and simple pattern of life or direct public activities in order to make people good. Its main goal is a minimalist one: to set strictly procedural conditions that make it possible for *cives* to interact and associate as free citizens while pursuing unhindered their private interests and projects. Above all, *civitas* as a rule-articulated association is a type that does not force its members to pursue substantive aims established in light of a set of overarching goals. There are no ends that all individuals may ever be obliged or forced to pursue in a free society; what the state may do is only to prescribe the manner in which various individual ends can be pursued, while laws and associations must always remain nonpurposive.

This explains why Oakeshott paid special attention to defining as accurately as possible the rules of conduct allowing people to cooperate in a civil and peaceful manner. "The language of civil intercourse," he argued (1975: 124), "is a language of rules" that represent "moral conditions" (in a broad sense of the word) that are, however, not instrumental to the satisfaction of substantive wants. The authority of the laws does not derive from their moral content, be that the Golden Rule, categorical imperatives, laws of reason, or natural law;[13] nor can it be deduced from their alleged utility or any other instrumental considerations. This explains why the actual terms of practices of civility are not logical conclusions derived from "a pretended *summum bonum civile* or 'ideal' justice" (1975: 176). Nor are they to be understood as logical inferences from "theorems about the so-called natural conditions of human life, from theorems about the dispositions of human character, from theorems about contingent human wants, purposes, and imagined satisfactions, or from theorems about 'social ideals' or so-called 'critical' morality" (1975: 176). It is the very fact that people recognize these rules as noninstrumental laws of conduct that is essential for the appearance of civility. These laws are neither directives, commands, orders nor behests, prohibitions, injunctions; they are mere general rules of conduct that allow individuals with diverse interests, desires, and abilities to find a minimal common ground, though not necessarily the common good.[14]

Here is what Oakeshott had to say about this issue in the second essay of *On Human Conduct*: "The civil condition is an enactment of human beings; a continuous, not once-and-for-all enactment. And what is enacted and continuously re-enacted is a vernacular language of civil understanding and intercourse; that is some historic version of what I have called the language of civility. . . . [This is] the instrument of that conversation in which agents recognize and disclose themselves as *cives* and in which *cives* understand and continuously explore their relation with one another" (1975: 122). The presence of civility is all the more important because it allows those with divergent interests and different needs and backgrounds to cooperate with each other in a manner that would have been otherwise impossible. The rules of civility are recognized to be the conclusions and maxims adopted by free individuals responding to contingent situations and seeking to find grounds on which they can reach common decisions. As such, this mode of civil intercourse is ideally suited to the conditions of modern polities marked by diversity, pluralism, and disagreement.

It is a characteristic and a virtue of civility that "being independent of both rivalry and of tender concern, it may subsist where the one is present or where the other is absent" (1975: 123). Civility has a moderating effect on our actions and the manner in which we pursue our interests and cooperate with others. Although historic practices of civil intercourse may also be understood in terms of general legal concepts and moral ideas about what constitutes and defines civil conduct, they do not form an ideology properly speaking, neatly organized for the purpose of bringing about social cohesion and collective action. In fact, the practice of civility undergoes constant transformation and has a certain degree of imprecision; it cannot escape "being ragged at the edges, intimating situations to which it has no precise response" (1975: 177). Civility describes a certain mode of attachment of the individual to other fellow citizens and society as a whole; it informs a certain style of political action that recognizes that our opponents are members of the same society to whom we owe proper respect and consideration even when we disagree with their moral and political views.[15]

As such, Oakeshott's theory of civil association has a close relationship with political moderation since the rules of civility act as a substitute for the absence of substantive agreement on a putative common good and tend to promote self-restraint and balance. Civility is also compatible with a skeptical disposition in politics, well suited to the pluralistic condition of modern polities consisting of individuals pursuing many different and often divergent purposes and who nevertheless must live together and cooperate with each other on civil terms. Closely related to all this is the fact that the rules of civility undergirding Oakeshott's theory of civil association do not form an ideology that would foster destructive forms of partisanship and would make civility difficult, if not altogether impossible. "There are some general ideas ready to be invoked," Oakeshott argued, "although they do not pull in the same direction" and do not pretend to offer final solutions or demonstrative conclusions that are necessarily impossible (1975: 178). When attempting to offer definitive solutions to political issues, ideologies spell the end of politics, civility, and moderation.

Oakeshott's Critique of Rationalism and Ideological Politics

The previous discussion helps us understand better the opposition between moderation and ideological politics, one of the main themes of this book. The articles of faith of ideological thinking can be described as follows: "First and all, the assumption that politics should be conducted from the standpoint of a coherent, comprehensive set of beliefs which must override every other consideration. These beliefs attribute supreme significance to one group or class—the nation, the ethnic folk, the proletariat—and the leader and the party as the true representative of these residences of all virtue, and they correspondingly view as the seat and source of all evil a foreign power, an ethnic group like the Jews, or the bourgeois class" (Shils, 1997: 26). Ideologies offer an array of ideas, premises, viewpoints, and conclusions through which the social and political world is to be interpreted and eventually changed according to a predetermined plan. They view the world through rigid Manichaean lenses and tend to be intolerant toward alternative interpretations. Ideologies also seek to simplify reality and control the spontaneity of life by elevating one single value or principle—equality, solidarity, integrity, purity, and so forth—to the rank of a single supreme criterion for the most important political, economic, social, and moral choices to be made. Their map of means and ends is made of stark contrasts that leave no room for nuances and balancing acts.

As such, ideological politics are opposed to compromise and bargaining, and their principles often tend to go to the extremes. They are not limited to the political sphere; instead, they radiate into every sphere of life, including that of the everyday and private life. This type of politics aims at covering everything, from sexual and family life, culture, and religion to the economic and political sphere. It is not a mere coincidence that many of those prone to ideological thinking also display a discernable tendency toward abstractions and endorse monistic conceptions of politics. They have difficulty coming to terms with value pluralism and often manifest deep distrust toward independent institutions and intermediary bodies, which they seek to abolish so that they can better control every nook and cranny of society. By contrast, the main concern of the proponents of a politics of moderation (and civility) is to protect the economic, social, cultural, and political pluralism and reconcile the divergent interests and values promoted by various groups in society in such a way that the ship of the state may be kept on an even keel in times of turmoil.[16]

While commenting on the decline of civility in modern politics, Oakeshott was also concerned with highlighting the roots and implications of a major intellectual trend in the history of post-Renaissance Europe—the growth of rationalism in politics—whose influence, he hoped, might be limited and reversed. His main goal was not to refute rationalism in politics, whose errors, he claimed, were widely acknowledged at the time of writing "Rationalism in Politics" that first appeared in 1947. Oakeshott admitted that almost all politics today had become Rationalist or near-Rationalist (1991: 5), and claimed that the rationalist disposition of mind had invaded deeply our political thought and practice. He viewed rationalism as predicated upon the belief that all forms of human activity should be guided by unhindered reason seen as a sovereign, authoritative, and infallible guide in political activity. Oakeshott was skeptical toward the claims that reason can intuit supreme values or goals, and that the aim of politics is to help build a state and a society that would properly achieve them. The rationalist, he wrote, has a specific attitude toward reality and assumes that all types of rational conduct must spring from a specific purpose or rules of behavior clearly defined in advance. In reality, rationality properly understood is something else, "the certificate we give to any conduct which can maintain a place in the flow of sympathy, the coherence of activity, which composes a way of living" (1991: 130). This form of rationality is not the work of—nor is given by—an outside source called "Reason"; it is something intrinsic to the conduct itself that cannot be fabricated at will.[17]

Although tradition plays a key role in this regard, to a rationalist "nothing is of value merely because it exists (and certainly not because it has existed for many generations), familiarity has no worth. . . . And this disposition makes both destruction and creation easier for him to understand and engage in, than acceptance or reform" (1991: 8). In place of a tradition of ideas and practice, the rationalist, who is a believer in infinite human perfectibility, puts something of his own making—an ideology that is the formalized abridgment of the ideas, customs, and norms contained in a specific tradition. He favors perfectionism and uniformity and believes that the role of government is to lead people toward perfection; if needed, he is ready and willing to lend his support to accomplishing this task.

As a perceptive commentator recently remarked (Malcolm, 2012: 223), for Oakeshott the category of rationalists was quite generous and included all idealists and those who embraced one of the many forms of the "politics of faith." What they all had in common was a belief in the superiority of technical knowledge consisting of clearly formulated principles, rules, and directions and the corresponding certainty that it is possible to use these principles and rules to devise rational solutions to most, if not all, social and political problems. As such, "political activity is recognized as the imposition of a uniform condition of perfection upon human conduct" and is driven by a desire to start from tabula rasa: "The only way to have good laws is to burn all existing laws and to start afresh" (Oakeshott, 1991: 9). Accordingly, the rationalist who believes in the possibility of unlimited social improvement and the sovereignty of technique assimilates politics to bureaucratic management and the imposition of a single comprehensive set of goals and pattern of activity upon a diverse and pluralistic community. There is no place in his scheme of things (dominated by the rationalist philosophies of Bacon and Descartes) for traditional and practical knowledge not susceptible of rigorous formulation.[18] Such an imprecise form of knowledge is dismissed as "not knowledge at all" and "nescience" (1991: 15, 16) because it cannot bring about certainty, the undisputed goddess of the rationalist mind.

Oakeshott's conservative and moderate disposition was entirely opposed to this worldview seeking certainty and imbued with the belief in the superiority of technical knowledge. The contingencies and complexity of the human world, he believed, cannot be reduced to a simple set of universal and abstract formulas that might be quickly taught and conveniently summed up in a short book. Oakeshott's target was the managerial conception of government and politics,[19] suffused with the language of efficiency and uniformity that gives preference to technocratic rule, extensive state action, and detailed regulations, and uses an extensive bureaucratic apparatus and planning for the conscious and deliberate selection of economic and social priorities. On this account, the discussion of principles is replaced by arguments about which techniques are most appropriate and effective in each context.

Oakeshott viewed with similar skepticism the unlimited confidence in reason and the quest for certainty in philosophy. Our experience, he thought, is always unique, partial, incomplete, and unfinished, and the richness and complexity of the world around us can never be fully captured by—and conveyed with the aid of—statistics, algorithms, and equations. Not surprisingly, Oakeshott had a long-standing and persistent antipathy toward philosophical abstractions; he insisted that they are abridgments of concrete activities and traditions and can never act as substitutes for the latter. Detached from real experience, they do little to advance our understanding of the complexity of political life. That is why, Oakeshott believed, it would be an error to try to apply principles such as natural law or the maximum of happiness for the greatest number to various contexts without regard to the uniqueness of each situation. Society is not made of interchangeable "pieces of machinery" (1991: 55) to be arranged at will as pieces of a jigsaw puzzle. The standard to be pursued in many cases is less conformity to some general rules, maxims of behavior, or a strict philosophy of life than proper respect for traditions of political inquiry and behavior.[20] This perspective, in turn, implies several important things. It promotes humility, modesty, and moderation, signals a clear preference for incremental change, and rejects large-scale social and political engineering. Finally, it opposes those forms of ideological politics that display a strong propensity toward abstractions along with deep distrust of traditional institutions (family, churches, economic and civil associations, or schools), political parties, and parliamentary politics.

In the end, what undergirds Oakeshott's political moderation is a combination of humility, prudence, and pragmatism, allied with a conservative temper. The moderation I have in mind here is not to be equated with the "bad" form of moderation, which he criticized in his notebooks. It is rather a distinctively political type of moderation defined as the opposite of all attempts seeking to reduce the entire social and political world to one single principle, which is the root of ideological fanaticism. "Obsession with a single problem," Oakeshott wrote (1948: 476), "however important, is always dangerous in politics; except in time of war, no society has so simple a life that one element in it can, without loss, be made the centre and circumference of all political activity." This applies to all issues, be they political, social, economic, or moral. Our task, Oakeshott affirmed elsewhere, is to refrain from judging the conduct or the merit of a particular proposal for reform by referring it to a unique norm. We should rather try to determine "the relative importance, in the given circumstances, of the numerous, competing normative and prudential considerations which compose our tradition. What is sought is a decision which promises the most acceptable balance in the circumstances between competing goods" (2008: 184).

The use of the word "balance" in this passage is far from accidental and deserves our attention. This metaphor is essential here as well as elsewhere in Oakeshott's works because it is closely linked to his own political moderation and his critique of rationalism in politics. Oakeshott was notoriously skeptical toward the use of apodictic principles as normative grounds for our beliefs and actions, and preferred instead to rely upon what is familiar and close to us and engages our sympathy. His skepticism toward foundational principles can be explained in light of the fact that the justification of such principles as grounds for normative judgments is often a function of our personal preferences and as such is problematic and open to question. "A principle is not something which may be given as a reason or as a justification for making a decision or performing an action," he claimed (2008: 186), "it is a short-hand identification of a disposition to choose" and carries strong subjective or emotivist connotations. The view of politics that emerges from all this goes beyond the conventional account that focuses on who gets what, how, and when. As Oakeshott wrote in a beautiful passage, "In political activity, men sail a boundless and bottomless sea; there is neither harbor for shelter nor floor for anchorage, neither starting-place nor appointed destination. The enterprise is to keep [the ship] afloat on an even keel; the sea is both friend and enemy; and the seamanship consists in using the resources of a traditional manner of behavior in order to make a friend of every hostile occasion" (1991: 60).

Oakeshott's reasons for rejecting the ideological politics should be obvious by now. The most important one has to do with the fact that an ideology is an expedient abstraction from—and an abridgment of—political experience that can be neatly and conveniently summarized into clear and simple formulas *ad usum populi*. The second main reason refers to the fact that the proponents of ideological politics maintain that politics should always be conducted from the unique standpoint of a comprehensive set of beliefs and must be allowed to pervade all spheres of life, having monopoly over the setting of the "right" moral and political priorities. Oakeshott took issue with this view, which he found both inadequate and dangerous. In politics, he maintained in one of his best essays ("Political Education"), every enterprise is "a consequential enterprise, the pursuit not of a dream, or of a general principle, but of an intimation. What we have to do with is something less imposing than logical implications or necessary consequences" (1991: 57). Political judgment cannot be based on mistake-proof arguments or apodictic assumptions; it ought to pursue intimations of traditions of behavior and can at best offer a modest contribution to an ongoing conversation, which must always remain open. Because there are certain features of political activity that can never be eliminated or entirely corrected, our judgments should therefore be circumstantial, revolving around contingencies and traditions of behavior: "[W]e have no resources outside the fragments, the vestiges, the relics of

[our] own tradition of behavior" (Oakeshott, 1991: 59). As such, political judgment is "not designed to reach universal conclusions, but to recommend or justify a proposal about what to do now" (2008: 186). Political argument seeks to both justify a set of policies or values and induce agreement.

It is no secret that Oakeshott viewed ideologies as expressions of the very rationalism he criticized in "Rationalism in Politics." The proponents of ideological politics think they possess an infallible measuring rod and tend to evaluate all proposals for social and political change "against a single, unambiguous, universally valid measure" (1991: 83) that is given the status of an undisputed axiom. In so doing, they seek, in fact, to emancipate politics from opinion and conjecture by conducting themselves according to "iron laws" of history and social change. Because they approach ideas and principles *sub specie aeternitatis*, they have difficulties handling the ever changing contingencies of political life. Needless to say, Oakeshott was not the first one to oppose ideological politics; in this regard, he was a man of his own time who shared a lot in common with other thinkers, equally concerned with the rise of political intransigence and dogmatism in the age of mass society and the Cold War. Like Raymond Aron and Isaiah Berlin, Oakeshott sought to inoculate his fellow citizens against the seduction of utopianism and extremism. He was a political moderate who did not believe that the proper answer to the pathologies of faith was an even stronger belief in the "right" values. Therefore, the solution he proposed was not a new, stronger, or better faith, but a nuanced politics of skepticism tempered by an original conservative temperament.[21]

This moderate agenda came out clearly in several texts of Oakeshott, and the one that I would like to discuss briefly here is his review of Aron's *The Opium of the Intellectuals* (1955), a book that the English thinker liked a great deal and with which he found himself in broad agreement, in spite of a few quibbles with its author. Noting the "silly turn" that the heated debate on communism had taken in France at that time, Oakeshott deplored the fact that it had ceased to be a dialogue and turned instead into a monologue full of invectives and recriminations. As such, it risked becoming a "fascinatingly foolish spectacle" (2008: 141) that set a high price on rhetoric and mere intellectual virtuosity measured by increasingly tenuous links with reality. Many French thinkers on the Left, Oakeshott believed (2008: 141), were engaged in little else than a "display of perversely ingenuous fireworks," which gave only the appearance of serious reasoning. He approved of Aron's critique of their "quixotic longing to transpose the contingent into the idiom of a set of metaphysical notions, part Marxists, part Existentialist" (2008: 141). In Oakeshott's view, the best proof of their literary type of politics was their reluctance to concern themselves seriously with economics or the real aspects of communism and their Marxist preference for "a teleological interpretation of history in which abstractions are substituted for events" (2008: 142).

What accounts for both the attractiveness and shortcomings of Marxism as an ideology, Oakeshott argued, is that it cannot offer anyone "a doctrine capable of verification" (2008: 143). This would be enough to guarantee its permanent appeal in spite of its divorce from reality and its intransigently Manichaean vision of history and social change. Unlike Aron, to whom he attributed this view, but whose thinking on this issue was in reality much more complex than that, Oakeshott did not believe that mankind was in the process of coming free from the war of ideologies, nor was he convinced that ideological politics were losing "their charm and cogency" (2008: 143). Drawing upon his reading of the history of European civilization, he believed that the conditions that generated this style of politics were much older and much more deeply rooted than Aron supposed. They had been with us for more than four centuries and were not likely to vanish or retreat suddenly.

If Oakeshott's forecast seems to have been on the mark, the solution he proposed should be taken with a grain of salt and is open to question. "What have we to put in the place of the faith, the optimism, and the devotion of the fanatic?," he asked in the review of Aron's book. This question did not have then a single or simple answer. A radical rejection of modern civilization would have been a quixotic gesture doomed to failure. Two other more promising solutions were skepticism and political moderation. "M. Aron sees the possibility of a faith purged of the fanatical urge to convert the world," Oakeshott wrote (2008: 144), encouraged by the fact that the Frenchman was alive to the virtues of skepticism. The conclusion of *The Opium of the Intellectuals* was, in fact, a timely call to an enlightened form of skepticism and political moderation, born out of prudence, toleration, and doubt. Such a cast of mind, both Aron and Oakeshott believed, could successfully challenge the confident faith professed by the radical prophets of extremism and redemption.

Moderation and the Conservative Disposition

There are several ways in which Oakeshott's skeptical moderation informed his conservative temperament. He was reluctant to use the conventional labels of Left and Right, which he regarded as expressions of the political rationalism that he rejected. Oakeshott doubted that conservatism properly understood could offer a full-fledged philosophy of life and had reservations about equating conservatism with the political Right in the traditional sense of the term. While he denied that conservatism constitutes an ideology in the literal meaning of the word, he was aware that certain forms of conservatism are not immune to ideological politics and may partake some of the most serious shortcomings of political rationalism.[22]

Any reader of Oakeshott's well-known essay "On Being Conservative" will easily note that he was no conventional conservative and that his use of tradition was sui generis, distinguishing him from other conservative thinkers and politicians of his (and perhaps our) time. To be conservative, according to Oakeshott, is first and foremost to display "a propensity to use and to enjoy what is available rather than wish for or to look for something else; to delight in what is present rather than what was or what may be" (1991: 408). It means to be grateful for what one has and to acknowledge it as a precious gift. As such, "to be conservative is to prefer the familiar to the unknown, to prefer the tried to the untried, fact to mystery, the actual to the possible, the limited to the unbounded, the near to the distant, the sufficient to the superabundant, the convenient to the perfect, present laughter to utopian bliss" (1991: 408). A conservative mind prefers familiar attachments to "the allure of more profitable attachments" (1991: 408–9) and does not privilege acquisition over cultivating and enjoying what one already has.

Delighting in the present and preferring the familiar (or the tried) to the unknown (or the untried) are recurrent phrases in Oakeshott's writings that require further scrutiny. He made it clear that a conservative disposition does not imply an obligation to submit blindly to existing hierarchies and social norms. It does not amount to idealizing the status quo, and it does not deny or oppose the need for change and reform. On the contrary, Oakeshott claimed, a true conservative always "recognizes change to be unavoidable" (2008: 81) and cannot afford to ignore the need for gradual adjustments in due course. What the conservative mind opposes, however, is an uncritical embrace of large-scale changes and the assumption that all innovations would inevitably bring about progress and improvement. To be conservative, in Oakeshott's understanding (1991: 410–11), implies skepticism toward bold novelties as well as a prudent manner of accommodating oneself to change. The true conservative spirit "is not worried by the absence of innovation, and is not inclined to thinking that nothing is happening unless great changes are afoot" (2008: 81). Many innovations that resemble or promise growth and progress entail, in fact, long-term loss. Since "there is no such thing as unqualified improvement" (1991: 411), conservatives tend therefore to prefer small, limited, incremental changes to large and ambitious ones. They are not very adventurous and have "no impulse to sail uncharted seas" (1991: 412); prudence is their cardinal virtue, along with moderation.

In spite of its commitment to these two virtues, Oakeshott's brand of conservatism was unlikely to please everyone, and the uniqueness of his position must be duly underscored here.[23] He refused to equate the conservative disposition with any party affiliation or support for a particular set of policies. He took his fellow conservatives to task for displaying a pronounced tendency to seek remedies to our cultural, political, and social problems in general beliefs that form an all-embracing and self-assured system of thought promising a deceiving form of moral clarity. But the most salient feature of Oakeshott's conservatism is that he preferred to refer instead to the "conservative disposition," which, in his opinion, was not necessarily connected with any particular beliefs about the universe, the afterlife, and human conduct in general. He insisted that it is possible to combine political conservatism—that is, the belief in the need to limit and disperse power in society—with a radically bohemian temperament and immoderate soul. "There is indeed no inconstancy in being conservative in politics and 'radical' in everything else," he once wrote (2008: 84). His redefinition of what it means to be conservative presents special interest for us, since it suggests the possibility that one can simultaneously be a political moderate (with regard to thinking about the proper tasks and limits of government) and a radical spirit in thought and ethos.[24]

Oakeshott's recently published notebooks covering almost six decades of his life shed fresh light on this point. They abound in fascinating reflections on the importance of living a full life and enjoying the present with its delights, sometimes even without moderation.[25] Several passages give voice to Oakeshott's skepticism toward a certain type of moderation, which he sought to eschew. "Is not excess involved in all greatness?" he wrote in a note from 1944, before asking whether a certain frigidity and incapacity for enthusiasm might not be involved in the conventional understanding of the Aristotelian mean.[26] Almost a decade and a half later, he wondered whether or not men "handicap themselves with all kinds of 'virtues,' like honour, decency, moderation, honesty, consistency" (2014: 409) which they could forgo. The ideal encouraged by modern civilization, he mused, is a superficial and lame individual, "a shallow, pseudo-sympathetic mind" (2014: 377), easily satisfied with comfort and ready-made solutions to life's most complex questions. In reality, solving the latter requires an adventurous and sometimes even immoderate mind, a wandering spirit that prefers quality to quantity and thirsts for discovering "the sort of immortality that belongs to us," that is, "the ability to find joy in the flying moment" (2014: 374).

Needless to say, such an unconventional position was unlikely to gain many adherents among Oakeshott's readers on the Right, especially among those who tended to view conservatism as a fighting ideology against communism during the Cold War. The position of Oakeshott toward Russell Kirk, a leading American conservative of his time, is a good case in point. In his essay on Kirk's influential *The Conservative Mind*, which he described, not without a touch of irony, as a "long and vigorous book" (2008: 81), Oakeshott reiterated again his view of what the true conservative spirit involves. He mentioned that a conservative mind displays caution toward improvement, is prudent and not apt to initiate change too easily, favors a slow tempo, and is averse to large or sudden and large-scale changes. Up to this point, one could imagine that Oakeshott should have been a follower of Burke, one of Kirk's favorite authors. But what is conspicuously missing from Oakeshott's list (but was present on Burke's) is religion, which, he believed, should *not* be regarded as an essential part of conservatism. Oakeshott did not think that conservatism necessarily implies support for a particular religion or set of comprehensive religious doctrines. "What I think Mr. Kirk never makes clear," he wrote (2008: 83), "is that the conservative disposition *in politics* (that is, in respect of government and the instruments of government) does not need to be buttressed by the kind of speculative beliefs (such as a belief in a Providential Order) which the conservative in general has often favoured."

Note the caveat introduced by Oakeshott here: he reflects on the conservative *disposition* in politics and this detail is significant. If he found religious and cultural beliefs unnecessary in politics, it was not because he thought such beliefs were unimportant in themselves; it was because he limited himself to speaking from a strictly political view. In reality, Oakeshott had a strong religious sensibility that manifested itself early on in some essays published in the 1920s and 1930s. Religion remained a persistent object of reflection for Oakeshott throughout his entire life, and there is no doubt that he viewed himself as a Christian sui generis committed to a modern form of Anglicanism.[27] His professed ideal was to combine the skeptical temperament of Montaigne with the religious outlook of Pascal. At the same time,

Oakeshott was skeptical toward those forms of religion to which we feel attracted most intensely only when in danger; he thought, in Pascal's footsteps, that the best and simplest definition of religion is "an experience of God" (2014: 139). He was critical of those who demand a reality "more solid than that of the religious consciousness" (2014: 137), and he spent a lot of time thinking about the meaning of death in the larger context of living "an integrated life" (2014: 149). The entries in his *Notebooks* from these periods are full of detailed reflections on religious topics such as sin, mortality, the doctrine of the Trinity, or the presence of evil in the world. They show him reflecting on and struggling with the tensions between spiritual, religious, and worldly values and principles.

The other equally unorthodox claim Oakeshott made regarded the founding fathers of conservatism. It would have been more fortunate and better for everyone, he argued, if the conservative movement had paid more attention to Hume the skeptical moderate and less to Burke the staunch defender of the virtues of the Old Regime (in France). This claim is likely to surprise not only because Hume is not often viewed as a conservative thinker (in light of his extreme form of philosophical skepticism and his hostility to religion), but also because he was, all things considered, a rather discrete presence in Oakeshott's writings.[28] Nevertheless, a closer look reveals significant affinities between his brand of conservatism and the skepticism of the individualist tradition of Montaigne and Hobbes. Oakeshott's defense of liberty did not rest on a doctrine of abstract individual rights supposed to protect individuals against unlimited state power; he preferred instead to view them as "abridgments" of liberty-protecting practices that develop slowly over time.[29] In a similar vein, Oakeshott had little use for the doctrine of natural law that, in his view, left much to be desired. For all its simplicity, he wrote (1948: 475), the doctrine of natural law "is too abstract to offer much practical guidance" and does not go beyond suggesting controversial external limits or vaguely defined thresholds. Elevated to the status of an infallible yardstick for social and political behavior, natural law risks therefore to become a rigid normative criterion inapplicable to practice. Oakeshott's rejection of natural law separated him from the North American disciples of Russell Kirk and those interested in providing transcendental justifications for the existing social and political order. It also led him to redefine the concept of tradition, which, in his view, has nothing to do with glorifying a bygone era, or offering a miraculous cure to the problems of modernity.

There is, to be sure, little political nostalgia in Oakeshott's writings, unlike in the works of many of his conservative contemporaries. In his private diaries, he celebrated the ability to live in the present "for the sake of life and freedom" and remarked that a genuine attachment to what is eternal "belongs neither to the past nor to the future but to a permanent present" (2014: 193). In another note, he wrote: "Each present has its politics; all true politics are politics of the present" (2014: 312). Oakeshott contemplated the spectacle of the modern world with a mixture of delight and anxiety and, all things considered, felt at home in its midst, even if, as a conservative mind, he remained critical of some of its keys features, especially the quick pace of life that makes deep attachments difficult, if not impossible.[30] The crime of our civilization, Oakeshott noted in his diaries, is to render us incapable of appreciating "the sweetness of the present day, the light of today." We come to love only "what is gone or is to come" and "we do not understand what is simply for itself" (2014: 148).

As a remedy of sorts, Oakeshott recommended the cultivation of those habits of thought and heart that allow us to enjoy and cherish not only fleeting pieties and evanescent loyalties but also the pluralism of interests and options as well as the diversity of the modern world. Political conservatism, he argued (2008: 83), has a particularly important role to play in modern society in an age of incessant innovation and ever accelerated change. If conservatism as disposition may not be appropriate to all aspects of human conduct, "there still remains a certain kind of human conduct for which this disposition is not merely appropriate but a necessary condition" (1991: 415). Some activities, for example, like friendship,[31] along with certain rules of conduct, require this conservative disposition; "each person has his 'season,'" he once wrote (2014: 185), and that is why we must make time for the important things that we really enjoy in life. The same applies to politics where a conservative disposition often seems to be appropriate in an age of rapid technological and scientific progress. But in other spheres of life, such as commerce, culture, and economics, one need not have this conservative disposition and must even sometimes embrace radical stances for a while.

It is not a mere accident that Oakeshott never referred to tradition as a storehouse of wisdom opposed to the small stock of individual reason, as Burke had done before him. Oakeshott believed that tradition and practice, if approached in the right way, could be liberating, but if approached dogmatically, might be stifling. Any tradition of behavior, he insisted, involves a great deal of contingency and is eminently fluid, being neither fixed nor inflexible. As such, "a tradition of behavior is not a groove within which we are destined to grind out our helpless and unsatisfying lives" (1991: 60).[32] Consequently, Oakeshott distanced himself from those who viewed Burke as the author of a "charter" (or "canon") of modern conservatism and believed that everywhere conservatism must follow his disposition. Burke, Oakeshott admitted, displayed political moderation but lacked speculative moderation, a virtue that Oakeshott valued highly in Montaigne and Hume. If he preferred the latter to Burke, this does not mean that he misunderstood or underappreciated the genius of the latter. Quite the contrary. Oakeshott admired the Burke's symphonic tune even if he was skeptical toward his interpretation of tradition. If the author of *Reflections on the Revolution in France* was not "a great composer," he was "a great intellectual melodist whose tunes were all the sweeter because they owed so much to the intellectual folk-music of Europe" (2008: 84).

The question remains: does the conservative disposition in politics naturally or necessarily lead one to espouse moderation? Oakeshott thought so, but a caveat is in order here: not all conservatives are moderates, and not all moderates are conservatives. A skeptical attitude like the one recommended by Oakeshott can lower expectations for what can be achieved in politics and may promote moderation into political debates. It can also help restrain and deflate tensions, promote compromise, and reduce the intensity of passions and conflict when the latter threaten to unravel the social and political fabric of society. And it may inspire people to be cautious and meet others' claims with a doubtful cast of mind. Being conservative, in Oakeshott's view, is however much more than having a certain (prudent) disposition or temperament; it translates into a set of political views about the nature and the role of government and politics in general.

Some might wonder at this point whether Oakeshott did have a real theory of power and of the political. His appreciation for Hobbes and the particular attention he gave to analyzing the rise of the modern state and concepts such as legitimate authority must be taken into account when trying to answer this question. Oakeshott's essay "Talking Politics" (1991: 438–61) is an excellent example that shows how careful Oakeshott was to distinguish between power and authority, and how he sought to rethink the vocabulary of politics to reflect what he took to be the real essence of politics. He dismissed the doctrine that "ruling is the exercise of power" as a "half-baked affair" (1991: 447), which has no place for the idea of legitimate authority and hence cannot properly distinguish between legitimate and illegitimate power. "The office of rule in a modern state," Oakeshott wrote (1991: 448), "cannot be understood as merely the authorized custodian and operator of an apparatus of power." The proper exercise of power and authority depends on a specific view of politics that gives priority to the relationship between the members of the political community to one another and to the office of rule. It is therefore obvious that a theory of politics does exist in Oakeshott's books, but it is important to add that he worked with a specific view of the role and task of politics that drew on Hobbes and was influenced to a certain degree by the ethos of the Cold War.

The office of government, Oakeshott claimed, must not seek to impose a set of beliefs upon its subjects nor make them moral or good; it must neither tutor them nor try to make them happier. The main role of government is "merely to rule" over those engaged "in a great diversity of self-chosen enterprises" (1991: 429), and the best way to do this is by embracing political moderation. Hence, the role of government, Oakeshott wrote, is "not to inflame passion and give it new objects to feed upon, but to inject into the activities of already too passionate men an ingredient of moderation: to restrain, to deflate, to pacify, and to reconcile; not to stoke the fires of desire, but to damp them down. And all this, not because passion is vice and moderation virtue, but because moderation is indispensable if passionate men are to escape being locked in an encounter of mutual frustration" (1991: 432). As already mentioned, this conception requires a chastened type of politics whose main goal is to consider "the arrangements and rule which give shape to an association of human beings" (1991: 438). It also presupposes a self-restrained form of government entrusted with the limited task of providing redress and means of compensation and facilitating reasonable compromises and trade-offs. The appropriate attitude to such a government is not unconditional love or total devotion, but a combination of loyalty, respect, prudence, and suspicion. Such a government, Oakeshott wrote (1991: 433), must be "strong, alert, resolute, economical and neither capricious nor over-active." It is not concerned with moral right or wrong or with promoting moral clarity, but is content to act like a referee who enforces the rules of the game but, much like Hobbes's *Leviathan*, remains indifferent to the actual beliefs and substantive activities of its subjects.

The image of the government as a referee whose main task is to enforce the rules of the game might at first sight seem identical to the view of government held by free-market conservatives and the libertarian proponents of the minimal state. Yet, Oakeshott was careful to distance himself from them all, and his reasons for doing so are not difficult to surmise. His main preoccupation was to eliminate the arbitrary state rather than build a minimal state, and in so doing, he refrained from using the term "capitalism," which seemed to him ideological and excessively controversial. Oakeshott made clear that he was concerned not so much with the quantity of government intervention and the size of the state, as is the case of libertarians, as with the *mode* of state involvement in economy and society.[33] To this effect, he emphasized the importance of the diffusion of power in society among a wide array of groups and noted that, beginning with the seventeenth century, many of the traditional resources of resistance to the growth of state power have been converted into an ideology of resistance. As a result, it had become de rigueur to have a doctrine of either encouraging or resisting this trend if one wanted to be taken seriously in the public realm.[34] The example Oakeshott chose in order to demonstrate this point was Hayek's *The Road to Serfdom*, a book he read with interest and with which he agreed in many respects, especially in its focus on liberty, the rule of law, and limited government.

On the surface, the similarities between the two thinkers cannot be denied. Writing about the policies of full employment proposed by the Labour Party in the mid-1940s, Oakeshott showed no less patience than Hayek for central planning, which he described as "the product of an academic ignorance of how the business world works, and a common ignorance of how society lives" (1948: 478). A centrally planned society, he added, building upon a point made a few years earlier by Hayek, would be in the eyes of many an appealing ideal because of its simplicity that glosses over the many complex ways in which individuals form and pursue their plans and cooperate with each other. This has been, in fact, the ideal of all rationalistic politics that have dominated Europe for the past several centuries. Economically, Oakeshott explained, such an ideal "is based upon a simplified, mechanistic conception of production and distribution. . . . Politically, it is based upon the naïve idea that power can be controlled only by setting up some greater and uncontrolled power to do the controlling. And socially it is based upon a simplified view of human life, a mental horizon which includes 'the individual' and 'the government' of the day and nothing else" (1948: 478). And yet, Oakeshott did not fully endorse all of Hayek's views, and in at least one important respect parted company with him. Commenting on the main significance and appeal of *The Road to Serfdom*, Oakeshott wryly noted that they did not lie so much in the ideas of the book, pertinent and timely as they may have been, as in the fact that Hayek put forward a well-rounded political doctrine meant to countervail the rise of collectivism throughout Europe. This, he suggested, was both a major virtue and a serious shortcoming of Hayek's book and agenda. "A plan to resist planning may be better than the opposite," Oakeshott remarked (1991: 26), "but it belongs to the same style of politics."

The implicit charge of ideological dogmatism, albeit in the service of an allegedly good cause (liberty), should not go unnoticed here. Oakeshott was suspicious of those who used principles of all sorts as if they were universal and apodictic axioms that could be applied anywhere and at any time. In his view, Hayek's political agenda was single-mindedly predicated upon rolling back the frontiers of the state, and as such it worked with what Oakeshott took to be a simplified and distorted view of the proper tasks of government. The role of government, he insisted (2008: 39), is not so much to promote a specific type of freedom (as freedom from interference) as "to maintain that peace and order without which civilization is impossible." Once again, it is not primarily the size of the government but the manner of intervention that distinguishes civil association from enterprise association; the first conceives of government as an "activity of secondary order," the second as an "activity of primary order."[35] Any doctrine, Oakeshott concluded, whether liberal or conservative, that ignores this fundamental distinction between the two different orders of activity makes a grave error and must be criticized for that.

This accounts for Oakeshott's skepticism toward our conventional political vocabulary, a topic he explored in a long essay, "The Concept of Government in Modern Europe." The ambiguities of our political vocabulary with regard to key concepts such as freedom, justice, rights, and security reflect the ambivalence of our views on the role of government.[36] As previously mentioned, the distinction between civil and enterprise associations was much more important for Oakeshott than concepts such as Left and Right, democracy, socialism, or capitalism. The latter tend to make us lose sight of the fact that the seemingly opposed poles of the political spectrum can—and, in fact, often do—share an enterprise conception of *respublica* in tension with individual freedom.[37]

The Politics of Faith and the Politics of Skepticism

If Oakeshott spent so much time refuting the claims of rationalism in politics, his deepest concern was about the rise of ideological politics related to what he called the "politics of faith." Because the latter might give rise to misinterpretations, it is important to begin by making clear that, on Oakeshott's account, this concept should be understood only as one of the two poles between which politics have been moving for the past five centuries (the other one has been, in his words, "the politics of skepticism"). Both styles of politics have been present from the beginning of modern history and should be regarded as coeval, since neither of them has managed to fully dominate alone the political scene for a long time. The history of modern politics has been, in fact, a *concordia discors* of these two styles of politics, which are "the stepchildren of that enlargement of power which marks the beginning of modern times."[38] In the tradition of the politics of skepticism, Oakeshott included thinkers as diverse as Spinoza, Pascal, Hobbes, Hume, Montesquieu, Burke, Paine, Bentham, Hegel, Coleridge, Calhoun, and Macaulay (1996: 80). The eclecticism of this list that brings together authors as diverse as Burke and Paine, usually seen as opposites, is quite surprising and raises a few interesting questions about what kind of "faith" and "skepticism" Oakeshott had in mind when drawing this distinction.

The politics of faith and the politics of skepticism, he insisted, should not be seen as alternative styles of politics among which there is no overlap. Each of them makes intelligible the ambivalence of our conception of government as well as the ambiguity of our political vocabulary. In Oakeshott's view, the two poles do not correspond to the usual categories Left/Right or liberalism/conservatism. Each designates a particular manner of going about the business of governing and a manner of understanding our governing practices; neither of them may be identified with the ever shifting differences, divisions, antagonisms, and parties that compose the surface of modern politics. The two forms of politics do not adequately reflect all the differences exhibited by political parties, but rather two rival manners of thinking about the act of governing. They stand therefore for ideal types and theoretic extremes in conduct and understanding and are to be seen as "shorthand expressions," "ideals," and "horizons of activity" (1996: 18; 21) that have coexisted for several centuries and have often been ill distinguished from one another. "Each, in the abstract, may have the virtue of simplicity," Oakeshott wrote (1996: 120), "but neither, as we know them, is capable of being by itself a concrete style of political activity." Each of the major triumphs of faith in the modern world has provoked, in fact, a corresponding movement in the opposite direction. Consequently, they must be regarded neither as simple unvarying doctrines nor as fixed conditions in our practice of government. We must not be surprised then to discover both the politics of faith and the politics of skepticism appearing in many versions and degrees of completeness, reflecting the changing conditions of Europe during the past five hundred years.[39]

It would be an error to regard faith simply as a reaction against skepticism and skepticism as a mere reaction against faith, and to understand them only as opposite poles seeking to destroy each other. They are, in fact, complementary and intertwined in complex ways that are not always easily visible. "The two styles of politics have shared a common vocabulary," Oakeshott wrote (1996: 38–39). "They speak the same language and for the most part they theorize the same familiar institutions of government." And yet, their communication has been for the most part at cross-purposes, missing from view the commonalities between them. If one of the two poles were to be relieved of the pressure and partnership of its opponent, it would lose its raison d'être and would defeat its purpose, as neither of them can exist without the other or is self-sufficient: "Each is not less the partner than the opponent of the other, each stands in need of the other to rescue it from self-destruction, and if either succeeded in destroying the other, it would discover that, in the same act, it had destroyed itself" (1996: 92). That is why each style of politics reacts upon the other and modifies it, triggering reciprocal reactions and counter assertions, similar to a pendulum that constantly changes but always makes sure that political activity never takes for long one direction "without being recalled by the pull exercised by the other pole" (1996: 90).

The faith invoked by Oakeshott should not be equated with religious faith. It is a different type of faith that he had in mind, such as when, for example, he described the language of rationalism based on a belief in the capacity of human beings to perfect themselves through their own efforts and various techniques of social control and design.[40] This is a distinctively modern and mostly secular type of faith, one that reflects the immense power at the disposal of modern governments and is made possible by a new conception of human power and reason undergirding a Promethean vision of politics suffused with the idea of infinite perfectibility. In modern times, Oakeshott remarked, the politics of faith has had, in fact, not one but several idioms related to each other. The clearest example of the religious version of the politics of faith appeared in the history of Puritan politics, with Calvinism being the most famous type that regarded the office of government as the guardian of God's glory destined to create a City of God on earth. All religious versions shared one thing in common beyond their natural differences: the powers of the government came to be enlarged and employed in minute detail in imposing upon their subjects a unique, absolute, and mandatory pattern of behavior, belief, and activity that comprehended the totality of their existence. The government ceased to be seen as a neutral referee settling the disputes between its subjects; its new role and duty was to impose holiness upon its subjects and preserve moral purity among them. This was a form of the politics of moral clarity taken to extremes, the result of which was that "every activity was made to contribute to a mundane condition of human circumstance denoted by the word 'righteousness'" (1993a: 93). It was this ideology that provided, among others, the background that made possible a few centuries later the emergence of Marxism as a secularized version of the politics of faith.[41]

The religious version, Oakeshott remarked, is intelligible and possible only in the context of the modern age, when the idea of government being entitled to impose a single pattern of activity (believed to be *the* right one) has gained legitimacy; premodern governments lacked the power and resources necessary to achieve the level of control characteristic of the politics of faith.[42] According to Oakeshott, the chief architect of the politics of faith was Francis Bacon, whose "doctrine of cosmic optimism" (1996: 23) was inspired by the possibility of acquiring new forms of knowledge and discovering new techniques that promised a progressive enlargement of mastery over nature. "With Francis Bacon," Oakeshott wrote (1996: 53), "an immense vista of human improvement is opened up before us, and government [becomes] the chief agent in a pursuit of perfection." To be sure, Bacon displayed in detail many of the subsidiary characteristics of the politics of faith: "an absence of scruple, a suspicion that formality in government and an insistence on the letter of the law will hinder the enterprise, a dislike of amateur meddling in government, a preference for prevention over punishment, no abhorrence of retrospective legislation, and a predominant interest in the future" (1996: 56–57). At the core of the new attitude that originated in Bacon's works lay the belief that "human power is sufficient, or may become sufficient, to procure salvation" (1996: 26) and the confidence that the new engineers of the human soul and body, in light of their allegedly superior knowledge and techniques, are on the right road and should be trusted by the others who lack this knowledge. Since the politics of faith understands governing "as an endlessly proliferating activity, integrating all the activities of the subject" (1996: 28), the act of governing becomes an unlimited activity that requires omnipotence and absolutism (two different concepts) in order to fulfill its mission. Thus, the government turns into the agent of human improvement and perfection and, in light of its self-appointed soteriological mission, sees itself entitled to concentrate all the power and resources of the community upon itself. It will therefore seek to be "minute, inquisitive, and unindulgent; society will become a *panopticon* and its rulers *panoverseers*" (1996: 29).

In the economic version of the politics of faith, the powers of government are employed in "directing and integrating all the activities of the subjects so that they converge in the pursuit of . . . 'well-being,' or 'prosperity'" (1996: 61). The key words now become social engineering, planning, and management, and the task of the government is redefined as the organization and direction of a "productivist" society" (1996: 62) promising to offer security and welfare to its subjects. To this effect, those who hold power develop techniques of oversight and control to maximize the exploitation of resources to be controlled and properly overseen by expert agents. In this style of politics, the business of the government is equally minute and manifold: "to supervise industry and trade, to improve agriculture, to eradicate idleness and waste, to regulate prices and consumption, to distribute wealth, to endow learning, to settle religion, . . . to preserve order and guard against a foreign foe" (1996: 56). Governing in this style is, much like in the case of the religious politics of faith, a godlike adventure that requires "the conviction that the necessary power is available or can be generated, and the conviction that, even if we do not know exactly what constitutes perfection, at least we know the road that leads to it" (1996: 26). The upshot is a certain "nervousness about the exercise of power" (1996: 36) and an unwillingness on the part of those who exercise power to accept limits and practice self-restraint. On this view, checks and balances can only hinder the pursuit of perfection: "Since this office [of the government] can be sustained only by a minute and zealous control of human activities, the first need of government in the politics of faith is power to match its task" (1996: 45). This, in turn, fosters a climate in which various forms of radicalism, extremism, and immoderation are likely to appear and flourish. When this happens, individual rights are going to be replaced by "a single, comprehensive Right—the right to participate in the improvement which leads to perfection" (1996: 29); in turn, political opposition will be viewed with skepticism and accepted at best as a temporary expedient that will have to be eliminated when the truth becomes apparent to all. Most importantly, such a style of politics will require sincere love and unconditional adoration from its subjects, while the absence of enthusiasm, duly noted and promptly denounced, will be reported and considered a punishable crime.[43]

Whatever one's ultimate judgment on this style of politics may be, three things stand out in this regard and deserve closer attention. First, most versions of the politics of faith have a propensity to self-destruction because they tend to overemphasize the political side of every activity and thus risk abolishing politics in the normal sense of the word, which denotes a limited and pragmatic activity.[44] Second, the politics of faith have a distinctively utopian quality because they search for perfection as opposed to mere improvement. The easiest way to distinguish improvement from perfection is by verifying if a single road or method is extolled or imposed at the exclusion of all others, and whether the activity of governing is seen as serving the "perfection" of mankind, which is to be achieved in this world solely by human effort unassisted by grace or Providence. Third, according to this understanding of politics, "the institutions of government will be interpreted, not as means for getting things done or for allowing decisions of some sort to be made, but as means for arriving at the 'truth,' for excluding 'error,' and for making the 'truth' prevail" (1996: 27).

If left alone, the politics of faith that consider governing as the pursuit of absolute moral clarity or purity are self-defeating since any attempt to impose top-down a single pattern of activity and behavior upon an entire community is likely to be a ruinous enterprise. Moreover, this type of politics is at odds with the pluralism inherent in the European civilization, characterized by an enduring multiplicity of activities, groups, and interests lacking any single direction or purpose. And it displays an immense hubris, always recognizable by the eccentricity of its design that seeks to achieve lasting achievements and total certainty even when these are impossible to achieve. Its overconfident style makes this type of politics of faith unable to correct itself by making tentative and gradual adjustments and explorations.[45] This style of faith, Oakeshott claimed (1996: 114), "when it stands alone, is not susceptible of degrees . . . and is incapable of the kind of self-criticism which would enable it to defend itself against its own excesses. It is the politics of immortality, building for eternity."

If we turn next to the politics of skepticism, we discover that governing is understood as a limited and self-contained activity unrelated to the pursuit of perfection. Aware of the limits of human knowledge, the proponents and practitioners of the politics of skepticism display prudence and diffidence toward channeling the resources of society in only one direction. Sometimes this prudence can also become excessively timorous. "Here is a style of government," Oakeshott writes (1996: 109–10), "which recognizes a multiplicity of directions of activity, and yet expresses approval of none; which assumes 'imperfection' and yet ventures upon no moral judgment. It sets a high value on precedent, but does not believe that the path of precedent leads to any specific destination. It pretends to be determined by 'expediency' but in so refined a manner that it will not surrender itself to the pursuit of 'perfection.'" Hence, government is no longer seen as a chief architect of society, and its main role is now merely to preserve order and balance by doing whatever is necessary "to lessen the severity of human conflict by reducing the occasions of it" (1996: 32).

Viewed from this minimalist perspective, the activity of governing becomes first and foremost a "judicial activity" (1996: 33) by means of known and settled laws and an established system of rights. "In this style of governing," Oakeshott notes (1996: 36–37), "a high degree of formality will be appropriate, and there will be considerable attention paid to precedent" and technicalities. Power ought to be used economically and sparingly and formalities will be valued over purity of motive and other moral considerations. The insistence on formality and orderliness is justified as an inexpensive and effective way of avoiding excess and promoting moderation and self-restraint, "without turning civil society into a badly managed classroom" (1996: 37) composed of obedient pupils easy to manipulate.

In the case of the politics of skepticism, the activity of governing does not require enthusiasm and adoration for its services, nor does it demand godlike qualities from rulers who no longer inhabit a particularly elevated (and unaccountable) space above the mortals.[46] Governing involves only a small and limited amount of power needed for tackling emergencies and contingencies and providing remedies for wrongs suffered. It sheds the self-assured and arrogant style characteristic of the politics of faith that allow for no dissent and no serious contestation. Now, government is expected to be prudent, self-restrained, and moderate, displaying judiciousness in its use of resources, willingness to evaluate and correct its steps, and openness to debate and publicity. Although it is not regarded as a means of discovering the truth, political discussion is now strictly conceived as an opportunity to become familiar with and understand diverse points of view in the hope of being able to engineer a modus vivendi between them.[47] Everything in this style of government is therefore pragmatic and provisional and is constructed flexibly "so that it may be enlarged or diminished as unfolding circumstances demand" (1996: 115).

The shrinking of the scope of government in the politics of skepticism is partly due to the fact that the skeptic has "the imagination of disaster," and consequently never forgets that order is both invaluable and fragile and might easily collapse when power is either abused or insufficient. That is why the office of the government is understood as the "maintenance of rights" and the redress of wrongs rather than the imposition of a comprehensive pattern of activity upon all subjects.[48] The proponents of the politics of skepticism are not blind defenders of the status quo; they seek, when appropriate, "to improve the system of rights and duties and the concomitant means of redress." This type of cautious, step-by-step improvement "is merely part of the articulation of maintaining order" and eschews big plans seeking to revamp entire societies: "Here what is to be improved is not human beings, or the conduct of human beings, . . . but the existing system of rights, duties, and means of redress" (1996: 34).

Nevertheless, Oakeshott's skeptic is no mere eulogist of the legal order and is aware that there may be "a barbarism of order no less to be avoided than the barbarism of disorder" (1996: 35). The first type tends to appear when "order is pursued for its own sake and when the preservation of order involves the destruction of that without which order is only orderliness of the ant-heap or the graveyard" (1996: 35). Although order is vital for social life, we must never forget that it is not everything. Consequently, the proponents of the politics of skepticism "will be suspicious of a great love of symmetry and an overbearingly eager impulse to abolish anomalies" (1996: 35) and will be ready to promote the necessary reforms while continuing to insist upon formalities and rules in the conduct of affairs. All victories and advances will be seen as tentative and temporary, and in permanent need of mending and adjustment.

If the politics of faith alone, as we have seen, tend to abolish politics altogether, then the politics of unbounded skepticism unassisted by faith also have their own shortcomings that may not be overlooked either. It is difficult to be really enthusiastic about skepticism, which is usually inclined to understatement; by contrast, faith is always prone to overstatement and is ready to seize every occasion and transform it into an emergency from which it stands to profit. Moreover, skepticism tends to underappreciate the need for change and might self-destruct itself, lacking the *gravitas* of faith, which is always serious, and often excessively so. By contrast, skepticism tends to be playful and sometimes excessively moderate.[49]

It would seem then that, for all their virtues, skepticism and moderation, in competition with faith and immoderation, would be unlikely to elicit popular support and admiration. Oakeshott acknowledged this point when arguing that "while faith suffers from the nemesis of excess, skepticism is deprived of its authority by its moderation" (1996: 109). Demanding respect rather than love or gratitude, the skeptical style of government is likely to be most often met with a combination of indifference, distrust, and contempt. And yet, the virtues of the politics of skepticism and moderation cannot be denied and derive from the ability of those who practice them to trim between extremes, avoid excess, and calm down passions.

The most important implication of Oakeshott's distinction between the two types of politics is that, since we are called "to find some means of being at home in the complexity we have inherited" (1996: 120), we must seek a combination of both types of politics—faith *and* skepticism—rather than the definitive triumph of one over the other. This, in his view, can be achieved only through moderation and political trimming. Oakeshott borrowed the last concept from Halifax, who, as already mentioned, penned the classical definition of the trimmer in a famous essay, "The Character of a Trimmer."[50] Oakeshott claimed that trimmers have a close affinity to skepticism and maintained that their motto is "neither Dionysus nor Apollo, but each in his place and season" (1996: 124). Instead of adopting and inflaming the passions of those around them, they try to diffuse among all parties their own spirit of moderation and skepticism. Although they find themselves in the middle of the political fight, their natural home is not necessarily in a middle party, as it is often thought.[51] Trimmers seek to promote necessary compromises, but they do much more than that; they also take into account and seek to preserve the most important commitments of all sides, which is a difficult and sometimes dangerous task. They are able to recognize the need and opportunities for change, which, in turn, makes them able to deal effectively with contingencies and emergencies. Their knowledge of the polarity of the politics and their perceptive discernment allow them to seize the opportunities that arise and grasp the appropriate directions of action.

According to Oakeshott, the task of trimmers can be described as follows:

> The trimmer is one who disposes his weight so as to keep the ship upon an even keel. . . . Being concerned to prevent politics from running to extremes, he believes that there is a time for everything, and that everything has its time. . . . He will be found facing in whatever direction the occasion seems to require if the boat is to go even. Nevertheless, his changes of direction will neither be frequent, sudden nor great; for the changes his movement is designed to counterbalance are

> not, for the most part, either frequent or sudden. Further, he will recognize the necessity of others facing in a different direction from himself; the mean in action is never to be achieved by a general surge this way or that; indeed, such surges are precisely what it is designed to exclude. . . . Success he will observe with suspicion, and he will lend his support more readily to weakness than to power; he will dissent without dissidence; and approve without irrevocably committing himself. In opposition, he will not deny the value of what he opposes. Only its appropriateness; and his support carries with it only the judgment that what is supported is opportune. (1996: 123–24)

On this view, trimmers seek to identify the trends at work in society and devise countervailing forces in order to restore the balance between competing ideas, interests, and groups. They understand that "the balance of a society in which power is distributed in its exercise among a great number of beneficiaries is always precarious" (1996: 87) and needs constant attention and mending. If trimmers often attempt to reconcile the claims of all significant parties in the state, they are not supposed to be indifferent spectators located in a hypothetical middle party.[52] They can fight with determination on both sides of the political spectrum for preserving the constitution or defending liberty against its enemies.

According to Oakeshott, trimmers must also have a sense of what is lost forever, what ought to be discarded or set aside for some time, and what should be preserved at all costs in certain circumstances and specific contexts. For example, faced with an unbalanced context entirely determined by the legacy of the past, they must restore the equipoise by promoting a form of politics that pays heed to both the needs of the present and the demands of the future in such a way that "while one or other of them may on occasion properly prevail, none is given exclusive attention" (1996: 87). One thing that trimmers must do is to be clear-sighted so that they can recognize the need for change in due time while the imbalance created by institutions or groups is still small; at the same time, they should also suggest and take appropriate redemptive measures before it is too late. Trimmers are uniquely positioned to do all that because, unlike the practitioners of a politics of faith and an ethics of absolute ends, they do not rely rigidly on a doctrine that ascribes a falsely permanent and universal character to a particular set of institutions, values, or class. Since all political actors and institutions have the tendency to overreach, trimmers believe that the task of government is to maintain the balance by keeping them in their proper place in such a way that none of them ever manages to triumph over the others.

Consequently, the trimmers' actions and initiatives aim at restoring "the understanding of the complexity of modern politics" by fighting against the ascendancy of the politics of faith and its drive toward simplicity, and by renewing "the vitality of political skepticism."[53] As trimmers, they sometimes dispose their weight against the prevailing current, "not in order to make it flow to the opposite extreme, but to recall our political activity to that middle region of movement in which it is sensitive to the pull of both its poles and immobilizes itself at neither of its extremes" (1996: 128). Finally, trimmers also work against the tendency to remove the ambiguity of our political vocabulary. This ambiguity is essential and ineradicable, and one must learn how to live with it and benefit from it; it is the politics of faith alone that fear ambiguity and dismiss it as evil.

Oakeshott made it clear that trimming is a difficult and potentially dangerous attitude that requires a great deal of courage, firmness, insight, and determination. Because trimmers operate in a climate of uncertainty and have only limited knowledge, they may sometimes be confused about the poles between which they must trim and may take into account irrelevant or inadequate reasons in their political decisions. Nonetheless, they never turn into ideologues and always retain an empirical and flexible approach, distrusting grand schemes and abstract theories. As such, they are always ready to receive light from many other minds and think that dialogue is possible and desirable even in the direst circumstances.

An Open Future?

If Oakeshott has been praised for the elegance of his writings, the clarity of his style is deceptive and he remains a notoriously difficult author among political philosophers. While he seemed to relish writing long and carefully crafted essays, they, too, require the sustained attention of his readers, who are invited to follow his musings and intimations with the patience of a skilled detective searching for lost treasures. All of Oakeshott's published works, and above all *On Human Conduct*, have a tight structure and put forward an original view of what political philosophy can and should do. They make it clear that understanding our present condition requires that we reflect responsibly and without ideological blinders on the complex legacy of hope, pride, progress, and war bequeathed by the twentieth century. Yet, Oakeshott refused the posture of a prophet who sought to convince others to take specific courses of action or endorse particular policies. Instead, he left his readers free to respond as they thought fit to his writings, even when he came out against some of the most salient intellectual and political tendencies of his age that, in his view, stood in need of urgent correction.

Some who have read only a few pages of his writings may think that he gave in a little too much to the temptation of binary thinking (in either/or terms), that he worked with an unrealistic view of politics, tradition, and conservatism, or that he was too elitist in his preferences and politics. Still others might wonder whether Oakeshott's rejection of ideological thinking does not contain, in turn, a certain form of disguised ideology that leads him in the end to embrace the status quo. Urbane and civilized, Oakeshott may indeed be an acquired taste, but in spite of his professed conservatism, he continues to attract a surprisingly diverse readership on both sides of the political spectrum. This, I argue, is due to his political moderation, which has a special ring to it.

Oakeshott invited his readers to acknowledge the complexity and ambiguity of our political tradition and called upon them to resist simplistic calls for moral clarity and purity that interpret the world though Manichean lenses. He was aware that moderation is not for everyone and has its own limits. "It is always difficult to be enthusiastic about moderation or passionate about self-control and skepticism" (1996: 109), he once admitted. In his private diaries, he went so far as to denounce an allegedly bad and weak form of moderation imposed upon us by old age and poor health. He also had harsh words for the superficial moderation of academics, who tend to turn their duties into doubts and "never believe any one thing strongly enough to lose consciousness of everything else" (2014: 143). "To rein in one's beliefs and desires," he wrote (1991: 436), "to acknowledge the current shape of things, to feel the balance of things in one's hand, to tolerate what is abominable, to distinguish between crime and sin, to respect formality even when it appears to be leading to error: all these are difficult achievements," he remarked, but also necessary ones, without which the survival of our polities would not be possible.

As a face of political moderation, trimming, too, might appear as unappealing and unimpressive to those who prefer authenticity to self-restraint and regard reasonableness, patience, and foresight as superfluous bourgeois virtues to be replaced with a novel set of virtues suited to our postmodern age. Moreover, the trimmers' changes of direction are likely to baffle observers, who might reject them as expressions of opportunism or lack of conviction. The question is then what kind of trimming, if any, we might need in our present world, in which most, if not all, parties agree that democracy is the name of the new game in the global town, and the old forms of the politics of faith seem to be for now a thing of the past. Might it then be the case that Oakeshott's distinction between the politics of skepticism and the politics of faith was suitable to the Cold War era, but is out of sync with the current landscape? And would it not be possible to argue that Oakeshott misinterpreted the politics of faith, underestimating perhaps the degree to which certain types of faith and pluralism are compatible?[54]

Oakeshott was conscious of the relativity of his own views and was aware of the degree to which his writings bore the stamp of his own (extreme) age. I believe that if he were alive today, he would welcome the fact that secure foundations for our beliefs can no longer be found, even if many still search for them in philosophy, art, religion, or politics. He would also welcome the fact that the politics of faith seem to have lost their once powerful appeal and are unlikely to regain their lost power anytime soon, in spite of the surge of terrorism and fundamentalism around the world. At the same time, he would probably continue to advise us to resist the temptation to put "too high a value on political action, too high a hope on political achievement" (2014: 316). He would also encourage us not to see the political world in simple black-and-white contrasts and cultivate instead a sense of the relativity of our values that "discourages the attempt to achieve great ends quickly when the cost is disproportionate to the ends achieved" (2014: 319).

Finally, Oakeshott would remind us of the congenital instability of modern liberal democratic societies stemming from their chronic democratic deficit and the insatiable demand for more autonomy, freedom, and equality. He would insist that our contemporary world remains particularly sensitive to the claims of utopia. If older utopias have left the scene by now, the abstract hope of a brilliant future and the possibility of the emergence of new forms of politics of faith remain on the horizon of our postcolonial and postmodern world. How should we navigate the troubled waters of postcommunism will be the subject of the next and final chapter of this book.

CHAPTER 6

Radical Moderation and the Search for Moral Clarity

Adam Michnik's Lesson

> We are neither from the left camp nor from the right camp; we are from the concentration camp.
>
> —Vladimir Bukovsky

A Rebellious Mind

Navigating the deep and muddy waters of communism in Central and Eastern Europe represents a fascinating chapter in the history of the twentieth century. Where and when the communists came to power, they created an intricate network of control and surveillance that produced suffering, injustice, and crimes that continue to haunt us today. What made communist regimes particularly outrageous and reprehensible was the fact that their proclaimed allegiance to noble ideals such as equality, justice, and freedom was accompanied by large-scale terror and constant surveillance. They erected a pervasive power apparatus that subjected societies to minute and ruthless control. Communist regimes in Eastern Europe, Russia, and Asia executed people without trial and induced famine meant to crush the resistance of dissenters; they resorted to mass deportations, built concentration camps, and relentlessly persecuted the clergy while systematically banishing religious symbols. As a result, the image of communism may no longer be separated from the millions of victims left behind, some of whom were condemned to hard labor in remote and isolated places from which they never returned to vindicate their honor and rights.[1]

With the benefit of hindsight, it is obvious today, as François Furet once claimed, that communism's power "came not from its material or military strength—although they were important factors—but from its hold over the political imagination of twentieth-century men and women" (Furet, 2014: 5). The ashes of cynicism and skepticism never entirely extinguished in the dreamers' hearts the hope for a brilliant future entirely free of the sins of the past. Their communist faith resembled the candles that moths use to circle before throwing themselves into their flames, which pretended to offer collective warmth and a sense of belonging. Arthur Koestler was right to point out that "devotion to pure Utopia and revolt against a polluted society are the two poles which provide the tension of all militant creeds" (1952: 14). In the Western world, disillusioned with the shortcomings of liberal democracies, some became typical converts embracing enthusiastically the principles of communism while having the privilege of observing it only from distance or through carefully orchestrated visits in the communist universe. Those who had to live there were confronted directly with the iron hand and the ideological intransigence of the communist Leviathan and had to resort to a variety of survival strategies, some more successful than others. A good number of them came to reluctantly accept the dogmas of the communist orthodoxy and were resigned to live with them. Some genuinely embraced the new faith, while many did so opportunistically seeking power and personal privileges. Still others were inclined to either withdraw into the private sphere or seek a pragmatic accommodation with the system, giving Caesar his due without selling their souls. For the more politically inclined ones, a possible strategy, though not free from considerable risks, was antipolitics, which defended the values of open society.[2] It reflected the ethos of civil society as a space of freedom and as a "parallel polis," to use Václav Benda's phrase. The most effective expression of antipolitics was the doctrine of "living in truth" and the "power of the powerless" in the writings of Václav Havel and the other members of the Charter 77, an informal civic initiative in Czechoslovakia founded in 1976 to protect human and civil rights.

Regardless of the path taken, many of those who lived under real communism behind the Iron Curtain shared one thing in common: the communist world forced them to see and interpret the world in stark contrasts, usually black and white, between "us" and "them," leaving little or no room for nuances and degrees. There seemed to have been little confusion about who the "maggots" and "angels" were and what distinguished the ones from the others. Alliances were drawn and survival strategies were chosen accordingly. It was unclear, however, if and how the "power of the powerless" could ever become a visible force in the public realm, challenging the authority of communist governments.

Few have dealt better with these challenges than Adam Michnik (b. 1946), a prominent member of the former Polish opposition, revered editor in chief of the influential *Gazeta Wyborcza*, and undoubtedly one the most important personalities of Polish public life still active today. Goethe once said that "there are few people who know how to deal with the immediate past. Either the present takes hold of us forcefully or we lose ourselves in the remote past and attempt to recreate what has been wholly lost."[3] Michnik belongs to this small category, and, within it, he is a part of an even smaller elite of trimmers who have managed to combine skepticism and faith, homelessness and rootedness in an original and (most of the time) effective way.

Many have sought to explain the essence of Michnik's personality, only to find themselves puzzled by his complex persona. Born into a family of committed communists, he eventually became an icon of the anticommunist resistance in Poland, one of the most respected former dissidents across Eastern Europe who served several terms in prison, where he wrote no fewer than five books. He was portrayed in turn as "a Polish Luther" (Ken Jowitt),[4] "a hero of our time" (Paul Wilson),[5] or "the Sisyphus of democracy" (Philippe Demenet).[6] None of these terms can fully account, however, for the complexity of Michnik's fascinating and absorbing personality.

The best we can do is to listen to his own words in order to identify the secret chain that links the different periods of his life. This seems to be his rebellious and antiauthoritarian spirit opposed to intransigent orthodoxies and any form of fundamentalism and extremism, on both the Left and Right. "I've remained faithful to my anti-authoritarian ideals," Michnik once told Daniel Cohn-Bendit, the leader of the 1968 student revolts in France. "I think that 'anti-authoritarian' is the key word. We rebelled against different authorities, but the sense of rebellion was the common denominator" (1998: 64, 67). We can also consider the following self-portrait from the same dialogue: "I don't like words like inflexibility or martyr, I'm not comfortable in that role. . . . I became trustworthy only if I behave like a kamikaze. This kind of thinking reflects a certain philosophy of life, and of political life also. . . . So I chose confrontation for myself while calling for political compromise" (1998: 65).

Such a combination of a political moderate, a rebellious mind, and an immoderate (at times, even "extremist") temperament is likely to create plenty of dilemmas and tensions, but we should not forget that dilemmas, tensions, and contradictions are inscribed in the biographies of all intellectuals, especially Eastern European ones. Among the former communist countries, Polish public life has often been quite difficult to follow and understand because of the complex configuration of political forces and their sometimes overlapping and conflicting political agendas. Notions such as patriotism, nationalism, humanism, Marxism, and the West along with institutions such as the Catholic Church were subject to intense public debates and controversies. In that part of the world, responsibility and integrity were (and still are) special terms that require peculiar hermeneutical skills and fine judgment. Polish intellectuals faced a particular situation, standing between a totalitarian communist state that required total loyalty and obedience, and a firm Catholic Church that demanded submission to its dogmas and hierarchy.[7] Occupying the space in between and defining oneself simultaneously as an antiauthoritarian and independent spirit, as a freethinker who respects the Catholic Church (without condoning its antiliberal practices and tendencies) and rejects the communist orthodoxy, would be a major challenge for anyone, but in Michnik's case, all this seems to have come naturally. This milieu helped him develop and practice a bold and radical form of political moderation that has transformed him into a revered hero across Eastern Europe and beyond.[8]

To be sure, Michnik has always felt a particular kinship with the image of the trimmer who acts as a Socratic gadfly in society. His belief has been that intellectuals must be simultaneously pious, humble, and bold, and he has advised them to maintain a healthy dose of skepticism in their political involvements. During the long years of resistance to communism, he enjoined them to "participate in the anti-totalitarian community," but at the same time he wanted them to maintain their homelessness and resist Manichean thinking and any form of moral fundamentalism that would divide the world into alleged "maggots" and "angels."[9] In Michnik's case, such a moderate attitude was (and still is) demanded by the complex nature of the world in which he has lived, a world that contains many—perhaps too many—shades of gray. "Remain faithful to your national roots," he once called upon his fellow intellectuals (Michnik, 1998: 95), "but cultivate your permanent rootlessness. Bring the clear simplicity of the commands of the Gospel (where yes means yes and no means no) into a world of unstable moral norms, but fill the bland world of officially codified values with the laughter of the jester and the doubts of the skeptic." He recommended combining irony and skepticism so that we can "remain faithful to lost causes, to speak unpleasant truths, and to rouse opposition" (1998: 95).

Kołakowski's Example

It might be worth remembering that such a moderate position had previously been recommended and defended by one of Michnik's heroes and friends, Leszek Kołakowski (1927–2009), one of the most important liberal interpreters of Marxism and author of the seminal three-volume *Main Currents of Marxism*.[10] There were significant differences between the two thinkers, most notably with regard to their religious views. In the last decades of his life, Kołakowski became more and more interested in religion and turned into an advocate of Pope John Paul II. He had been a Marxist philosopher in his youth, but beginning with 1956, he came to realize that communism was a road to nowhere and that Stalinism, in spite of its claim to be a regime based on wide popular support, was in its essence a fanatic and intolerant sect defending a few myths. In the mid-1960s, Kołakowski became an inspiration for many Polish students, including Michnik, and was known to young dissidents as "King Leszek I."[11] He chose to leave Poland after 1968 for political reasons, eventually settling in Chicago and Oxford, where he passed away in 2009.

One of Kołakowski's essays that resonated with his younger friends was titled "The Priest and the Jester," written in 1968. In this compelling text, he called upon them to combine the faith of the priest, who perpetuates the absolute and is vigilant to keep the reverence for it in society, with the skeptical philosophy of the jester who systematically questions the accepted truths. As the guardian of the absolute, the priest "sustains the cult of the final and the obvious as acknowledged by and contained in tradition." On the other hand, the jester is he who "moves in good society without belonging to it, and treats it with impertinence; he who doubts all that appears self-evident" (Kołakowski, 1968: 33). That is why, in order to properly fulfill his task as a gadfly, the jester "must stand outside good society and observe it from the sidelines in order to unveil the nonobvious behind the obvious, the non-final behind the final" (1968: 34). As such, Kołakowski maintained (1968: 34), "the jester's constant's effort is to consider all the possible reasons for contradictory ideas" and he is not shy of coming up with mixed solutions to complex problems. Looking to expose "as doubtful what seems most unshakable" in the eyes of the common sense, the jester ranges "through all the extremes of thought" (1968: 34), ready to criticize anyone who tries to interpret the multiplicity of facts "by means of a single ordering principle" (1968: 35) deemed to be absolute and sacred. In particular, he dislikes and is suspicious toward all those organizations that demand total submission, label their critics as heretics, and tend to punish them severely. In the jester's eyes, such organizations tend to become ideological, political, moral, or religious sects that threaten to spread their fanaticism into the whole fabric of society.

Nevertheless, Kołakowski admitted, no philosophy can ever fully dispense with absolutes of some kind, and the skepticism of the jester must be tempered by the priest's (and the believer's) commitment to transcendence. We always thirst for the absolute, Kołakowski wrote, and we can never turn our ears deaf to its calls and signs. Moreover, we often need to appeal to transcendent principles in order to draw courage to live in accordance with our self-chosen values. On this view, belief properly understood is not the antithesis, but the complement of reason and knowledge.[12] And yet, it should not be forgotten that the priest can sometimes violate the mind as much as the jester: one with "the garrote of catechism," the other with "the needle of mockery" (1968: 35).

If so, what we need then is a philosophy of action that offers a possible middle ground between the two attitudes, an intermediate position between the priest and the jester that can protect us against their excesses while also allowing us to live in—and with—dignity. Such an attitude, which requires combining respect for truth with skepticism toward those who claim to possess it, would avoid interpreting the multifarious nature of reality by means of a single ordering principle or value. It would seek to combine the active imagination of the jester, while avoiding his excessive confidence in reason and irony, with the seriousness of the priest, while refusing "the stilts of lofty morals"[13] and the immoderate search for absolute moral clarity at all costs. As such, it would promote "courage without fanaticism, intelligence without discouragement, and hope without blindness" (1968: 37).

More importantly, this middle ground would allow us to find a balance between the quest for the absolute and the flight from it, or between reverence for the past and tradition and openness to a form of progress that does not promote a utopian vision of the world. The role of this moderate position would be to nurture the spirit of truth and inquisitiveness by encouraging individuals "never to stop questioning what appears to be obvious and definitive, always to defy the seemingly intact resources of common sense, always to suspect that there might be 'another side' in what we take for granted."[14] To cite Kołakowski once again, what we need is both "diggers" who seek the ultimate foundations of the world and "healers" who seek to root prejudices out of our minds and souls, both "reckless adventurers and cautions insurance brokers" (1990: 136).

This original credo was admirably and courageously put in practice by Michnik and his friends, first by the Workers' Defense Committee (also known as KOR, founded in 1976) and, several years later, by the Solidarity movement. The distinctive characteristics of these two seminal organizations must be duly underscored because they combined radicalism and moderation, pragmatism and idealism in an original and surprisingly effective way. Undergirding their activities were the twin concepts of "new evolutionism," the title of one of Michnik's most important essays, written in 1976 and published in *Letters from Prison*, and "self-limiting revolution."[15] Both terms highlight Michnik's political moderation and give us a chance to understand how he avoided the trap of extreme partisanship and moral fundamentalism while strongly challenging the legitimacy of the communist system. More importantly, the two concepts became key elements of the political vocabulary that made possible the events of 1980 and 1981 in Poland that eventually energized the opposition to communism all over Eastern Europe.

The reformist program of the Polish anticommunist opposition addressed to an independent public outlined a new political vision and offered concrete means capable of making improvements possible. Previous revisionist attempts limited themselves to speaking only to those in charge of the state and party apparatus and failed because they depended for their most part on the changing whims of the communist elite, itself in constant flux and rarely (if ever) committed to change. It was therefore unrealistic to assume that the communist system of power could be democratized top-down, beginning with its constantly threatened liberal wing. Such a belief in the possibility of a positive evolution within the Polish Communist Party, Michnik noted (1987: 137), was based on little else than childish "delusions." The moment of 1968, including the tragic end of the Prague Spring, discredited revisionism forever in Poland and showed that the top-down reforms initiated by few well-intentioned bureaucrats had exhausted their potential, especially in the realm of economics.

In this regard, Michnik and his friends were influenced by one of the foundational texts of the Polish opposition, Kołakowski's short but incisive essay "Hope and Hopelessness." A model of clarity, realism, and sound political judgment, this was, according to a perceptive interpreter, "a compelling call-to-arms" (Falk, 2003: 165) that few could ignore. Written in the late 1960s, it was published first in the Paris-based *Kultura* magazine, and an English translation appeared in 1971 in *Survey: A Journal of East & West Studies*. In this timely and insightful text, Kołakowski demonstrated with powerful arguments why the communist social system could not be reformed and explained clearly why the time for revisionist strategies from above had passed. He insisted that the communist system had the tendency to destroy all independent forms of life and wage constant war against its own people. Moreover, the system was based on chronic misinformation "built into the system" (Kołakowski, 1971: 39), a flawed allocation of resources and false setting of priorities. As such, the system tended to systematically distort or destroy historical memory and manipulated all types of information, starting with economic data and ending with misinformation about the opposition.

Freedom of information, Kołakowski asserted, is a pillar of open society and is "naturally unthinkable without the ruin of the whole system of government, which, in conditions of the free exchange of information, would inevitably collapse in a short period" (1971: 38–39). The functioning of the communist system depended on a perverse and negative natural selection as long as the members of the nomenklatura were chosen based not upon their expertise or competence, but upon their "servility, cowardice, the lack of initiative, readiness to obey superiors, readiness to inform on people, indifference to social opinion and public interest" (1971: 40). Competent individuals and experts were systematically weeded out and replaced by obedient members. Finally, the system was poised to constantly invent new enemies and conspiracies, at home and abroad, to justify its oppressive policies and constant surveillance; as such, the party-state was engaged in a constant and reprehensible war against its own people.

Any reader of Kołakowski's courageous essay might have concluded that an all-or-nothing maximalist approach would have been the only effective and realistic option in the fight against communism, given the failure of previous top-down reformist attempts. Nonetheless, the real significance of Kołakowski's essay, for all its firm denial of the reformability of the communist system, lies elsewhere, and its genius consisted precisely in articulating a moderate agenda of gradual reform that was the opposite not only of defeatism and civic apathy but also of anticommunist zealotry. Such a moderate reformist position, he argued, was not absurd if understood as "an idea of active resistance exploiting inherent contradictions of the system" (1971: 42). Here Kołakowski was thinking of "a reformist orientation in the sense of a belief in the possibility of effective gradual and partial pressures, exercised in a long-term perspective, a perspective of social and national liberation" (1971: 49). The strength and stability of the system, he observed, had to be taken with a grain of salt insofar as they depended partly on the degree to which the people living under it were convinced of its strength. Nonetheless, Kołakowski claimed, the immense concentration of power that tends to occur in any communist system could (and should) also be seen as a source of weakness, especially in light of the internal conflicts between rival groups within the communist apparatus.

Thus, Kołakowski's essay that proclaimed the futility of revisionism ended paradoxically on an optimistic note giving reasons for hope. "Despotic socialism," he insisted (1971: 49), "cannot be seen as a totally inflexible system, for there are no such systems." It was inevitable that the scope of its ideological control would diminish over time along with the breaking down of rigid orthodoxies and the routinization of charisma as manifested by the waning of rules, taboos, and enthusiasm. Appearances notwithstanding, the alternative solution—docility, passivity, and nonresistance—would have been a recipe for defeat that would have strengthened the inflexibility of the regime. Instruments of pressure, Kołakowski pointed out, were widely available, at nearly everybody's disposal. They consisted in drawing obvious conclusions from the most simple precepts—those that "forbid silence in the face of knavery, servile subservience to those in authority" (1971: 52). Under these circumstances, the solution was to resort once again to classical concepts such as freedom, independence, law, justice, truth, and to use them creatively and legally in such a way that they could be effectively turned against the bureaucratic tyranny.

Michnik never lost sight of Kołakowski's hopeful message when formulating his own theory of "new evolutionism" a few years later.[16] From his older colleague, he learned that the fight against the communist authorities was not a matter of an "all-or-nothing" strategy as the most inveterate anticommunists believed, and that the future, far from being predetermined or set in stone, was, in fact, up for grabs. Borrowing an idea from Tomasz Burek, a charismatic left-wing secular critic in the 1960s, he insisted that there are no laws of history that might invalidate an ethic of individual duty and personal responsibility. "There are no meaningless moments or deeds in history,"

Burek wrote in an influential text ("On the Razor's Edge") published in 1968, "history happens at every moment, [and] is determined in every gesture of every individual life. This sense that we live . . . on the razor's edge, totally and ruthlessly, believing that everything about us is always the result of human choice and the drive to humanity within each person—this is not theology or historical determination but a realistic approach."[17] Such a form of realism required among other things that people acknowledge that the old dilemma "reform or revolution" was no longer the real quandary faced by the Polish opposition to communism. "To believe in overthrowing the dictatorship of the party by revolution," Michnik went on (1987: 142), "and to consciously organize actions in pursuit of this goal is both unrealistic and dangerous." Another route had to be invented and taken, and a new epoch was about to begin in the annals of twentieth-century Poland and Eastern Europe.

KOR and Solidarity: The "New Evolutionism" and the "Self-Limiting Revolution"

This is where the Workers' Defense Committee (KOR)[18] stepped in and brought a seminal contribution that will guarantee it a major chapter in the history of the twentieth-century opposition to communism. The Polish opposition of which KOR became a key player in the mid-1970s understood that its main goal was not to seize power or try to topple the communist hierarchy. Such an ambitious agenda would have been unrealistic and dangerous in those late decades of the Cold War and would have met with a low chance of success, given the daunting coercive power of the Polish communist state apparatus and the pervasive military and political influence of Poland's major neighbor, the former Soviet Union, which still stationed troops on the Polish soil at that time.[19]

The twin concepts of "self-limiting revolution" and "new evolutionism" allowed KOR and Solidarity to envision concrete steps toward political change and identify the most effective means of forcing the communist leaders to respect the rule of law along with other basic civil liberties such as freedom of association, expression, and the press. The real means for making social and political change, its members assumed after having learned from the failure of the revisionism of the 1960s, were public opinion and civil society. The vision that motivated these movements was not a militant and crusading doctrine aiming at conquering power and evolving into the strongest center of power in society. Such an attempt to dismantle communism might have had unforeseen and tragic consequences, triggering most likely a Soviet intervention that would have threatened the independence of the Polish state and nation. Dismantling communism was the goal that the self-limiting revolution had to forgo, at least for the time being, while continuing to press with determination for punctual reforms. This was a remarkable lesson of political moderation that would later have a significant impact elsewhere in Eastern Europe, culminating with the historical Round Table Accords in 1989.

As such, the political vision of KOR and Solidarity was an original combination of civil courage, freedom from fear, anti-utopianism, humility, and moderation that displayed flexibility in action and resilience in pursuing a set of clearly defined limited goals. Their members saw civil society as a framework for addressing social conflicts and promoting gradual reform in a peaceful manner according to legal rules. Michnik captured this in the following memorable words that deserve to be quoted *in extenso*:

> This mighty and spontaneous social movement, deprived of examples, changing from one day to the next amid incessant conflicts with the authorities, did not possess a clear vision of piecemeal goals or a well-defined concept of coexistence with the communist regime. . . . Solidarity knew how to strike but not how to be patient; . . . it had overall ideas but not a program for short-term actions. It was *a colossus with legs of steel and hands of clay*. . . . Across from it sat its partner, which could not be truthful, run an economy, or keep its word, which could do only one thing: break up social solidarity. . . . This partner, the power elite, was a moral and financial bankrupt and was unable, because of its political frailty, to practice any type of politics. . . . The Polish communist system was *a colossus with legs of clay and hands of steel*.[20]

Through its determined actions, the colossus with "legs of steels and hands of clay" created a pluralistic and decentralized network of self-organized groups that successfully challenged the authority of the Leviathan with "legs of clay and hands of steel." Real concessions on expanding civil liberties were achieved not through violent upheaval or conspiratorial activities aiming at the destruction of the communist system, but by applying "steady pressure" upon the government in a process of "gradual and piecemeal change"

(Michnik, 1987: 142–43). The key point was to identify correctly and delineate "the area of permissible political maneuver" (1987: 144) in which the interests of those in power could overlap and align with those in opposition, making open conflict less probable and compromise more likely. This was no small matter as long as the colossus disposed of an efficient security apparatus that constantly arrested and blackmailed people, banned many from working in their professions, and fabricated compromising materials to discredit its opponents.

Faced with all that, KOR proposed a new style and venue of direct political action in society that started from the grassroots level. As Jan Lipski remarked, "KOR meant social and not political activity [and] KOR's dominant role was in the area of social work" (1985: 62). Because its main goal was "to stimulate new centers of autonomous activity in a variety of areas and among a variety of social groups independent of KOR" (1985: 64), it was different from the classical formula for revolution, "first seize power and then try to change things." In the Polish case, the order was reversed and the Polish opposition began with the small things at the grassroots level before eventually turning its attention to the state. As Jonathan Schell pointed out, "Its simple but radical guiding principle was to start doing the things you think should be done, and to start being what you think society should become. Do you believe in freedom of speech? Then speak freely. Do you love the truth? Then tell it. Do you believe in an open society? Then act in the open. Do you believe in a decent and humane society? Then behave decently and humanely" (2004: 371). In turn, Michnik stressed on many occasions the essentially anti-utopian nature of both KOR and the Solidarity movement that affirmed "the primacy of practical thought over utopian thought."[21] "Our movement," he told a French journalist (2001: 48), "like that of Czechoslovakia's Václav Havel, Russia's Andrei Sakharov, Solidarity did not strive for utopia. What we wanted was a return to 'normality.'" The irony is that such a return to normality was perhaps the most difficult task that one could have imagined four decades ago in Eastern Europe.

Consequently, KOR steadfastly focused on the plight of those individuals and families that needed financial, legal, and medical assistance; in most cases, they were victims of repression, abuse of power, or unfair governmental policies. As the movement matured and transformed itself, a couple of years later, from the Workers' Defense Committee into the Social Self-Defense Committee, it also got involved in the founding of the Initiative Committee of Free Trade Unions (September 1977 to April 1978). The leaders of KOR understood from the outset the far-reaching implications of their policy of modest and limited goals. Putting money in the hands of persecuted people in desperate need, seeking to improve work safety and to limit work time, or struggling to amend the Labor Code were legal and highly effective ways of challenging the communist regime on the very terrain of daily life, which was otherwise so politicized and tightly supervised.[22] Another successful activity partly related to KOR was the so-called Flying University that functioned in Warsaw for many years, offering unofficial lectures in private apartments across the capital. Still another one was the publication of the "Black Book on Censorship in the Polish People's Republic" (1977) and the "Documents of Lawlessness" (1978) that made plain the extent to which the communist authorities sought to stifle any independent political activity in Poland.[23]

Arguably the most astonishing thing about KOR for students of political moderation and grassroots politics was the fact that it was composed of people of various ideologies,[24] who, in spite of their differences, managed to find common ground (in face of a common enemy) and were able to cooperate effectively to achieve clearly defined limited goals. The opposition to communism undoubtedly provided the impetus for all that, but this was far from being a merely "negative" agenda directed against the communist state. In fact, the ethos of the movement was a positive one, and it is no accident that Jacek Kurón, one of KOR's most prominent members, called upon his colleagues not to burn down committees, but to found their own new ones. According to Lipski and others, the most important task was to make possible and foster the appearance of new foci of autonomous activity and self-government in society, the renewal of social ties at both a micro and macro scale, while rejecting any form of cheap patriotic exhibitionism. "Nothing instructs the authorities better than pressure from below," Michnik maintained (1987: 144), and "pressure from the working classes is a necessary condition for the evolution of public life toward a democracy." As such, the essence and significance of KOR and Solidarity lay in their attempt to reconstruct civil society and restore indispensable social bonds outside of the framework provided by official institutions.

KOR's focus on reaching out to public opinion and civil society was accompanied by the use of nonviolence whose ethos also characterized the activities of Solidarity a few years later. In August 1980 when the latter emerged as a formidable force on the political stage, the priority was to gain autonomy and social capital "without violence or fanatical hatred" (Michnik, 2011: 30). The genius of the movement led by Lech Wałęsa lay in its having imagined and implemented a bold agenda that eschewed violence and direct confrontation with the communist authorities. Indeed, it mattered a lot that the Polish opposition was entirely committed to using only *nonviolent* means and pursuing a policy of openness, truthfulness, meticulous factual precision, genuine autonomy of action, and trust. "KOR's doctrine," Lipski noted (1985: 64), "was to trust everyone within the bounds of the common sense. . . . There was agreement that in a movement such as KOR, an atmosphere in which everyone suspected everyone else would ultimately be more dangerous than the possibility of overlooking a few agents."

As a result, one of the fundamental principles was that the KOR members refused to lie in the struggle with the authorities and were determined to stick to the truth without compromise. They agreed not to suggest anything "beyond what was actually being asserted directly" and not to "color the fact or fill in gaps in information with empty phrases" (1985: 70). They courageously refused to testify during interrogations while also refraining from giving false testimony. Revealing important details about the actual work of KOR was to be avoided in keeping with the principle of discretion strictly enforced (1985: 66–67). More importantly, the KOR members rejected the classical conceit of dissidents—to think that "whoever is not with us is against us, since only we are good and noble" (1985: 74)—and stayed clear of political Manichaeism and the related obsession with moral clarity at all costs, which would have made compromise virtually impossible. They admitted the possibility of different parties being right in the sense that each had a limited yet legitimate claim to the truth. Consequently, they refused to try to evaluate and resolve in a general manner questions about anyone's alleged guilt, although the KOR members were not blind to the existence of opportunism and perfidy around them. The means they used eventually became ends in themselves, in such a way that refusing to denounce a colleague or helping a member overcome a critical personal situation became acts that had powerful social and political reverberations at large. As such, KOR's reformist program addressed to an independent public represented not just a revolution challenging the communist regime on the terrain of daily life, but a revolution in conceptualizing the very notion of revolution itself.[25]

With the benefit of hindsight, it was extremely important that the Polish opposition, influenced (to a significant extent) by Christian ethics, engaged in the struggle against communist authorities while rejecting violence and the use of force.[26] If KOR (and later Solidarity) had responded to the provocations of the government with hatred and violence, it would have lost a great deal of its appeal and it might have even been doomed to failure. The very concept of "self-limiting revolution" would have also been jeopardized by any recourse to violence. Refusing the latter made KOR and Solidarity more willing and open to compromise and allowed them to remain faithful to their desire to create rather than destroy. Affirming that violence cannot be redeeming and acceptable also cemented the tactical alliance between Solidarity and the Catholic Church and strengthened the internal unity and focus of the Polish anticommunist opposition. Even in dark times characterized by uncertainty, long years of underground work, and constant repression, Solidarity "never allowed itself to be broken or pushed into the extremism of a fanatical sect that feeds on the sense of injustice and the drive for revenge" (Michnik, 2011: 29). This is all the more significant since the evolution of Solidarity was not always a smooth one, being marked at times by tensions between its commitment to the self-limiting revolution and the need to respect internal hierarchy, pluralism, and disagreement. The movement also had to come to terms with the nonnegligible discrepancy between its significant political power and capital and its relatively weak economic force.[27]

Even more significant perhaps was the fact that in spite of its firm anticommunist stance that prevented Solidarity from compromising on certain key principles, its leaders were obliged, by reason of state and geo-strategic considerations, to act with a good dose of self-restraint and prudence. The movement, Martin Malia observed, "was forced by circumstances, if not to lie itself, at least not to speak the whole truth."[28] While putting pressure on the government to respect civil liberties and extend social and economic rights, Solidarity leaders and members had to refrain from pushing their claims and demands too hard or too far out of fear of a possible Soviet military reaction. At the same time, with regard to protecting civil and individual rights, the movement could not afford to be self-limiting and had to remain intransigent and uncompromising in its commitment to legalism and factual accuracy. As Malia (1982) put it, "Solidarity found itself in the anomalous position of being a revolution that dared not speak its name, and that dared not name its enemy." It had to remain true to the image of a self-limiting revolution, but in some respects it could not afford the luxury of being "self-limiting." Solidarity leaders recognized their daunting task when admitting that what they were doing was at first sight impossible and, at the same time, necessary, which is the dilemma of all moderates everywhere.

It is therefore all the more remarkable that, faced with all these constraints, Solidarity more than tripled its membership, from three million in

September 1980 to ten million urban members (both workers and intellectuals) by January 1981 (the Communist Party had only three million registered members at that time; out of them one-third is alleged to have belonged to Solidarity). New organizations were set up at the local level, and by early 1981 Solidarity could count on over forty thousand regular staff members, an efficient system of communication, and its own newspaper.[29] Strong support for the ideals of Solidarity was also registered among the peasants who, to quote Bronislaw Geremek (1992: 4), "made up in anticommunist intensity what they lacked in organization." The extraordinary courage of Solidarity members, starting with those in prison who refused to capitulate and finishing with the ordinary members who faced daily persecutions and repression, was ennobled by their openness to seeking nonconfrontational solutions at a point in time when some encouraged them to resort to violent action. Uplifted by the historic visit of Pope John Paul II to Poland in June 1979, the shipyard workers in Gdańsk in the long summer of 1980 "took the first bricks out of the Berlin Wall" (Michnik, 2011: 27). In so doing, they solidified the distinction between civil society, the realm of openness, trust, and truth, and power, the sphere of the state and its oppressive apparatus, the realm of wooden language, propaganda, lies, and distrust. From that moment on, as Geremek remembered a decade later, Solidarity could legitimately claim to speak in the name of "We, the People."

The famous twenty-two-point Gdańsk Accords, signed in late August 1980, showed the entire world how a system (hypocritically) claiming to represent the interests of the working class could be successfully and courageously challenged by a mass strike staged by the very workers whose interests the system was supposed to defend and protect but failed to do so. For the first time ever in the history of communism, the authorities were willing to sign an accord with the same civil society it had previously refused to acknowledge and respect. The agreements marked and ratified for the first time in the history of communist Poland the creation of labor unions independent of the communist state apparatus, which vowed not to attempt to interfere with the unions and let them function freely. In fairness, making sure that the Gdańsk Accords were being strictly implemented was not an easy task, and by February 1981 only two of the twenty-two points had been partially implemented. Nonetheless, social ties were being restored and civil society and self-government were given fresh impetus. With the benefit of hindsight, it is now clear that the crisis of August 1980 was the epic culmination of a long process and the sequel to other previous episodes of protest and social unrest.

It eventually paved the way for the dismantling of communism all over Central and Eastern Europe a decade later.

In the end, the self-limiting and anti-utopian revolution proved to be surprisingly bolder and much more extensive than its actors originally envisaged and also more controversial. Heated arguments persisted within the opposition between those who advocated a policy of moderation and those who distrusted negotiations with the communist authorities and preferred a more inflexible and radical approach. Such tensions appeared, for example, after the Bydgoszcz crisis of March 1981 that triggered the resignation of Karol Modzelewski, a close associate of Lech Wałęsa, who accused the latter as behaving like a feudal lord within Solidarity after having called off the national strike following tense negotiations with the communist leaders who brought up the card of a possible Soviet invasion. These tensions reflected the peculiar constraints faced by the anticommunist camp in Poland, which had to carve out and follow a prudent path between its threat to plan national strikes and the attempt to find terms on which it could reasonably compromise with the authorities. But Solidarity also derived much strength from the fact that it brought together three great political cultures: Catholic nationalism, working-class populism, and the democratic culture of the intelligentsia. Its surprising combination of pragmatism and idealism, prudence and courage, moderation and realism,[30] made possible the emergence of a new genuine power *within* society (as opposed to a power *distinct* from society) that would play a key role in the politics of the last communist decade and would finally decide the outcome of the Round Table negotiations in the spring of 1989.[31]

Reversing the new tide unleashed by the new evolutionism and the self-limiting revolution advocated by both KOR and Solidarity proved in the end to be impossible, and communism fell in Poland, in a nonviolent manner, "without a single barricade, without a single shot fired, without a single casualty" (Michnik, 2011: 30). By helping society self-organize around a clearly defined agenda and become "the executor of its own interests and aspirations" (Michnik, 1987: 158), the Polish opposition managed to peacefully dismantle the communist Leviathan, something that had been judged impossible before. The Round Table negotiations and accords of 1989 were a historic triumph of political moderation that represented "the most important and successful Polish political accomplishment of the twentieth century" (Michnik, 2011: 53). They brought about a peaceful and previously unthinkable change of regime without violence and blood. The dialogue between the government and the opposition ended a long and often stormy chapter in the

Polish-Polish hostilities and the compromises reached between former political opponents demonstrated that elites could put aside their differences in order to think (for once) in terms of the common good.

Postcommunist Democracy and Its Challenges

When the Iron Curtain fell in the *annus mirabilis* 1989, as the entire world, glued to their television screens, watched the astonishing and unexpected events in Central and Eastern Europe, the future seemed open again. The inauguration of the first noncommunist government in Poland in August 1989 followed by the dismantling of the Berlin Wall a few months later took the whole world by surprise, reminding everyone that human actions do have unintended and unpredictable consequences that may sometimes break the "iron" laws of history.[32] A past that in the eyes of many had seemed until then eternal collapsed in a few months in the front of dazzled spectators. Almost overnight, as Ira Katznelson, a prominent American scholar and friend of Michnik, remarked, "a geography of apprehension had been transformed into a geography of hope" (1996: xi).

Yet, finding one's bearings in the new and strange postcommunist world has proved to be a surprisingly difficult challenge. It is enough, for example, to read Václav Havel's sober reflections on this period in order to realize its puzzling complexity. The previously stark contrasts between "maggots" and "angels" became suddenly blurred and a new political and moral compass seemed necessary for navigating the muddy waters of postcommunism. For many observers and analysts of the momentous transformations in Central and Eastern Europe, the exit from communism and the uncertain start of most postcommunist democracies have been an unexpected opportunity to reassert their own wishful thinking and claim that their predictions had been confirmed by the course of history. With the benefit of hindsight it is obvious that many of their arguments were a particular combination of sincere beliefs, ideology, intellectual myopia, and wishful thinking that often displayed a noticeable propensity to Manichaeism and lacked nuance.[33] Such a dualistic pattern of thought could no longer render justice to a new and rapidly evolving world, and it was itself, to some extent, the legacy of a bygone universe dominated by black-and-white contrasts. Yet, at least in one respect, the postcommunist Cassandras were right. Almost everywhere, the fledgling democratic regimes turned out to be mostly gray, messy, and confusing, lacking the stark contrasts and colors of the previous totalitarian democracies.

To be sure, one thing that has seemed to be missing from the new post-communist world has been heroism. The members of the previous anticommunist opposition had believed that since communism was "a coherent system of pointless prohibitions and abridgments of freedom,"[34] it must also be inherently evil; from here, they inferred that the resistance to communism was always and unconditionally good, heroic, and noble. There was a lot of truth about all that, and the split world in which Michnik and his friends had lived before 1989 had probably given them an idealized image of the anticommunist oppositional circles.[35] This was also the attitude espoused by some of those who embraced "antipolitics" as an alternative understanding of politics that sought to relocate the political realm to society and away from the state, while championing the notions of human dignity, honor, and responsibility.[36] Because life under communism, Michnik told a French journalist in 2001, "was a struggle between Good and Evil, between total Truth versus Absolute Lies" (2001: 48), the choice facing any human being endowed with moral sense was relatively simple: one had to be "an idiot or a hoodlum" to ignore the differences between the "good" and "evil" political actors. A certain form of "moral absolutism" and moral clarity were therefore needed and justified as a means of living in truth. As such, the special political significance of morality under communism was a phenomenon that was unusual and had significant implications for the subsequent transition to democracy.

Yet, if moral absolutism had been a great strength for individuals and groups fighting against the communist system, Michnik asserted (1998: 323), it has become after 1989 "a weakness for individuals and groups active in a world in which democratic procedures are being built on the rubble of totalitarian dictatorship." Defending "the power of the powerless" in the new context has taken new forms, and the previous spirit of resistance has had to be combined with the ethos of compromise and moderation. Rebuilding civil society after 1989 has demanded a significant effort to reach across the aisle and strike compromises with former opponents. It has required finding one's compass in an imperfect and hybrid world of clashing viewpoints and conflicting interests in which the primary color has been neither red, nor brown, but gray.

The latter, Michnik insisted, is by definition the very color of democracy; it may not be as dazzling as other colors, but it has its own beauty and subtlety. "Only gray democracy, with its human rights and institutions of civil society, can replace weapons with arguments," he argued (1998: 326). This form of imperfect democracy presupposes, above all, a protracted struggle between competing interests and an often painful reconciliation of differences that require and test the ability to critically assess one's own views along with the willingness to revise them in light of rational evidence. It demands from all political actors that they accept the inevitability of political and ideological pluralism, conflict and disagreement, and acknowledge the possibility that their opponents might be right and prevail in the end if their arguments are sounder and gain more popular support. Democracy, Michnik explained,

> is neither black nor red. Democracy is gray, it is established only with difficulty, and its quality and flavor can be recognized best when it loses under the pressure of advancing red or black radical ideas. Democracy is not infallible because in all debates all are equal. That is why it lends itself to manipulation, and may be helpless against corruption. This is why, frequently, it chooses banality over excellence, shrewdness over nobility, empty promise over true competence. Democracy is a continuous articulation of particular interests, a diligent search for *compromise* among them, a marketplace of emotions, hatreds, and hopes; it is *eternal imperfection, a mixture of sinfulness, saintliness, and monkey business.* (1998: 326, emphases added)

This may appear as an excessively sober, cynical, or disenchanted view of democracy in the eyes of some, but it is not a despairing or pessimistic account of how democracy works in reality. It has a close affinity with Judith Shklar's "liberalism of fear," a fear inspired by "an acute sense of hell" and the dark side of "man's excessive dynamism" (Michnik, 1998: 85). Such a minimalist defense of democracy would never satisfy the thirst for absolutes of those who seek perfect moral clarity and are unwilling to make necessary compromises with the degrees of "evil" present in the world. Such intransigent spirits often do not feel at home in democratic societies, even when they endorse their institutions, principles, and rules of the game. Because they tend to believe that they are always and unconditionally right, they lack the capacity to question their own beliefs and, when needed, to correct their own mistakes.

In Michnik's opinion, the reemergence of new forms of fundamentalism and extremism has been one of the most unsettling aspects of postcommunist politics. In all of its three forms—national, religious, and moral—fundamentalism draws on the belief that there is such a thing as "the single best way" accompanied by an allegedly infallible method or technique for solving all social, moral, and political problems, even the most apparently intractable ones. It assumes that every political act can and must be translated into a strict moral language and a simple scale of moral values, without paying due attention to the complexity and diversity of the political world. And it confidently affirms that "one can build a world without sin; and that this can only happen if the state is governed by sinless individuals who are equipped with the doctrine of the one and only correct project for organizing human relations" (Michnik, 2014: 31). The key point in all these maximalist views is that there is a discernible single "correct" project or agenda for social and moral reform that every rational and well-intended person should pursue. Such ideas, Michnik claimed, are deeply flawed and inimical to liberty. Freedom properly understood always means open "debate, a multiplicity of viewpoints, pluralism of opinion" (2014: 35); only dictatorships can afford the luxury of imposing monologue and banishing dialogue. For their part, democracies are condemned to live in the Tower of Babel, where all languages and dialects are spoken at once and all groups are represented and free to pursue their interests as they think fit, as long as they accept and follow the rules of the game.

An important example of Michnik's political trimming and rejection of moral absolutism has been his controversial position on lustration and decommunization. Few could have had a stronger reason for promoting lustration after 1989 than Michnik who had spent considerable time incarcerated—he served his first term in prison at the age of eighteen—and unfairly suffered at the hands of communist authorities. Yet, much to the surprise of many, Michnik, who had been in his own words "not only an anti-Communist extremist but also an anti-Jaruzelski extremist" (1998: 262), came out early on *against* lustration and argued for amnesty and inclusion. He became a partner of dialogue and defender of the civil rights of the very person—General Wojciech Jaruzelski—who had thrown him into prison several times and whom Michnik had previously attacked as an obstacle that "had to be removed before there could be any possibility of change for the better in Poland" (1998: 262).

Let there be no doubt: Michnik was (and is) no naïve idealist.[37] On numerous occasions, he claimed that the virus of communism had contaminated his fellow countrymen so profoundly that the Bolshevik mentality came to be deeply ingrained in their minds, either as apparatchiks, prisoners, simple citizens, informers, accomplices, or torturers. But lustration, he argued, was not going to be an effective way of restoring the health of the political community. In opposing a course of action whose overzealous proponents have shown "the virus of anti-communism with a Bolshevik face" (2014: 32), Michnik treaded a very narrow path that alienated him from some of his previous friends and admirers. He was aware that many of those who contested the desirability of lustration did it out of purely selfish reasons because they had ugly skeletons to hide in their own closets and their secret files. Allying oneself with such dubious characters would have undoubtedly been a great dishonor for Michnik, and he was fully mindful of this risk when making public his critical stance. It would be absurd to suspect him of attempting to hide a stain in his own past or that of others and nothing could be further from the truth.[38] As one of Michnik's most interesting recent essays ("The Ultras of the Moral Revolution") suggests, his reasons for opposing lustration should not be separated from his arguments in favor of a profound and responsible reckoning with the past. They had to do with his principled political moderation and trimming attitude, based upon the assumption that "the basic condition for understanding is the juxtaposition of various narratives," which must always be given proper consideration (2014: 49) and ought to be analyzed without bias or rancor.

To understand the complexity of Michnik's moderate position and his "angerless wisdom"[39] we must examine closely his arguments and particularly his position on "moral clarity," a highly controversial concept. In Michnik's opinion, there is no easy formula or algorithm for dealing with such a complicated topic as decommunization and the past. He has been skeptical toward issuing top-down official condemnations of communism because such acts risked being an empty act of the politics of faith based on what he considered a simplistic Manichaean understanding of the world. It is not a mere coincidence that Michnik was not among the original signatories of the controversial Prague Declaration of June 3, 2008, which asked for "the establishment in European states, which had been ruled by totalitarian Communist regimes, of committees composed of independent experts with the task of collecting and assessing information on violations of human rights under totalitarian Communist regime at the national level with a view to collaborating closely with a Council of Europe committee of experts."[40] Publishing a detailed black book of communism, giving material compensation to former victims, and creating museums on the site of former prisons as places of education for the new generations offer, in Michnik's view, much more effective ways for dealing with the past.

Michnik has always been open to paying close attention to historical precedents in the hope that we could learn something valuable from them. He felt, for example, a profound affinity with the heroes of Stendhal who often complained of being up to their ears in mud in a bourgeois world in which everything became for sale overnight and lost its value. Yet, at the same time, because the recourse to history has its own challenges and dangers, Michnik has been wary of drawing and relying upon too many historical analogies in his writings. He has acknowledged that there are certain limits to our ability to use historical precedents to set our present priorities and solve our political dilemmas. In particular, he has argued, one must denounce and oppose the attempts to turn the past into "a baseball bat for destroying political opponents [and] a method for intimidating public opinion" (2014: 43). In reality, the study and interpretation of history must afford the opportunity to enter into a dispassionate dialogue with other individuals and epochs that had different perspectives and priorities. This, Michnik insisted, requires from us a willingness to listen and an effort of empathy accompanied by humility. To study history properly "is always a *conversation with the Other*, the one who *thinks differently*, who is *differently situated*, and who has been differently shaped by his or her social position. To want to understand means to understand the other" (Michnik, 2014: 49, emphases added). That is why the historian must cultivate a spirit of heresy and be bold while also displaying a certain degree of prudence and moderation. "He has to believe that the truth is worth caring for; and that only the truth has the power to liberate" (2014: 52); yet, at the same time, he must study how different contexts provide individuals with various opportunities to act on their beliefs and pursue their own interests.[41] It is this moderate and nuanced approach to history that Michnik has applied to the controversial and complex issue of postcommunist lustration and decommunization. If he expressed publicly his skepticism toward them, he did it, as he acknowledged, *in spite of* his own feelings and sentiments. This is a remarkable and puzzling confession that warrants a closer look.

As a historian, Michnik could not have forgotten that past revolutions seeking justice, equality, and freedom had often produced executions, mass-scale violence, and terror; this was the case of England in 1648–49, France in 1793–94, and the former Soviet Union after 1917. These revolutions "begotten of freedom" had far-reaching unintended consequences and Michnik wondered whether lustration, too, might not have similar perverse effects in spite of the good intentions of the political actors defending such measures. Consequently, he kept an open mind and refused to join the choir of those who adopted an intransigent stance on this thorny issue by invoking the need for moral clarity. In fact, what distinguished Michnik's position on lustration from others was precisely his moderation that refused to see the world in black-and-white, "us versus them" contrasts and did not dismiss opposite views as primitive, naïve, or wicked. Ranging himself among "the malcontents from the sects of the eternally unsatisfied and afraid," Michnik warned against "further moral revolutions; a tightening of the reins; special commissions to track down the enemies of virtue or the divine order; the proscription list of enemies, those who are suspected of animosity" (2014: 98). Adopting more modest goals and being prepared to make reasonable compromises, he believed, would be preferable to searching for perfect moral clarity on complex, divisive, and ultimately unsolvable political issues. "We the malcontents dream of just such a patchwork of compromise and good sense," Michnik declared. "We the malcontents do not want further revolutions in a country that has not yet recovered from the last several of them" (2014: 98).

The difficulty of properly judging the others and the past in an impartial manner has been revealed by the opening of the archives of the former intelligence services, which has paradoxically been accompanied by inefficient forms of moral maximalism and various attempts to blackmail political opponents. The rhetoric of lustration and decommunization has created the illusion that they would be able to answer all problems while, in fact, it has solved little or nothing.[42] In some cases, Michnik pointed out, decommunization has even had an "anti-democratic" character (2001: 49) because it has led to unacceptable discriminatory measures against former civil servants or party activists. While protesting against applying "excessive moral rigor" to judging past deeds, Michnik admitted that he did not like "the practice of judging intellectuals who became involved in Stalinism, because this practice does not take into account earlier or later parts of their biographies" (1987: 184), nor does it leave room for any form of political learning or genuine change of mind.

Hence, it is against this complex background that we must judge Michnik's call for inclusion and reconciliation while keeping alive the memory of past tragedies. "Amnesty," he affirmed, "doesn't mean amnesia" (2001: 49), and it is preferable to seeking revenge by settling scores against previous enemies. Lustration was supposed to carve out a much-needed path to finding the truth about communism, but it has turned out to be precisely the opposite, that is, "a way of annihilating this truth," sometimes in spite of all the good intentions of those seeking to set the historical record straight (2014: 27). Our philosophy, Michnik wrote, "is just the opposite of the spirit of revenge. We're for reconciliation, because it's impossible to take a step ahead when you are looking back. . . . We must reject one camp's domination over another, with endless settlings of scores. Our country must make room for everybody."[43] An inclusive and moderate approach on the issue of lustration, Michnik claimed, is all the more justified because it reflects the essence of democracy, which is nothing but "an endless search for compromise, eternal imperfection" (2001: 48). Democracy does not claim infallibility or saintliness and is predicated upon openly admitting human fallibility and working with, in Kant's famous words, "the crooked timber of humanity." Its strength comes from the fact that it is "an alternative to civil war" (2001: 48) that can effectively replace weapons by arguments. It has no place for moral absolutism because "a democratic world is a chronically imperfect one. It's a world of freedom (sinful, corrupt, and fragile) that came after the collapse of the world of totalitarian necessity (also, luckily, imperfect)" (1998: 323). As such, democracy demands not only passion and commitment, but also moderation and prudence, two virtues always in short supply. That is why democratic regimes must be appreciated for what they are worth, without unjustified enthusiasm or puritanical indignation.

For all the differences between Michnik and his famous friend, the late Václav Havel, the former president of Czechoslovakia and, after the velvet separation of 1992, of the Czech Republic, their positions on lustration and decommunization shared a few important things in common while also differing in some regards.[44] Commenting on the virtues and limits of a policy that would draw a thick line between the past and the present, Havel acknowledged the need for espousing a thoughtful form of moderation when judging what had occurred before 1989. As he told Michnik in 1991:

> You have to steer a course somehow between Scylla and Charybdis. . . . Our history teaches us that we pay dearly whenever we take the approach that we should not concern ourselves with the past, that it is of no importance. . . . It seems to me that the need to cut it out, to see that justice is done, is completely justified and natural. At the same time, however, we mustn't open the door to lawless revenge and witch-hunts; this would simply be another version of what we've just left behind.[45]

The point that Havel stressed—and with which Michnik entirely agreed—was the need for balance between looking at the past in the face without self-pity and illusions, and drawing the appropriate conclusions from it, "honestly, with circumspection and tact, with magnanimity and imagination."[46] The principle of collective guilt, Havel insisted, must be rejected, and only that of individual responsibility should be preserved. Michnik echoed Havel's position. "I do not believe in any collective responsibility except a moral one," he wrote. "What I meant is that I can blame myself for the acts of others, but I would not give anyone else the right to blame me for those same acts."[47] The need for moderation and trimming is justified by the fact that, to use Havel's words again, the boundary between Scylla and Charybdis may be defined only by something vague—"something like sensitivity, taste, forbearance, circumspection, wisdom"—that cannot be adequately captured by legal norms or abstract reasoning. This poses significant challenges even to those animated by the best intentions in their search for the fine and elusive line where justice ends and the desire for revenge begins. This limit, Havel remarked, is extremely difficult to find, as demonstrated by the some of the debates on various drafts of lustration laws that were the result of hasty deliberations that led to situations in which everybody could publicly accuse anybody and turn it into a public scandal or execution. If we allow ourselves to be guided by prudence and moderation, it might be possible to find that fine line. "It's a vital problem, and the boundary is difficult to define, as evidenced by the lustration law, which I consider an abortive effort," Havel argued. "The law shows how difficult it is to define this boundary in legal terms, but at the same time it must be defined in legal terms because even worse than a rigid law is a state of lawlessness in which everyone can lustrate and publicly slander everyone else."[48]

To conclude, Michnik's trimming position on lustration had its own logic and justification, but it is, of course, open to question much like the intransigent attitude of those asking for absolute moral clarity at all costs. As always, the truth may be in the nuances. Michnik's affinity with the anticommunist camp is clearest in his emphasis on the need for having an open debate about and a honest reckoning with the past. These, Michnik believed, would remain empty words in the absence of a "clear identification of good and evil" (1998: 297), and all attempts to blur the picture in this regard would have to be looked at with justifiable skepticism. At first sight, this attitude seems to contradict Michnik's embrace of eclecticism and skepticism toward calls for absolute moral clarity. But we should not forget that Michnik insisted that no one may claim any monopoly on virtue or vice, for that matter. "The communists didn't have a monopoly on wicked goods," he reminded his readers (1998: 297), and those who stood apart "weren't all paragons of virtue" either. Just as no one could be officially declared an "angel" or written off as a "maggot," no one could claim to be entirely without some degree of guilt. Moreover, Michnik feared that once started, the project of unmasking the "sinful" ones could pave the way for an intransigent moral revolution that would contradict two fundamental principles of open society, inclusiveness and fairness to everyone.

It is no mere coincidence that Michnik insisted that we may never begin to judge the alleged sins of others before we start reckoning first with our own political choices and moral failings. This is all the more important since people have the tendency to be partial and one-sided and often deceive themselves by being inclined to reject any personal guilt or blame. In so doing, they lose sight of the moral complexity of the issues they face and abandon the humility and moderation that alone could prevent them from becoming self-righteous and intransigent toward others. That is why Michnik has preferred to use such concepts as responsibility, courage, and honor rather than moral clarity or purity. The latter are likely to remain abstract notions while responsibility, courage, and honor are always within our reach and, hence, more or less attainable in practice.

The Prerequisites of Dialogue and Compromise

The foregoing account has shown that the genius of the Polish anticommunist opposition lay in its decision to act incrementally and avoid an open confrontation with the authorities by limiting the immediate goals of civil struggle and skillfully working to increase the range and likelihood of possible concessions and tactical compromises. As already mentioned, the "new evolutionism" theorized by Michnik sought a gradual and steady expansion of civil liberties and human rights and was open to striking, whenever necessary and possible, limited compromises with the communist authorities in the pursuit of those limited goals. Compromise, Michnik believed, is necessary for a healthy public life, provided that it is real rather than fake compromise, both in substance and in the public eye. Of course, not all compromises are acceptable, and Michnik, who possesses the temperament and imagination of a (moderate) politician, has always been careful to point out the limits and conditions of legitimate compromise in keeping with his own philosophy of dialogue.

Compromise and conciliation, he insisted (1987: 141), would make sense and ought to be pursued only if both sides were prepared to take them seriously and honor them. This condition was all the more important since the concept of compromise did not really exist in the language of the Polish ruling communist elite. Every concession made by the opposition was likely to be treated by the government as an opportunity and invitation to make even harsher demands upon the latter. In reality, there was no indication that the communist leaders would be prepared to share power "even with its most loyal and obedient ally,"[49] let alone with those who openly challenged their legitimacy and policies. A conciliatory or moderate approach was also likely to be self-defeating when applied to the tense relations between citizens and authorities.

Signing declarations of loyalty demanded by the communist government in exchange for personal favors was, in Michnik's view, morally unacceptable and politically ineffective. Every such declaration signed as a price for being released from prison, for example, would have been an unqualified "evil" and an affront to human dignity and common sense: "To forsake your dignity is not a price worth paying to have the prison gates opened for you."[50] There are certain things that may never be subject to compromise because negotiating them would be tantamount to self-betrayal. With every small capitulation on our part, the other camp gains power and influence over us. "When a compromise is seen by the public as renunciation of conviction or as flagrant treason," Michnik wrote (1987: 13), "it is no longer a compromise. It becomes a falsehood or a misunderstanding." Hence, in relation to the communist power whose political vocabulary lacked the word "conciliation," a policy of compromise and concessions could have had any meaning at all only if it was conducted by the opposition from a position of legitimacy and strength. Otherwise, a policy of conciliation risked leading the opposition to immoral capitulation and political suicide.

Worth noting here is the combination of courage, flexibility, and integrity that can be found at the core of Michnik's animated moderation and accounts for its success before 1989. No one else highlighted its originality better than his former opponent, General Jaruzelski, who told Michnik in a conversation they had in 1992: "You were like a cross between a lizard and a tiger. The lizard signified cunning and shrewdness, and the tiger was going to bite us."[51] Jaruzelski's memorable description of the proverbial versatility of the former dissident may be on the mark, but it should not make us lose sight of the fact that Michnik's actions always followed a logic of personal integrity and honor that was anything but Machiavellian. "There is only one thing I worry about: being right with myself," Michnik once admitted (1998: 66). "Everything else is God's affair. . . . Being morally irreproachable. For the rest I put my faith in God; it's his affair."

Moreover, Michnik's emphasis on defending honor and individual dignity was grounded in a particular ethics of dialogue that he shares with several other authors studied in this book. Michnik did not merely theorize the need for dialogue from the perspective of a disengaged or neutral observer; he was directly involved in the events he described in his writings and participated actively in the controversies and debates surrounding them. As such, his reflections were intrinsically tied to the dramatic unfolding of the events that had gradually changed the political map of Central and Eastern Europe beginning with the mid-1970s. Michnik rejected as bogus the attempts at dialogue between inflexible doctrines and worldviews that do not seek genuine compromise but only try to outwit each other in an incessant struggle for power. True dialogue, he affirmed, is not to be equated with reaching a compromise that would miraculously solve all tensions between different interests and viewpoints. It is, in fact, an indispensable method for an ideologically diverse society to become aware of its internal diversity and try to reach an overlapping consensus on its main values and principles.

Michnik's ethics of dialogue presupposes several things at once. First, it requires that we be engaged in an active and open search for truth and never stop questioning; on this view, we must be willing to acknowledge and correct our errors in addition to pointing out the mistakes of others.[52] Second, we should try to identify areas and issues on which we might be able to compromise with our opponents when this becomes necessary. In this regard, Michnik has been close to liberal Catholics such as Tadeusz Mazowiecki who became the first noncommunist Polish prime minister in August 1989. According to Mazowiecki, dialogue is possible only if and where there is "a readiness to understand the validity of someone else's position and to enter into a different way of thinking; that is, whenever there is an openness to the values embodied in other points of views."[53] A true dialogue does not always lead to compromise, nor does it imply washing away doctrinal differences or smoothing out rough edges: "It is, instead, an attempt to discover a new dimension of the matter at hand, to find a new plane of discourse in which it is possible to meet." As such, genuine dialogue should be seen as a method by which individuals living in an open and free society can learn to live together and it represents a way "to overcome mutual human isolation"[54] brought about by ideological intransigence.

All this is nicely captured by the following fragment taken from Michnik's essay "The Accusers and the Non-civic Acts," a text about the relevance of the great Polish writer and Nobel Laureate Czeslaw Miłosz (1911–2004). Lamenting the transformation of civic dialogue into monologue in Polish public life after 1989, Michnik described the nature of authentic dialogue as follows:

> The person of dialogue attempts to transform the enemy into an opponent and the opponent into a partner. An opponent is for him one who presents challenge, who wants and asks to be understood. The person of dialogue believes that dialogue is the only way to be understood by others. So he makes an effort to look at the world through his opponent's viewpoint, to "change hats with him," and to "step into his shoes." . . . He does not shy away from defending his own arguments and is not afraid of the truth, but, invariably, he puts respect for human dignity first. . . . Each partner accepts that the dignity of the other is of immensurable value. This presupposes the ability to strike a compromise, whenever possible, the readiness to admit that one is not in possession of the sole and complete [truth], and the willingness to accept somebody else's reasoning and to change one's own attitudes. (2011: 123)

The moderation undergirding Michnik's profession of faith in this fragment may be a reasonable and admirable ideal, but the question remains whether it is also realistic and attainable. At the end of his long conversation with General Jaruzelski, Michnik argued that the maturity of a society is to be judged by the capacity of its members to talk about controversial topics, past and present, "without hatred, without hostility, and with mutual respect" (1998: 285), while also trying to reexamine *sine ira et studio* their past commitments and actions. This was the direction in which he and other former dissidents hoped that the Polish society would evolve and eventually create "a permanently open society," the avowed goal of the former opposition. Unfortunately, postcommunist societies have not lived up to these lofty standards, in Poland or elsewhere. "It is impossible today to speak about a political opponent with respect," Michnik admitted (2014: 14). "It is impossible to seek a compromise that would lead to the common good; it is even impossible to converse without an internal conviction that our adversary is but a cynical cheat." The trend has been toward "a revival of hatred for adversaries in public life" (1998: 152), permanent suspicion, doctrinal intransigence, fanatical partisanship, and extremism.

"A Cross Between a Lizard and a Tiger"

Few metaphors capture better Michnik's personality than the trimmer who seeks to keep the ship on an even keel and is concerned with finding a proper balance between moral testimony and political calculation, between faith and skepticism. To be sure, Michnik had brilliantly played the role of a trimmer—"a cross between a lizard and a tiger" to quote again Jaruzelski's memorable phrase, or a revolutionary moderate—in different circumstances before 1989 as well as after the fall of the Iron Curtain, combining a resilient ethos of resistance and a strong commitment to human dignity with a pragmatic ethos of compromise and realism. He has done all this with his charming propensity to mix honesty, irony, modesty, skepticism, and humor, combining anecdotes, historical examples, and serious engagement with difficult political issues, and never forgetting that the complexity of the latter requires that we approach them with prudence and without ideological biases.[55]

If Michnik has never been shy at affirming his own, sometimes idiosyncratic, views and has always given clear indications about where he stands on controversial topics from lustration to the Jewish-Polish relations, he has always sought to understand, as best he could, all sides of the debates to which he contributed. To his credit, he has attempted to take into account all the arguments put forward by different groups holding opposing views, as has been the case with the complex Jewish-Polish relations.[56] Consider, for example, the position of the Catholic Church toward the Kielce Pogrom of 1946, which had remained for decades a taboo subject in Polish history. The pogrom took place on July 4, 1946, after several Jewish citizens from Kielce were accused of having kidnapped and detained a young boy who had disappeared for a few days from his home in a neighboring village. It is almost certain that the boy fabricated the whole kidnapping story in order to escape punishment on his return home. The authorities silently condoned the pogrom, in which over forty people were killed.

The official position of the Church left a lot of dark corners untouched and contained a good number of questionable statements, such as Bishop

Kaczmarek's controversial report that affirmed that those participating in the pogrom were "peaceful people" (Michnik, 2011: 203) rather than pathological killers. This was a morally unacceptable and callous claim given what had happened on the ground, and Michnik was quick to reprimand the bishop for espousing a degenerate type of "patriotism of anti-Semites" (2011: 203). At the same time, Michnik also went to great length to remind his readers that "when thinking about those years, those people, and their intellectual failures, it is necessary . . . to make the effort to understand their experience, to empathize with them, and to look at the world through the eyes of the Different One, the Other" (2011: 202).

The reason for Michnik's trimming attitude was simple. While acknowledging the importance of truth and moral testimony, he was skeptical toward moralizing postures and self-righteous calls for moral purity that displayed a considerable dose of narcissism and extremism. Denouncing what he called "the egotism of suffering" (2011: 199), Michnik admitted that collective suffering may also be egotistic and exploited by shrewd populists who in the end lock people in their own fortresses of memories and narratives of suffering and create a climate of "hatred and vengefulness" (2011: 199). That explains why he has refused to accept and believe in such concepts as collective guilt or collective responsibility, "apart from moral responsibility" (2011: 209). His own condition as a Pole with Jewish roots, situated between the two worlds, made him particularly aware of all this and enabled him to act as a trimmer in this case as well as in others.[57]

Perhaps the most remarkable thing about Michnik's trimming attitude is that it has been free of any trace of self-righteousness, hypocrisy, or vanity. He has openly acknowledged the virtues of eclecticism, recognizing that we often face conflicts of loyalty and are, therefore, "doomed to inconsistency." Divided in two, "we are doomed to live in a state of tension, uncertainty, permanent risk," he once admitted (1998: 155). Yet, recognizing these challenges and admitting one's fallibility do not amount to being neutral since there are many things that we also know that allow us to act responsibly. For example, we know not only that "the truth of politics resides, in the end, in the politics of truth" (1998: 155), but also that imperfection is an essential and ineradicable part of every political order that we must prudently accept rather than attempt to eliminate it altogether. We also know the high cost of political utopia while being conscious that "our future is an imperfect society, a society of ordinary people and ordinary conflicts—but, precisely for this reason, a society that must not renounce its ethical norms in the name of political illusions" (1998: 155). When Michnik did not know the answers to the questions he faced, he was not shy at confessing his own ignorance; in some cases, he also publicly admitted that he changed his mind, as it was the case with his attitude toward General Jaruzelski. His long experience of dealing with communist authorities had taught him that the real danger is not openly admitting one's ignorance, but precisely the opposite, the self-assured, vain, and arrogant attitude of those who believe that they have answers to all problems in all circumstances.

From the many possible examples that shed additional light on Michnik's political moderation, in addition to his position on decommunization discussed above, I would like to comment briefly on another one that reflects quite well his mindset as a trimmer: his views on the dialogue between the Left and the Catholic Church during the communist period. To be sure, the reckoning with the past has always been an enormously complicated problem in Poland, and few issues had been more complex and intricate than the relations between society and the Catholic Church. The very fact that Michnik, who came from a Jewish background and maintained a healthy skepticism toward using religious arguments in public debates, chose to write a book titled *The Church and the Left* was no mere accident. His willingness in bringing the two sides closer together was indicative of his commitment to moderation and ecumenical dialogue. Finding a common ground with the Catholic Church in the struggle against the communist authorities in Poland was sometimes extremely difficult, in spite of the fact that both the Left and the Church courageously fought for freedom and human dignity in their opposition to communism. The presence of powerful conservative groups within the Church who were dismissive of the "Godless intellectuals" on the Left, allegedly corroded by liberal secular values, delayed and, at times, blocked the dialogue. Moreover, many conservative intellectuals were never able to break free from the powerful gravitational hold of Catholicism, and some of them overreached in their defense of traditional religious values, triggering, in turn, a corresponding overreaction on the Left.

Nonetheless, these tensions proved to be beneficial in the end, giving birth to important debates and controversies within the Polish civil society. "Everything of value in Polish culture," Michnik admitted (1998: 69), "has taken shape at the intersection of its great historical paths, at the point where Christianity encounters the freethinking spirit, in the mutually enriching conflict between these two worlds." He spent a great deal of time analyzing the competing and sometimes conflicting narratives of Polish history advanced by the Catholic Church and the thinkers on the Left. He paid close attention not only to the differences between their accounts but also to the overlap between them, especially with regard to their common commitment to civil liberties and individual dignity.[58] Michnik's goal was to try to convince the two sides that they should talk to each other instead of remaining hostile or skeptical toward each other's intentions. At the same time, he came to reevaluate his own views of the Church in such a way that his earlier radicalism gave way to a more moderate and balanced position. Speaking for those situated on the noncommunist Left, Michnik admitted: "We have traditionally believed that religion and the Church were but synonyms for reaction and dim-witted obscurantism. From that perspective, we considered indifference to religion to be a natural by-product of moral and intellectual progress. This view, which I once shared, I now consider false" (1993: 181). This was a courageous act for Michnik, who risked alienating some of his former friends without necessarily gaining the esteem of those in the opposite camp. Religious indifference, he insisted, "entails no particular practical attitude" (1993: 181) and should not be seen as an a priori obstacle in the struggle against dictatorship. Its social implications may be quite diverse, and the absence of belief is in itself no more dangerous than the presence of fanaticism. With regard to religious belief, Michnik admitted that "only those forms of religious belief that are 'anti-values,' that lead to fanaticism and intolerance, are objectionable" (1993: 181) and should therefore be opposed. "I would nevertheless be afraid to live in a world without conservative institutions and values," he confessed, speaking like a true moderate (1998: 109). "A world devoid of tradition would be nonsensical and anarchic. The human world should be constructed from a permanent conflict between conservatism and contestation; if either is absent from a society, pluralism is destroyed."

Turning to his colleagues on the Left, Michnik called upon them to acknowledge the Catholic Church as a valuable partner in the fight against injustice and despotism and engage in an open and unbiased dialogue with its members according to the principles of individual responsibility and dignity. This was all the more relevant given the embattled situation of the secular Left fighting for freedom and human dignity in communist Poland. The central component of the doctrine of the Left in a totalitarian state, Michnik believed, was and could only be antitotalitarianism, and that is why it had to be open to—and engage with—other antitotalitarian ideas and groups. As a result, the secular Left had to be ready to defend the Church and shed its traditional anticlericalism while maintaining a vigilant attitude toward the Church's authoritarian tendencies. This was necessitated by the fact that, as Michnik himself insisted, the enemy of the Left was totalitarianism rather than the Catholic Church. Accordingly, he believed that thinkers on the Left ought to support an open and tolerant Church that did not compromise its values vis-à-vis the communist state by preaching, for example, that people must always bow their heads under the power of the latter. We should want to join with Christians, Michnik told his friends on the Left, not in spite of their religious beliefs, but precisely because of those beliefs that made the Catholic Church stand up for freedom and individual dignity against the totalitarian state.

Although the idea of a "Church-Left" alliance might have been a distant goal at the time when Michnik wrote his book in the 1970s, he did not seem to be too concerned by that. His appreciation of Christian ethics and morality was linked to his opposition to communism and his reasoning remained first and foremost political.[59] What mattered in his eyes was not only that the Catholic Church as an institution courageously opposed the ideology of the Communist regime, but also that it embraced a universal language and democratic ethos that could be shared by secular and religious spirits alike, regardless of their religious affiliations or philosophical persuasion. What really mattered was the fact that there was a large enough ground on which the two sides (the Church and the Left) along with other secular and religious groups in society could meet and cooperate in their common opposition to the communist Leviathan.[60]

Moderation and "Inconsistency"

Michnik's political trimming has elicited both admiration and criticism over the years. It is possible, for example, to be skeptical of his opposition to calls for moral clarity after 1989 and question whether Eastern Europe has really gone too far in the direction of political witch hunts and vendettas feared by the Polish thinker. Others, closer to the worldview of his great friend, the late Václav Havel, might want to challenge some of the nuances Michnik introduced in the discussion on the relationship between morality and politics. Havel was wedded to a stronger view of moral purity and authenticity that seemed at times to come into conflict with the political moderation advocated by his Polish colleague.[61] As such, Havel's ideal of authenticity did not appear to have much room for the type of trimming theorized and practiced by Michnik, who could have been taken to task for his alleged inconsistency and, possibly, opportunism.

We should certainly resist the temptation of turning Michnik into a saintly figure. Whether or not one agrees with his trimming mindset, one thing is clear: it has been an integral part of his political moderation and constitutes a bold attitude that involves significant risks and requires a great degree of courage in face of adversity. Such an attitude is obviously a matter of personal temperament, which is different from Aristotle's famous golden mean often taken as the standard image of political moderation. It bears repeating that Michnik has espoused a *radical* form of moderation rather than a middle-of-the-road approach. His moderation has been, in fact, the exact opposite of middlingness construed as a search for a comfortable and lukewarm center that avoids conflict and confrontation.

The question remains: what kind of moderation does best characterize Michnik's vision? On the one hand, his standpoint on key political issues has been firm, clear, and, at times, uncompromising. This last term must be taken, however, with a grain of salt since it refers not so much to Michnik's convictions as to his own style. "If you are defending an idea," he once told Daniel Cohn-Bendit (1998: 64–65), "you first have to show, by your own behavior, that you believe in it; in other words, you have to bear witness." Michnik's record has been unambiguous in this regard, and it would be impossible to accuse him of having failed to bear witness or to defend his moral and political beliefs. He never struck immoral compromises with the communist authorities for personal gain. In fact, even when he engaged in (mostly polemical) exchanges with the communist authorities, he consistently refused to use the term "dialogue" since the latter, in his view, was not an adequate way of describing the profoundly unequal relationship with those in power.[62] Furthermore, for Michnik the ethical point of view defending values such as integrity, decency, and justice was not to be regarded as external to politics as long as the communist authorities had launched an open attack on civil society and the truth itself, thus threatening people's freedom, rights, and dignity. In his essay "What Is Dialogue?" he openly admitted that sometimes "the only effective way to deal with the communist authorities is through firm resistance" (1993: 180). A certain form of moral absolutism was, therefore, permitted, and even necessary, in the opposition to dictatorship and represented a great strength for individuals and groups fighting against oppression.

Michnik acknowledged that he, too, had practiced a certain form of moral absolutism in the past when he opposed the communist authorities. Writing from his prison cell in the 1980s to General Kiszczak, the chief of police who had tried through an intermediary to convince him to sign an agreement in order to be released from prison and be permitted to go into exile on the French Riviera, Michnik gave a firm and unambiguous answer that highlighted the undeniable moral and political differences between them. "I know very well, General, why you need our departure," he courageously wrote. "So that you can besmirch us in your newspapers with redoubled energy as people who have finally shown their true faces, who first executed foreign orders and then were rewarded with capitalist luxuries. . . . So that you can proclaim with relief: after all they are no better than us" (1987: 67). To such a hypocritical position, Michnik insisted, there was only one possible answer: a firm denial of any compromise. "To offer to a man, who has been held in prison for two years, the Côte d'Azur in exchange for his moral suicide, one would have to be a swine," he went on challenging the powerful communist leader.

Michnik knew that in his place, the latter would have chosen the Riviera rather than his honor. But, he added, that was the difference between them: Kiszczak and the other communist leaders were "pigs" devoid of conscience and sheer opportunists ready to sell their souls in exchange for tangible material benefits. Words like "good," "evil," and "honor" meant nothing to them. By contrast, Michnik and his friends loved their country even from the prison cells where they were punished for their courageous dissent. They had no intention of leaving Poland because for them words like "honor," "responsibility," and "conscience" mattered a lot. To Michnik, there was no middle ground or compromise on the issue of integrity, and Kiszczak's tempting offer had to be turned down unconditionally and firmly.

Such a radical position was justified by the fact that, as Michnik himself put, "in the life of every honorable man comes a difficult moment . . . when the simple statement this is black and that is white requires paying a high price" (Michnik, 1987: 68). In such extreme or critical situations, any decent person who wants to retain his or her humanity should unconditionally affirm "that white is white and black is black" against the insinuations of those who would like to blur the line between them. The imperative of moral clarity under extreme circumstances is dictated and justified by the need to maintain one's conscience bound by its obligation to the truth. The latter will always whisper to our ears that there are certain things that we may not do and it will remind us that communism is both an illusion and a lie. The illusion was inseparable from the pretention, belied by reality, that communism represents a more humane future for humanity. The lie, referring to the glaring contradictions between words and deeds, was a collective and deliberate act of deceit by which the communist leaders sought to mislead their own citizens and their observers abroad through a vast and well-funded propaganda apparatus and systematic brainwashing. On the other hand, Michnik's position was surprisingly flexible and nondogmatic, leaving the door open to dialogue and compromise with his former political opponents. This applied even to General Kiszczak, the architect of the martial law regime in 1981, who eight years later became a key protagonist of the Round Table negotiations that led to the peaceful demise of the communist regime in the summer of 1989.

Michnik's openness to dialogue was neither a concession of defeat nor an expression of political opportunism on his part. It had its roots in a few fundamental beliefs that he never surrendered during his long public career and which have defined his political moderation to this day. The first one, connected to his modesty and humility, admits that we must always resist the temptation to believe in the righteousness of our views and ought to hold in check any form of moral egotism and arrogance that might creep in our views, however legitimate they might (appear to) be at some point. "The angel who demands heroism not only of himself but of others," Michnik cautioned (1987: 196), "who perceives the world with a Manichaean simplicity and despises those who have a different concept of obligations toward others—this angel, loving heaven as he may, has already started on the path that leads to hell." He was repeating an old favorite trope of Pascal, who warned us that those who pretend to behave like angels risk becoming fanatic beasts in the end. The second fundamental belief derives from Michnik's understanding of politics as "the art of achieving political goals—of achieving what is possible in a given situation, that is, in a situation that has its conditions and its limits."[63] Such a view leaves room for a particular degree of creativity within certain—moral, legal, and political—bounds in keeping with one's sense of responsibility, integrity, and honor.

Third, and perhaps most importantly from the viewpoint of moderation, Michnik has defended the need for dialogue and compromise by invoking the impossibility of finding a magic universal formula or standard for dealing with complex and controversial topics such as justice, liberty, or fighting evil. "Everyone has to answer in his own conscience the question of how to counter the evil, how to defend dignity, how to behave in this strange war that is a new embodiment of the age-old struggle of truth and lies, of liberty and coercion, of dignity and degradation," Michnik wrote in 1982, a few months after the imposition of martial law in Poland. "In this struggle there are *no final victories*, but *neither* are there—and here is a slight reason for optimism—*any final defeats*" (1987: 40, emphases added). This is a refreshing combination of realism, moderation, and optimism reminiscent of Isaiah Berlin's rejection of determinism in history and his insistence that the latter has no predetermined libretto that all individuals must follow.

Finally, there is also an epistemological justification of Michnik's political moderation and his ethics of dialogue based on human fallibility and imperfect knowledge. It starts by recognizing that we are surrounded by multiple and diverse voices defending a variety of positions, interests, and worldviews, some incompatible with each other, but each containing a valuable grain of truth. The dialogue with these voices is all the more important since their plural perspectives can always suggest alternative arguments, paths, and solutions to the problems we attempt to solve. No ideological scheme, however sophisticated it may be, can adequately reflect the vibrant pluralism of the real world, nor can it fully capture the polyphonic truth of history. We must first try, as best we can, "to understand the other side" (Michnik, 1998: 285) and should take into account as many views and voices as possible, without distorting them and without any trace of wishful thinking on our part.[64]

What made Michnik's moderate position remarkable is that he developed and practiced it in the heat of the political battle rather than ex cathedra or in a comfortable ivory tower, far away from the sound and fury of the world. Even more puzzling, he has been an unconventional political moderate who has sometimes practiced different forms of moral absolutism. He reacted to a world of extremes that contained many contradictions and tensions and in which, in order to preserve his dignity, he was not afraid of being, at times, moderately inconsistent. This very topic—the inconsistency between general principles and their application—had, in fact, been previously discussed by Michnik's predecessor, Leszek Kołakowski, in a splendid text, "In Praise of Inconsistency." In this short but incisive essay, he sounded the alarm against the intransigence of those who, overconfident in their beliefs, always seek "to carry their assumptions to their utmost logical conclusions and loudly voice their judgments on every matter in which their principles were engaged" (Kołakowski 1968: 211). Such people, following the ethics of absolute faith, never vacillate or change course once they make up their minds; their consistency and firmness of purpose elicit admiration and praise even when their positions are, in fact, entirely predictable and often dogmatic. The ever present danger lurking behind this form of moral and political autism is fanaticism manifested, among other things, by the unwillingness to open a dialogue with one's opponents and the constant preoccupation with finding conspiracies and punishing heretics. Toleration, flexibility, and pluralism are three words often absent from the vocabulary of these priests of truth; they are, in fact, seen as expressions of mental or moral confusion and inexcusable weakness that must be combated at all costs.

Next to this race of severe ideological priests stands another one, "the race of those who vacillate and are soft, the inconsistent people" (1968: 213). These are those who, being skeptical of the ethics of absolute ends, are reluctant to carry their assumptions to their final logical conclusions and, most of the time, shy away from seeking moral and political clarity. Some may accuse these persons of opportunism and pusillanimity, but for the most part, these are honest and decent individuals who believe in the superiority of moderation over any form of ideological or doctrinal intransigence. If they believe "in God and the superiority of eternal salvation over temporal well-being," they do not demand that "heretics be converted at the stake" (1968: 213). Moreover, they are prepared to make prudent accommodations in order to live with imperfection and error, which makes them liable of being accused of inconsistency. In Kołakowski's view, this race of "inconsistent" people is one of the greatest sources of hope for the survival of mankind, and their moderation is a good omen for the future of the planet.

It is not a mere coincidence that in the postcommunist context, this praise of inconsistency and moderation in the search for moral clarity and purity can be found in the writings of two distinguished Eastern European intellectuals who struggled to maintain their dignity and independence of mind in a tough world that sometimes allowed for no middle ground between recklessness, cowardice, and heroism. This is one of the most precious gifts that former dissidents offered us: a persuasive illustration of "fragility as a mode of historical existence" within the larger "geography of pain" in Central and Eastern Europe.[65] On this map, the traditional categories of Left and Right were blurred beyond recognition and eventually became irrelevant. As the former Russian dissident Vladimir Bukovsky once wryly remarked, speaking for the millions who lived under the communist regimes of the past century, "We are neither from the left camp nor from the right camp; we are from the concentration camp."[66]

For those who came from this dark world, performing small acts of daily resistance that reaffirmed their humanity and decency was sometimes much more important than being faithful to a certain ideology; it was also the way in which they could effectively defend and maintain their dignity and freedom. For them, acting "heroically" in their daily lives often meant little more than treating others with civility, gentility, and respect, refusing even for a single second to side with the guardians and the officials against their fellow citizens. Sometimes, as in the case of those thrown into prison for being dissenters to the official line, it was enough to share with their fellow prisoners the little they had, for example, a cup of soup or a glass of water. At other times, resisting in prison meant washing one's face, or keeping one's clothes as tidy as possible in an environment in which shapeless clothes given to prisoners were part of a deliberate attempt to humiliate them and deprive them of their personality. These "weapons of the weak"[67] became hugely important and acquired a symbolic dimension that empowered defenseless individuals and gave them the power to survive.

In the murky corners of that (now bygone) world, "ordinary heroes"[68] like Michnik and Kołakowski learned a few important lessons that eventually turned them into political moderates. First, they discovered that in order to survive, one must always be unpredictable and on the move, maintaining as much as possible a rebellious attitude and mindset. For Michnik, this lesson learned under communism became an asset after 1989 when he turned into a major political actor. He understood that life often opens many doors on us and tries to lure us into one single direction at times, closing our mind forever. But we must resist being pushed down this path and should remain (as much as possible) unpredictable, free, and open-minded, much like the famous "Flying University" and its members in communist Poland. Even Havel once described himself as an "eternal rebel and protester," always unsure of himself, an eternal dreamer and skeptic, rational and systematic but also "oversensitive [and] almost a little sentimental," a neurotic "eternally doubting the rightness of his place in the order of things" (1990: 203–5). All this implies a certain degree of calculated performance and eclecticism not incompatible with political moderation.

Second, in a world led by prophets of extremity who claimed to know the road to heaven, our moderates came to understand that, appearances notwithstanding, a certain form of syncretism might be a precious asset providing "a consciously sustained reserve of uncertainty, a permanent feeling of possible personal error, or if not that, then of the possibility that one's antagonist is right" (Kołakowski, 1968: 214). It is not a mere accident that both Michnik and Kołakowski wrote in praise of political (not moral) eclecticism, refusing stark labels and black-and-white categories. A deliberately provocative expression of this "odd mix of the most curious opposites"[69] was a playful essay written by Kołakowski in which he tried to demonstrate that one can simultaneously be a "Conservative-Liberal-Socialist." These labels, far from being incompatible with each other, may, in fact, be combined in such a way that they "are no longer mutually exclusive options" (Kołakowski, 1990: 227) with regard to key issues such as justice, liberty, equality, or security.

Finally, our ordinary heroes learned that a certain form of inconsistency may be the best attitude we can adopt in order to find our way in a world characterized by an eternal and ineradicable antinomy and conflict of values. In such a universe, it would be wrong and illusory to assume "that a reasonable mind can harmonize what to the immoderate one appear to be contradictions" (Kołakowski, 1968: 216). Such contradictions and tensions (either/or) are inherent in both the world at large and human nature. They are created by individuals who, whenever they are allowed to act freely, are likely to abuse their principles and transgress borders. "These contradictions inhere in the world of values and cannot be reconciled in any synthesis," Kołakowski acknowledged (1968: 216), taking up a major theme that had also appeared in Isaiah Berlin's writings. "Reasonable inconsistency does not seek to forge a synthesis between extremes, knowing it does not exist, since values as such exclude each other integrally. The real world of values is inconsistent; that is to say, it is made up of antagonistic elements." It would therefore be impossible and futile to try to make sense of the multifarious nature of reality by means of a single ordering principle, be that justice, moral clarity, or purity. Again, we are doomed to inconsistency, uncertainty, and political moderation.

Nevertheless, like any other principle, inconsistency itself must not be abused and ought to be espoused with prudence and a grain of skepticism. "When we are not always inconsistent, only then do we become absolutely inconsistent," Kołakowski admitted (1968: 220). "Inconsistent inconsistency . . . is actually consistent inconsistency." To some, this may sound like an incomprehensible paradox or cheap aphorism. But to those who lived in surreal conditions for decades, it was a daily way of life and sometimes even a matter of life and death. In their effort to maintain their dignity and liberty, they could find no better compass than political moderation, a fighting and bold virtue for noncaptive minds.

Epilogue

Beyond the Golden Mean

> Having political opinions is not a matter of having an ideology once and for all; it is a question of taking the right decisions in changing circumstances.
>
> —Raymond Aron

It is time to complete our journey by returning to the metanarratives that undergird the arguments presented in this book. Although the different aspects of moderation—personal, institutional, and political—are related to each other and, taken together, might point to a thin (as opposed to a thick) definition of this concept, I have preferred to highlight the complexity and diverse faces of this elusive virtue, leaving the question of its precise definition open. I showed that in all of its incarnations, political moderation has a distinct content and style and forms a diverse tradition of thought, resembling an archipelago consisting of various islands represented by a wide array of ideas and modes of argument and action.[1]

The moderate thinkers discussed in these pages affirmed several basic attitudes that allow us to begin describing the school of moderation to which they belonged, beyond their inevitable personal and intellectual differences. The agenda of moderation promotes social and political pluralism and endorses trimming and balance between competing values and principles. It rejects monist conceptions of the public good and the good life and opposes Manichaeism. It prefers gradual reforms over radical revolutionary breakthroughs and sometimes—though not always—searches for a *juste milieu* or "golden mean" between extremes that would maintain the equipoise of the community. Less obvious but equally important, moderation also denotes a certain style of political action, often manifested by the propensity to seek conciliation and find balance between various ideas, interests, and groups. As trimmers seeking to keep the ship of the state on an even keel, the moderates discussed in this book were prepared to make compromises and concessions on both prudential (political) and normative (philosophical) grounds. Starting from the premise that there cannot be in principle only one single correct (or valid) way of life on which we all might agree, these thinkers reconciled themselves to the fact that there are no definitive solutions to intractable social and political problems. They eschewed perfectionism and made a special effort to listen to all sides of the debate, keeping the conversation open with their friends, critics, and opponents. They accepted that most political and social issues often involve tough trade-offs and significant opportunity costs, and require constant small-scale adjustments and gradual steps. And while realizing the relative validity of their convictions and ideas, they were also prepared to stand for them unflinchingly, but without becoming dogmatic zealots obsessed with moral purity and excessively preoccupied with achieving perfect consistency in their beliefs and attitudes.

The *first* metanarrative of the book is that moderation has many related faces—personal, ethical, institutional, constitutional, and political—that form a distinctive political style and agenda. This is a key point sometimes neglected by those who tend to equate moderation with a mere (individual or national) character trait, state of mind, vaguely defined ethos, or personal disposition. Moderation is, in fact, much more than that. It would be difficult to deny that political moderation is partly a matter of intellectual temperament and character, but we need to admit that it is sometimes possible to mix radical thinking with a bohemian personality in private life and still endorse at the same time political moderation in the public arena. As a certain form of sensibility or disposition, moderation is a cardinal virtue related to civility, self-control, equipoise, temperance, and prudence. By being simultaneously an act of self-restraint and an attempt to restrain others, it can serve—in most, though not all, circumstances—as antidote to moral absolutism, fanaticism, zealotry, ideological thinking, and extremism. When we try to examine moderation as a character trait in further detail, its flexibility and protean qualities become even more obvious. It is possible to have an immoderate temperament and still uphold moderation in political matters by defending the principles of constitutionalism, rule of law, and so forth. One can be moderate not only by temperament (Bobbio),[2] but also out of fear (Shklar), out of necessity (Michnik), or as a matter of principle (Aron and Berlin).

Furthermore, nothing prevents one from being a moderate simultaneously out of fear and from principle, or from being moderate in some respects and radical or immoderate in others (Oakeshott's private notebooks reveal him as an immoderate person in his youth).[3] Finally, it is important to stress that moderation can also be the outcome of an arduous process of political learning, involving experience, changes of mind, and reevaluations of previous attitudes. At the same time, in addition to its ethical (moral) meaning, moderation also has a distinctively constitutional and institutional dimension reflected by the choice of institutions, rules, and practices. Political moderation has traditionally been linked to the separation and balance of powers, the use of the executive veto, bicameralism, neutral power (or third power) as well as to the adoption of declarations or bills of rights.[4]

The *second* metanarrative of the present book sheds light on the connection between moderation and thinking politically as well as on the opposition between political moderation and ideological thinking. By arguing that moderation implies a certain form of judgment and a complex balancing act not unlike the art of walking along a thin wire or rope (illustrated on the cover of the book), I have sought to move the discussion beyond the (negative) definition of moderation as a form of opposition to extremism, fanaticism, and zealotry. While there are important differences among the thinkers studied in this book, they all agreed on an important point: namely, that when thinking about politics or acting in the political sphere, one must start from the facts themselves and acknowledge that there are certain structural tensions between values and principles that cannot be fully solved or eliminated forever. These are permanent antinomies, not transitory ones, and often the best way to deal with them is by using prudence and moderation in attempting to find the best approach in each context.

As the opposite of ideological thinking, according to which politics can and should be conducted strictly "by the book," that is, from the standpoint of a single set of criteria and beliefs relevant to all spheres of life, moderation presupposes making constant judgments about how to balance the values in each sphere and situation and how to navigate between the inevitable frictions and contradictions of political life. This is probably what Keynes had in mind when he wrote these lines in praise of political expediency that must be distinguished from sheer opportunism in the worst sense of the term. "It is fatal for a capitalist government to have principles," he wrote. "It must be opportunistic in the best sense of the word, living by accommodation and good sense."[5] In an important essay from 1925 ("Am I a Liberal?"), originally given as an address to the Liberal Summer School at Cambridge, the English economist had this to say: "A party program must be developed in its details, day by day, under the pressure and the stimulus of actual events; it is useless to define it beforehand, except in the most general terms."[6] This way of approaching change is the opposite of ideological thinking, a term that denotes a closed system of thought that takes its standards for evaluating society and politics as eternal principles or infallible dogmas, not to be discussed critically or challenged by anyone. Ideologies shape how people (ought to) think by providing conceptual lenses to interpret the world in a specific way. They tell their followers what to do and what not to do, and they seek to provide remedies, some imaginary, and some real, to the problems of society. As Backes pointed out, extremist ideologies defined as ideocracies "unfold a bipolar Manichaean world view that assigns the spiritually deviant to the 'kingdom of evil' and thus justifies a clear friend-foe differentiation" (2010: 184) with significant political implications.

Thinking politically (as opposed to thinking ideologically) represents a form of "dissent" from the political orthodoxies of one's epoch.[7] It follows the fluid contours of reality without an infallible compass and requires both a form of judgment and an act of moderation. To give just a couple of examples, it recognizes that "liberties and rights vary with times and circumstances, and admit of infinite modification, [and] cannot be settled upon any abstract rule" (Burke, 1968: 151). And it acknowledges that the political sphere is a whirlpool of passions and shifting interests in which nothing can be settled forever into a system governed by rigorous laws, as in geometry. Our political judgments and choices must therefore take into account this fundamental and permanent changeability and malleability of the world around us. Yet, arguing that what is right in each context cannot be judged in light of an absolute truth or doctrine that claims to have monopoly over the right ordering of life does not amount to endorsing relativism, as one might think. An important criterion to be followed in most circumstances is the need to preserve the balance and constitutional order of the political community, and this requires a flexible approach seeking what is appropriate, possible, and right in each moment in order to achieve this goal. This is again similar to the case of a tightrope walker who needs to be attentive and alert at all times in order to maintain his or her equipoise and avoid falling.

One of the best means of preserving the balance of political community and promoting the necessary social and political changes is by keeping the dialogue open with all the political actors who accept the basic rules of the game and are committed to preserving the basic values of the society. This is the *third* metanarrative, which explains why many of the thinkers studied in this book, from Aron and Bobbio to Michnik, successfully practiced the art of dialogue across the aisle and refused to see the world in black-and-white contrasts. If they adopted the role of committed or engaged spectators, they also maintained a certain degree of detachment and skepticism in their attitudes and political judgments. Their invitation to dialogue and their willingness to speak to their critics illustrated their courage and determination not to look for "safe spaces" and lukewarm solutions. Instead, they saw themselves as mediators whose duty was to open a line of communication with their opponents who disagreed with them. The dialogue they staged was at times difficult and frustrating, and their belief in the (real or symbolic) power of discussion was an open act of defiance against the crusading spirit of their age, marked by political sectarianism, monologue, and ideological intransigence. Aron and the other moderates studied here were convinced that we can improve ourselves not so much by seeking a fictitious harmony with our critics as by engaging in an open debate with them, as long as we all remain committed to civility and rational critique. In this regard, they all acted as true disciples of Montaigne, who once acknowledged that "no premise shocks me, no belief hurts me, no matter how opposite to my own they may be. . . . When I am contradicted it arouses my attention not my wrath."[8] This is exactly how Aron and the other moderates felt and behaved. They were open to being challenged and did not shy away from correcting others when they thought fit. Yet, in so doing, they did not simply seek to refute or defeat their opponents' arguments, being aware that the truth is almost never the monopoly of a single camp or group.

A *fourth* related metanarrative has to do with the eclecticism of moderation, which is an upshot of its syncretism and dependence on context. In stressing this point, I want to remind the reader that according to circumstances, moderation can have both radical and conservative connotations that may vary with time and place and make it virtually impossible to speak of moderation as a fixed ideology or closed belief system. The latter seems to be a common misunderstanding among many interpreters of moderation, and it is important to emphasize that moderation should not be conflated with any ideology. Accordingly, I have done my best to highlight both the liberal and conservative sides of moderation, and the selection of authors was made with this goal in mind.

The eclecticism of moderation is best illustrated by its relationship with trimming between extremes, that is, a way of keeping the ship of state on an even keel and maintaining the fragile balance between competing ideals, groups, and interests in society. This represents the *fifth* metanarrative of the book. As already mentioned, trimmers are quite different from opportunists. They start from acknowledging the existence of deep antinomies in political life and admit that often there is no "right way" in the abstract. They distrust those who pursue single-mindedly their ethics of absolute ends and seem uninterested in making necessary and timely compromises and adjustments. As a result, trimmers recognize that most of the time in politics we cannot—and should not—think dogmatically, that is, by the book (whatever the latter might be). Trimming (as a face of moderation) overlaps to some extent with the issues of the center and the *juste milieu* between extremes, but it is not identical with them, and should therefore be distinguished from them. It delineates the broad contours of a complex political agenda that is different from Centrism, in spite of their affinities. Like centrists who "try to transcend the pursuit of essentially self-interested politics, attempting to find a mutually beneficial balance of rights and responsibilities consistent with the creation of a more civil society" (Avlon, 2004: 448), moderates practice the art of balance aiming at maintaining and strengthening the political communities to which they belong.[9] Nonetheless, moderation should not be narrowly identified with the political center since those committed to this virtue can exist on both aisles of the political spectrum; some moderates prefer to locate themselves in the center, other do not. They are often difficult to pin down and belong, as it were, to a party sui generis without banners or ideology in the stronger sense of the term.[10]

The *sixth* and last metanarrative is, in fact, a veiled critique of moderation throughout the book. This might surprise those would expect to find here a panegyric of this virtue according to which moderates are infallible heroes always placed on the "right" or "good" side of history. In spite of my genuine appreciation for moderation as a political virtue, I believe that such a view would be inadequate and wrong. Moderation is neither a panacea nor a substitute for pragmatic partisanship; politics cannot function without strong contestation and deep disagreement, and we should resist the temptation of sometimes overpraising moderation, Centrism, and bipartisanship. I take seriously into account what the critics of moderation have to say about it and do not exclude the possibility that the promotion of moderation might have implied at some point in history "aggressive" interventions by agents of power leading to "dangerous excesses in Church, state, and society."[11]

That is why the present book seeks to respond to those who are skeptical about moderation as a political virtue by openly admitting that moderation is *not* a virtue for all people and all seasons, and that various forms of political radicalism acting in the framework of legality can occasionally give fresh impetus to necessary and timely course corrections.[12] I acknowledge the existence of important links and affinities between some types of emancipatory politics and forms of political behavior sometimes unfairly stigmatized as extremist or fanatical by their opponents. As the example of the civil rights movement showed, some calls for moderation made during the 1950s and 1960s were mostly intended to rebuff legitimate challenges to pernicious forms of racial injustice and entrenched privileges.[13] With the benefit of hindsight, it is now clear that what might have passed at some point as "moderation" was, in reality, little else than hypocrisy and dissimulation and functioned as a tool of coercion and control used by shrewd political actors to block necessary reforms.

Therefore, the image that emerges from the present book is that of a virtue that is simultaneously necessary (in light of the overwhelming historical experience and the fact that we have lived until recently in a world of extremes), limited (given the fact that this is not a universal virtue), and difficult to practice (because moderation requires judgment and lacks a precise algorithm or manual that could teach it to those willing to learn it). Moreover, moderation is not only necessary but simply inevitable in political life, since contradictions in human attitudes and between values and principles are inherent in the world rather than caused by our lack of reasonableness.[14] Like temperance, political moderation is a human, ordinary, and humble virtue "all the more necessary when the times are good, . . . to be practiced on a regular rather than exceptional basis."[15] It demands a good dose of reflexivity, lucidity, and discernment that offer a necessary compass to orient ourselves in the labyrinth of public and political life by choosing honorable ends and assessing the appropriate means to pursue them. Yet, because it is a flexible, mixed, and fluid virtue, political moderation also has its own inherent limitations. It may sometimes be (or appear to be) insufficiently democratic and does not always guarantee political success in spite of its reasonableness. Furthermore, moderates can give the impression of being too detached, ironical, or excessively uncertain about the best course of action. Their eclecticism makes it difficult for any moderate to be a disciplined and regimented party person.

Nonetheless, if the thinkers discussed in these pages were for the most part detached from party platforms, just as they were too skeptical to engage in conventional party politics, they did not shy away from courageously fighting political battles or engaging in public controversies. They all were caught in the orbit of—and reacted to—the struggle against the twin totalitarianisms of the twentieth century: fascism and communism. It is in response to these two doctrines that a tradition of political moderation as an art of balance emerged over time in defense of the values and principles of open society.[16] Nonetheless, it would be wrong to believe that moderation is simply a circumstantial virtue, even if at times it may appear as dependent upon the configuration and strength of extremes. Moderation is, as Joseph Hall put it four centuries ago, "the silken string running through the pearl-chain of all virtues."[17] It is a cardinal virtue in the absence of which the normal functioning of political life would simply be impossible to imagine.

The Benefits of Moderation

Moderation may have many indisputable benefits, but one thing that it does not (and cannot) guarantee is the moral clarity demanded by members of different vice squads across the world engaged in relentless crusades in the name of the truth. Moral clarity has appeared at different points in this book and is a perfect example of the challenges faced by all political moderates. It would be impossible to deny that there are issues on which the line separating light from darkness is quite clear. Moral clarity has been used by many politicians and journalists to justify a strong stance in the fight against communism (beginning with the 1950s) and, most recently, in the current war on terror.[18] It is in the name of moral clarity that politicians of all colors (but especially those on the Right) have denounced the axis of evil, and the war on terror has been described as a cosmic struggle between good and evil that requires near constant mobilization, a burning faith, and unlimited resources.

Yet it would be wrong to think that calls for moral clarity have remained confined to the conservative side. On the Left, philosopher Susan Neiman has argued that moral clarity presupposes taking moral questions seriously rather than dismissing them ironically. In her view, moral clarity is the opposite of embracing a relativistic stance according to which there is no right and wrong as universal moral categories since everything is relative to context. At the same time, according to Neiman, moral clarity is the opposite of moral fundamentalism and simplicity. The latter assumes that a certain religious or political authority has settled moral questions once and for all, leaving no ambiguities whatsoever on the "right" set of priorities and values that we should follow. Neiman acknowledged, however, the dangers associated with the search for moral clarity. "The language of good and evil," she wrote (2008: 371), "is vulnerable to exploitation because . . . [n]othing moves men and women more deeply and surely, for better and worse." While it is important to strive for moral clarity, we should never assume that we possess it, because that would give us a false and dangerous sense of self-righteousness. Moral clarity is not a moment of instant enlightenment, but a normative goal that we should work for our entire life to achieve: "Every situation and every dilemma needs to be thought through individually. That's what moral clarity, as opposed to moral simplicity, demands."[19]

It would be an understatement to say that moral clarity is an extremely complex concept that can be interpreted in various ways to serve different political agendas. According to its conventional meaning, moral clarity implies having an unambiguous sense of what is right and wrong in each case. Such a confident view may work in some circumstances and settings, but it becomes problematic as soon as it is applied universally. It risks justifying dangerous moral crusades when those who call for moral clarity go a step further to argue that the current confusion about our values is a deeper sign of the crisis of modern society and cultures that must be dealt with in a forceful and uncompromising manner. Not surprisingly, moral clarity has had its own vocal critics. For example, analysts of America's foreign policy adventures in the Middle East have warned that moral clarity is "an attractive-sounding but disingenuous concept"[20] that we should avoid precisely because of its potential for self-delusion and hypocrisy. Others have claimed that moral clarity is easier preached than practiced and have criticized it for being excessively idealistic and unable to render justice to the untidiness of the world made of many shades of gray. Those who have called for moral clarity have also been suspected of trying to bully their critics, simplify reality, and espouse an unjustified air of superiority over those who do not see the world through Manichaean lenses.

Regardless of whether or not these critiques are right, it cannot be denied that many people call for moral clarity and embrace this concept because the latter promises to offer exactly what moderation seems unable to do: that is, to put some order in a confusing world, full of clashing values, beliefs, and interests. Moderation is, indeed, the opposite of all that: it is a humble expression of our imperfection and limitations as well as a constant reminder that we should never assume the moral righteousness of our causes or believe that God is on our side. Moderation is also a refusal to simplify reality, which happens when we try to interpret the latter in light of a particular value or standard, be that justice, liberty or equality. The authors discussed in this book believed that like goodness itself, the good society and the good life can never be reduced to one single principle, and that (moral, social, and political) pluralism is the necessary precondition of all open societies.[21]

If I were to select one final quote to illustrate the complex spirit of moderation, I would choose the following words of Camus who once admitted: "I lack the assurance that allows one to settle everything. . . . One has a right to hesitate and to weigh the pros and cons."[22] This is a wonderful statement that captures quite well the essence of moderation as the opposite of the self-assured tone and highbrowed moralism of those who are certain of the rectitude of their beliefs and act according to the rule "No compromise on principles." Some of Camus's contemporaries, for example, believed that violence can sometimes be regenerative and aesthetically pleasing and argued that radical forms of politics were the best means of creating a new world and a better humanity.[23] Their endorsement of violence in an "age of extremes"[24] was often accompanied by a dogmatic belief in the righteousness of their causes, which, in their eyes, legitimized the means used to achieve them.

While the authors and texts studied in this book pointed out that moderation is a rare and difficult virtue, they also reminded us of its real benefits, to which I would like to turn next. First, arguably the greatest advantage of moderation derives from the fact that it is not an ideology with fixed contours,[25] and, as already mentioned, is also much more than the proverbial golden mean between the extremes. Aron, Berlin, Oakeshott, Bobbio, Kołakowski, and Michnik belonged to the pluralist camp that rejects unitary and simplistic definitions of the political good. Their moderation was neither an ideology of control nor an aggressive tool for blocking reforms. On the contrary, it was a means for promoting reform and change rather than defend the status quo. If one were to look for at least one element of continuity in their works, that would be their staunch refusal to define "one single best way"[26] and their opposition to ideocracies of all sorts. The diversity of their viewpoints on the issue of the political good suggests that there is no single model of political moderation. As previously discussed, moderation has affinities with different political traditions and moderates of various persuasions can (and did) exist on the left side, in the center, as well as on the right side of the political spectrum. In light of its inherent heterogeneity, it can accommodate a wide range of political ideas, views, and forms of government. This flexibility arguably constitutes one of its greatest advantages and benefits because it allows moderates to get things done where others, following a particular ideology, fail to do so.[27]

Second, far from being of mere historical interest, political moderation is particularly relevant and important in a postideological age such as ours, when old political doctrines and ideas have lost their sharp contours and new forms of extremism are on the rise. All moderates share the following quality that distinguishes them from their opponents: they tend to feel and understand well the opposite sides of life, and this ability gives them a panoramic view of politics that others often lack. This trait can be particularly helpful today. Moderation promotes a flexible, antiperfectionist, and balancing mindset that can make us better prepared to engage in difficult but necessary trade-offs between different values and principles. We do have the right to hesitate, compare, and balance them in each situation in accordance with the limited knowledge and information at our disposal. The best that can often be done, as a general rule, is not to strive for perfection, but to try "to maintain a precarious equilibrium that could prevent the occurrence of desperate situations, of intolerable choices—that is the first requirement for a decent society" (Berlin, 1998b: 15). If moderates are sometimes prepared to sacrifice the better for what is decent, they do it in keeping with a larger goal, defending the pluralism of ideas, principles, and interests essential to maintaining and nurturing freedom in modern society.

Moderation can also serve as a significant normative stance in the fight against various forms of fundamentalism because it does have a universal appeal across borders and continents; it is rooted in—and is the expression of—the collected wisdom of many generations that had witnessed the dangers and consequences of political and religious fanaticism and extremism. Many different political traditions, cultures, and religions are able to accommodate moderation; the latter is at home not only in an Aristotelian or Christian framework, but also in a Jewish, Confucian, and even Islamic setting,[28] although it is likely to espouse a different form in each context. To be sure, a fundamental idea can be found in all major moral and religious traditions: namely, that safety lies in taking the middle course in life by seeking to achieve through moderation a balance between deficiency and excess, between indulgence and parsimoniousness. The assumption is that we can taste the joys of life in abundance only if we are moderate and temperate in our desires and pursuits. In most (if not all) of its incarnations, moderation enables us to place things in the right perspective and see what is good and proper to pursue in each case.

Third, moderation has the great advantage of being a virtue tailored to human nature that aims neither too high nor too low. Montaigne once remarked that our main business is to live our lives fittingly, *à propos*,[29] that is, with moderation, something that is always in our power to do if we apply our attention and will to it. As the "union of life with measure, of spirit with reasonableness" (Bagehot, 1872: 201), moderation makes our minds simultaneously firm and flexible and promotes a mindset favorable to compromise and dialogue.[30] It weeds out rigidity and dogmatism and enlivens and civilizes social life by giving the latter that kind of temper, common sense, and vivacity conducive to "civil politics."[31] As such, it is a distinctively human virtue that protects us against becoming self-righteous and teaches us self-restraint and humility. The following aphorism of a wise man, simply identified (by Czeslaw Miłosz) as an old Jew from Galicia, describes well the way most moderates think. "When someone is honestly 55% right," the wise man said, "that's very good and there's no use wrangling. And if someone is 60% right, it's wonderful, it's great luck, and let him thank God. But what's to be said about 75% right? Wise people say this is suspicious. Well, and what about 100% right? Whoever says he's 100% right is a fanatic, a thug, and the worst kind of rascal."[32]

Moderation is a virtue that protects us precisely against this type of fanaticism of self-righteousness. Described as "a mixture of discretion and charity in one's judgment,"[33] it is based on the conviction that others may be wrong, but nonetheless are entitled to voice and share their views, and that we stand to learn something important even from their (and our) mistakes. And it manifests itself in the determination to refrain from using violence or the effort to subvert legitimate social institutions. Moderation also has its own rules regarding measure, civility, and self-restraint, combining the search for truth with a tolerant respect for others' opinions. Like the art of conversation, it requires a talent for speaking, listening, and keeping silent, along with a good sense of irony and courtesy needed to prevent futile quarrels or violent episodes.[34] As the opposite of ideological intransigence, moderation demands civility, intuition, psychological awareness, quick understanding, and wit. A certain joyous spirit presides over it, one that is never morose or boring, but playful, skeptical, ironic, and serious at the same time; its style is characterized by lightness of touch combined with elegant gravity and a sense of responsibility.

Fourth, as a virtue opposed to fanaticism and extremism, moderation is also connected to the concepts of balance and compromise and goes hand in hand with an antiperfectionist cast of mind that often works well in normal politics. When asked to pass judgment on the virtues and limits of the newly drafted U.S. Constitution in 1787, Benjamin Franklin had this to say: "I doubt too whether any other convention we can obtain may be able to make a better Constitution: for when you assemble a number of men to have the advantage of their joint wisdom, you inevitably assemble with those men all their prejudices, their passions, their errors of opinion, their local interests and their selfish views. . . . Thus, I consent Sir, to this Constitution because I expect no better, and because I am not sure that this is not the best."[35] These are the words of a political moderate who humbly acknowledged his limited knowledge and abilities as well as the complex nature of politics and who was deeply aware of the fragility of political liberty and the complexity of social order. A moderate of this kind has "a permanent feeling of possible personal error, or if not that, then of the possibility that one's antagonist is right" (Kołakowski, 1968: 214).

Fifth, having experienced many instances in which better information, new experiences, and additional evidence oblige them to amend or nuance their views, moderates remain open to changing their minds and learning from experience. Sometimes their open-mindedness takes the form of a peculiar "propensity to self-subversion,"[36] a milder way of living dangerously that may be necessary to espouse from time to time in order to stay alive. Self-subversion can, in fact, become the "principal means of self-renewal"[37] and creativity, allowing us to correct errors and misconceptions and cast aside dogmatic beliefs. One might then say that moderation is a constant effort to outwit or "cheat" life, which tries to straitjacket us by committing us to a certain position, agenda, or single direction.[38] The moderates versed in the art of self-subversion develop a systematic habit of questioning and nuancing some of their views, and are not embarrassed to acknowledge that what they once thought to be right turned out, in fact, to be wrong. They also pay due attention to the unintended consequences of their (and others') ideas and actions, recognizing the complexity of social relations and the unpredictability of life in general.

As such, moderates feel an obligation to fight the intransigent dogmatism of those who believe that changing one's mind is unacceptable or sinful and are unwilling to revisit and amend their beliefs, even when they are belied by reality. Moderates attempt "to disintoxicate minds and to calm fanaticisms even when this is against the current tendency" (Camus, 1974: 121). They refuse to opportunistically join the strongest party in power and try to distinguish in each camp "the respective limits of force and justice" while combating "the simplifications of hatred and prejudice."[39] As such, moderates rarely, if ever, take the line of the least resistance that would imply creating around them "safe spaces" and surrounding themselves with "safe" people who reiterate and reaffirm their own beliefs. Finally, they believe that while it is often impossible to demonstrate the truth in political affairs, it is always possible to make sensible and reasonable decisions based on the limited knowledge and information at our disposal.

Last but not least, moderation presupposes a constant reserve of uncertainty and a permanent feeling of imperfection that can act as an effective and permanent countervailing force to all kinds of excesses.[40] Because of that, moderates can often turn their challenges and failures to their advantage. As Ortega y Gasset once nicely put it, "consciousness of shipwreck, when it becomes the truth of life, is already salvation. That is why I believe only in the thoughts of shipwrecked men."[41] While it is not necessary for moderates to always hold power or enjoy political success in the conventional meaning of the term, their ideas, initiatives, and actions may have salutary and tempering effects on those in power and beyond. Although they sometimes operate under the radar, moderates often work toward promoting social justice and humanitarian causes. For example, they can record and expose the lies, euphemisms, and omissions of those in power who seek to deliberately obscure the real problems and prevent us from seeing them in their real light and addressing them effectively. They can also seek to redress injustices, sometimes by swimming against the current or changing their positions and alliances as demanded by circumstances.

Camus highlighted well this last benefit of moderation in his Algerian chronicles in which he took distance from a certain fanaticism of principles that may sometimes become counterproductive. "If anyone . . . still thinks heroically that one's brother must die rather than one's principles," he once wrote, "I shall go no farther than to admire him from a distance. I am not of his stamp" (1974: 113). Camus's pragmatic type of moderation represented a much-needed injunction against the highbrowed moralism of many of his fellow (French) intellectuals who rigidly followed an ethics of absolute ends. His remark was also an acknowledgment that a certain degree of humility in political matters is always desirable and necessary so that "the language of reason may again be heard."[42]

Can We Really Be Moderate?

Today we no longer have to perform heroic acts of political acrobatics in order to allow the voice of reason to be heard again in political life. But the courageous form of moderation praised by Camus remains as relevant as ever. Such a moderate and bold political vision transcending our black-and-white categories was sketched by Leszek Kołakowski in a short essay with a provocative title—"How to Be a Conservative-Liberal-Socialist: A Credo"[43]—and, more recently, by Karol Soltan, who has explicitly drawn upon Kołakowski's ideas in his own spirited defense of moderation.[44] On Soltan's view, moderation requires a complex and eclectic center, qualitatively different from the center identified with a pragmatic and shortsighted politics of compromise and balance of powers that attempt to achieve a precarious and unstable equilibrium among dominant interests and groups in society.[45] The type of moderation that makes possible the politics of the center presupposes a firm commitment to moral and political pluralism and an uncompromising opposition to violence.[46] It also requires self-control, inflexible courage, patient calculation, and adequate knowledge of all available options. This may sound appealing, one could say, but it is important to remember that even the most generous forms of moderation can sometimes degenerate into a mere arithmetic of deal making. In order to be both honorable and inspiring, the complex center must therefore have a pole star, and I would like to claim that that might be precisely what Walter Bagehot once dubbed "animated moderation."[47]

In principle, such a fluid center in which moderates of all colors would meet might help us navigate a world in flux characterized by conflicting and competing principles and values. I emphasize *might* because I am not sure whether this is a realistic goal or yet another utopian ideal. One conclusion of the present book is that it would be inaccurate to always equate political moderation with a centrist agenda. Looking at the political reality around us today, it is hard to deny that the center has not held well in many parts of the world, and has remained in many instances an abstract concept devoid of much substance. For example, the growing partisanship in American politics in the past decade has led to the weakening of the center and the silencing of many moderates on both aisles whose willingness to compromise and work with the other side has frequently put them out of step with their own parties and decreased their chances of being (re)elected. There may be another reason for the declining appeal of moderation: it is much more difficult to be a moderate than to think and act ideologically, especially if one wants to gain power and stay in office. It requires constant balancing and weighing various principles in every situation rather than relying on a single set of universal principles or values or a ready-made algorithm. Moderation presupposes reasoning and deliberation, but it can never rely on reasoning alone; it also demands a combination of intuition, foresight, and flexibility, complemented sometimes by good luck.

Can we appreciate and practice this (or any other) type of political moderation? Montesquieu, for one, thought that all things considered, human beings tend to accommodate themselves better to moderation than to extremes, but the historical record suggests a less optimistic story. Most of us are, in general, unwilling (and unlikely) to fall in love with the nuances of gray which characterize the universe of moderation. We often seek, to use Tocqueville's words, "what is ingenuous and new instead of what is true, being very appreciative of good acting and fine speaking without reference to the play's results, and finally, judging by impressions rather than reasons" (1986: 67). In particular, philosophers find it difficult to reconcile the demand for efficiency with the commitment to morality and truth, and they are torn and divided in two, being "doomed to live in a state of tension, uncertainty, permanent risk" (Michnik, 1998: 154–55). Some may be inclined to embrace moral absolutism by blurring the distinction between moral norms and the specific rules of politics. In so doing, they forget that a democratic world is a chronically imperfect one, a fragile world of freedom coexisting with corruption, and which can survive only if the main political actors do not act as if their positions and ideas were absolute and universally valid.

Moreover, moderation might not be popular in times of crisis when many are inclined to pursue agendas that express and correspond to their fears of chaos and longing for order, simplicity, and security. Yet, as the authors studied in this book showed, crises and strong ideological clashes are not necessarily bad for moderation. Under the cross fire of their opponents, Aron, Berlin, Bobbio, and Michnik courageously defended their visions of a free and decent society against their opponents. If their approaches were sometimes eclectic, they were based on a principled commitment to creating and maintaining institutional and political balance and liberty. They often refrained from pursuing "the best," being aware that they had to choose the least unfavorable course of action. In so doing, they also acknowledged that nothing in the political world is valid in an absolute way, but only in a relative manner depending on time and circumstances. Furthermore, they understood that no question may ever be decided only by taking into consideration one single principle, value, or viewpoint. For human actions have unintended consequences that can jeopardize the implementation of even the best plans and most generous ideas.

I believe that this moderate vision remains relevant in a world that cannot properly function without moderation and compromise. An intelligent politics of moderation suitable to our condition today would still require opposition to all types of moral absolutism,[48] and would maintain a healthy dose of skepticism toward all forms of zealotry and agendas trying to simplify the complex reality of political and social life. It would reject all attempts to impose the rule of a single idea or program that defines itself as the single "best way." By opposing simple systems that seek to transform the diversity of the world into a neatly organized and uniform universe governed by general and rigid rules or criteria, such a moderate agenda would favor social, political, and moral complexity and promote a mixture of institutions, ideas, and principles such as pluralism, balanced constitutions, and mixed forms of government. This is certainly not going to be a high-profile and flamboyant platform advocating large-scale political and social change. It is likely to be a more modest program, predicated upon the assumption that politics are often a messy and mundane business that has little in common with the romantic quest for ultimate truths and certainty that can inspire the masses. Yet, after having suffered the tyranny of sharper and bolder colors advocated by prophets of extremity, we should be prepared to admit that gray, too, can be beautiful. Is that really the case?

Rather than trying to answer this question, I would like to give the last word to a moderate close to my heart who would have deserved an entire chapter in this book (if I had more space). In a lecture given in Lisbon in January 1997, half a year before his untimely death, the distinguished French historian François Furet, one of the world's leading authorities on the French Revolution, reminded us of the power of attraction that utopias have always had on the human imagination. Our fascination for utopia may have subsided after the fall of communism, he argued, but the story is far from being over. In light of their inherent imperfection, liberal democracies are always going to encourage some to imagine a better world in which genuine human communities and authentic forms of solidarity might flourish one day. While old-style communism may be a closed chapter for now, Furet concluded, we can expect that modern democracies will not be able to live without some form of utopia in the long term. The interesting question then is which new type of utopia stands the best chance of reappearing on our political horizon and when and where this might actually happen.[49]

These are, of course, the unknowns of history about which we can only speculate now, but one thing seems difficult to deny. Moderates will always be needed to calm passions, give a sense of possibilities, and remind us that extremism in the pursuit of liberty can sometimes be a vice, while moderation in the pursuit of justice and equality might also be a virtue under some circumstances. In times of crisis, these are the very individuals who, when the intensity of conflict reaches dangerous limits, call for prudence, promote armistices, and negotiate necessary compromises that can save lives, reduce suffering, and avert chaos. This is no small achievement, and it is due to a virtue—moderation—that still awaits to be fully rediscovered and properly appreciated at its real value.

NOTES

Prologue

1. I prefer to refer to the "moderate mind" rather than the "middling mind" in order to distinguish the former from the pejorative connotations associated with the latter, as discussed in Curtis White's polemical *The Middle Mind* (2003).

2. In a subsequent book, I plan to develop the ideas of the epilogue of the present volume and comment on the contemporary relevance of moderation in today's politics.

3. I use here the phrase coined by Judith Shklar in her essay with the same title, originally published in 1989 and reprinted in Shklar (1998). The concept of "liberalism of fear" was also analyzed in Williams (2005).

4. The title of a famous book by Schlesinger originally published in 1949 and reprinted later in several editions.

5. On Keynes's middle way, see Skidelsky, 1994: 218–41.

6. Ortega y Gasset as quoted in Marías, 1970: 237.

7. A caveat is in order here. I do *not* seek to offer a transcendental ideal of moderation, nor do I intend to make a case for an "eternal" moderation that might exist everywhere as a permanent political option. My goal is only to highlight a few relevant faces of moderation in the history of the twentieth-century political thought.

8. Michnik, for example, might be described as both a moderate revolutionary and a revolutionary moderate.

Chapter 1

1. I note in passing that the epigraph to Schlesinger's *The Vital Center* (1962) contains the same fragment from Yeats's famous poem.

2. Also see the surprisingly similar account of the aftermath of the revolution in Corcyra given by Thucydides in *The History of the Peloponnesian War*, 3.82.3–5 (Thucydides, 1996: 199–200).

3. This form of tyrannophilia was analyzed by Lilla (2001).

4. On the distinction between "weak" and "strong" virtues, see Bobbio, 2000: 26.

5. On this issue, see Lake (1982) and Shagan (2011). They argued that moderation did function as a "profoundly coercive tool of social, religious, and political power" and that concepts such as "moderation," the "golden mean," and the "middle way" became a controversial "moral language by which power in state, Church, and society was justified" in early modern England (Shagan, 2011: 3).

6. Also see Craiutu, 2012c: 13–32.

7. See Plato, *The Republic*, 329a–e (trans. T. Griffith).

8. See Smith (2013). An analysis of the chances of moderation in the Middle East can be found in Muasher (2009). Backes (2010) offered a pertinent analysis of extremism from the perspective of the *Begriffsgeschichte* (history of concepts) school. Another older title deserves a brief mention here. Hartshorne (1987) articulated a "philosophy of the middle way," but it left out politics almost entirely. Only four pages of the book were devoted to political moderation. Susan Haack's *Manifesto of a Passionate Moderate* (1999) is equally uninterested in political moderation and is a collection of disparate essays on various philosophical and epistemological questions.

9. See Strauss, 1975: 39.

10. Nietzsche, 1967: 159. On Nietzsche's critique of moderation, also see Clor, 2008: 90–95.

11. See Goodheart, 2001: 49–50.

12. Weil also added: "Equilibrium alone destroys and annuls force. Social order can be nothing but an equilibrium of forces" (1997: 224).

13. I borrow here Camus's own words from the preface to his Algerian chronicles included in *Actuelles III* (Camus, 1974: 115). On Camus as social critic, see Walzer, 2002: 136–52.

14. See Toscano (2010) and Olson's defense of "democratic fanaticism" in 2007: 685–701. Both authors challenge us to revisit the common pejorative association of zealotry and fanaticism with irrationality, intolerance, fundamentalism, and terrorism.

15. I borrow this phrase from Friedman (2003).

16. The title of one of Martin Luther King Jr.'s most famous sermons (republished in King, 2010: 1–10.

17. For an overview of Steinhardt's life and writings, see Craiutu (1997b) and (2012a).

18. Camus, 1956: 301. Note the affinity between Camus and Simone Weil on the need for balance, equilibrium, and social harmony (see Weil, 1997: 223–31).

19. As Shils argued, "Good manners in direct relationships of individuals in the public sphere are not civility. . . . Good manners, courtesy, temperate speech in relationships face-to-face, cannot be identical with the civility which is a part of civil society" (1997: 80). On civility, also see Calhoun (2000) and the essays collected in the volumes edited by Rouner (2000) and Sarat (2014).

20. See Shils, 1997: 80.

21. I return to this concept in Chapter 6 and the epilogue.

22. According to Shils, "moral separatism arises from the sharp, stable, and unbridgeable dualism of ideological politics which makes the most radical and uncompromising distinction between good and evil, left and right, national and unnational, American and un-American. Admixtures are intolerable, and where they exist they are denied as unreal, misleading, or unstable" (1997: 28). Also: "The ideological outlook is preoccupied with the evil of the world as it exists; it believes in the immiscibility of good and evil. It distinguishes sharply between the children of light and the children of darkness" (1997: 37).

23. Might moderation sometimes promote "rotten" compromises? To answer this question one must examine the complex relationship between moderation and compromise. One can be a radical or extremist, and still engage in compromises without being a moderate or adopting a moderate tone. At the same time, moderates often (though not always) recommend and justify compromises for the sake of restoring balance in society. On compromise, see Margalit (2009), Gutmann and Thompson (2012), and Fumurescu (2013).

24. This section and the next draw upon and develop some arguments from Craiutu (2015a).

25. See Brown's general introduction to Halifax, 1989: 1: xix–xliii; also Goodheart, 2013: xii–xiii.

26. Halifax, 1969: 50. For additional information about the various meanings given to the word "trimmer" in seventeenth-century England, see Halifax, 1989: 1:42–43.

27. See Sunstein, 2009: 1065–68. He sees trimmers as committed to "clarity" and minimalists as committed to leaving many issues unresolved (2009: 1081). The trimmers discussed in this book point to a different conclusion. They acknowledge that the majority of moral, social, and political issues we face are hazy and bound to remain unresolved.

28. As quoted in Hamburger, 1966: 6n83.

29. Aristotle, *Nicomachean Ethics*, 1106b17–34 (trans. Terence Irwin).

30. I elaborate on this distinction in Chapter 5.

31. Goodheart, 2001: 49. He added that "a trimmer's party is something of an oxymoron" and the choices and actions of trimmers always have "a provisional and skeptical cast" (2001: 49; 50).

32. See Halifax, 1969: 54.

33. Halifax, 1969: 101; also see the following statement: "Our Trimmer is far from idolatry in other things, in one thing only he cometh near it; his country is in some degree his idol" (1969: 96).

34. Halifax, 1969: 54; also see 1969: 210.

35. The metaphors of the "priest" and the "jester" (borrowed from the writings of Leszek Kołakowski) are discussed in Chapter 6.

36. See Ortega y Gasset, 1958: 142, 145.

37. On the "captive mind," see the classic book (with this title) of Czeslaw Miłosz (1955).

Chapter 2

1. Claude Lévi-Strauss, "Aron était un esprit droit," in Aron, 1985a: 122.

2. As quoted in Baverez, 2005: 385.

3. Kissinger ended his foreword with these words: "It was an honor to have been his contemporary" (Kissinger in Aron, 1990: xii).

4. In the United States, the situation was somewhat different. Here, Aron's writings were translated and read during the Cold War, at least by political scientists interested in war and international relations and sociologists studying the nature of modern industrial societies. It did not go unnoticed that Aron understood and appreciated what America did during the Cold War in defense of liberty, in spite of the errors of its foreign policy in Vietnam and Latin America. Yet, Aron repeatedly referred to the United States as an "imperial republic" and claimed that some of its foreign policy initiatives historically bore part of the responsibility for the conflicts and unrest in Latin America and in the Pacific.

5. I have previously commented on this metaphor in Craiutu (2007).

6. For more details, see Baverez, 2005: 496–500.

7. In this section, I draw upon and develop some of the arguments originally presented in Westler and Craiutu (2015).

8. On Aron and Germany, see Oppermann (2008).

9. See Aron, 2005: 209–10. All quotations from this book are from the Gallimard edition (Quarto series); the translations are mine, unless noted otherwise.

10. In his memoirs, Aron recalled the words of a German colleague: "You will always be a spectator, a critical spectator, you will not have the courage to commit yourself to action that carries the movement of crowds and of history" (1990: 49).

11. See "Aron's essay "L'avenir des religions séculières," in Aron, 1985a: 369–83.

12. Aron's "États democratiques et états totalitaires" was published in Aron, 2005: 55–106. It was translated into English and included as an afterword to Aron, 1997b: 325–47. For more details on this important text, see Mahoney, 2011: 165–67. Aron's comparison between the Nazi and the Soviet regimes was further developed in *Democracy and Totalitarianism*; following the critique advanced by Alain Besançon in "On the Difficulty of Defining the Soviet Regime" (1976), Aron revised his thesis and concluded in his *Memoirs* that communism was no less hateful to him than Nazism.

13. See Aron, 2005: 77. The notion of heroism was also mentioned by Jacques Maritain in the public debate that followed Aron's lecture (Aron, 2005: 78).

14. See Aron, 2005: 137.

15. See Aron, 2005: 137; also see Westler and Craiutu (2015).

16. Benda, 1955: 21. On Benda as social critic, see Walzer, 2002: 29–44.

17. The phrase is from Marx's *Nationalökonomie und Philosophie* as quoted in Wilkinson, 1981: 90.

18. This passage is taken from Merleau-Ponty's *Humanisme et terreur* as quoted in Wilkinson, 1981: 92.

19. See Coole, 2007: 56.

20. *Apud* Trilling, 1973: 123.

21. See Schumpeter, 1950: 127–28.

22. On this issue, see Aron, 1990: 214–25; 2001: 210–12.

23. On this issue, also see Craiutu (2007).

24. Pierre Manent also insists on Aron's debt to Aristotle in his foreword to Aron, 2013: 5–26.

25. "Evasion of a decision about the Soviet Union, or a combination of yes and no," Aron wrote, "is quite obviously a violation of the imperative of commitment" (1990: 221).

26. Aron refused to think in black-and-white terms even when judging the degree of guilt of Marshal Pétain during World War II. This was certainly not a case of moral indecision or lack of moral clarity on Aron's part. As both a Jew and a French citizen, he could have never endorsed a regime that had in fact been imposed by the Nazis and allowed for the deportation of the Jews. For more details, see Aron, 1997b: 82.

27. Aron, 1997b: 162, 164–66. Also see Judt's introduction to Aron, 2002a: xvii–xx.

28. Aron wrote: "As for the philosophy of history, whether it derives from Bossuet or Hegel, Marx or Toynbee, it is at best regarded more as a literary than a scientific exercise, fit perhaps for writers but not for respectable thinkers" (2002a: 463). On Aron's understanding of history and his intellectual dialogue with Spengler and Toynbee, see Simon-Nahum (2015).

29. See Simon-Nahum, 2015: 113.

30. See Aron, 1984: 248.

31. See Aron, 1984: 243.

32. See Michnik, 1998: 326. On this issue, also see Aron, 1997b: 263.

33. In this section, I am drawing upon and developing the arguments originally presented in Craiutu (2011).

34. Sartre's text, "Les Bastilles de Raymond Aron" was published in *Le Nouvel Observateur* (June 19, 1968).

35. Aron, 2005: 618. Aron's *La Révolution introuvable* was reprinted in Aron (2005); all translations from this book are mine. The English translation of *The Elusive Revolution* by Gordon Clough is occasionally inaccurate.

36. The first one to describe the events of 1968 as a psychodrama had been no one else than a man of the Left such as Alexandre Kojève. For all their ideological differences, Kojève was on good terms with Aron. He called Aron on May 29, 1968 to assure him that the unfolding events were not a revolution—after all, nobody wanted to kill anyone, Kojève remarked—but rather "a ruissellement de connerie" (Kojève as quoted in Baverez, 2005: 388). For an account of the larger implications of the 1968 moment in France, see Wolin, 2010: 70–108, 350–70.

37. As quoted in Aron, 1990: 313.

38. See Aron, 2005: 658; 1990: 314.

39. Here is what Aron wrote in his articles from that period: "Aujourd'hui, dans l'Université comme dans la République, un impératif et un seul: en finir avec la mascarade révolutionnaire, avec les comités d'action, les assemblées plenières et les assemblées générales, caricatures au troisième degré de la Commune jacobine, en bref, revenir à la légalité . . . pour permettre enfin la distinction entre ceux qui veulent reformer et ceux qui veulent manipuler" (2005: 755). Also: "Il importe d'abord restaurer le sens de la légitimité démocratique, c'est-à-dire, en notre siècle, de la legitimité électorale, seule protection contre la guerre civile et le totalitarisme" (2005: 732–33).

40. One of Furet's articles on Aron from 1959 was titled "Raymond Aron, professeur d'une droite qui ne l'écoute pas" (Furet, 2007: 301–5).

41. See Aron, 1997b: 257.

42. As quoted in Aron, 1990: 460.

43. See Aron's essay "Marx's Messianism and Its Misadventures" in Aron, 1985b: 137–64. On Aron and Marx, also see Craiutu (2015b) and Mesure (2015).

44. Here is Aron's self-portrait from a speech on the occasion of his admission to the Institute (Academy of Moral and Political Sciences) in 1965: "Un sans parti, dont les opinions heurtent tout à tour les uns et les autres, d'autant plus insupportable qu'il se veut modéré avec excès, et qu'il dissimule ses passions sous des arguments" (as quoted in Baverez, 2005: 338). Also see Aron, 1997b: 301.

45. This statement appeared in Ortega's "Prologue" to the French edition of *La rebelión de las masas* and was published in English as a chapter, "Unity and Diversity of Europe," in *Toward a Philosophy of History* (Ortega y Gasset, 2002: 43–83). The claim is on p. 70 of that edition.

46. This aspect of Aron's personality was precisely what made him appealing to two younger readers who although they did not share his political preferences, decided to invite him to dialogue in December 1980: "Ce qui nous a peut-être le plus séduit chez Raymond Aron c'est le caractere anti-conformiste, par rapport aux schemas de droite et de gauche, de ses analyses des grands événements contemporains" (Missika and Wolton's introduction to Aron, 1981: 16).

47. Aron, 1997b: 101. In turn, de Gaulle perceived the differences that separated him from Aron. In a conversation with Malraux, the General acknowledged that Aron was never a Gaullist attached to him by a kind of "feudal" tie.

48. These are Pierre Hassner's words as quoted by Pierre Manent in a dialogue with Nicolas Baverez, "Raymond Aron, le dernier philosophe des Lumières," published in *Le Figaro*, October 17, 2003, marking the passing of two decades since Aron's death.

49. Aron, 1990: 256. The phrase is taken from an article of Aron in which he commented on

de Gaulle's constitutional plans. The expression "absolute and limited" came from Charles Maurras.

50. In Aron's view, one of its expressions is the claim that the principles of the ideal order are identical only with a certain set of institutions and incompatible with all others (2001: 332–34). Also see Aron, 1970: 49–99, where he discussed the differences between "formal" and "real" freedoms.

51. Aron, 1984: 243.

52. On this issue, also see Mahoney, 2011: 177–81.

53. See Aron, 1998a: 71–136. For the English translation, see Aron (1970).

54. In the preface to *Essais sur les libertés*, Aron asked in a Tocquevillian tone: "In a society in which conditions will be more and more equal, will freedom be safeguarded? . . . In a society that is carried along by the dynamism of economic growth and technological progress, what will become of freedom?" (1970: 7).

55. See Aron, 1994: 82. This is from Aron's essay "The Liberal Definition of Liberty: Concerning F. A. Hayek's *The Constitution of Liberty*."

56. See Aron, 1998a: 228–30. On Aron's attitude toward Hayek, see Mahoney, 1992: 87–88, 118–19. Interestingly, a similar critique was advanced by Oakeshott (1991: 26).

57. Aron, 1994: 85; also see 1994: 83. For an interpretation of this topic, see Mahoney, 1992: 73–90.

58. A similar position was held by Norberto Bobbio as discussed in Chapter 4.

59. See Aron, 1970: 158. On Aron's critique of presenting the rule of law or political participation as the *single* legitimate criterion of political liberty, also see 1970: 127–33.

60. Aron, 1970: 48. Also: "It is essential to achieve a compromise between conflicting demands, which carried to extremes, would be totally incompatible" (2001: 21).

61. See Aron, 2013: 54–60.

62. For further discussions of Aron and convergence theory, see Mahoney, 1992: 65, 113; Manent, 1994: 25–26.

63. Aron's interlocutor was Samuel Pisar. Aron's text, "Réponse à un missionaire de la foi" (*Le Figaro*, June 16–17, 1973) was republished in Aron, 1997a: 1229–31.

64. See Pierre Manent's essay "Raymond Aron—Political Educator," in Aron, 1994: 1–23.

65. On the relationship between Aron and Sartre, see Sirinelli (1995).

66. See the chapter on Tocqueville in Aron, 1998b, I: 237–302.

67. "We only know and can only know but fragments of the milieu in which we live" (Aron, 1975: 212).

68. See Aron, 2002a: 46. On Aron's debt to Kant, see Hassner (2015).

69. I borrow this phrase from Judt (1998).

70. See Aron, 1975: 159.

71. Note here the similarity between Aron and Wilhelm Röpke's defense of economic humanism (Röpke, 1998: 1–35).

72. See Bloom (1985) and Fawcett (2014).

73. For more details on Aron's method, also see Aron, 1997b: 201, 250.

74. For a critique of the French obsession with political engagement, see Judt (1992), especially chapters 1, 3, 6–7.

Chapter 3

1. Berlin as quoted in Ignatieff, 1998: 301.

2. These were Michael Oakeshott's words; the antipathy between the two was reciprocal (see Franco, 2003: 485).

3. These are Berlin's own words from the transcript of a message sent on cassette tape to his biographer, Michael Ignatieff, on December 30, 1996 (Berlin, 2015: 15).

4. Collini, 1997: 3. Also see Cherniss 2006: xxxvi–xxxvii and the essays from the special issue dedicated to Berlin in *European Journal of Political Theory*, 12: 1 (January 2013).

5. *Apud* Ignatieff, 1998: 233.

6. On Berlin's moderation, see Cherniss, 2013: 112–30; I have reviewed this book in Craiutu (2014).

7. On Cold War liberalism, see Cherniss, 2013: 67–87; Hacohen, 2010: 502–10; Müller (2010 and 2011). On Berlin's reaction to the critics who accused him of engaging in Cold War rhetoric, see Berlin (2015).

8. Also see Cherniss, 2013: 14–20.

9. Berlin, 1998b: 14; also see Berlin, 1999: 35–39.

10. See Berlin, 1998b: 13–14. Note the similarity here with Oakeshott's description of the secularized version of the "politics of faith" (Oakeshott, 1993a: 93–94).

11. Berlin, "A Letter to George Kennan," in Berlin, 2002: 341; also see 2002: 337.

12. See Berlin, 2006: 153–54.

13. On this issue, see Cherniss, 2013: 18–19.

14. On the romantic notion of liberty, see Berlin, 2006: 170–77.

15. On Berlin's theory of pluralism, see Gray, 1996: 38–75.

16. As quoted in Cherniss, 2013: 200.

17. Other thinkers whom Berlin placed in the pluralist camp were Montesquieu, Giambattista Vico, Johann G. Herder, and, to some extent, Max Weber.

18. On this issue, see Gray, 1996: 61ff.

19. On this issue, see Berlin's important letter to Alan Dudley from March 17, 1948, in Berlin, 2009: 44–48.

20. See Berlin, 2009: 240. Berlin published an article about Stalin in 1952 under the pseudonym "Utis," which means "nobody" in Greek.

21. Berlin, 2009: 100. Note the similarity with Raymond Aron's position on this issue discussed in Chapter 2.

22. See Cherniss, 2013: 7. It is a pity Berlin passed away just as the *Black Book of Communism* was being published in France. It is impossible to know for sure what he would have made of it.

23. Berlin, 2009: 350. On Berlin and Hayek, see Cherniss, 2013: 181–82.

24. Worth noting is the similarity with Adam Michnik's views on this issue discussed in Chapter 6.

25. For an extensive discussion of Berlin's thought in the context of Cold War liberalism, see Cherniss, 2013: 67–87, 170–87.

26. A similar perspective can be found in "Extremism as a Way of Life" included in Ortega y Gasset, 1958: 138–58.

27. For a recent account, see Fawcett (2014).

28. I borrow this term from Emerson's essay "The Conservative" published in 1841.

29. See Popper, 1964: vii. Popper's most famous political book, *The Open Society and Its Enemies*, was originally published in 1945 (fifth ed., 1971).

30. This quote is from an essay published by Schlesinger in the *New York Times* in 1948 in which he summarized the main tenets of his book, *The Vital Center*. In 1997, he had a chance to revisit the themes of his book in an interesting article published in the *Slate*. Taking some distance from Bill Clinton, Schlesinger argued that his middle of the road of the third way doctrines was not the vital center as he conceived it; it was rather "the dead center." In the same article, he endorsed a bold center and vigorous leadership: "Still, if you want to change things, you can count on the hostility of those who benefit from the way things are. No great president was a middle-of-the-roader. 'Judge me,' said FDR, 'by the enemies I have made'" (Schlesinger, 1997). Schlesinger's political eclecticism is discussed in Lester, 2014: 198–210.

31. "People who know they alone are right find it hard to compromise," Schlesinger wrote (1962: 174), "and compromise is the strategy of democracy."

32. On the similarities and differences between Berlin and Talmon, see Cherniss, 2013: 172–75.

33. See Hacohen, 2010: 450.

34. See Müller, 2010: 55–57.

35. Shklar quotes here from the poet C. Day Lewis; see Kateb, 1998: ix. For a critique of Shklar's account of ordinary virtues, see Elshtain (1985).

36. See Hess, 2014: 111.

37. Shklar as quoted in Hess, 2014: 99.

38. As quoted in Berlin, 2002: 92.

39. Berlin as quoted by Aileen Kelly in her posthumous tribute reprinted in Berlin, 1999: 137.

40. "To crush all diversity and even conflict in the interest of uniformity is to crush life itself" (Berlin, 2013: 49).

41. In the sense of the feverish affirmation of one single value or principle at the expense of all others.

42. Berlin as quoted in Ignatieff, 1998: 234.

43. Schumpeter as quoted in Berlin, 2002: 217.

44. Berlin himself commented on the challenges of being caught in the middle. His statement can be found in Ignatieff, 1998: 246.

45. Berlin, 1997: 25. On this issue, also see Berlin's essay "Realism in Politics" in Berlin, 2000: 134–42; also see Cherniss, 2013: 113–21 and Hanley (2004).

46. Berlin as quoted in Cherniss, 2013: 80.

47. Berlin, 2008: 192. I am using here the words chosen by Berlin to describe Herzen.

48. See, for example, Bell (1976). Nevertheless, Berlin's ideas overlapped to some extent with Bell's analysis of the pluralism of spheres characteristic of modern society.

49. On anti-managerial liberalism, see Cherniss, 2013: 88–111.

50. See Berlin, 2008: 302.

51. As a matter of fact, Ignatieff remarked that "no one could tell where Berlin started and Herzen, Turgenev, Tolstoy, or Disraeli stopped" (1998: 224). On the similarities between Berlin and Turgenev, also see Ignatieff, 1998: 256–57.

52. One example was Berlin's essay on Joseph de Maistre (originally published in *The Crooked Timber of Humanity*) whom he interpreted as a precursor of fascism and Nazism.

53. "What stands up to the ravages of time," Berlin once wrote to the Labour politician Richard Crossman, "is intellectual depth and power" (as quoted in Kelly, 2013: 9).

54. In his foreword to Shklar, 1998: xvii.

55. For a similar point, see Niebuhr, 1960: 151–52.

Chapter 4

1. Bobbio, 2001: 28; 30. For a brief presentation of Bobbio's life and works, see his obituary published in the *Guardian* on January 13, 2004: http://www.theguardian.com/news/2004/jan/13/guardianobituaries.obituaries. Another excellent portrait of Bobbio can be found in Einaudi (1994). In the main body of this chapter, I am quoting, where applicable, from the existing English translations of Bobbio's books. The translations from the other books of Bobbio available only in Italian (especially *Politica e cultura*, 1955) are mine.

2. Bobbio, 2001: 38. The title of one of his essays was "Il dovere di essere pessimisti" included in Bobbio (1981). Today, Bobbio wrote four decades ago, pessimism is "a civil duty" (Bobbio, 1981: 161).

3. For more information, see Bobbio's "Intellectual Autobiography" in Bobbio, 2001: 44–59. Bobbio wrote a letter to Mussolini in 1935 to dissociate himself from some extremist antifascist circles and protect his fledgling teaching career. The letter was published in *Panorama* in 1992 and caused him a great deal of shame and suffering. Excerpts from the letter can be found in this detailed account published in the influential newspaper *La Repubblica*: http://ricerca.repubblica.it/repubblica/archivio/repubblica/1992/06/16/bobbio-tanti-anni-fa.html (accessed September 28, 2015). Special thanks to Nadia Urbinati for calling my attention to this point.

4. This was the most important political party to which Bobbio belonged. In 1968, he joined the ill-fated Unitary Socialist Party that resulted from the reunification of the Socialists and the Social Democrats. The Center-Left did not hold for a long time as the electorate moved to the Right in response to the student unrest that began in Turin and then moved to the rest of the country.

5. Bobbio, 2002: 68. Among the other intellectuals in the party were Guido de Ruggiero (1888–1948), a prominent historian of European liberalism and rector of the University of Rome (1943–44), and Luigi Salvatorelli (1886–1974), a respected historian and publicist.

6. Guido Calogero was one of the leading exponents of this current of thought (that began to crystallize around 1936), along with Aldo Capitini at the Scuola Normale Superiore di Pisa. A comprehensive selection of his political writings can be found in Calogero (1972) which includes the two original manifestos of liberalsocialism from 1940 and 1941 (pp. 199–226) as well as Calogero's review of Rosselli's book on liberal socialism (pp. 231–36).

7. On Rosselli's liberal socialism, see Nadia Urbinati's introductory study to Rosselli (1994). Rosselli's political manifesto, "The Revolutionary Program of *Giustizia e Libertà*," was drafted in 1932.

8. The Italian thinkers of the period, starting with Benedetto Croce and Luigi Einaudi, made a famous distinction between social liberalism and *liberismo*, understood as laissez-faire capitalism, allowing only a small role for state intervention in economy.

9. After the fall from power of the Parri government in November 1945, the leader of the Christian Democrats, Alcide de Gasperi, became prime minister a month later. On the history of the Action Party, see De Luna (1982); Bobbio, 2001: 51–52; Bobbio, 2002: 65–70. On Italy in the larger context of early postwar Europe, see Wilkinson, 1981: 218–38; Judt, 2005: 65–66, 78–79.

10. See De Luna (1982) and Bobbio, 2002: 66–68.

11. See Bobbio, 2002: 114, 116. The Schmitt-Bobbio letters (nine written in German by Schmitt and eleven written in Italian by Bobbio) were edited and published by Piet Tommissen in *Diritto e Cultura* (5: 1, January–June 1995).

12. On Solari's teaching inspired by the civic role of the philosophy of law, see Bobbio, 2002: 21.

13. Bobbio was awarded the prestigious Balzan International Plan (1994) and the Agnelli International Prize (1995).

14. On the intellectual dialogue with Kelsen, see Bobbio, 2001: 74–79.

15. For a short history of liberal socialism in European perspective, see Audier (2006). An anthology covering various national traditions of liberal socialism was edited (in French) by Canto-Sperber and Urbinati in 2003.

16. Some of Bobbio's most important articles from the 1970s were collected in *Le ideologie e il potere in crisi* (1981).

17. Similar reservations about the value of journalism were expressed by Raymond Aron.

18. This appears with clarity in Bobbio (2000). It is worth noting here Bobbio's affinity with Judith Shklar's "liberalism of fear," discussed briefly in Chapter 3.

19. See Bobbio, 1981: 93–95; 1993: 215.

20. See Bobbio, 1993: 215–16. Contrary to Machiavelli, Bobbio believed that "il mezzo malvagio corrompe anche il migliore dei fini" (1981: 95).

21. See the essay "Che cos'è il pluralismo" in Bobbio, 1981: 3–7. An excellent summary of Bobbio's political philosophy can be found in *Teoria generale della politica* (1999). Edited by Michelangelo Bovero and organized in six parts, it explores the legacy of the classics, the relationship between politics, morality, and law, values and ideology, democracy, the rights of man, and peace and war.

22. "I have always considered myself a man of the left and therefore, for me, the term 'left' has always had a positive connotation" (Bobbio, 1996: 82–83). Bobbio believed that the division between the Left and the Right is not arbitrary and rests upon a set of different conceptions of a broad range of topics from economy to culture, education, and religion. On Bobbio's conception of the Left and Right, see Anderson (2005).

23. Bobbio noted, among others, the contribution of German Ordoliberals such as Wilhelm Röpke on the "third way" debate (Bobbio, 1981: 142).

24. See Bobbio, 1981: 126.

25. See Urbinati, 2003: 585–86.

26. As quoted in Bobbio, 1995: 166.

27. Bobbio argued: "We are faced with the great problem of our times: the division of the world into opposing blocs. The European Society of Culture does not acknowledge this division. Its members have expressed their will not to be subject to one or the other and favour an attitude that we have defined as 'both over here and over there.' . . . We must always distinguish between ordinary politics and the politics of culture, which is another way of saying 'Render unto Caesar that which is Caesar's and render unto God what is God's.' It is not a question of synthesizing opposites but transcending them. It is not a question of reconciling on a higher plane what is good in one with what is good in the other, which is the illusion held by the Third Force. The Society is not a third force. It challenges the reason of state with its reason of the conscience. . . . So it is . . . a moral force" (Bobbio, 2001: 93).

28. See Bobbio, 1955: 34–35; 2002: 8.

29. See Bobbio, 1955: 34, 36.

30. See the statement (in French) given in Bobbio, 1955: 34.

31. See Bobbio, 1955: 41, 43.

32. The task is, in Bobbio's words, "di rispondere, ai seminatori di discordie, col supremo tentativo di invitare gli uomini, non ancora accecati dal fanatismo, al colloquio, e di lasciare ai guerreri, ai politici, agli uomini di parte e di passione, l'iniziativa e la responsabilità delle crociate" (1955: 46).

33. See Bobbio, 2002: 145.

34. As quoted in Bobbio, 2002: 89; the original text appeared in *Italia civile*, published in 1964.

35. Bobbio as quoted in Urbinati (2003); the passage is taken from Bobbio's essay "Politica ideologica." Also see the preface in Bobbio (1969).

36. In Bobbio's words: "Rifiutare di porsi i problemi in termini di rigide alternative: 'o di qua o di là,' no significa risolverli in termini di bassi accomodamenti, 'un piede di qua, un piede di là'" (Bobbio, 1955: 19).

37. Bobbio wrote: "Non vi è per l'intellettuale che una forma di tradimento o di diserzione: l'accettazione degli argomenti dei 'politici' senza discuterli, la complicità con la propaganda, l'uso disonesto di un linguaggio volutamente ambiguo, l'abdicazione della propria intelligenza all'opinione settaria, in una parola il rifiuto di 'comprendere'" (1955: 20).

38. Writes Bobbio: "Al di là del dovere di entrare nella lotta, c'è, per l'uomo di cultura, il diritto di non accettare i termini della lotta cosí come sono posti, di discuterli, di sottoporli alla critica dell'indagine" (Bobbio, 1955: 17). Bobbio went on to cite the following passage from Gramsci: "Comprendere e valutare realisticamente la posizione e la ragioni dell'avversario . . . significa appunto *essersi liberati dalla prigione delle ideologie* (*nel senso deteriore, di cieco fanatismo ideologico*), cioè porsi da un punto di vista 'critico,' l'unico fecondo nella ricerca scientifica" (in Bobbio, 1955: 17, emphases added).

39. It could also be interpreted to mean "Neither for Them, nor Against Them."

40. See Urbinati, 2003: 585.

41. Bobbio, 2001: 51; also Bobbio, 1995: 151–52.

42. See Bobbio, 1993: 213ff.; and Bobbio, 2002: 83.

43. Also see Bellamy, 2014: 260–64.

44. On Bobbio's critique of Marx's views on the relationship between democracy and dictatorship, see Urbinati, 2003: 588. On the use of nondemocratic means to promote democratic ideals, see Bobbio's essays, "Difesa della libertà" and "Dialogo tra un liberale e un communista" (1955: 47–57 and 58–71), and "Ancora sullo stalinismo: alcune questioni di teoria" written in 1956 and republished in Violi, 1997: 28–29.

45. See Bobbio, 1955: 170–71.

46. The key text here is "Della libertà dei moderni comparata a quella dei posteri," included in Bobbio, 1955: 160–94.

47. The original text, "Libertà e potere," was reprinted in Bobbio (1955: 269–82), and this quote appears on pp. 281–82. I use here the translation provided by Anderson (1988, emphases added).

48. A responsible intellectual, Bobbio argued, can only endorse "i diritti del dubbio" against the pretensions of dogmatism, propaganda, and blind faith (1955: 16).

49. This point is made by Bobbio in his important essay "Intellettuali e vita politica italiana," originally written in 1954 and included in Bobbio, 1955: 121–36.

50. Bobbio wrote: "L'importante è che l'uomo di cultura, quando è impegnato nella sua funzione che è quella di capire, non si lasci frastornare dagli zelatori di ogni ortodossia o dai pervertiti di ogni propaganda" (1955: 20).

51. See Bobbio, 1955: 15.

52. In Bobbio's own words, the intellectuals' duty is "no sottomettersi supinamente alla verità di una parte sola" (1955: 9).

53. See Bobbio, 1987: 72.

54. See Bobbio, 2000: 34.

55. See Bobbio, 2000: 26.

56. See Bobbio, 2000: 4.

57. Bobbio, 2000: 29. On the question of "meekness or mildness," see the justification for choosing *mitezza* in Bobbio, 2000: 23–24.

58. As quoted in Bobbio, 2000: 2, from a commentary made by Giuliano Pontara on Bobbio's praise of meekness (Pontara, 1994). In *La personalità nonviolenta* (1996), Pontara listed the capacity for dialogue and meekness among the ten characteristics of the nonviolent personality, the others being the rejection of violence, the capacity to identify violence, the capacity for empathy, the rejection of authority, trust in others, courage, abnegation, and patience (Pontara, 1996: 40). The disposition to dialogue and meekness are discussed on pp. 58–63 of this volume.

59. See the description of the meek by Pontara as quoted in Bobbio, 2000: 2.

60. Pontara as quoted in Bobbio, 2000: 2–3.

61. Bobbio, 2000: 32. The same applies to "altruism, kindness, generosity, and mercy, all of which are social as well as unilateral virtues" (2000: 32).

62. See Bobbio, 1955: 189. He also wrote: "Il tempo dunque sembra dar ragione non a coloro che vedevano o tutto rosso o tutto nero, ma a quelli che non hanno avuto timore di insinuar qualche dubbio nei troppo eccitati difensori dell'una o dell'altra parte. A coloro, vorrei dire, che accusati, a volta a volta, di aver fatto il gioco di questa o quella parte, si vien dimostrando al contrario che stavano facendo . . . il gioco di nessuno, che è poi il vantaggio di tutti" (1955: 10–11).

63. This aspect of Bobbio's personality and writings is well discussed in Einaudi, 1994: 50–51.

Chapter 5

1. Surprisingly, the concept of moderation does not appear on the index of a few important books on Oakeshott's political thought: Franco (1990), Gerencser (2000), and Campbell Corey (2006). Nor is moderation mentioned in the index of the two recent companions on Oakeshott edited by Franco and Marsh (2012) and Podoksik (2012).

2. "What I write," Oakeshott confessed (2014: 154), "is merely a kind of justification of my temperament. If I wrote it to persuade others, I should be guilty of self-contradiction: I write it to persuade myself, & because no man can be said to be master of himself until he had made clear to himself." Also see the following self-portrait: "Oh! If only I knew what I wanted! . . . My mind is a picture without a design; a chaos of warring desires. I know what I want. I want freedom. But since I can only grope for freedom blindly, . . . I cannot be said to know what I want" (2014: 179). Grant (2012) has been at work writing a biography of Oakeshott that promises to give the full measure of his complex personality.

3. On Oakeshott and Arendt, see the brief discussion in Beiner, 2014: 36–40.

4. See Gamble, 2012: 166.

5. Oakeshott as quoted in Franco, 1990: 141–42.

6. See Oakeshott, 1993b: 91.

7. Oakeshott 2014: 315. The idea that "politics are an inferior form of human activity" (2014: 303) appears in many entries in Oakeshott's notebooks. On the limited and secondary role of politics, see 2014: 315–16, 390–93.

8. See Oakeshott's introduction to Hobbes's *Leviathan*, reprinted in Oakeshott, 1991: 221–94; also see Timothy Fuller's "Introduction" to Oakeshott (1991) and Gerencser, 2000: 77–98.

9. For an analysis of the relationship between Oakeshott's skeptical politics and his theory of civil association, see Gerencser, 2000: 125–52; Campbell Corey, 2006: 175–88.

10. See Luke O'Sullivan's introduction to Oakeshott, 2008: 31–32, and Devigne, 2012: 283.

11. On this issue, see Franco, 2003; and Villa, 2012: 335–37. Oakeshott once introduced Berlin to a crowd at the London School of Economics as "a Paganini of ideas." In turn, Berlin acknowledged privately that he never bothered to read Oakeshott's works (*apud* Franco, 1990: 485).

12. See Oakeshott, 2014: 121, 144.

13. See Oakeshott, 1975: 174.

14. Note the affinities with Hayek's position on this issue in *The Constitution of Liberty* and *Law, Legislation and Liberty*.

15. Note the similarity on this point between Oakeshott and Shils's views on civility (see Shils, 1997: 340).

16. For a similar view, see Crick, 1964: 54–55.

17. See Oakeshott, 1991: 121, 130. On his critique of rationalism, see Campbell Corey, 2006: 155–64; Franco, 1990: 107–56.

18. On the distinction between technical and practical knowledge, see Oakeshott, 1991: 12–17; also Franco, 1990: 109–15. "The significance of Rationalism," Oakeshott wrote, "is not its recognition of technical knowledge, but its failure to recognize any other: its philosophical error lies in the certainty it attributes to technique and in its doctrine of the sovereignty of technique" (1991: 25).

19. Note here the similarity with Berlin's critique of managerial liberalism; see Cherniss, 2013: 88–95. For a different view that emphasizes the differences between the two thinkers, see Franco, 2003: 486.

20. "A philosophy of life is a meaningless contradiction," Oakeshott once wrote (1933: 54).

21. A good example is Oakeshott's review of Burckhardt's correspondence in Oakeshott, 2008: 69.

22. My argument goes against the interpretation proposed by Gamble: 2012: 154 and Anderson, 2005: 3–28. On the relationship between Oakeshott and the Left, see O'Sullivan (2014: 473–78), who demonstrated that in his youth, Oakeshott had socialist leanings and was influenced by Bernard Bosanquet's reworking of Rousseau's discourse of the general will.

23. See Franco, 1990: 148–50.

24. "Any man who has a passionate interest other than politics will be disposed to be a conservative in politics" (Oakeshott, 2014: 390).

25. Here is a revealing passage: "Some people love life, other are in love with life, but the rare few make love with life in every moment" (Oakeshott, 2014: 415).

26. See Oakeshott, 2014: 354.

27. "I don't know whether I believe in God," he wrote in 1958. "But I believe in the Virgin Mary, Jesus Christ, St Michael and the devil" (2014: 415).

28. For example, there is only one very brief reference to Hume in the Harvard lectures from 1958 on morality and politics in modern Europe.

29. See Oakeshott, 2008: 83; Galston, 2012: 223.

30. "Pieties are fleeting," Oakeshott waxed lyrically, "loyalties evanescent, and the pace of change warns us against too deep attachments" (1991: 414).

31. In his notebooks, Oakeshott once wrote that true happiness "is to be found only in the society of a few indispensable friends" (2014: 185).

32. Also see Franco, 1990: 138–40.

33. On this issue, see Oakeshott's essay, "The Political Economy of Freedom" in Oakeshott, 1991: 384–406; also see Galston (2012) and O'Sullivan's introduction to Oakeshott, 2008: 19.

34. See Oakeshott, 1991: 27.

35. On the distinction between government as an activity of primary and secondary order, see Oakeshott's essay "The Concept of Government in Modern Europe," in Oakeshott, 2008: 98–100.

36. Oakeshott remarked that there are many types of conservatives around, even "conservative" Stalinists, and the vagueness of this term makes its use problematic and confusing.

37. See Oakeshott, 2006: 26.

38. Oakeshott, 1996: 46. On the distinction between the two types of politics, see Campbell Corey, 2006: 164–74.

39. See Oakeshott, 1996: 17–18, 70.

40. Also see Fuller's introduction to Oakeshott, 1996: xi.

41. Oakeshott's description of Marxism as a secularized form of the politics of faith can be found in 1993a: 95–96. Note here the overlap with Voegelin's account of the secularization of modern politics and Aron's critique of secular religions. On Oakeshott and Voegelin, see Campbell Corey, 2006: 189–214.

42. See Oakeshott, 1996: 47.

43. See Oakeshott, 1996: 29.

44. "When government is understood as an activity of limitless control, it finds itself with nothing to control. . . . This self-destruction is inherent in the uninhibited character of the politics of faith" (1996: 94).

45. See Oakeshott, 1996: 96.

46. See Oakeshott, 1996: 38.

47. See Oakeshott, 1996: 72.

48. See Oakeshott, 1996: 79; also see Teles and Kaliner (2004) for what a concrete politics of skepticism might entail.

49. See Oakeshott, 1996: 108–11.

50. For more details, see Chapter 1.

51. It is true that centrist parties often claim to promote the spirit of moderation, but most often, theirs is "a spurious moderation which has nothing to do with the mean in action" (Oakeshott, 1996: 124).

52. See Oakeshott, 1996: 124.

53. Oakeshott, 1996: 128.

54. Regarding the last question, it might be profitable to contrast Oakeshott's political

moderation with that of Jacques Maritain (1882–1973), long celebrated (along with Étienne Gilson) as the architect of the Thomistic revival in the twentieth century. The reason for bringing these two thinkers together would be that both of them defended political moderation during their long careers, but they did it from two different perspectives: skepticism and faith. From Maritain's writings, of particular interest here would be *Integral Humanism* (1936) as well as his "A Letter on Independence" (1935), *Man and the State* (1948), and *Principles of a Humanist Politics* (1944).

Chapter 6

1. See, for example, Courtois et al. (1999), Applebaum (2004).

2. György Konrád, a leading Hungarian dissident, described antipolitics as follows: "Antipolitics is the political activity of those who don't want to be politicians and who refuse to share in power. Antipolitics is the emergence of independent forums that can be appealed to against political power; it is a counterpower that cannot take power and does not wish to" (1984: 230–31).

3. Goethe as quoted in Hirschman, 1995: 9.

4. See Jowitt's foreword to Michnik, 1998: xvi.

5. The title of Wilson's review of two books by Michnik in the *New York Review of Books* (Wilson, 2015).

6. See Michnik (2001).

7. See Michnik's essay "The Dilemma" in Michnik, 1998: 68–95, influenced by Kołakowski's essay "The Priest and the Jester."

8. Michnik's star has recently declined, as Polish politics have become once again highly polarized and more ideological.

9. "Maggots and Angels" was one of Michnik's most famous essays included in *Letters from Prison* (1987).

10. The significance of Kołakowski's writings as "a source of hope amidst hopelessness" is discussed in Falk, 2003: 157–65. She also pays attention to Kołakowski's influential essays "The Priest and the Jester" and "Hope and Hopelessness" as well as his book *The Presence of Myth* (1966/1972). The religious side of Kołakowski and its connection with his political skepticism are discussed in Heidrich, 1995: 185–236.

11. The detail is reported in Connelly (2013).

12. See Heidrich, 1995: 302–35.

13. Kołakowski, 1968: 88. His position changed over time. If he initially declared himself "in favor of the jester's philosophy and thus vigilant against any absolute" (1968: 36), he eventually became an ardent defender of the values of the Catholic Church and Pope John Paul II. This evolution is discussed in Connelly (2013) and Heidrich, 1995: 237–335.

14. Kołakowski, 1990: 135. Note here a possible affinity between political moderation (as described in this passage) and Karl Popper's philosophy of science and politics (see Popper, 1964 and 1971).

15. Some have attributed the invention of the term "self-limiting revolution" to the sociologist Jadwiga Staniszkis (who wrote a book on this issue), while others have credited Jacek Kuroń for coining this phrase.

16. Havel must have been familiar with Kołakowski's essay; his seminal "The Power of the Powerless" (1977) had a similar message.

17. Burek as quoted in Michnik, 1993: 205–6.

18. KOR was founded on September 23, 1976, following the repression of the workers' demonstrations in Ursus and Radom earlier that year. The founding document was an "Appeal to Society and to the Authorities of the PRL" made public on September 23. It is reproduced in Lipski, 1985: 467–69, along with the Declaration of the Workers' Defense Committee (Lipski, 1985: 469–72). The movement dissolved on September 23, 1981, after the formation of the Solidarity. On the activities of KOR, the key role of Jacek Kuroń, and the concept of "new evolutionism," see Falk, 2003: 177–92.

19. All these tensions and limits became obvious in the tense negotiations between the Solidarity leaders and the Communist Party after the workers' demonstrations in Bydgoszcz in March 1981 that had dashed the hopes for a three-month moratorium on strikes called for by General Wojciech Jaruzelski, freshly minted as the country's prime minister. Mostly out of prudential considerations that turned out to be quite controversial among his colleagues, Lech Wałęsa decided to call off a national strike for fear of a possible Soviet military intervention to restore order in Poland.

20. Michnik as quoted in Schell, 2004: 373–74, emphases added.

21. Michnik, 1998: 64. He jokingly added about Solidarity: "Its only utopia were the Ten Commandments and the Gospels—except for the commandment about adultery" (1998: 64).

22. See the concrete program in Lipski, 1985: 492–95.

23. For more information, see Lipski, 1985: 208–22.

24. It might be worth saying a few words about Michnik's activity before 1968. In the club that Michnik organized in his high school, he invited as speakers and fellow readers a quite eclectic audience consisting of bishops, philosophers, Marxists, and anti-Marxists. He had always reached out to people from different quarters of life, inviting them to support his projects. Thanks to Irena Grudzińska Gross (who participated in those events) for bringing this detail to my attention.

25. For a similar argument, also see Schell, 2004: 356.

26. "The principle of rejecting hatred," Lipski acknowledged (1985: 71), "was not accepted without resistance." On nonviolence as theory and practice in the case of the Polish opposition, see Falk, 2003: 180–84. The case for nonviolence was clearly made by Michnik in his "Letter from the Gdańsk Prison" (included in 1987: 76–99).

27. On this issue, see Staniszkis, 1984: 137–38.

28. See Malia (1982).

29. I use here the data provided by Malia (1982); also see Falk, 2003: 180–98.

30. These traits are also highlighted in Michnik, 2011: 28. It might be worth mentioning that a significant overlap existed among the Catholic nationalists, the working class, and the intelligentsia groups that composed Solidarity. Another interesting aspect was that many of its members were, at least initially, committed to a romantic vision of a working-class type of socialism adapted to Poland. On these issues, see Staniszkis, 1984: 140–46. She highlighted Solidarity's political moralism, which, in her view, had a strong impact on the activities of the movement. This moralism manifested itself, again on her account, by "a tendency to see politics in black and white terms" and perceive every compromise as "very painful" (1984: 141).

31. The Polish context is discussed in Judt, 2005: 604–8; Garton Ash, 1990a: 25–46, and 1990b: 47–60, 221–26, 286–93, 309–19.

32. As late as 1984, a leading voice in comparative politics, Samuel P. Huntington, declared emphatically that the likelihood of democratic development in Eastern Europe was virtually nil.

The complexity of the political situation in Eastern Europe is highlighted in Judt, 2005: 585–633; and Tismaneanu, 1992; 1998.

33. Consider, for example, the debates on whether the events of 1989 can properly be called revolution or restoration. Various terms were proposed, from "rectifying revolution" to "unfinished revolution" to "refolution," the term coined by Garton Ash for reforms from above in response to the pressure for revolution from below (1990b: 309–24).

34. These are Konrád's own words (1984: 236). In truth, he had a more nuanced view than other former dissidents (1984: 35).

35. See Michnik, 1998: 322.

36. Also see Ost, 1990: 16–17.

37. On this issue, see Dalecki (1997) who emphasized the importance of Michnik's essay, "The Presence of Liberal Values."

38. Lech Wałesa has recently been accused by the new Polish leaders of betraying his fellow anti-Communists and having collaborated with the former secret police in the 1970s. The new accusations (denounced by Wałesa as fabricated) were based on newly released documents obtained from the widow of the last Communist interior minister, the late General Kiszczak. This is not the first attempt to tarnish Wałesa's reputation. An earlier wave of accusations occurred in 2000 when he was officially cleared of any alleged collaboration.

39. I borrow here Antoni Slonimski's phrase as quoted in Schell, 2004: 383. On this issue also see Cherniss, 2014: 356ff.

40. The original text of the Prague Declaration of June 3, 2008, can be found here: http://defendinghistory.com/the-original-prague-declaration-of-3-june-2008 (accessed December 29, 2015). The Prague Declaration of June 2008 (initiated by Václav Havel, among others) also asked that the "many crimes committed in the name of Communism . . . be assessed as crimes against humanity serving as a warning for future generations, in the same way Nazi crimes were assessed by the Nuremberg Tribunal."

41. Michnik's credo was summarized by Paul Wilson as follows: "history is a 'teacher of life'; . . . it is 'always a conversation with the Other, the one who thinks differently, who is differently situated, . . . differently shaped by his or her social position'; . . . 'the truth of history is often polyphonic'; . . . 'historical wounds can only heal in a climate of free debate, in which everyone can cry out about one's own wrongs, pains, and sufferings'; and the core of his beliefs, that history is not just about the past because it is constantly recurring, and not as farce, as Marx had it, but as itself" (Wilson, 2015: 74).

42. See Michnik, 1998: 270.

43. Michnik, 2001: 49, 50. For a different position on lustration and decommunization, see Tismaneanu, 1998: 111–40. On inclusion and the ethics of combating political extremism, see Kirshner (2014) with brief comments on Michnik.

44. On Havel's political philosophy, see Tucker (2000) and Popescu (2012).

45. Havel as quoted in Michnik, 1998: 227.

46. Havel as quoted in Michnik, 1998: 227. He added: "When we're faced with confessions of guilt and expressions of repentance, there ought to be room for forgiveness" (*apud* Michnik, 1998: 227).

47. This passage is taken from an exchange between Adam Michnik and Leon Wieseltier published in the *New Republic*, June 4, 2001: 24.

48. Havel in Michnik, 1998: 229.

49. Michnik, 1993: 180. Also see the essay "What Is Dialogue?" in Michnik, 1993: 172–87.

50. Michnik, 1987: 6. Also: "For me there was a price beyond which we couldn't pay for a compromise, a price that was equal to betrayal" (Michnik, 1998: 63).

51. As quoted in Michnik, 1998: 273.

52. On this issue, also see Cherniss, 2014: 353ff.

53. Mazowiecki as quoted in Michnik, 1993: 183. Falk also quotes this important passage in 2003: 171–72 and offers a discussion of Michnik's views on dialogue (2003: 165–77). On Mazowiecki's social and political thought, see Kosicki (2013).

54. As quoted in Michnik, 1993: 183.

55. For a slightly different view, see Dalecki (1997: 238ff.). The ambiguity of Michnik's position, Dalecki argued, is that the historical examples he invoked can justify both anti-Manichaeism as well as extreme forms of Manichaeism. Dalecki discussed, among other works, Michnik's *On the History of Honor in Poland*, an important book not yet translated into English.

56. His position on the complex Polish-Jewish matters was outlined in two texts on the Kielce Pogrom of July 1946 and the Jedwabne wartime episode. Both essays were published in Michnik, 2011: 173–212.

57. "I feel like a perfect schizophrenic," Michnik confessed (2011: 210). "I am Polish and my shame over the murder in Jedwabne is a Polish shame; but I also know that had I happened to be there at the time I would have been murdered as a Jew."

58. Also see Falk, 2003: 173–75; Dalecki, 1997: 157ff.

59. Michnik's understanding of religion was also sui generis. As Dalecki remarked (1997: 159–60), for Michnik, religion means not so much a private affair as a certain way of engaging with the world.

60. As of the time of sending this book to press, the situation has deteriorated in Poland to the point that a prominent populist politician such as Lech Kaczynski, the leader of the governing Law and Justice Party, has recently claimed that "every hand raised against the Church is a hand raised against Poland."

61. On this issue as well as on Heidegger's influence on Havel's ideas, see Havel (1990).

62. See Michnik, 1993: 175ff.

63. Michnik, 1998: 151. This passage is from Michnik's essay "After the Revolution," an article written for the *New Republic* after the fall of the Berlin Wall.

64. Also see Cherniss, 2014: 352ff.

65. On the relevance of the political thought of the former Eastern European dissidents, see Isaac (1998).

66. As quoted by Michnik in his essay "Letter from the Gdansk Prison," published in *The New York Review of Books*, July 18, 1985, http://www.nybooks.com/articles/1985/07/18/letter-from-the-gdansk-prison/ (accessed March 20, 2016).

67. The title of James C. Scott's book. An unforgettable account can be found in Steinhardt's *The Diary of Happiness* (1991), one of the most memorable books published in Eastern Europe since 1989; for more details, see Craiutu (2012a).

68. I borrow this term from Jowitt's introduction to Michnik, 1998: xxxiii.

69. This is Havel's own phrase (1990: 205).

Epilogue

1. For a more detailed discussion on this issue, see Craiutu, 2012c: 6–7, 13–19.

2. The quintessential example of a temperamental moderate was Benjamin Franklin, who

listed moderation among the fundamental thirteen virtues in his celebrated *Autobiography*. "Avoid extremes; forbear resenting injuries so much as you think they deserve" was his advice to all seekers of wisdom and success in life. For more details, see Franklin, 1993: 84–86.

3. See Craiutu, 2012c: 240–42.

4. The constitutional dimension of moderation loomed large in Craiutu (2012c).

5. Keynes as quoted in Skidelsky, 1994: 224.

6. This essay was included in Keynes's *Essays in Persuasion*, http://www.gutenberg.ca/ebooks/keynes-essaysinpersuasion/keynes-essaysinpersuasion-00-h.html#Am_Liberal (accessed January 14, 2016).

7. I am paraphrasing here a point made by John Avlon with regard to Centrism (2004: 3).

8. Montaigne, 1991: 1046–47 (from his essay "On the Art of Conversation").

9. Thanks to Alexander Smith for stressing this point in our exchanges on moderation.

10. Moderates should not be equated with independent voters either.

11. Shagan, 2011: 4. My perspective challenges the general image of moderation as a "profoundly coercive tool of social control" as described by Shagan (2011) and Lake (1982).

12. That is why it would be inaccurate to claim that moderation is *the* solution to the persistence of extreme forms of partisanship in contemporary politics.

13. On the complex nature of fanaticism, see Toscano (2010) and Olson (2007).

14. As Kołakowski noted (1968: 216), this is what makes Aristotle's appreciation for moderation and the middle somewhat alien to us. Unlike him, we believe that these contradictions are inherent in the world of values and cannot be reconciled; our world of values is inconsistent because it is made up of antagonistic elements.

15. I borrow here Comte-Sponville's description of temperance as that form of "moderation which allows us to be masters of our pleasure instead of becoming its slaves" (2001: 39).

16. It would be a mistake to believe that moderates are (always) on the good side of history, while opponents of moderation are (always) on its dark side. It would be equally inadequate to a priori identify moderation with reasonableness and immoderation with unreasonableness.

17. I borrow Joseph Hall's phrase from *Christian Moderation* (1640), as quoted in Calhoon, 2009: 274.

18. The main reference here is to William Bennett's *Why We Fight: Moral Clarity and the War on Terrorism* published in 2002, at the outset of the intervention of the United States in the war against terror. On the need for moral clarity in foreign policy, also see Safire (2002).

19. From an interview with Susan Neiman taken by Vidushi Sharma and published in "Moral Clarity: The Real-World Legitimacy of Idealism," *Huffington Post*, October 28, 2012, http://www.huffingtonpost.com/kidspirit/moral-clarity-the-real-world-legitimacy-of-idealism_b_1825235.html (accessed January 3, 2016).

20. See Corn (2002).

21. See Judt and Snyder, 2012: 213.

22. Camus, 1974: 112–13. A similar expression of moderation can be found in the following statement of François Furet: "Je me sens ambigu et double, et je ne pense pas qu'il puisse en être autrement" (2007: xxii).

23. The list is long and includes, in addition to Jean-Paul Sartre, Frantz Fanon, Alain Badiou, and Slavoj Žižek, to name just a few prominent names. On Sartre's statements declaring that violence can be moral, see Wolin, 2010: 205–7. As Mao once put it, "A sheet of blank paper carries no burden. The most beautiful characters can be written on it, the most beautiful pictures painted" (Mao as quoted in Wolin, 2010: 229).

24. I borrow here the title of Hobsbawm's well-known account of the twentieth century (1996). Compare with Judt (2005), Courtois et al. (1999), and Applebaum (2004).

25. For a similar perspective applied to compromise, see Gutmann and Thompson, 2012: 29.

26. On this issue, see Hirschman, 1995: 76.

27. For a similar point about Centrism, see Avlon, 2004: 448-49.

28. The idea of moderation was present in various forms in the writings of Al-Ghazali (especially in *Moderation in Belief*) and Maimonides. The existence of an Arab tradition of political moderation was discussed in Marwan Muasher's book on the center in Middle Eastern politics (2009).

29. See Montaigne, 1991: 1258–59.

30. On the distinction between uncompromising and compromising mindsets, see Gutmann and Thompson, 2012: 69–90.

31. See Shils, 1997: 48–53.

32. This was the epigraph chosen by Miłosz for his famous book *The Captive Mind* (1955: 2). On the traits of the self-righteous mind, see Haidt (2012).

33. Thomas Fuller as quoted in Calhoon, 2006: 275.

34. On the art of conversation, see Montaigne, 1991: 1044–69.

35. This passage is from Franklin's speech at the Constitutional Convention on September 17, 1787, reprinted in Franklin, 1993: 350–51.

36. I borrow here the title of one of Albert O. Hirschman's last works (1995). I commented on the importance of "self-subversion" as a practice of moderation in Craiutu (1997a).

37. See Hirschman, 1995: 92.

38. Kołakowski argued that a certain form of (wisely practiced) inconsistency is a means to "cheat life" (1968: 214) when the latter wants to make us one-dimensional.

39. Camus, 1974: 121. Camus also highlighted the affinities among moderation, courage, and self-control.

40. Also see Kołakowski, 1968: 214. It is possible to have "moderate" communists as well as "moderate" capitalists, socialists, conservatives, and liberals.

41. Ortega y Gasset as quoted in Marías, 1970: 8.

42. Camus, 1974: 124. In this last paragraph, I am paraphrasing Camus's words (1974: 122–24).

43. For more details, see Chapter 6. The essay was reprinted in Kołakowski, 1990: 225–28.

44. See, in particular, Soltan (2002) and (2008).

45. I borrow the phrase "complex center" from Soltan (2002), whose view of moderation differs from mine in some respects. A conservative defense of a "radical center" different from Soltan's can be found in Halstead and Lind (2001). The relationship between the moderate mind, the middle ground, and Centrism needs further elaboration. For a passionate defense of Centrism, see Avlon (2004; 2014). He defines the Centrism as "far more than a collection of cautious gestures toward the middle ground," "a principled political philosophy" and a form of "practical politics" that offer "both a principled vision of governing and a successful strategy for winning elections (2004: 2).

46. See Soltan, 2008: 96–116. In Soltan's view, the constitutionalist practice might be better served by a theory of moderation and a complex center rather than by procedural liberalism.

47. See Bagehot (1872).

48. See Soltan, 2002: 20–21. He gives as examples of "moral absolutism" the following ones:

the slogan "one nation, one party, one leader," laissez-faire market radicalism ("the more market, the better"), and democratic radicalism ("the more democracy, the better"). It is possible, of course, to think of other examples as well, such as the tendency to view the U.S. Constitution as a sacred and unalterable document and the excessive idolatry of the First and Second Amendments to the point of blocking any further discussion of possible reforms.

49. On this issue, also see Furet's important essay, "Les feuilles mortes de l'utopie" (April 1990), republished in Furet, 2007: 376–81.

BIBLIOGRAPHY

Adams, Henry (1960). *The Education of Henry Adams*. New York: Modern Library.

Adams, John (1954). *The Political Writings of John Adams*, ed. George A. Peek. Indianapolis: Bobbs-Merrill.

Al-Ghazālī (2013). *Moderation in Belief*, trans. Aladdin M. Yaqub. Chicago: University of Chicago Press.

Anderson, Brian C. (1997). *Raymond Aron: The Recovery of the Political*. Lanham, Md.: Rowman & Littlefield.

Anderson, Perry (1988). "The Affinities of Norberto Bobbio." *New Left Review*, 270 (July–August). http://newleftreview.org/I/170/perry-anderson-the-affinities-of-norberto-bobbio (accessed January 6, 2016).

———(2005). *Spectrum: From Right to Left in the World of Ideas*. London: Verso.

Applebaum, Anne (2004). *Gulag: A History*. New York: Anchor Books.

Aron, Raymond (1957). *Espoir et peur du siècle. Essais non partisans*. Paris: Calmann-Lévy.

———(1969). *The Elusive Revolution: Anatomy of a Student Revolt*, trans. Gordon Clough. New York: Praeger.

———(1970). *An Essay on Freedom*, trans. Helen Weaver. New York: New American Library.

———(1975). *History and the Dialectic of Violence*, trans. Barry Cooper. Oxford: Basil Blackwell.

———(1981). *Le Spectateur engagé. Entretiens avec Jean-Louis Missika et Dominique Wolton*. Paris: Julliard.

———(1984). *Politics and History: Selected Essays*, 2nd ed., ed. and trans. Miriam B. Conant. New Brunswick, N.J.: Transaction.

———(1985a). "Raymond Aron (1905–1983): Histoire et politique." Special issue of *Commentaire* (Paris), 28–29.

———(1985b). *History, Truth, Liberty: Selected Writings of Raymond Aron*, ed. Franciszek Draus. Chicago: University of Chicago Press.

———(1988). "The Revolt of the Masses." *Partisan Review*, 55: 3: 359–70.

———(1990). *Memoirs: Fifty Years of Political Reflection*, trans. George Holoch. New York: Holmes & Meier.

———(1994). *In Defense of Liberal Reason*, ed. Daniel J. Mahoney. Lanham, Md.: Rowman & Littlefield.

———(1997a). *Les Articles du Figaro, Tome III: Les Crises, 1965–1977*, ed. Georges Henri Soutou. Paris: Éditions de Fallois.

———(1997b). *Thinking Politically: A Liberal in the Age of Ideology*, ed. Daniel J. Mahoney and Brian C. Anderson. New Brunswick, N.J.: Transaction.

——(1998a). *Essais sur les libertés*, ed. Philippe Raynaud. Paris: Hachette.

——(1998b). *Main Currents of Sociological Thought*, 2 vols., ed. Daniel J. Mahoney and Brian C. Anderson. New Brunswick, N.J.: Transaction.

——(2001). *The Opium of the Intellectuals*, ed. Daniel J. Mahoney and Brian C. Anderson. New Brunswick, N.J.: Transaction.

——(2002a). *The Dawn of Universal History*, trans. Barbara Bray, ed. Yair Reiner. New York: Basic Books.

——(2002b). *Le Marxisme de Marx*, ed. Jean-Claude Casanova and Christian Bachelier. Paris: Éditions de Fallois.

——(2005). *Penser la liberté, penser la démocratie*, ed. Nicolas Baverez. Paris: Gallimard (Quarto).

——(2006). *Les sociétés modernes*, ed. Serge Paugam. Paris: PUF.

——(2006–7). "Autoportrait." *Commentaire*, 116 (Winter): 903–7.

——(2013). *Liberté et égalité*. Paris: EHESS.

Avlon, John P. (2004). *Independent Nation: How Centrists Can Change American Politics*. New York: Three Rivers Press.

——(2014). *Wingnuts: Extremism in the Age of Obama*. New York: Beast Books.

Audier, Serge (2006). *Le socialisme libéral*. Paris: La Découverte.

Backes, Uwe (2010). *Political Extremes: A History of Terminology from Ancient Times to the Present*. London: Routledge.

Bagehot, Walter (1872). *Physics and Politics*. London: King & Co.

Baverez, Nicolas (2005). *Raymond Aron*. Paris: Flammarion.

Beiner, Ronald (2014). *Political Philosophy: What It Is and Why It Matters*. New York: Cambridge University Press.

Bell, Daniel A. (1976). *The Cultural Contradictions of Capitalism*. New York: Basic Books.

Bellamy, Richard (2014). *Croce, Gramsci, Bobbio and the Italian Political Tradition*. Wivenhoe Park, UK: ECPR Press.

Benda, Julien (1955). *The Betrayal of the Intellectuals*, trans. Richard Aldington. New York: Beacon.

Bennett, William (2002). *Why We Fight: Moral Clarity and the War on Terrorism*. New York: Regnery.

Berkowitz, Peter (2013). *Constitutional Conservatism: Liberty, Self-Government, and Political Moderation*. Stanford, Calif.: Hoover Institution Press.

Berlin, Isaiah (1948). *Karl Marx*, 2nd ed. Oxford: Oxford University Press.

——(alias O. Utis) (1952). "Generalissimo Stalin and the Art of Government." *Foreign Affairs*, 30: 2: 197–214.

——(1997). *The Sense of Reality: Studies in Ideas and Their History*, ed. Henry Hardy. London: Pimlico.

——(1998a). "Isaiah Berlin in Conversation with Steven Lukes." *Salmagundi*, 120 (Fall): 52–134.

——(1998b). *The Proper Study of Mankind: An Anthology of Essays*, ed. Henry Hardy and Roger Hausheer. New York: Farrar, Straus and Giroux.

——(1999). *The First and the Last*, ed. Henry Hardy. New York: New York Review Books.

——(2000). *The Power of Ideas*, ed. Henry Hardy. Princeton, N.J.: Princeton University Press.

——(2002). *Liberty*, ed. Henry Hardy. Princeton, N.J.: Princeton University Press.

——(2004). *Flourishing: Letters, 1928–1946*, ed. Henry Hardy. Oxford: Oxford University Press.

———(2006). *Political Ideas in the Romantic Age*, ed. Henry Hardy. Princeton, N.J.: Princeton University Press.
———(2008). *Russian Thinkers*, rev. ed., ed. Henry Hardy. London: Penguin.
———(2009). *Enlightening: Letters, 1946–1960*, ed. Henry Hardy and Jennifer Holmes. Oxford: Oxford University Press.
———(2013). *Building: Letters, 1960–1975*, ed. Henry Hardy. London: Chatto & Random House.
———(2014). "A Message to the Twenty-First Century." *New York Review of Books*, October 23. http://www.nybooks.com/articles/archives/2014/oct/23/message-21st-century/ (accessed August 28, 2015).
———(2015). "Among Important Persons: Two Letters." *Times Literary Supplement* (August 21 & 28): 14–16.
Bloom, Allan (1985). "Le dernier des libéraux." *Commentaire* 28–29: 174–81.
Bobbio, Norberto (1955). *Politica e cultura*. Torino: Einaudi.
———(1969). *Saggi sulla scienza politica in Italia*. Bari: Laterza.
———(1971). *Una filosofia militante. Studi su Carlo Cattaneo*. Turin: Einaudi.
———(1981). *Le ideologie e il potere in crisi. Pluralismo, democrazia, socialismo, comunismo, terza via e terza forza*. Florence: Felice Le Monnier.
———(1987). *The Future of Democracy*, trans. Roger Griffin, ed. Richard Bellamy. Minneapolis: University of Minnesota Press.
———(1989a). *Il terzo assente. Saggi e discorsi sulla pace e la guerra*. Turin: Sonda.
———(1989b). "The Upturned Utopia." *New Left Review*, 177 (September–October): 37–39.
———(1993). *Il dubio e la scelta. Intelletualli e potere nella società contemporanea*. Rome: Carocci.
———(1995). *Ideological Profile of Twentieth-Century Italy*, trans. Lydia G. Cochrane. Princeton, N.J.: Princeton University Press.
———(1996). *The Age of Rights*, trans. Allan Cameron. Cambridge: Polity.
———(1999). *Teoria generale della politica*, ed. Michelangelo Bovero. Turin: Giulio Einaudi.
———(2000). *In Praise of Meekness: Essays on Ethics and Politics*, trans. Teresa Chataway. Cambridge: Polity.
———(2001). *Old Age and Other Essays*, trans. Allan Cameron. Cambridge: Polity.
———(2002). *A Political Life*, ed. Alberto Papuzzi, trans. Allan Cameron. Cambridge: Polity.
———(2009). *Quale democrazia?*, ed. Mario Busi. Brescia: Morcelliana.
Boudon, Julien (2011). *La passion de la modération*. Paris: Dalloz.
Brooks, David (2011). "Does Moderation Work?" *New York Times*, January 12. http://opinionator.blogs.nytimes.com/2011/01/12/does-moderation-work/ (accessed September 15, 2015).
———(2012). "What Moderation Means." *New York Times*, October 25. http://www.nytimes.com/2012/10/26/opinion/brooks-what-moderation-means.html?nl=todaysheadlines&emc=edit_th_20121026&_r=0 (accessed September 15, 2015).
Burke, Edmund (1968). *Reflections on the French Revolution*, ed. Conor Cruise O'Brien. Harmondsworth: Penguin.
———(1992). *Further Reflections on the French Revolution*, ed. Daniel E. Ritchie. Indianapolis: Liberty Fund.
———(1993). *Pre-Revolutionary Writings*, ed. Ian Harris. Cambridge: Cambridge University Press.
Calhoun, Cheshire (2000). "The Virtue of Civility." *Philosophy & Public Affairs*, 29: 3: 251–75.

Calhoon, Robert McCluer (2006). "On Political Moderation." *Journal of the Historical Society*, 6: 2: 275–95.

——(2009). *Political Moderation in America's First Two Centuries*. New York: Cambridge University Press.

Calogero, Guido (1972). *Difesa del liberalsocialismo e altri saggi*, ed. Mario Schiavone and Dino Cofrancesco. Milan: Marzorati.

Campbell Corey, Elizabeth (2006). *Michael Oakeshott on Religion, Aesthetics, and Politics*. Columbia: University of Missouri Press.

——(2012). "The Religious Sensibility of Michael Oakeshott." In *A Companion to Michael Oakeshott*, ed. Paul Franco and Leslie March, 134–50.

Camus, Albert (1956). *The Rebel*, trans. Anthony Bower. New York: Vintage.

——(1974). *Resistance, Rebellion, and Death*, trans. Justin O'Brien. New York: Vintage.

——(1991). *The Plague*, trans. Stuart Gilbert. New York: Vintage.

Canto-Sperber, Monique and Nadia Urbinati, eds. (2003). *Le socialisme libéral: Une anthologie. Europe-États-Unis*. Paris: Éditions Esprit.

Carrese, Paul (2016). *Democracy in Moderation*. New York: Cambridge University Press.

Cherniss, Joshua (2006). "Isaiah Berlin's Political Ideas." In Isaiah Berlin, *Political Ideas in the Romantic Age*, xxi–liv.

——(2013). *A Mind and Its Time: The Development of Isaiah Berlin's Thought*. Oxford: Oxford University Press.

——(2014). "Political Ethics and the Defense of Liberalism in Twentieth-Century Political Thought." Ph.D. dissertation, Department of Government, Harvard University.

Clor, Harry (2008). *On Moderation: Defending an Ancient Virtue in a Modern World*. Waco, Tex.: Baylor University Press.

Colen, José and Elizabeth Dutartre, eds. (2015). *The Companion to Raymond Aron*. New York: Palgrave Macmillan.

Collini, Stefan (1997). "Against Utopia." *Times Literary Supplement* (August 22): 3–5.

Colquhoun, Robert (1986). *Raymond Aron: The Sociologist in Society, 1955–1983*. Beverly Hills, Calif.: Sage.

Comte-Sponville, André (2001). *A Small Treatise on the Great Virtues*, trans. Catherine Temerson. New York: Henry Holt.

Connelly, John (2013). "Jester and Priest: On Leszek Kołakowski." *Nation*, September 3. http://www.thenation.com/article/176016/jester-and-priest-leszek-kolakowski# (accessed April 14, 2015).

Coole, Diana (2007). *Merleau-Ponty and Modern Politics After Anti-humanism*. Lanham, Md.: Rowman & Littlefield.

Corn, David (2002). "Searching for Moral Clarity." *Nation*, April 23. http://www.thenation.com/article/searching-moral-clarity/ (accessed December 29, 2015).

Courtois, Stéphane, et al. (1999). *The Black Book of Communism: Crimes, Terror, Repression*, trans. Jonathan Murphy and Mark Kramer. Cambridge, Mass.: Harvard University Press.

Craiutu, Aurelian (1997a). "Is Self-Subversion the Elixir of Eternal Youth?" *Government and Opposition*, 32: 3: 442–47.

——(1997b). "N. Steinhardt (1912–1989)." In *The Encyclopedia of the Essay*, ed. Tracy Chevalier. London: Fitzroy Dearborn, 813–15.

——(2007). "Faces of Moderation: Raymond Aron's Committed Observer." In *Political Reason in an Age of Ideology*, ed. Bryan-Paul Frost and Daniel J. Mahoney. New Brunswick, N.J.: Transaction, 261–83.

———(2011). "Thinking Politically: Raymond Aron and the Revolution of 1968 in France." In *Promises of 1968: Crisis, Illusion, and Utopia*, ed. Vladimir Tismaneanu. Budapest: Central European University Press, 101–27.

———(2012a). "On Happiness in Unusual Places: N. Steinhardt's Uplifting Lesson." In *Philosophy, Society and the Cunning of History in Eastern Europe*, ed. Costica Bradatan. London: Routledge, 83–97.

———(2012b). "Raymond Aron and the French Tradition of Political Moderation." In *French Liberalism: From Montesquieu to the Present Day*, ed. Raf Geenens and Helena Rosenblatt. Cambridge: Cambridge University Press, 271–90.

———(2012c). *A Virtue for Courageous Minds: Moderation in French Political Thought*. Princeton, N.J.: Princeton University Press.

———(2014). "The Center and the Margins." Review of Joshua Cherniss' *A Mind and Its Time*. *Los Angeles Review of Books*, March 26. https://lareviewofbooks.org/review/center-margins / (accessed May 15, 2015).

———(2015a). "Political Moderation and the Lost Art of Trimming." *The Island* (Tasmania, Australia) 140 (March): 38–43.

———(2015b). "Raymond Aron and Alexis de Tocqueville: Political Moderation, Liberty, and the Role of the Intellectuals." In *The Companion to Raymond Aron*, ed. José Colen and Elizabeth Dutartre, 261–74.

Crick, Bernard (1964). *In Praise of Politics*. Harmondsworth: Penguin.

Crowder, George (2004). *Isaiah Berlin: Liberty and Pluralism*. Cambridge: Polity.

Dalecki, Jacek (1997). *The Political Evolution of Polish Dissident Adam Michnik*. Ph.D. dissertation, Department of Political Science, Indiana University, Bloomington.

De Luna, Giovanni (1982). *Storia del Partito d'Azione. La rivoluzione democratica, 1942–1947*. Milan: Feltrinelli.

Devigne, Robert (2012). "Oakeshott as Conservative." In *A Companion to Michael Oakeshott*, ed. Paul Franco and Leslie Marsh, 268–89.

Dutartre, Élisabeth, ed. (2007). *Raymond Aron et la démocratie au XXIe siècle*. Paris: Éditions de Fallois.

Egginton, William (2011). *In Defense of Religious Moderation*. New York: Columbia University Press.

Einaudi, Giulio (1994). "Norberto Bobbio, el testimonio de un contemporaneo." In *La figura y el pensamiento de Norberto Bobbio*, ed. Ángel Llamas, 41–52.

Elshtain, Jean Bethke (1985). "Ordinary Scholarship." *Yale Law Journal*, 95: 5: 1270–84.

Emerson, Ralph Waldo (1841). "The Conservative." http://www.bartleby.com/90/0108.html (accessed September 23, 2015).

Falk, Barbara J. (2003). *The Dilemmas of Dissidence in East-Central Europe: Citizen Intellectuals and Philosopher Kings*. Budapest: Central European University Press.

Fawcett, Edmund (2014). *Liberalism: The Life of an Idea*. Princeton, N.J.: Princeton University Press.

Forrester, Katrina (2012). "Judith Shklar, Bernard Williams, and Political Realism." *European Journal of Political Theory*, 11: 3: 247–72.

Franco, Paul (1990). *The Political Philosophy of Michael Oakeshott*. New Haven, Conn.: Yale University Press.

———(2003). "The Shapes of Liberal Thought: Oakeshott, Berlin, and Liberalism." *Political Theory*, 31: 4 (August): 484–507.

Franco, Paul and Leslie Marsh, eds. (2012). *A Companion to Michael Oakeshott*. University Park: Pennsylvania State University Press.

Franklin, Benjamin (1993). *Autobiography and Other Writings*, ed. Ormond Seavey. Oxford: Oxford University Press.

Friedman, Thomas (2003). "Wanted: Fanatical Moderates." *New York Times*, November 16. http://www.nytimes.com/2003/11/16/opinion/16FRIE.html (accessed September 17, 2015).

Fumurescu, Alin (2013). *Compromise: A History*. New York: Cambridge University Press.

Furet, François (2007). *Penser le XXe siècle*. Paris: Laffont.

———(2014). *Lies, Passions, and Illusions: The Democratic Imagination in the Twentieth Century*, ed. Christophe Prochasson, trans. Deborah Furet. Chicago: University of Chicago Press.

Gallipeau, Claude (1994). *Isaiah Berlin's Liberalism*. Oxford: Clarendon.

Galston, William (2012). "Oakeshott's Political Theory: Recapitulation and Criticisms." In *The Cambridge Companion to Oakeshott*, ed. Efraim Podoksik, 222–44.

Gamble, Andrew (2012). "Oakeshott's Ideological Politics: Conservative or Liberal?" In *The Cambridge Companion to Oakeshott*, ed. Efraim Podoksik, 153–76.

Garton Ash, Timothy (1990a). *The Magic Lantern*. New York: Random House.

———(1990b). *The Uses of Adversity*. New York: Vintage.

Geremek, Bronislaw (1992). "Civil Society Then and Now." *Journal of Democracy*, 3: 2: 3–12.

Gerencser, Steven Anthony (2000). *The Skeptic's Oakeshott*. New York: St. Martin's Press.

Goodheart, Eugene (2001). "In Defense of Trimming." *Philosophy and Literature*, 25: 1: 46–58.

———(2013). *Holding the Center: In Defense of Political Trimming*. New Brunswick, N.J.: Transaction.

Gracián, Baltasar (1993). *The Art of Worldly Wisdom*, trans. Joseph Jacobs. Boston: Shambala.

Grant, Robert (2012). "The Pursuit of Intimacy, or Rationalism in Love." In *A Companion to Michael Oakeshott*, ed. Paul Franco and Leslie March, 15–44.

Gray, John (1996). *Isaiah Berlin*. Princeton, N.J.: Princeton University Press.

Greco, T. (2000). *Un itinerario intelletuale tra filosofia e politica*. Rome: Donzelli.

Gutmann, Amy and Dennis Thompson (2012). *Compromise: Why Governing Demands It and Campaigning Undermines It*. Princeton, N.J.: Princeton University Press.

Haack, Susan (1999). *Manifesto of a Passionate Moderate: Unfashionable Essays*. Chicago: University of Chicago Press.

Hacohen, Malachi (2010). *Karl Popper: The Formative Years, 1902–1945*. New York: Cambridge University Press.

Haidt, Jonathan (2012). *The Righteous Mind: Why Good People Are Divided by Politics and Religion*. New York: Pantheon Books.

Halifax, Marquis of (1969). *Complete Works*, ed. J. P. Kenyon. London: Penguin.

———(1989). *The Works of George Savile Marquis of Halifax*, vol. 1, ed. Mark N. Brown. Oxford: Clarendon.

Halstead, Ted and Michael Lind (2001). *The Radical Center: The Future of American Politics*. New York: Anchor Books.

Hamburger, Joseph (1966). *Intellectuals in Politics: John Stuart Mill and the Philosophic Radicals*. New Haven, Conn.: Yale University Press.

———(1976). *Macaulay and the Whig Tradition*. New Haven, Conn.: Yale University Press.

Hanley, Ryan (2004). "Political Science and Political Understanding: Isaiah Berlin on the Nature of Political Inquiry." *American Political Science Review*, 98: 2: 327–39.

Hartshorne, Charles (1987). *Wisdom as Moderation: A Philosophy of the Middle Way*. Albany: State University of New York Press.

Hassner, Pierre (2015). "Raymond Aron and Immanuel Kant: Politics Between Morality and History." In *The Companion to Raymond Aron*, ed. José Colen and Elizabeth Dutartre, 197–204.

Havel, Václav (1990). *Disturbing the Peace. A Conversation with Karel Hvíždala*. New York: Knopf.

———(1991). *Open Letters: Selected Prose, 1965–1990*, ed. Paul Wilson. London: Faber and Faber.

Heidrich, Christian (1995). *Leszek Kolakowski: Zwischen Skepsis und Mystik*. Frankfurt: Verlag Neue Kritik.

Hess, Andreas (2014). *The Political Thought of Judith N. Shklar: Exile from Exile*. Houndmills: Palgrave Macmillan.

Hirschman, Albert O. (1991). *The Rhetoric of Reaction: Perversity, Futility, Jeopardy*. Cambridge, Mass.: Harvard University Press.

———(1995). *A Propensity to Self-Subversion*. Cambridge, Mass.: Harvard University Press.

Hobsbawm, Eric (1996). *The Age of Extremes: A History of the World, 1914–1991*. New York: Vintage.

Ignatieff, Michael (1998). *Isaiah Berlin: A Life*. New York: Henry Holt.

Isaac, Jeffrey C. (1998). *Democracy in Dark Times*. Ithaca, N.Y.: Cornell University Press.

Jahanbegloo, Ramin and Isaiah Berlin (1992). *Conversations with Isaiah Berlin*. New York: Charles Scribner's Sons.

Jowitt, Kenneth (1998). "In Praise of the Ordinary." Foreword to Adam Michnik, *Letters from Freedom*, xiii–xxxiii.

Judt, Tony (1992). *Past Imperfect: French Intellectuals, 1944–1956*. Berkeley: University of California Press.

———(1998). *The Burden of Responsibility: Blum, Camus, and the French Twentieth Century*. Chicago: University of Chicago Press.

———(2005). *Postwar: A History of Europe Since 1945*. New York: Penguin.

———(2010). *Ill Fares the Land*. New York: Penguin.

Judt, Tony and Timothy Snyder (2012). *Thinking the Twentieth Century*. New York: Penguin.

Kabaservice, Geoffrey (2012). *Rule and Ruin: The Downfall of Moderation and the Destruction of the Republican Party, from Eisenhower to the Tea Party*. New York: Oxford University Press.

Kateb, George (1998). Foreword to Judith Shklar, *Political Thought and Political Thinkers*, vii–xix.

Katznelson, Ira (1996). *Liberalism's Crooked Circle*. Princeton, N.J.: Princeton University Press.

Kelly, Duncan (2013). "Lessons in Liberty." *Financial Times* (August 10–11): 9.

Keynes, John Maynard (1964). *The General Theory of Employment, Interest, and Money*. New York: Harcourt, Brace & World.

King, Martin Luther, Jr. (2010). *Strength to Love*. Minneapolis, Minn.: Fortress Press.

Kirshner, Alexander S. (2014). *A Theory of Militant Democracy: The Ethics of Combatting Political Extremism*. New Haven, Conn.: Yale University Press.

Koestler, Arthur (1952). "The Initiates." In *The God That Failed*, ed. Richard Crossman. New York: Bantam Books, 13–75.

Kołakowski, Leszek (1968). *Toward a Marxist Humanism: Essays on the Left Today*, trans. Jane Zielonko Peel. New York: Grove Press.

———(1971). "Hope and Hopelessness," *Survey: A Journal of East & West Studies*, 17: 3: 37-52.

———(1990). *Modernity on Endless Trial*. Chicago: University of Chicago Press.

Konrád, György (1984). *Antipolitics*. San Diego: Harcourt Brace Jovanovich.

Kosicki, Piotr H. (2013). "After 1989. The Life and Death of the Catholic Third Way." *Times Literary Supplement* (December 13): 13–15.

Lake, Peter (1982). *Moderate Puritans and the Elizabethan Church*. Cambridge: Cambridge University Press.

Lester, Emily (2014). "British Conservatism and American Liberalism in Mid-Twentieth Century: Burkean Themes in Niebuhr and Schlesinger." *Polity*, 46: 2: 182–210.

Lilla, Mark (2001). *The Reckless Mind: Intellectuals in Politics*. New York: New York Review Books.

Lipski, Jan Jósef (1985). *KOR. A History of the Worker's Defense Committee in Poland, 1976–1981*. Berkeley: University of California Press.

Llamas, Ángel, ed. (1994). *La figura y el pensamiento de Norberto Bobbio*. Madrid: Instituto de derechos humanos Bartolome de las Casas.

Macaulay, Thomas Babington (1913). *The History of England from the Accession of James the Second*, ed. Charles H. Firth. London: Macmillan.

Madariaga, Salvador de (1954). *Essays with a Purpose*. London: Hollis & Carter.

Mahoney, Daniel J. (1992). *The Liberal Political Science of Raymond Aron: A Critical Introduction*. Lanham, Md.: Rowman & Littlefield.

———(2011). *The Conservative Foundations of the Liberal Order*. Wilmington, Del.: ISI Books.

Malcolm, Noel (2012). "Oakeshott and Hobbes." In *A Companion to Michael Oakeshott*, ed. Paul Franco and Leslie Marsh, 217–31.

Malia, Martin (1982). "Poland: The Winter War." *New York Review of Books*, March 18. http://www.nybooks.com/articles/archives/1982/mar/18/poland-the-winter-war/ (accessed May 15, 2015).

Manent, Pierre (1994). "Raymond Aron—Political Educator." In *Political Reason in an Age of Ideology*, ed. Bryan-Paul Frost and Daniel J. Mahoney. New Brunswick, N.J.: Transaction, 11–32.

Mannheim, Karl (1936). *Ideology and Utopia: An Introduction to the Sociology of Knowledge*, trans. Louis Wirth and Edward Shils. New York: Harcourt, Brace.

Margalit, Avishai (1996). *The Decent Society*. Cambridge, Mass.: Harvard University Press.

———(2009). *Compromises and Rotten Compromises*. Princeton, N.J.: Princeton University Press.

Marías, Julían (1970). *José Ortega y Gasset: Circumstance and Vocation*, trans. Frances M. López-Morillas. Norman: University of Oklahoma Press.

Matynia, Elzbieta, ed. (2014). *An Uncanny Era: Conversations Between Vaclav Havel and Adam Michnik*. New Haven, Conn.: Yale University Press.

Merleau-Ponty, Maurice (1969). *Humanism and Terror: An Essay on the Communist Problem*, trans. John O'Neill. Boston: Beacon.

Mesure, Sylvie (2015). "Aron and Marxism: The Aronian Interpretation of Marx." In *The Companion to Raymond Aron*, ed. José Colen and Elizabeth Dutartre, 217–30.

Michnik, Adam (1987). *Letters from Prison and Other Essays*, trans. Maya Latynski. Berkeley: University of California Press.

———(1993). *The Church and the Left*, trans. David Ost. Chicago: University of Chicago Press.

———(1998). *Letters from Freedom*, ed. Irena Grudzińska Gross, trans. Jane Cave. Berkeley: University of California Press.

———(2001). "Adam Michnik: The Sisyphus of Democracy." Interview with Philippe Demenet, *Courrier Unesco* (September): 47–51.

———(2011). *In Search of Lost Meaning: The New Eastern Europe*, ed. Irena Grudzińska Gross, trans. Roman Czarny. Berkeley: University of California Press.

———(2014). *The Trouble with History: Morality, Revolution, and Counterrevolution*, ed. Irena Grudzińska Gross, trans. Elzbieta Matynia et al. New Haven, Conn.: Yale University Press.

Miłosz, Czeslaw (1955). *The Captive Mind*. New York: Vintage.

Minogue, Kenneth (2012). "The Fate of Rationalism in Oakeshott's Thought." In *A Companion to Michael Oakeshott*, ed. Paul Franco and Leslie Marsh, 232–47.

Montaigne, Michel de (1991). *The Complete Essays*, trans. M. A. Screech. London: Penguin.

Muasher, Marwan (2009). *The Arab Center: The Promise of Moderation*. New Haven, Conn.: Yale University Press.

Müller, Jan-Werner (2010). "Fear and Freedom: On 'Cold War Liberalism.'" *European Journal of Political Theory*, 7: 1: 45–64.

———(2011). *Contesting Democracy, Political Ideas in Twentieth-Century Europe*. New Haven, Conn.: Yale University Press.

Neiman, Susan (2008). *Moral Clarity: A Guide for Grown-Up Idealists*. Orlando, Fla.: Harcourt.

———(2012). Interview with Vidushi Sharma. In Sharma, "Moral Clarity: The Real-World Legitimacy of Idealism." *Huffington Post*, October 28. http://www.huffingtonpost.com/kid spirit/moral-clarity-the-real-world-legitimacy-of-idealism_b_1825235.html (accessed January 3, 2016).

Niebuhr, Reinhold (1960). *The Children of Light and the Children of Darkness: A Vindication of Democracy and a Critique of Its Traditional Defense*. New York: Charles Scribner's Sons.

Nietzsche, Friedrich (1967). *The Will to Power*, trans. Walter Kaufmann. New York: Vintage.

Oakeshott, Michael (1933). *Experience and Its Modes*. Cambridge: Cambridge University Press.

———(1948). "Contemporary British Politics." *Cambridge Journal*, 1: 474–90.

———(1975). *On Human Conduct*. Oxford: Clarendon.

———(1991). *Rationalism in Politics and Other Essays*, 2nd enlarged ed., ed. Timothy Fuller. Indianapolis: Liberty Fund.

———(1993a). *Morality and Politics in Modern Europe*, ed. Shirley Robin Letwin. New Haven, Conn.: Yale University Press.

———(1993b). *Religion, Politics, and the Moral Life*, ed. Timothy Fuller. New Haven, Conn.: Yale University Press.

———(1996). *The Politics of Faith and the Politics of Skepticism*, ed. Timothy Fuller. New Haven, Conn.: Yale University Press.

———(2006). *Lectures on the History of Political Thought*, ed. Luke O'Sullivan. Exeter, UK: Imprint Academic.

———(2007). *The Concept of a Philosophical Jurisprudence: Essays and Reviews, 1926–51*, ed. Luke O'Sullivan. Exeter, UK: Imprint Academic.

———(2008). *The Vocabulary of a Modern European State*, ed. Luke O'Sullivan. Exeter, UK: Imprint Academic.

———(2014). *Notebooks, 1922–86*, ed. Luke O'Sullivan. Exeter, UK: Imprint Academic.

Olson, Joel (2007). "The Freshness of Fanaticism: The Abolitionist Defense of Zealotry." *Perspectives on Politics*, 5: 4: 685–701.

Oppermann, Matthias (2008). *Raymond Aron und Deutschland: Die Verteidigung der Freiheit und das Problem des Totalitarismus*. Ostfildern: Thorbecke.

Ortega y Gasset, José (1958). *Man and Crisis*, trans. Mildred Adams. New York: Norton.

———(1994). *The Revolt of the Masses*. New York: Norton.

———(2002). *Toward a Philosophy of History*. Urbana: University of Illinois Press.

Ost, David (1990). *Solidarity and the Politics of the Anti-Politics: Opposition and Reform in Poland Since 1968*. Philadelphia: Temple University Press.

O'Sullivan, Luke (2014). "Michael Oakeshott and the Left." *Journal of the History of Ideas*, 75: 3 (July): 471–92.

Plato (2000). *The Republic*, ed. G. R. F. Ferrari, trans. Tom Griffith. Cambridge: Cambridge University Press.

Podoksik, Efraim, ed. (2012). *The Cambridge Companion to Oakeshott*. Cambridge: Cambridge University Press.

Pontara, Giuliano (1994). "Il mite e el nonviolento. Su un saggio di Norberto Bobbio." *Linea d'ombra*, 93 (March): 67–70.

———(1996). *La personalità nonviolenta*. Turin: Edizioni Gruppo Abele.

Popescu, Delia (2012). *Political Action in Václav Havel's Thought: The Responsibility of Resistance*. Lanham, Md.: Lexington Books.

Popper, Karl (1964). *The Poverty of Historicism*. New York: Harper Torchbooks.

———(1971). *The Open Society and Its Enemies*, 5th ed. Princeton, N.J.: Princeton University Press.

———(1994). *The Myth of the Framework: In Defense of Science and Rationality*, ed. M. A. Notturno. London: Routledge.

Ringen, Stein (2002). "Helvétius and His Friends" (review of Isaiah Berlin's *Freedom and Its Betrayal and Liberty*). *Times Literary Supplement* (September 15): 26.

Röpke, Wilhelm (1998). *A Humane Economy: The Social Framework of the Free Market*. Wilmington, Del.: Intercollegiate Studies Institute.

Ross, Kristin (2004). *May 68 and Its Afterlives*. Chicago: University of Chicago Press.

Rosselli, Carolo (1994). *Liberal Socialism*, ed. Nadia Urbinati, trans. William McCuaig. Princeton, N.J.: Princeton University Press.

Rouner, Leroy S., ed. (2000). *Civility*. Notre Dame, Ind.: University of Notre Dame Press.

Ruiz Miguel, Alfonso (1994). "Bobbio: Las paradojas de un pensamiento en tension." In *La figura y el pensamiento de Norberto Bobbio*, ed. Ángel Llamas, 53–75.

Russell, Bertrand (1950). *Unpopular Essays*. New York: Simon and Schuster.

Ryan, Alan (2013). "Isaiah Berlin: The History of Ideas as Psychodrama." *European Journal of Political Theory*, 12: 1: 61–72.

Safire, William (2002). "Moral Clarity." *New York Times*, May 12. http://www.nytimes.com/2002/05/12/magazine/12ONLANGUAGE.html (accessed December 29, 2015).

Sarat, Austin, ed. (2014). *Civility, Legality, and Justice in America*. New York: Cambridge University Press.

Schell, Jonathan (2004). "Introduction to *Letters from Prison* by Adam Michnik." In *The Jonathan Schell Reader*. New York: Nation Books, 335–86.

Schlesinger, Arthur M., Jr. (1948). "Not Left, Not Right, But a Vital Center." *New York Times*, April 4. http://www.nytimes.com/books/00/11/26/specials/schlesinger-centermag.html (accessed December 23, 2015).

———(1962). *The Vital Center: The Politics of Freedom*, new ed. Boston: Houghton Mifflin (first ed., 1949).

———(1997). "It's My 'Vital Center.'" *Slate*, January 10. http://www.slate.com/articles/briefing/articles/1997/01/its_my_vital_center.html (accessed January 16, 2016).

Schumpeter, Joseph A. (1950). *Capitalism, Socialism, and Democracy*. New York: Harper & Row.

Shaftesbury, Antony, Third Earl of Shaftesbury (2001). *Characteristikcs of Men, Manners, Opinions, Times*, 3 vols., foreword by Douglas Den Uyl. Indianapolis: Liberty Fund.

Shagan, Ethan H. (2011). *The Rule of Moderation. Violence, Religion, and the Politics of Restraint in Early Modern England*. New York: Cambridge University Press.

Shils, Edward (1985). "Raymond Aron: A Memoir." In Raymond Aron, *History, Truth, Liberty*, 1–20.

———(1997). *The Virtue of Civility*, ed. Steven Grosby. Indianapolis: Liberty Fund.

Shklar, Judith (1957). *After Utopia: The Decline of Political Faith*. Princeton, N.J.: Princeton University Press.

———(1984). *Ordinary Vices*. Cambridge, Mass.: Harvard University Press.

———(1998). *Political Thought and Political Thinkers*, ed. Stanley Hoffmann. Chicago: University of Chicago Press.

Simon-Nahum, Perrine (2015). "Raymond Aron and the Notion of History: Taking Part in History." In *The Companion to Raymond Aron*, ed. José Colen and Elizabeth Dutartre, 105–18.

Sirinelli, Jean-François (1995). *Deux intellectuels dans le siècle: Sartre et Aron*. Paris: Fayard.

Skidelsky, Robert (1994). *John Maynard Keynes: Volume Two: The Economist as Savior, 1920–1937*. London: Penguin.

Smith, Alexander Thomas T. (2013). "Democracy Begins at Home: Moderation and the Promise of Salvage Ethnography." *Sociological Review*, 61: S2: 119–40.

Smith, Alexander Thomas T. and John Holmwood, eds. (2013). *Sociologies of Moderation*. Oxford: Wiley-Blackwell.

Smith, Steven B. (2012). "Practical Life and the Critique of Rationalism." In *The Cambridge Companion to Oakeshott*, ed. Efraim Podoksik, 131–52.

Soltan, Karol (2002). "Liberal Conservative Socialism and the Politics of a Complex Center." *Good Society*, 11: 1: 19–22.

———(2008). "Constitutional Patriotism and Militant Moderation." *International Journal of Constitutional Law*, 6: 1: 96–116.

Staniszkis, Jadwiga (1984). *Poland's Self-Limiting Revolution*, ed. Jan T. Gross. Princeton, N.J.: Princeton University Press.

———(1992). *The Ontology of Socialism*. Oxford: Clarendon.

Steinhardt, Nicolae (1991). *Jurnalul fericirii* [*The Diary of Happiness*], ed. Virgil Ciomoş. Cluj: Dacia.

———(2009). *Articole burgheze* [*Bourgeois Articles*], ed. Viorica Nişcov. Iaşi: Polirom Press.

Strauss, Leo (1968). *Liberalism Ancient and Modern*. Chicago: University of Chicago Press.

———(1975). *An Introduction to Political Philosophy: Ten Essays by Leo Strauss*, ed. Hilail Gildin. Detroit: Wayne State University Press.

Sunstein, Cass (2009). "Trimming." *Harvard Law Review*, 122: 4 (February): 1051–95.

Talmon, Jacob L. (1961). *The Origins of Totalitarian Democracy*. London: Mercury.

Teles, Steven and Matthew Kaliner (2004). "The Public Policy of Skepticism." *Perspectives on Politics*, 2: 1: 39–53.

Thompson, Norma (2001). *The Ship of State: Statecraft and Politics from Ancient Greece to Democratic America*. New Haven, Conn.: Yale University Press.

Thucydides (1996). *The Landmark Thucydides: A Comprehensive Guide to the Peloponnesian War*, ed. Robert B. Strassler. New York: Free Press.

Tismaneanu, Vladimir (1992). *Reinventing Politics: Eastern Europe from Stalin to Havel*. New York: Free Press.

———(1998). *Fantasies of Salvation: Democracy, Nationalism, and Myth in Eastern Europe*. Princeton, N.J.: Princeton University Press.

Tocqueville, Alexis de (1986). *Recollections*, ed. J. P. Mayer and A. P. Kerr, trans. George Lawrence. New Brunswick, N.J.: Transaction.

Toscano, Alberto (2010). *Fanaticism: The Uses of an Idea*. London: Verso.

Trilling, Lionel (1955). *The Liberal Imagination*. New York: Mercury Books.

———(1973). *Sincerity and Authenticity*. Cambridge, Mass.: Harvard University Press.

Tucker, Aviezer (2000). *The Philosophy and Politics of Czech Dissidence from Patočka to Havel*. Pittsburgh: University of Pittsburgh Press.

Urbinati, Nadia (1994). "Another Socialism." Introduction to Carlo Rosselli, *Liberal Socialism*, xiii–lxv.

———(2003). "Liberalism in the Cold War: Norberto Bobbio and the Dialogue with the PCI." *Journal of Modern Italian Studies*, 8: 4: 578–603.

Villa, Dana (2012). "Oakeshott and the Cold War Critique of Political Rationalism." In *The Cambridge Companion to Oakeshott*, ed. Efraim Podoksik, 319–44.

Violi, Carlo (1997). *Né con Marx né contro Marx*. Rome: Editori Riuniti.

Walzer, Michael (2002). *The Company of Critics: Social Criticism and Political Commitment in the Twentieth Century*. New York: Basic Books.

Weil, Simone (1997). *Gravity and Grace*, trans. Arthur Wills. Lincoln: University of Nebraska Press.

Westler, Brendon and Aurelian Craiutu (2015). "Two Engaged Spectators: José Ortega y Gasset and Raymond Aron." *Review of Politics*, 77: 4: 575–602.

White, Curtis (2003). *The Middle Mind*. San Francisco: Harper.

Wilkinson, James D. (1981). *The Intellectual Resistance in Europe*. Cambridge, Mass.: Harvard University Press.

Williams, Bernard (2005). "The Liberalism of Fear." In *In the Beginning Was the Deed*. Princeton, N.J.: Princeton University Press, 52–61.

Wilson, Paul (2015). "Adam Michnik: A Hero of Our Time." *New York Review of Books* (April 2): 73–75.

Wolin, Richard (2004). *The Seduction of Unreason: The Intellectual Romance with Fascism from Nietzsche to Postmodernism*. Princeton, N.J.: Princeton University Press.

———(2010). *French Intellectuals, the Cultural Revolution, and the Legacy of the 1960s*. Princeton, N.J.: Princeton University Press.

Wulf, Steven J. (2007). "Oakeshott's Politics for Gentlemen." *Review of Politics* 69: 2: 244–72.

Yeats, William Butler (1962). *Selected Poetry*, ed. A. Norman Jeffares. London: Macmillan.

INDEX

ACKNOWLEDGMENTS

I would like to express my renewed gratitude to all those who over the past few years have read and commented on various drafts of the chapters of this volume or my previous book on moderation in modern French political thought (1748–1830). The list is quite long and includes, in alphabetical order, Sorin Antohi, Michael Behrent, Paul Carrese, Ross Carroll, Joshua Cherniss, Harvey Chisick, Jacek Dalecki, Jan Drentje, Michael Drolet, Timothy Fuller, Alin Fumurescu, Alexandru Gabor, Venelin Ganev, Michael Gillespie, Irena Grudzińska-Gross, Christopher Guyver, Benjamin Hill, Lucien Jaume, Alan Kahan, George Kateb, Luigi Lacchè, Mathew Lamb, Alain Laquièze, Olivia Leboyer, Samuel Moyn, Matthias Oppermann, Catalin Partenie, H.-R. Patapievici, Melvin Richter, Helena Rosenblatt, Andrew Sabl, Rahul Sagar, Javier Fernandez Sebastian, Alexander Smith, Steven B. Smith, Karol Soltan, Vladimir Tismaneanu, David Tubbs, Nadia Urbinati, K. Steven Vincent, and Robert Zaretsky. As always, Daniel J. Mahoney has generously shared with me his knowledge of Aron and the French context, keeping me updated on new books essential for this project on moderation. Costica Bradatan has been a priceless friend and supporter with whom I discussed many themes of this book, and Vladimir Protopopescu has read the entire manuscript with his characteristic generosity and acumen. To all, my most sincere thanks!

I started working on and completed the first draft of the manuscript while on sabbatical from Indiana University as Ann and Herbert Vaughan Visiting Fellow in the James Madison Program in American Ideals and Institutions at Princeton University (September 2014–June 2015). Special thanks to its Director, Robert George, its Executive Director, Brad Wilson, the Visiting Fellows during the academic year 2014–15, and the wonderful staff of the Program, Elizabeth Schneck, Ch'nel Duke, Jane Hale, and Duanyi Wang, who provided exceptional research conditions for this project. Duanyi went far beyond her duty to assist me with her invaluable expertise and deserves a special note here. Thanks are also due to Radu Constantinescu and Isabela Mares for their warm hospitality in Princeton.

Over the past few years, I have been invited to present chapters of this book in various academic settings at Harvard, Yale, Duke, Indiana, the University of Wisconsin–Madison, American University, and the Research Triangle Intellectual History Seminar (at the National Humanities Center in North Carolina). I would like to thank my hosts for providing wonderful opportunities to share my ideas with their colleagues and students. The support of my colleagues (Dan Cole, Russell Hanson, Jeffrey Isaac, Mike McGinnis, and William Scheuerman) and graduate students (above all, Zach Goldsmith, Matthew Slaboch, and Brendon Westler) in Bloomington should also be properly acknowledged here.

Finally, a special note of thanks to Damon Linker, Noreen O'Connor-Abel, and their editorial team at the University of Pennsylvania Press who helped this manuscript become a book. Damon, who is also a fine political theorist himself and a public intellectual with a genuine appreciation for ideas, has been extremely supportive of the whole project from the outset. I have benefitted a great deal from our exchanges over the past couple of years. Three anonymous reviewers for the press provided valuable suggestions at different stages of this project, and I would like to take this opportunity to thank them all for their trust and endorsement.

Several chapters of this book discuss and develop various themes that I have previously touched upon in several essays and reviews. The original publications are gratefully acknowledged here, along with my renewed thanks for the opportunity to share my ideas with their audiences: "Michael Oakeshott's *Notebooks*," *Los Angeles Review of Books*, February 4, 2016; "Two Critical Spectators: José Ortega y Gasset and Raymond Aron" (with Brendon Westler), *Review of Politics*, 77: 4 (Fall 2015): 575–602; "Political Moderation and the Lost Art of Trimming," *Island* (Tasmania, Australia), 140 (March 2015): 38–43; "The Center and the Margins," *Los Angeles Review of Books*, March 26, 2014, https://lareviewofbooks.org/review/center-margins/; "Thinking Politically: Raymond Aron and the Revolution of 1968 in France," in Vladimir Tismaneanu, ed., *Promises of 1968: Crisis, Illusion, and Utopia* (Budapest: Central European University Press, 2011), 101–27; and "Faces of Moderation: Raymond Aron's Committed Observer," in Daniel J. Mahoney and Bryan-Paul Frost, eds., *Political Reason in an Age of Ideology* (New Brunswick, N.J.: Transaction, 2007), 261–83.

As always, my family—Sophia and Christina—has been a priceless source of support and encouragement. Sadly, my mother, Natalia, passed away before I began working on this book. No words can adequately express my gratitude and debt to her (as well as to my father, Adrian). I also regret that two good old friends from Romania, Silvia and Mihai Avram, are no longer with us to be able to see this book in print. Their personal trajectories that included exile, imprisonment, and life in relative marginality under dictatorship are perhaps the best illustration and justification of the need for political moderation.

I am honored to dedicate this book to my mother, Natalia, and to Silvia and Mihai in loving memory and as a token of my profound gratitude.

CPSIA information can be obtained
at www.ICGtesting.com
Printed in the USA
BVOW06s1023270118
506148BV00005B/3/P

9 780812 224092